STUDIES
IN
ANTHROPOLOGY

1

SOVIET ETHNOLOGY AND ANTHROPOLOGY TODAY

EDITED BY

YU. BROMLEY

Academy of Sciences of the USSR
N.N. Miklukho-Maklay Institute of Ethnography

1974

MOUTON · THE HAGUE · PARIS

377001

77662

Editorial Board:

Printed in The Netherlands by Mouton & Co., The Hague.

Contents

Preface

The scientific interests of Soviet ethnologists and anthropologists cover a broad field of topics ranging in time from anthropogenesis and sociogenesis to ethnic processes in modern society and in space embracing the whole ecumene.

The publication in English of selected recent works by Soviet authors in these fields from the scientific press of the USSR is an urgent and important task. The articles contributed to this collection are either forwarding the theory of ethnology and anthropology or summarizing the results of extensive investigations in certain areas. For lack of space there are numerous works dedicated to more detailed case studies which unfortunately are outside the limits of this collection. The editors hope that the twenty articles which constitute this volume can provide our colleagues throughout the world with a sufficiently adequate though incomplete outline of main trends in the development of ethnology and anthropology in the USSR in the last decade. The recent works of Soviet ethnologists are especially focused on the main object of study in this discipline, the ethnos. They aim at illuminating the concept of the ethnos and regularities of ethnic processes both in the past and in modern times. These problems have unequivocally become the central topics in the development of theoretical ethnology for the recent decade. This volume includes several articles which we hope will draw the keen interest of many scholars: the articles of Yu. V. Bromley and V. I. Kozlov, focusing on the general theory of ethnic entities, and articles by Yu. V. Arutjunjan, I. K. Vasiljeva, V. V. Pimenov, and L. S. Khristoljubova which represent some case studies dealing with the application of some original methods on ethnic processes among the contemporary peoples of the USSR.

The studies of social organization in primeval and early class society have undergone further development in recent years. A well-known Soviet expert in primitive society, A. I. Pershits, presents here an article which sums up certain results of long and fruitful researches of Soviet scholars in the history of the family and marriage. The article by A. M. Khazanov provides a new point of view on social organizations at the stage of the genesis of classes. Yu. I. Levin examines in his article an original method of a formal semantic analysis for kinship system terminologies.

At the same time the study of culture and especially of material culture and everyday life, a traditional branch in the whole of Russian and Soviet ethnology, remains a favorite theme for Soviet scholars. E. S. Markarjan presents here a summary of his book reflecting its philosophic and culturological concepts. The oldest Soviet ethnologist, S. A. Tokarev, deals in his article with a more restricted problem — the material culture and the main principles of the methods of its study. A more limited, but still important, insufficiently elaborated approach to the study of material culture is the subject of S. A. Arutjunov's article dealing with regularities in the interaction of traditional cultural traits with modern innovations. The recent trends in the development of ethnology resulted in a number of newly emerging synthetic disciplines. Two of them, ethnic mapping and ethnic onomastics, occupy a considerable place in the works of Soviet ethnologists. Examples of such studies are treated in articles by S. I. Bruk, D. V. Deopik, and M. A. Chlenov.

Ethnic or racial physical anthropology may be also regarded as a synthetic discipline and is represented in this volume by articles by the late G. F. Debets, V. P. Aleksejev, and A. A. Zubov. These works enable the reader to learn the principles of race classification which are applied in Soviet physical anthropology — the concept of two centers in the genesis of races and the utilization of odontological data in the science of the history of races. Some more generalized problems of physical anthropology are dealt with in the articles by V. V. Bunak, V. P. Jakimov, and Ya. Ya. Roginskij. The volume begins with two review articles by Yu. V. Bromley and V. P. Aleksejev aimed at introducing students of ethnology outside the USSR to the main stages in the development of Soviet ethnology and physical anthropology. The editors consider it their pleasant duty to express a deep gratitude to all institutions and persons who have rendered their assistance in the course of preparation of this book.

The Editors

Key to transliteration of the Cyrillic Alphabet

Cyrillic	Latin	Cyrillic	Latin	Cyrillic	Latin
а	a	л	l	ц	c
б	b	м	m	ч	č
в	v	н	n	ш	š
г	g	о	o	щ	šč
д	d	п	p	ъ	"
е	e	р	r	ы	y
ж	ž	с	s	ь	'
з	z	т	t	э	è
и	i	у	u	ю	ju
й	j	ф	f	я	ja
к	k	х	x		

PART I

Introduction

Ethnographical Studies in the USSR, 1965-1969

Yu. BROMLEY

The study of the origin, distribution, affinities, and differences of peoples is a science unto itself. In the USSR, as in many other countries, it is traditionally known as ethnography — "description of peoples". Termed as it is, ethnography is sometimes opposed to ethnology which is understood as a discipline dealing with the theoretical aspects of the study of the peoples of the world; however, the term ethnology has not gained a wide popular appeal in the USSR, and ethnography combines both the descriptive and theoretical levels. We do not possess a terminological differentiation between the study of our own people and the study of foreign peoples, and for this reason ethnography corresponds to what is covered by such disciplines as *Volkskunde* and *Völkerkunde* in the German-speaking countries. At the same time, the belief has long been current that in the English-speaking countries ethnography, as we understand the term, corresponds to cultural and social anthropology.[1] Even though the subject matter of these two disciplines and that of ethnography are not in fact totally identical, there is some reason in their coming together because they have a lot in common and some of their fields coincide.

In the Soviet Union, one of the largest multinational states, ethnographical studies have attained great momentum. The existence of the perennial traditions of ethnographical research in Russia before the 1917 Revolution was an important contributory factor.

In the USSR, as elsewhere, evidence on peoples and the distinctive features of their life can be found in the earliest records (e.g., in the writings of a 7th-century Armenian geographer, in the early 12th-century Russian

---

[1] In the USSR the term anthropology is commonly used in a narrow sense designating physical anthropology.

chronicle *Povest vremennykh let* [The Tales of Time-Honored Years], etc.). Evidence of this kind has been building up for centuries.

The official recognition of ethnography as a science in Russia dates from the first half of the 19th century. The most important milestone in the establishment of Russian ethnographical studies was the founding of the Russian Geographical Society with an ethnographical department in Petersburg in 1845. Since that date ethnographical material was gathered in a systematic manner; the Society maintained a special data-gathering program throughout the country. Initially the Society studied almost exclusively non-Russian nationalities of the Russian Empire, but gradually it began to concentrate more on the Russian people as well.

One of the special features of ethnographical studies in the middle of the 19th century was an interest in folk art, including oral folk art, traditionally called folklore in Russia. This brought ethnography right into close contact with folkloric studies, a tradition which has largely survived to this day. It was to this contact that the manifest influence of the mythological school on the Russian ethnographical studies of that time was partly due.

Later in the century ethnography tended to join the natural sciences. A vivid illustration of this was the founding of the Society of the Lovers of the Natural Sciences in Moscow in the 1860's, with Departments of Ethnography and Anthropology (already at that time by anthropology was usually meant the study of the variations in human physical types).[2] In 1867 the Society organized in Moscow the first All-Russia Ethnographical Show. The Ethnographical Department of the Society published a series of works dealing with the different peoples of Russia.

In the 1870–80's the ethnographers became more interested in the study of social life — family and community. This was largely due to the practical requirements of the Russian public after the abolition of serfdom in Russia. Russian populism (*narodnichestvo*) which idealized the communal system was coming into its own. Among other things, the study of common law attracted much attention; this was of great practical importance since the jurisdiction of the landlords had been abolished. The study of folk art was continuing, but now involved a critical approach to the mythological school and the popularity of the "theory of borrowings" (V. V. Stasov, V. F. Miller). Scientific expeditions to non-European countries, especially N. N. Miklukho-Maklay's expedition to Oceania, also left their imprint on ethnographical studies in Russia.

In the 1890's and the early part of the 20th century, the ethnographical museums at the centers (the Museum of Anthropology and Ethnography in Petersburg, the Dashkov Ethnographical Museum in Moscow, and the

[2]   The term was simultaneously used in a wider, philosophical sense.

Ethnographical Department of the Russian Museum in Petersburg) and in the provinces became more active. This prompted interest in the study of the material life of the people. Evolutionism, which had exercised some impact in the preceding decades, now became the leading ideological stream in Russian ethnography (M. M. Kovalevsky, N. N. Kharuzin, L. Ya. Shternberg, and others).

Many ethnographical traditions which were carried on in Soviet times, originated in fact in the pre-revolutionary period. There were, for example, no studies contrasting the country's dominant nation (Russia) and the other nations, a trend which was common in many countries especially in the colonialist countries. There were not sufficient grounds for that, because the status of the bulk of the Russian people (peasantry) differed little from that of the peoples living on the fringes of the empire. For the pre-revolutionary progressive Russian ethnographers it was utterly impossible to divide peoples into "historic peoples" and "non-historic peoples", nor were there conditions in Russia for the spread of racist views in ethnographical science.

Up to the Revolution of 1917, ethnographical studies, it should be noted, were carried on either by single-handed amateurs or by ethnographical societies with small memberships. No system of state ethnographical establishments grew up. At the few state-sponsored ethnographical museums research was on a small scale indeed; ethnography was not taught at the universities.

Of course, no single socio-political orientation of pre-revolutionary ethnographical studies was in existence. The central motive which kept the science going was the contest between the two principles: the conservative and the progressive which catered for the aspirations of the people. In ideological and theoretical matters, discord among the ethnographers was great. Even on the very concept of ethnography the views were many. Some held that the major task of ethnography was to find out the laws of man's development at the lowest stages; others defined ethnography as a science dealing with the culture of primitive peoples in general and with the survivals of this culture; and still others held that ethnography was to study the peculiarities of the material and spiritual life of individual peoples (Tokarev, 1966; *Ocherki*, 1956–1968).

The Revolution of 1917 radically changed the conditions in which ethnography was to develop in Russia. From the start Soviet ethnography drew upon the humanistic and democratic legacy of pre-revolutionary Russian ethnography, following the example set by its best representatives who took an active part in the building of the new life. Among other things which the Soviet ethnographers inherited from their pre-revolutionary fellow scientists were a broad outlook and interest in all the peoples of the world.

What, however, played a dominant part in the development of ethnographical studies in the post-revolutionary years was the dovetailing of these studies with the practical requirements advanced by the new social regime. The tasks of Lenin's national policy and the need for radical changes in the life and culture of the formerly backward peoples called for thorough research into the ethnic composition of their populations and the national peculiarities of their cultures.

To tackle the problem, several new ethnographical centers (first in the form of various commissions and committees, and later in the form of institutes) were set up in Leningrad and Moscow during the initial Soviet years; meanwhile, most of the scientific societies in which the majority of ethnographical studies were carried on before the revolution resumed their work. Of immense importance in the organization of ethnographical research was the establishment in 1926 of the journal *Etnografiya* (*Sovetskaya etnografiya* from 1931). By the close of the 30's the ramified network of ethnographical institutions had been broadly outlined: apart from the USSR Academy of Sciences' Institute of Ethnography,[3] corresponding research units in many of the Republics emerged. Local scientific manpower, including those coming from the native nationalities, were getting into their stride. In the post-war period this trend gained special momentum, and at present ethnographical teams are in existence in all Soviet Republics and in several cities of the Russian Federation (Guslistyj, 1958; Chitaja, 1948; Guliev, 1961; Akaba, 1961; Vardumjan, 1962; Vishniauskajte, 1960; Stepermanis, 1960; Vijres, 1960; Samarin, 1948; Pisarchik, 1954; Masanov, 1966; and Jershov, 1968). The museums contribute much to ethnographical research.[4] Annual archaeological and ethnographical sessions of the Department of History of the USSR Academy of Sciences, at which the results of field research for the past year are summarized, are of much importance in the coordination of the activity of Soviet ethnographers.

Of course, the development of Soviet ethnography over the past half century is not confined merely to the improvement of the research organi-

---

[3] Named in 1947 after N. N. Miklukho-Maklay, the well-known Russian explorer and ethnographer, the Institute is at present the major center of ethnographical research in the USSR.

[4] This applies both to the central museums (the Museum of Anthropology and Ethnography of the USSR Academy of Sciences, the State Museum of the Ethnography of the Peoples of the USSR) and to the republican museums (for example, the ethnographical museums at Tbilisi, Tartu, and Lvov). Numerous museums of regional ethnography also contribute to the ethnographical study of the country.

zation, the expansion of research, and the training of scientific personnel. The major trend of this development has been the establishment and assertion of Marxist methodology in ethnography. Already nearly complete as early as the pre-war years, this process in turn revolutionized our concept of ethnography itself, as well as the major problems and the status of ethnography in the scientific world.

In the first years after the 1917 Revolution, Soviet ethnography was noted for its wide divergence of theories. In the late 1920's and the early 1930's in the ethnographical field, as well as in most of the other humanities, numerous discussions were held in order to clear up the theoretical disagreements and assert Marxist principles.

Despite opposite extremes, the discussions on the whole were of much value for Soviet ethnography. The heated theoretical debates undoubtedly helped Soviet ethnographers to gain a better knowledge of Marxist methodology. In the course of these debates, Soviet ethnography determined itself as a field of historical science with its own particular range of sources and specific problems.

One of the distinctive features of the ethnographers' activity in those years was concentration on the problems of social organization, especially on the various forms of patriarchal and patriarchal-feudal relations. This was in large measure due to the ethnographers' striving to master Marxist-Leninist methodology.

Comparative historical studies of the general problems of primitive organization, the origin of exogamy, maternal clan and matriarchate, military democracy, etc., also attracted more attention (Kagarov, 1937; Krichevskij, 1936; Zolotarev, 1931, 1933; Tolstov, 1931; "*Voprosy ...*", 1936; and others). Data-collecting activities were carried out on a wide scale, especially in the little studied areas of the Far North (Bogoraz-Tan, 1932; Shternberg, 1933; Popov, 1931, 1936; Vasilevich, 1930; and others). At the same time, a tendency was in evidence to narrow the concept of ethnography as a science, eliminating those of its fields which formally are beyond the frame of the historical sciences. As a result, studies of the contemporary way of life of the peoples of the Soviet Union and other countries came virtually at a standstill.

The first post-war years witnessed a general rise of activity and a wide range of problems were studied in the field of ethnography (Tolstov, 1947b, 1957; Tokarev, 1958d). To cater for the practical problems which arose during the final stage of the war, the studies of ethnic borders and ethnic mapping began. In addition, work on the history of ethnography in the USSR and other countries was launched. The study of contemporary ways of life was advanced as a high priority problem. The belief gained wide currency among the ethnographers that they should and could study comprehensively contemporary culture and life by their own devices. This in turn affected the general concept of the subject matter of ethnography. More often than not, the realm of ethnography became too wide and ill-defined (Tokarev, 1958d). Yet a narrower definition of ethnography as a science dealing comprehensively with the peculiarities of culture and life of peoples was also in use (Tolstov, 1960).

The study of present-day ethnic processes both in the USSR and abroad came more into the foreground in recent years. At the same time the wide spectrum of concrete sociological studies, including the study of ways of life, enabled ethnographers to concentrate on the ethnic specifics of present-day cultural and social processes.

The concept of ethnography which is predominant in the USSR today is that of a science which deals with stable (ethnic) distinctive features of the everyday life of the peoples of the world, and with ethnogenesis and ethnic history up to the present time. Ethnography is regarded as one of the historical sciences, which as we have said, was already recognized during the pre-war discussions. Such a classification makes the most of the consistent historicism of Soviet ethnography derived from the methodology of historical materialism. Although Soviet ethnographers deal first of all with present-day peoples, they treat their ethnic peculiarities from a historical perspective — in the making. This, inevitably, brings into sight not only the peoples living at the moment, but also all peoples who ever existed in the past. Ethnography thus embraces the whole of man's history, exploring it from a certain ethnographical viewpoint.

While regarding ethnography as one of the historical sciences, Soviet ethnographers at the same time consistently emphasize its peculiar position in the sciences at large. This peculiarity is primarily due to the fact that in order to identify distinctive and typical traits in the life of each particular people we must learn about this life as a whole and not only the socio-cultural province in which these traits make themselves most vividly manifest. Hence the ethnographical study of peoples overlaps many of the "departmental" social and natural sciences. Indeed, no sharp demarcation line can be drawn between some of these and ethnography. It is not accidental that in this country, as in many others, a whole array of the borderline disciplines has come into existence: ethnic anthropology, ethnic geography, ethnic linguistics, etc. (Debets, Leving, Trofimova, 1952; Bunak, Kozlov, Levin, 1963; Yeremejev, 1967; Agajev, 1968). Further, Soviet ethnography is closely connected with the study of folklore (Chistov, 1968). Special emphasis on the study of present-day forms of social life makes ethnography, in the opinion of Soviet scientists, cognate with concrete sociological studies. Indeed, a new science — ethno-sociology — has been arising at the juncture of the two sciences in recent years. The main object of the new science, Soviet scholars believe, consists of the study of the interactions between ethnic and social processes with due regard to the specifics of ethnic processes in various social groups, and the specifics of social changes in various ethnic environments (Bromley, Shkaratan, 1969).

In our opinion, the science of ethnography is also remarkable for certain specific features of method: its integrated use not only of materials from all the historical sciences including archaeology, but also of data derived from diverse branches of knowledge; and its broad application of the method of direct observation of the present-day life of peoples, with special field research undertaken to this end. The dozens of expeditions commissioned annually by the central and local ethnographical institutions in all regions of the Soviet Union have gleaned a wealth of factual material, most of which first appeared in numerous publications and in museum expositions.

In the half-century of its development the major research trends of Soviet ethnography have taken shape (Pershits, Cheboksarov, 1967; Bromley, 1968). One of the trends may be defined arbitrarily as the historico-ethnographical study of the peoples of the world. The problems of the trend range from ethnogenesis to the present-day sociocultural and national processes; most of this range of problems are correlated with those which are studied by cultural anthropology in the English-speaking countries.

The problems of ethnic history, and, in the first place, ethnogenesis, take up a special place among the general historico-ethnographical studies of peoples. The investigation of these problems is of immense significance. They in fact show that all of the present-day peoples have grown from different ethnical components and have a mixed composition, thereby refuting the racist and chauvinist allegations of "racial purity", "primeval ancestors", and "national exceptionality".

For many decades now Soviet ethnographers have studied the problems of ethnogenesis in collaboration with anthropologists, archaeologists, and linguists. In the past, ethnogenetic problems were settled mainly on the strength of linguistic evidence and were largely confined to the history of languages, and their origin and distribution — with priority given to the migrations of peoples. Later, some of the primitive migratory theories of the origin of many peoples were revised under the impact of N. Ya. Marr's linguistic theory. This time the tables were turned: the role of migrations was denied altogether. The discussion of the problems of linguistics in 1950 helped to clear up this misunderstanding. Further, the increasingly wider

use of anthropological evidence enabled us to call in question the traditional conception that the sweeping majority of the migrations had entailed
nearly complete destruction or ousting of the local aboriginal population
(Aleksejev, Bromley, 1968). Thus ethnogenetic studies by no means un-
folded in a straightforward manner. Yet the integrated approach which
gained a wide appeal in the post-war years has proved fruitful in the investigation of concrete problems of the origin of separate peoples. What we
know today about the origin of many of the peoples of the Soviet Union
undoubtedly corresponds more to the historical reality than did the views
held some two or three decades ago. This is equally true of the peoples
inhabiting the most diverse historico-ethnographical regions of our country: the Baltic area, the Volga area, the Caucasus, Central Asia, Siberia,
the Far East, etc. (Tokarev, 1949; *Baltijskij* ..., 1956; *Voprosy*, 1959,
1960; *Trudy*, 1952–1959, 1956–1960, 1960–1966; Levin, 1958; Dolgikh,
1960, 1963; Guslistyj, 1963; Gurvich, 1963; *Proiskhozhdenije*, 1967;
Arutjunov, Sergejev, 1969).

Soviet scholars also concentrated on the problems of the origin of
foreign peoples, especially the peoples of America, Asia, Australia, and
Oceania (Bunak, Tokarev, 1951: Levin, Cheboksarov, 1951; Olderogge,
1952; Arutjunov, 1961, 1964; Butinov, 1962; Cheboksarov, 1964;
Jeremejev, 1967; Kabo, 1969).

The study of the history of the ethnic and above all sociocultural
peculiarities of individual peoples is a major activity of Soviet ethnographers. In the course of this study they often have to scan the culture and
life of a given people as a whole, for one cannot see the general without
learning the specific. Furthermore, the ethnographer usually finds himself
unsupported when studying peoples who have no written language
and therefore has to investigate all the aspects of the activity of such
peoples.

In their study of the cultures of all ethnic communities, irrespective of
their number, Soviet ethnographers have done a great deal for the comprehensive treatment of the contribution which different peoples of
the world have made to the overall cultural treasury of mankind.
Especially indicative in this respect is the study of material culture (*Kultura*, 1963, 1966, 1967a).

In the past fifty years a large number of special studies on the history
of farming technology, settlements, dwellings, clothes, and food appeared, covering many, if not all, the peoples of the USSR (Popov, 1948;
Belitser, 1951; Chitaja, 1952; *Vostochnoslavjanskij*, 1956; Krjukova,
1956; Gadzhieva, 1960; Antipina, 1962; Issledovanija, 1963; Stelmakh,
1964; Karakashly, 1964; Tarojeva, 1965; Krupjanskaya, Potapov,

Terentjeva, 1961; Pershits, 1964), as well as several foreign nations (Orlova, 1958; Olderogge, 1960b; Bogatyrev, 1964; Anokhin, 1964; Atutjunov, 1965; Starikov, 1967; *Tipy*, 1968).

Special historico-ethnographical regional atlases have been prepared by the joint efforts of ethnographers at the centers and in the republics to summarize the whole body of accumulated data on the history of the material culture of the Soviet peoples. In 1961 an atlas devoted to the peoples of Siberia came out (Levin and Potapov, 1961). In 1967 an atlas entitled *The Russians* was published (*Russkije*, 1967). In this publication, which has summarized abundant factual material, the major components of the material culture of the Soviet Union's largest people from the middle of the 19th to the early 20th century are characterized by a carto-graphical method. In the atlas each phenomenon is not charted statically, but developmentally (in the pre-Reform period and prior to the 1917 Revolution). In this way the atlas gives a clear idea of the major features of the unfolding of the Russians' material culture in the pre-revolutionary period. The seventy-five charts are accompanied with numerous tables and short explanatory notes. Atlases devoted to other peoples of the USSR are now in preparation (Guslistyj, Gorlenko, Priljapko, 1967; Kobychev, Robakidze, 1967; Studenetskaja, 1967).

As for the spiritual culture, the attention of Soviet ethnographers is primarily drawn to mass folk art — a field which they explore together with folklorists and art students. Ethnographical studies of the different forms of folk art of the minority peoples who reveal profound individuality in their art have made special progress (Ivanov, 1954, 1961, 1969; Kilchevskaja, Ivanov, 1959; Chernetsov, 1964; Vajnshtejn, 1967).

Because religion has molded many of the specific features of the present-day life of some peoples, Soviet ethnographers have consistently concen-trated on separate aspects of religion. They have contributed most of all to the study of the early faiths and cults noted for their special diversity in form, as well as the problems of the origins and classification of religions (Tokarev, 1957, 1964b,c; Bardavelidze, 1957; Kryvelev, 1961; Sharevskaja, 1964; Zhukovskaja, 1965; Snesarev, 1969). In recent years the study of such traditional ethnographical subjects as folk morals and customs has become more popular (Lobacheva, 1967; Saburova, 1967b).

The deciphering of some of the long-forgotten scripts is an important part of the ethnographical study of culture. The most world-renowned achievement in the field of ethnolinguistics is the work on the deciphering of the ancient Maya script (Knorozov, 1963). Research is also beginning in the study of the script of Easter Island, the proto-Indian texts originated by the forefathers of the Harappian culture, and the scripts of the Kitans and Jurjans (Kudrjavtsev, 1949; Olderogge, 1949; Butinov, Knorozov, 1956, 1964, 1965; Starikov, 1966).

There are numerous monographs, works by expedition members and special collections (*Trudy*, 1952–1959, 1956–1960; *Sibirskij*, 1952–1963; Rudenko, 1955; *Baltijskij*, 1956; *Voprosy*, 1956, 1959, 1960; Potapov, 1957; Levin, 1958; Aleksandrov, 1964; Gurvich, 1966; Busygin, 1966; Saburova, 1967a; *Etnografija*, 1969), reflecting the results of the historico-ethnographical studies both of separate peoples and whole regions of the Soviet Union. Of particular importance among the works of this kind are the historico-ethnographical monographs concerned with the minor peoples who possess no tradition of written language. It is the ethnographer commanding the materials of direct field observation who can reconstruct the history of such peoples by means of retrospective reconstruction and drawing upon all sources, including archaeological data. Indeed, the real dedication of the ethnographers has helped to restore the history of a few dozen peoples of our country who had either no written language at all or had it in a rudimentary form in the past. Over the last five years alone there appeared historico-ethnographical monographs on the Ulchi, Veps, Archintsy, Nivkhi, Chukchi, Nentsy, Orochi, and others (Larkin, 1964; Vdovin, 1965; Pimenov, 1965; Smoljak, 1966; Khomich, 1966; Sergejeva, 1967; Taksami, 1967; Vasilevich, 1969). There are also several historico-ethnographical monographs devoted to some foreign peoples, in particular the peoples of Latin America (Cuba, 1961; Ecuador, 1963; Brazil, 1963; Chile, 1965; Venezuela, 1967; Guiana, 1969).

The study of the present-day ethnic processes is today one of the central subjects of Soviet ethnographical research. The reason is obvious enough: the immense economic, social, and political changes that have taken place in the post-war period all over the world, and in particular in Africa, Asia, and Latin America, made the national and ethnic processes move at a faster rate. Interest in the present-day ethnic life of the peoples of the world has risen as never before, and the Soviet ethnographers are not remaining indifferent.

Soviet ethnographers concentrated with special care on the study of the sociocultural process in their ethnic individuality. Work in this field started as early as the 1920's and 1930's as the practical requirements of reconstructing the previously backward fringes of the country and collectivization demanded. By the close of the 30's research in this field, as we have said, was nearly at a standstill: the ethnographers' efforts shifted into the field of archaic studies. Revived in the late 1940's the ethnographical study of the present-day cultures and ways of life of the peoples of the Soviet Union was largely of descriptive nature.

Much progress on a wider scale was made in this field in the late 1950's and first half of the 1960's. Several monographs on the collective-farm way of life of the Russians, Tadziks, Uzbeks, Ukrainians, Latvians, Kirghizes, and other peoples of the Soviet Union were prepared and published in this period (*Kultura*, 1954, 1964, 1967b, 1968; Sukhareva, Bikzhanova, 1955; Selo, 1958; *Byt*, 1958; Terentjeva, 1960; Semja, 1962; Vardumjan, Karapetjan, 1963; Anokhina, Shmeleva, 1964a; Kuvenjova, 1966; Kubanskije, 1967, etc.; Krupjanskaja, Potapov, Terentjeva, 1961; Potapov, 1962; Vinnikov, 1969).

The scope of research gradually became wider: the lives of workers, and later of the whole of urban population, came to the fore as subjects for research (Krupjanskaja, 1960; Annaklycheb, 1961; Zinich, 1963; Krupjanskaja, Rabinovich, 1964; Anokhina, Shmeleva, 1964b; Chyrakzada, 1965; Kogan, 1967; *Etnograficheskije*, 1968; etc.). Methods of investigation improved as well. The study of exceedingly complex processes of modern life called for the collection of material on a mass scale; scientific questionnairing and computer techniques came into play (Rozhdestvenskaja, 1964; Anokhina, Shmeleva, 1968). What kind of ethnographical research should be carried on in the present-day culture and life of highly developed societies also received theoretical treatment in recent years (Tokarev, 1967a, b). At the same time, the problem of the relationship between ethnography and sociology in the study of present-day sociocultural processes is becoming increasingly compelling. Tentative yet vigorous steps in the field of ethnosociological investigation of these processes in the peoples of the USSR are being taken (Arutjunjan, 1968).

Of immense scientific interest are the ethnographical studies (drawing upon the evidence of linguistics and census records) of such processes of national consolidation as the disappearance of former isolation and seclusion, the confluence of separate cognate ethnic formations into nations, and the merging of small national groups into closely-knit ethnic communities. Studies of such vital ethnic processes as nationally mixed marriages, relationships between the native language and ethnic self-consciousness, bilingualism, etc. also made special progress in recent years (Gardanov, Dolgikh, Zhdanko, 1961; Smoljak, 1963; Zhdanko 1964; Gantskaja, Terentjeva, 1965; Monogarova, 1967; Smirnova, 1967; Gurvich, 1967; Terentjeva, 1969; Vasiljeva, 1969).

The study of the sociocultural and modern ethnic processes abroad, and in particular in Asia (Bruk, Cheboksarov, 1961; *Etnicheskije*, 1963; Ivanov, 1967; Cheboksarov, 1966; Arutjunov, 1968) and Africa (Potekhin,

1955, 1957; Smirnov, 1956; Ismagilova, 1963, Andrianov, 1964, 1967), are gaining more momentum. Work on the study of the present-day ethnic processes in the U.S.A., Canada, and Latin American countries has begun (Natsii, 1964; Berzina, 1968; Bogina, 1968). The study of the present-day ethnic life of West European peoples is gradually getting into its stride (*Kultura*, 1967a; Bromley Kashuba, 1969).

Ethno-demographical and ethno-geographical studies of modern peoples have become popular in recent years in the USSR. For example, several methods of the chart imposition of various ethnic and demographical indexes have been devised (Kushner [Knyshev], 1950; Terletskij, 1953). The new techniques enabled the ethnic charts of all parts of the globe to be completed within a relatively short time (Bruk, 1959a, b, 1960; Andrianov, 1961; Berzina, Bruk, 1962, etc.). The ethnic charting of the little investigated regions received special attention. Also, the summarizing chart *The Peoples of the World* (Andrianov, Berzina, Bruk, Vinnikov, Kamenetskaja, Kozlov, 1961) and *The Atlas of the Peoples of the World* (*Atlas*, 1964), which incorporated the results of many years of research, have been published. The most significant outcome of ethnodemographic research is the summarizing work entitled *The Numbers and Distribution of the Peoples of the World* (Chislennost, 1962), which furnishes a detailed description of the national composition of the population of all countries of the world, as well as the numbers of the different peoples and their territorial distribution.

The investigation of separate concrete ethnic and sociocultural processes and developments of different peoples of the world involves in the Soviet Union the elaboration of methodological matter of general nature. Thus, to understand the general laws of the development of specific features in the culture of different peoples of much importance is the doctrine developed by Soviet ethnographers on economic-cultural types and historico-ethnographical regions. In the first case the reference is to definite complexes of economy and culture, each of which is simultaneously basic to several peoples living sometimes in different parts of the ecumene. Although these complexes build up independently in different peoples, they prove to be uniform in type by virtue of approximately the same socio-economic levels of development and similar environments. By historico-ethnographical (or rather historico-cultural) regions are meant separate parts of the ecumene, the populations of which reveal similar sociocultural peculiarities by virtue of the community of socioeconomic development, sustained intercourse, and reciprocal influence (Levin, Cheboksarov, 1955; Andrianov, 1968).

In recent years Soviet ethnographers also concentrated on the theoretical elaboration of such ethnic processes and problems essential for understanding such general laws as the interrelation of cultures, the role of continuity, and innovation in the development of culture (Artanovskij, 1967; Pimenov, 1967).

Soviet ethnographers also took an active part in the theoretical work which recently was launched on the typologization of ethnic communities (Tokarev, 1964a; Kozlov, 1967a,b, 1969; Lashuk, 1967b; Cheboksarov, 1967; Khomich, 1969; Bromley, 1969). Special emphasis in this field is placed on the notion of ethnic community itself. Soviet ethnographers understand it in a wider sense than the term people because ethnic community can be applied both to a group of peoples cognate in language and culture and to a part of a people with language and cultural individuality.

Apart from the whole complex of historico-ethnic studies of the peoples of the world, the study of the history of society is a field of primary importance in Soviet ethnography (this field corresponds, to a certain extent, to social anthropology in the English-speaking countries).

At the early, archaic stages of social development in which production and family life are welded together, ethnic specifics permeate all life. For this reason the ethnographical study of pre-class and early class society usually covers all provinces of social activity. This in turn makes it possible to use ethnographical evidence obtained in the course of direct observation of archaic phenomena in order to reconstruct primitive history.

The identification of specimens of man's pre-class stages plays a major role in the elaboration and substantiation of the Marxist conception of social development. Soviet ethnographers from the very beginning focused their attention on primitive history, a field which they explored in collaboration with archaeologists and anthropologists. Over the past decade a vast amount of fresh evidence indicating the historical versatility of clan organization has been collected and put into scientific circulation by Soviet ethnographers; for example, the wide spread of dual organization as one of the basic features of the primeval clan has been proved. The later forms of primitive communal organization has been investigated more thoroughly: the complex structure of patriarchal clan has been ascertained, the typologization of the extended family started and abundant evidence on the segmentized form of this family — the so-called patronomy — has been brought to light and summarized (Zolotarev, 1931, 1939, 1964; Anisimov, 1936; Kisljakov, 1936; Kosven, 1948, 1957, 1963; Fainberg, 1964; Semenov, 1966b; Krjukov, 1967a; Robakidze, 1968; Bromley, 1968c; *Voprosy*, 1936; Rodovoje, 1951; *Problemy*, 1960).

The ethnographical study of military democracy and domestic serfdom has been of major importance in disclosing the concrete ways of the transition from pre-class to class society (Tolstov, 1935a; Averkieva, 1941, 1961; Potekhin, 1951; Kosven, 1960; Tokarev, 1958c; *Razlozhenije*, 1968).

As the materialist conception of primitive history developed and crystallized, it became clear that some of the particular contentions advanced by L. H. Morgan were obsolete. The elaboration of these contentions, a trend which began as early as the pre-war years and gained special popularity in the recent period, is all the more important since the attempts to disprove the materialist conception of primitive history is usually connected with the ascribing of Morgan's erroneous contentions to Marxism.

In the light of present-day ethnographical evidence, the pattern of development of the marriage relationship in the primitive family has been in particular greatly specified, leaving out of the court Morgan's hypothetically reconstructed stages of consanguine family and punaluan family (Tokarev, 1929; Zolotarev, 1940; Kosven, 1946; Olderogge, 1951; Tumarkin, 1954, etc.; Pershits, 1967). Many Soviet ethnographers refused to accept Morgan's view that the origin of exogamy is due to conscious efforts to avoid the harmful consequences of incest (Zolotarev, MSa; Zhakov, 1933; Tolstov, 1935b; Olderogge, 1947; Butinov, 1951); however, there is no single viewpoint as yet among Soviet ethnographers on this problem which is of vital importance in understanding the causes and mechanism of the transformation of the human herd into a clan community.

In the light of recent ethnographical and archaeological evidence it was also necessary to specify, as F. Engels foresaw, Morgan's periodization of primitive history. In the course of the post-war discussions, a number of new periodizations have been suggested (Tolstov, 1946; Kosven, 1952; Pershits, 1960; Butinov, 1960; Semenov, 1965a; Averkieva, 1967). Although the question has not yet been settled, the major result is already obvious. It is well known that this periodization must first of all be based on sociological indexes and not on cultural-historical ones. Among other matters which have given rise to lively discourse are the relationships of clan and clan community, the sequence of the rise of matrilineal and patrilineal computation, the historical place of disclocal marriage, the patterns of early forms of marriage relations, etc. (Olderogge, 1947; 1960a; Likhtenberg, 1960; Butinov, 1962; Semenov, 1965b; Krjukov, 1967b, etc.).

The study of archaic forms of social life, which survived in class and above all in early class societies, is closely associated with the elaboration of the problems of primitive organization. Perhaps the most important contribution which Soviet ethnographers have made in this field is the study of nomadic social organization (Tolstov, 1934; Bernshtam, 1934; Potapov, 1947, 1954; Abramzon, 1951; Efendiev, Pershits, 1955; Pershits, 1961a; Lashuk, 1967a,c). It is also necessary to mention the ethnographers' active participation in the discussion on early class society, as well as their contribution to the study of various types of community. The introduction of abundant new material characterizing various types of community and disclosing their roles in the life of peoples of diverse regions of the globe is another subject of attention (Karapetjan, 1958; Kharadze, 1960–1961; Maretin, 1961; Gardanov, 1967; *Obsjina*, 1967; Butinov, 1968, etc.).

It is worthwhile emphasizing that research became especially lively in recent years in the USSR in the study of Soviet ethnography (*Ocherki*, 1956, 1963, 1965, 1968; Tokarev, 1966). Foreign studies of ethnographical nature also have been investigated on a wide scale in the post-war decades, including works on social and cultural anthropology, and ethnology. Several papers published in periodicals and special collections, e.g., *Modern American Ethnography*, are devoted to their analysis (*Bibliografija*, 1967).

It is also necessary to draw attention to the fight of Soviet ethnographers against racists who sometimes try to derive their arguments not only from anthropology but also from ethnography. Matured as long ago as the pre-war period, the activity of Soviet ethnographers in this field recently took a new lease on life when the collective works *Protiv Rasizma* [Against Racism] (Moscow, 1967), *Net-Rasizmu!* [Racism. NO!] (Moscow, 1968), and the collection *Dokumenty oblichajut Rasizm* [Documents Exposing Racism] (Moscow, 1968) were published.

International contacts of Soviet ethnographers became especially wide in the post-war years. This was largely due to the 7th International Congress of Anthropological and Ethnographical Sciences held in Moscow in 1964 and attended by about two thousand Soviet and a thousand foreign scholars from fifty-five countries (Kitogam, 1965; Gurvich, 1965; Sokolova, 1965). The Soviet delegation took an active part in the work of the 8th International Congress of Archeological and Ethnographical Sciences held in Tokyo and Kyoto in 1968 and presented more than forty reports on a wide variety of ethnographical, anthropological and folkloristic matters (Averkijeva, Arutjunov, Bromley, 1969; Bromley, 1969a).

The cognitive significance of historico-ethnographical knowledge predetermined the Soviet ethnographers' close concern with the creation of summary descriptions of peoples in the form of summarizing works, textbooks, and popular science fiction. In particular, work on textbooks and teaching aids has made appreciable progress in recent years (Tokarev, 1958a; Gromov, 1966; Knyshenko, 1965; Kozlova, 1967; Aleksejev, Mongajt, Pershits, 1968). *Essays in General Ethnography*, a five-volume popular-science publication covering all the peoples of the world, has been completed (*Ocherki*, 1957; *Zarubezhnaja*, 1959, 1966; *Aziatskaja*, 1960; *Jevropejskaja*, 1968).

The thirteen-volume series *The Peoples of the World* (in eighteen books) under the general editorship of S. P. Tolstov was completed in 1966 and in a way summed up the development of Soviet ethnography. Each volume in this series furnishes detailed evidence based on the most recent sources about the ethnic composition of the population, the socio-cultural peculiarities of different peoples, as well as material on the history of their culture from ancient times to the present day (Tolstov, 1954–1966; Narody, 1956a, 1959, 1954, 1965b, 1964, 1964–1965a, 1962, 1957, 1956b, 1962–1963b, 1966, 1963a; Chislennost, 1962).

In their efforts to continue the thorough study of man's multifaceted image, Soviet ethnographers are convinced that such a study contributes to better international understanding.

Fifty Years of Studies in Anthropological Composition of Population in the USSR

V. ALEKSEJEV

Following A. Retzius's work on the use of the cranial index for the classification of skulls, measurements have become an integral part of anthropological science and the main method of anthropological studies. *Fundamentals of Cranioscopy* by K. Karuss, a German anatomist (Kanajev, 1963), which appeared in Russian translation in 1844, was among the first publications in this language to contain measurements applied to anthropology. The impact of this book on further progress was, however, insignificant, much like that of K. Baer's illustrious papers in craniology and his large-scale, concentrated effort aimed at setting up a collection of skulls representative of peoples inhabiting Russia. On the whole, the anthropological characteristics of the contemporary population of Russia were unknown. Purposeful investigations in this direction had not actually begun before 1863 when the Society of Lovers of Nature Study, Anthropology, and Ethnography — comprising an Anthropology Department — was established in Moscow. It was then one of Europe's first scientific anthropological associations.

Headed by A. P. Bogdanov, later followed by D. N. Anuchin, the Anthropology Department covered a wide field by its extensive activities. New aspects continue to come to light which had been omitted in the numerous historiographic and memorial papers concerned with the Department. This agency succeeded in drawing the attention of the Russian public to anthropological science, in procuring the necessary funds, and in sending large parties to various remote places of our country to undertake anthropological studies of the population. Discussions of the results obtained by these parties can be seen in the voluminous

First published in *Sovetskaja etnografija* N5 (1967)

Proceedings of the Anthropology Department which contain both collections on specific topics of anthropologies of individual peoples and large monographs (Gladkova, 1963).

Before the Great October Socialist Revolution of 1917, the Anthropology Department of the Society of Lovers of Nature Study, Anthropology, and Ethnography was without doubt the country's central anthropological agency which rallied the few peripheral specialists and set an example to be followed by most other anthropological associations and institutions. These included the Anthropological Society of the Military Medical Academy in St. Petersburg, the Russian Anthropological Society under Moscow University, the Society of Natural Scientists and the Society of Archaeology, History, and Ethnography under the University of Kazan, and the Caucasian and East Siberian Branches of the Russian Geographical Society (Aleksejev, 1964). Nearly every effort in the investigation of the anthropological composition of the peoples inhabiting Russia was concentrated within the above institutions since anthropology was not given the official status of a self-sustained discipline, either in the universities or at the Russian Academy of Sciences, and had no official control agency whatsoever. Collected materials were primarily published in the *Russkij antropologicheskij zhurnal (Russian Anthropological Journal)* started in 1900.

Besides the authors of numerous small-size publications on the anthropologies of individual peoples, one can recall many Russian anthropologists who have made the study of the anthropological composition of Russia the goal of their entire lives. R. F. Oerkert, I. I. Pantukhov, N. V. Giltchenko, and A. N. Gavakhov worked in the Caucasus; N. Yu. Zograff, V. V. Vorobjov, D. N. Anuchin, Yu. D. Talko-Grintsevich, A. G. Rozhdestvenskij, K. N. Ikov, F. K. Volkov, E. M. Chepurkovskij, and others wrote on the anthropologies of Russians and other Eastern Slavs; much fruitful research in the anthropology of the peoples inhabiting the Volga Basin was carried on by N. M. Malijev, S. M. Chugunov, and M. M. Khomjakov; A. P. Fedchenko, N. L. Zeland, A. N. Kharuzdin, and A. A. Ivanovskij were engaged in the anthropology of Central Asia within and outside Russia; the anthropological types of Siberian natives were studied by P. G. Matsokin, K. I. Gorosjenko, Yu. D. Talko-Grintsevich, I. I. Majnov, etc. Collected facts enabled Ivanovskij to write the first general paper on the anthropology of Russia which has been severely criticized (and with sufficient reason) from the methodological point of view, but which till now remains an invaluable source of information concerning the level of anthropological knowledge about peoples inhabiting Russia in pre-revolutionary times (Ivanovskij,

1904). Some years later Ivanovskij published an additional list of bibliography on the anthropology of Russia in his supplement to the anthropological synopsis of the entire world (Ivanovskij, 1911).

What, then, were the methodological standards of these numerous studies? On the whole, they conformed to contemporary scientific requirements. Subsequent results provided proof to the effect that even well-coordinated programs for the collection of anthropological data cannot fully eliminate subjectivism and lack of compatibility in information gained by different authors. Naturally enough, such subjectivism was characteristic of all the pre-revolutionary studies, and even more so when the methods applied varied widely and even measurement programs could not be coordinated. The situation was further aggravated when inadequate sampling in some investigated groups hindered comparisons of specific anthropological features peculiar to individual peoples and excluded satisfactory conclusions concerning their genetic relations. One should be careful, therefore, in one's analyses of the anthropological composition of the Soviet Union when using papers written by pre-revolutionary authors.

The above criticism in no way implies that no real achievements were made at that time in the field of method and gaining knowledge against a generally poor background. One must recall D. N. Anuchin's excellent paper on the stature of different local Russian groups based on anthropological measurements of recruits taken by draft boards (Anuchin, 1889; Bunak, 1932a). This classic study was perhaps the first in anthropology to provide a description of the spatial variations of a parameter based on uniform data, and it laid the foundations of the geographical method in the analyses of races.

The works of S. I. Rudenko and E. M. Chepurkovskij are another example of fruitful studies immediately before the October Revolution. Though Rudenko's program of Bashkir studies differs greatly from that adopted at present, the elaborateness of his program and the extremely representative broad coverage of diverse groups make his monograph a unique source of information about the anthropological composition of the Bashkir people even today (Rudenko, 1916). Chepurkovskij's results, drawn from his study of thousands of individuals living throughout nearly the entire habitat of the Russian people, enabled him to prove beyond doubt existing differences between the inhabitants of different areas based on head indices and skin color (Chepurkovskij, 1913). His papers are marked by highly correct methods and strict conformity to fact. Chepurkovskij made a valuable contribution to the geographical method, and was the first (fifteen years before the British biometrists) to demonstrate the incompatibility of results provided by different authors. He was also among the first to analyze and demonstrate the dissimilarity between intergroup and intragroup correlations, etc. Thus some advances in methods gained by pre-revolutionary anthropologists and some of the factual information collected by them have not yet lost their significance.

THREE STAGES IN THE HISTORY
OF SOVIET ANTHROPOLOGY

A final periodization of the history of anthropological studies in the USSR is not expected to be finally decided upon before a complete history of such studies, based on the exhaustive utilization of all available sources, has been written. At present a discussion of the major phases of such studies can be found only in more or less detailed articles devoted to certain memorial dates in the history of our State. In accordance with an already established tradition, three periods are generally distinguished (Levin, 1947; Debets, 1957).

The initial period of fifteen years began on the date of the Great October Socialist Revolution and lasted till 1932 when the reorganized *Antropologicheskij zhurnal (Anthropological Journal)* resumed publication after a year's break. This period was marked by some significant events. The country's first Chair of Anthropology was established at the Physics and Mathematics Faculty of Moscow State University in 1919, which also established the Anthropological Institute and Museum in 1922. Besides Moscow, active anthropological centers started operating in the Ukraine under Kharkov University and the Ukrainian Academy of Sciences in Kiev, and in Leningrad in the Museum of Anthropology and Ethnography, Academy of Sciences of the USSR. The theoretical standards of work carried on by the above centers differed but little from those of pre-revolutionary times, even though their methods had by then been raised to a noticeably higher level, particularly in Moscow University.

Higher theoretical standards in anthropological studies and a trend towards the practical application of their results to immediately meeting the needs of Socialist construction work are characteristic of the period to follow. The Fourth Congress of Zoologists, Anatomists, and Histologists held in Kiev in 1930 was a landmark: its Anthropology Section brought fundamental issues of Soviet anthropological theory to the fore for discussion. In this period, temporarily discontinued by the outbreak of the Great Patriotic War of 1941–1945, many major advances were made: theories of race and race analysis took shape, the labor anthropogenetic theory was developed and was improved in a number of respects, and some important papers on the cardinal problems of human morphology appeared.

Following the war Soviet anthropologists were provided with new possibilities for progress in their science. More institutions were set up: an Anthropology Department and later the Laboratory of Plastic Reconstruction of Face from Skull emerged at the in 1943 reorganized Institute of Ethnography, USSR Academy of Sciences in Moscow. This new Department concentrated on the study of the anthropological composition of the country's population; its standards were much superior to those of the pre-war period. General anthropological surveys of individual peoples were replaced by more thorough investigations of particular ethnic groups distinguished within peoples and investigation of local variations; in other words, it was a transition to much more detailed and thorough analyses of the spatial variability of anthropological parameters. Alongside these transformations, the overall volume of research showed a sharp rise; it was now facilitated by the new centers of anthropology within the Republican Academies of Sciences in Kiev, Tbilisi, Baku, Riga, Tallin, Alma-Ata, and Dushanbe.

In Kiev and Tbilisi these centers were given the status of independent units, whereas in the other places anthropologists worked within the ethnographic departments of their respective archaeological and historical institutes.

In the early sixties when preparations were underway for the forthcoming Seventh International Congress of Anthropological and Ethnographic Sciences to be held in Moscow, a new trend took shape among Soviet anthropologists: the application of physiological research techniques to anthropological investigations, similar to what was occurring elsewhere at the time. Anthropologists became morphophysiologically rather than morphologically-minded. True, such studies had been sometimes undertaken in the USSR in the earlier periods, during the first and second stages, but they were not resumed after the war when genetically-oriented research was practically eliminated. After the Congress this trend gradually gained in strength; now every anthropological institution of the country is pursuing an extensive program of study of the peoples of the USSR with respect to physiological features such as blood groups, serum types, the phenylthiocarbamide taste test, color blindness, oxygen and basal metabolism, etc. Morphological studies proper also increased in scope, as well as odontological and dermatoglyphic investigations. The broader and more solid foundation of anthropological pursuits makes them closely related to populational human genetics. All this shaped the outlines of the fourth stage in the history of Soviet anthropology starting from the early sixties, which can only be spoken of rather tentatively as yet.

ANTHROPOLOGICAL EXPEDITIONS OF THE FIRST STAGE

Even though many new anthropological centers were set up during this initial period, the organizational level of studies on the anthropological composition of the population of the USSR cannot be spoken of as having assumed a consistently planned pattern. Most of the expeditional undertakings of that time primarily reflected the individual inclinations of their initiators. All these expeditions can be classified into two categories: those sent by the central institutions to various parts of the country, and those locally-arranged parties led by peripheral scientists within their own national Republics. The results of this collection effort appeared in print partly in the years immediately following fieldwork and partly in the subsequent period.

Moscow-based anthropologists extended their activities into both near and remote regions of the country. In Eastern Europe they followed Chepurkovskij in studying diverse spatial Russian groups. Unfortunately, a greater part of the materials collected never appeared in print (Bunak, 1932c); nevertheless, they contributed to a fairly representative overall picture of the geographic variability of anthropological features drawn for Eastern Europe and made it possible to formulate a satisfactorily detailed classification of race variations among the Eastern Slavs. The genetic relations between these variants were mostly approached on a speculative basis because the necessary paleoanthropological information was then available in at best fragmentary form (Bunak, 1932b; Debets, 1934). The anthropological type of the Russian people was studied not only in general for the entire nation, but also with particular emphasis on certain ethnic groups which are of specific interest for the ethnic history of the Russian people due to their peculiar traditions (Bunak, 1922). At the same time expeditions sent by the Institute of Anthropology of Moscow University worked among the Finnish-speaking neighbors of the Russians of the Volga Basin. V. V. Bunak's paper referred to above distinguishes a peculiar anthropological type of the Vyatka-Kama area which is characteristic of these peoples and is expected to have formed by noticeable interbreeding with Mongoloid elements.

Siberia was another field of activity for Moscow anthropologists. Using modern techniques, Bunak began collecting data on Tuvinian anthropology (Bunak, 1928b); in the early 1930's, M. G. Levin obtained much anthropometric information (which appeared in print two decades later) on the indigenous peoples of the Sea of Okhotsk, the Evenks and Evens. Particularly fruitful were expeditions lead by A. I. Jarkho who covered every ethnic group of the Altai-Sayan Highlands. It was during these expeditions that the techniques of measurement and determination of descriptive parameters emerged and proved worthwhile. They were subsequently made the basis of almost all studies carried on by Soviet scientists. These were summed up in *Metodika antropologicheskikh issledovanij (Methods of Anthropological Studies)* edited by Bunak, a well-known guide to methodology which has appeared in three volumes. In the Volga Basin and the Urals area where Europoids contact Mongoloids, P. I. Zenkevich studied the Udmurt, Mari, and Chuvash peoples; he published his findings in the following decade. Active studies in Transcaucasia were led by Bunak, and in the North Caucasus by V. I. Levin.

Research in the anthropological composition of the population of the Soviet Union in this period is not to be reduced to what was done by Moscow anthropologists in spite of the wide scope and range of their field work. In Leningrad fruitful results were obtained by D. A. Zolotarev who collected much anthropological information on the peoples inhabiting the North European part of the USSR — the Karels, Saamo, and some groups of Russians. B. N. Vishnevskij scrutinized the distribution of blood type *ABO* factors among many peoples of the USSR (Rubashkin, 1929). In Soviet Central Asia a program of many years was started by L. V. Oshanin who published his findings on the Uzbeks and Kirghizes in the late twenties (Oshanin, 1927–1928; Oshanin, Jasevich, 1929). He proposed a promising, though at that time speculative, hypothesis concerning the dolichocephalic ancient settlers of Central Asia (Oshanin, 1926, 1928). A group of F. K. Volkov's followers worked in the Ukraine.

ANTHROPOLOGICAL EXPEDITIONS AND ANTHROPOLOGICAL INVESTIGATIONS OF THE POPULATION OF THE USSR DURING THE SECOND STAGE

Chronologically, the beginning of this period coincides with the appearance of A. I. Jarkho's paper on unification in the definition of descriptive parameters (Jarkho, 1932b). His article, supplied with a large number of graphic illustrations, contained an exhaustive description of models to be used in describing the structure of soft facial tissue. Bunak's well-known book of 1941 contained a detailed representation of the anthropometric technique. These two events are characteristic of the immense interest in the methods to be applied in anthropological studies of the Soviet Union during the pre-war decade. Rapid accumulation of relevant facts occasionally supplied by ethnographers helped realize infrequent incompatibility of data collected by different scientists which posed the need for careful control of compliance with the methodological requirements.

Studies in the anthropology of Eastern Europe continued on a large scale. M. A. Gremjatskij and P. I. Zenkevich examined the Komi-Permyaks of Inveny, the first among the Komi groups investigated by Soviet anthropologists after N. M. Malijev (Gremjatskij, 1941). G. F. Debets, P. I. Zenkevich, T. A. Trofimova, and N. N. Cheboksarov worked among diverse Russian entities within the so-called Eastern Great Russian habitat (Debets, 1933) in the region enclosed by the Volga and Vetluga Rivers (Aleksejeva, 1956) and in the European North of the USSR. Debets published extensive information on the anthropology of the Mordvinians and the Vepsas; Cheboksarov wrote on the Komi and the Kalmyks; Trofimova on the Tatars of West Siberia; Trofimova and Cheboksarov on the Mansi (1941); and S. A. Shluger studied the Moldavians (1936). The significance of these concrete materials far exceeds that of their narrow specific fields — they formed the basis for the reconstruction of the history of anthropological types and elucidation of their interaction in the genealogical aspect (Cheboksarov, 1936c; Debets, 1941).

In Soviet Central Asia Oshanin continued his fruitful studies covering more and more peoples. He obtained information on the local variation in anthropological features which is highly important for this region since isolation of these traits is characteristic of these parts. Oshanin released his findings in print soon after collection; they became available to the anthropological community within a short time and the results of their further development were applied in ethnogenetic programs. Concurrent with Oshanin, studies in Soviet Central Asia were conducted by Jarkho among the Kirghizes, Turkmenians, Uzbeks, and Kara-Kalpaks (Jarkho, 1933a, b, 1952) and by V.V. Ginzburg among Tadzik highland-ers. The latter author published his results in a separate monograph (Ginzburg, 1936, 1937a, 1949). Jarkho also studied the Azerbaidzanians in the Caucasus (Jarkho, 1932a).

In addition to the work of Trofimova, several expeditions operated in the Western regions of Siberia. Among these one of the most noteworthy was that led by Ya. Ya. Roginskij and M. G. Levin to the Evenki of the Baikal area. Their anthropological survey of the Evenki made it possible to discover a peculiar anthropological type distinct from that of the Central Asian Mongoloids, which later proved to be widespread among Siberian Mongoloids (Roginskij, 1934). Fruitful were A. M. Zolotarev's studies along the Amur River (Zolotarev, 1941), Debets' among the Selkups, and Shluger's among the Nentsi (Shluger, 1941). Debets is the author of the in 1934 published classification of Siberian Mongoloids later renounced by the author himself as inadequately supported by facts since it had been based primarily on the cranial parameter. For its time, the classification was progressive and played an important role as one of the first attempts at classifying all available information concerned with the anthropological composition of Siberia.

In addition to anthropometry and anthroposcopy, a prominent place in the programs of anthropological expeditions was occupied by collection of data in physiological anthropology. Thus, Ginzburg accumulated limited but highly representative information on the variations of ABO blood type factors among Tadzik highlanders and Turkmenians. His work is even now referred to for illustrations of sharp dissimilarities in a single feature compared for neighboring settlements isolated from one another (Ginzburg 1934, 1937b). He also undertook a comprehensive study of blood pressure among Tadzik highlanders (Ginzburg, 1936). Cheboksarov investigated variations of the ABO blood type factors and color blindness among the Komi (Cheboksarov, 1936b). Extensive dermatoglyphic research was carried out by M. V. Volotskij, who not only published numerous papers on methods used in dermatoglyphy but also compiled a representative survey of dermatoglyphic variations characteristic of many peoples, including those living in the USSR (Volotskij, 1937, 1941).

ANTHROPOLOGICAL STUDIES OF THE POPULATION OF THE USSR DURING THE THIRD STAGE

Many publications printed immediately after World War II presented materials collected prior to the war. For example, Trofimova's fundamental monograph on the ethnic anthropology of the Tatars and Nogai appeared in print in 1949. Other papers presented the results of programs started before the war; an anthropological study of the Kazakhs (Ginzburg, Debets, Levin, Cheboksarov, 1952) is an example. However, the third stage in the development of Soviet anthropology has a distinctive feature of its own, as far as studies in the anthropological composition of the USSR is concerned: investigation of the bodily parameters characteristic of various peoples was now raised to the status of a thorough analysis mandatory for all component ethnic groups. Thus it was only during the third period that spatial variability of anthropological parameters across the territory of the Soviet Union was finally given detailed and thorough consideration.

During the period 1952–1954 alone the Anthropological Party of the Joint Baltic Archaeological and Ethnographic Expedition, set up by the Archaeology and Ethnography Institutes of the Academy of Sciences of the USSR and the Institutes of History of the Estonian, Latvian and Lithuanian Academies of Sciences, covered over twenty Estonian, Lett, and Lithuanian spatial entities. The results of the study were summed up in a special book by M. V. Vitov, K. Yu. Mark, and Cheboksarov published in 1959. R. Ja. Denisova studied the Livonians (Denisova, 1956), Letts, Eastern Lithuanian groups, and Belorussians (Denisova, 1963); Yu. M. Aul published ample data on Estonian anthropology which he had gathered over many years (Aul, 1964d). He also studied the Letts (Aul, 1958, 1964b), Russians living in the North European part of the USSR (Aul, 1964a), and the Vod' and Izhora groups (Aul, 1964c). Vitov worked among the Saamo, Karels, and Russians of the North European part of the country, but, unfortunately his extensive collections have been made public only through partial publications (Vitov, 1964). Still unpublished are detailed anthropological data collected by Mark on the anthropology of all the Finno-Ugrian peoples living in the USSR, except the Mordvinians whose anthropological type was discussed in a special article (Mark 1960), collected by Mark.

Bunak worked in South Belorussia (Bunak, 1956a) and made a survey of the population in Transcarpathia (Bunak, 1948). A comprehensive study of the entire population in the Ukraine was not undertaken before an Anthropology Department was set up within the Institute of Arts, Folklore and Ethnography of the Academy of Sciences of the Ukrainian SSR. It took only a few years to cover every region of the republic in large-scale expeditional activities throughout the Ukraine in search of anthropological information. A summary of all collections was made in a separate monograph by V. D. Djachenko (1965). Somewhat earlier this author studied the Gagauz (Djachenko, 1953). The first post-war findings in the anthropology of the Russians were obtained by Aleksejeva in the Upper Volga region where, according to the chronicles, the ancient tribes of Muroma and Meshchera used to live (Aleksejeva, 1956, 1958). She also surveyed the Mishari Tatars (Aleksejeva, Vasiljev, 1959) and Chuvashes (Aleksejeva, 1955). The bulk of the anthropological survey of the Russians was carried on by the Russian Anthropological Expedition organized by the Institute of Ethnography of the Academy of Sciences of the USSR, which operated in the late fifties and early sixties under the general guidance of Bunak; the fieldwork was headed by Aleksejeva. The results gained were published in the form of a book (*Proiskhozhdenije*, 1965; Aleksejeva, 1965). Our review of studies undertaken in the Eastern Europe part of the USSR will be sufficiently complete if we mention A. N. Puljanos' paper on the Karaims (Puljanos, 1963) and R. S. Levman's on the Moldavians (Levman, 1948, 1950).

In the Caucasus, M. S. Akimova, M. A. Bulatova, and N. N. Miklashevskaja were the first to resume studies after the war. Akimova and Bulatova worked among the Avars and Lezgins (Akimova, Bulatova, 1947; Akimova, 1952), and Miklashevskaja among the Kumyk, Dargi, and Nogai (Miklashevskaja, 1953). Their efforts remained at a small party level and could not exhaust the great variety of anthropological types characteristic of the numerous peoples living in the Caucasus. Large-scale research in the Caucasus did not start before an Anthropology Department was established within the Institute of Experimental Morphology of the Georgian Academy of Sciences (later transferred to the Institute of History, Georgian Academy of Sciences). These programs were initially controlled by A. N. Natishvili, later replaced by M. G. Abdushelishvili, and covered almost every ethnic and spatial group of the North Caucasus in the Georgian and Armenian Republics (Abdushelishvili, 1964). At the same time anthropological materials were collected in Azerbaidzan, but these were published only in part (Kasimova, 1960). Scientific guidance of this expedition was offered by Debets, who also studied the anthropological types of peoples living in Daghestan with particular emphasis on the Western ethnic groups — the Avars and the Andy-didojans (Debets, 1956b). Detailed anthropological mapping of Daghestan was completed by A. G. Gadzhijev (1965).

Oshanin persistently expanded the field of his activities in Soviet Central Asia, finally covering all the peoples of this region (Oshanin, 1957). The rich data he collected in the expeditions of many years provided the basis for a synthetic representation of the ethnic anthropology and ethnic genesis of Central Asian peoples which he was fortunate to complete by the close of his amazing scientific career devoted to the anthropology of Soviet Central Asia and adjacent countries abroad (Oshanin, Zezenkova, 1953; Oshanin, 1957–1959; Nadzhimov, 1958).

Those peoples whose characteristics were not satisfactorily reflected in Oshanin's writings, the Kirghizes, for instance, were later considered by others. Thus, N. N. Miklashevskaja made a study of the Kirghizes while participating in the Joint Kirghiz Archaeological and Ethnographic Expedition of the USSR and Kirghiz Academies of Science. I. M. Zolotareva, another member of this expedition, succeeded in collecting in a single season information on all the peoples of Soviet Central Asia living in the Fergana Valley except the Turkmenians, and thus created a basis for subsequent comparisons of their anthropological peculiarities drawn from fully compatible materials. Yu. G. Rychkov worked in the Western Pamirs; unfortunately, the results of somatological measurements he collected still remain unpublished.

Referring to anthropological studies in Siberia, one must first and foremost recall works by Debets and M. G. Levin on the origin of peoples inhabiting East Siberia and the Soviet Far East as evidenced by anthropological facts. Containing much more than merely vast and original information, these books provide a review of the results of previous investigations and their further development and analysis viewed from the angle of an anthropological classification of Siberian peoples and the genesis of the Siberian Mongoloid types. In this respect, of a less general nature are the studies undertaken by M. G. Levin among the Yakuts, Toffalars, and Tuvinians; by Zolotareva among the Buryats, Nganassans (Zolotareva, 1962), and Dolgans (Zolotareva, 1965); by Rychkov among the Evenki; and by N. S. Rozov among the Selkups and the Turkic peoples of Western Siberia (Rozov, 1961). These studies contributed many new facts to our knowledge of the anthropological composition of Siberian peoples. Of immense importance are efforts by Bunak and G. M. Davydova in studying old-time Russian settlers of Siberia (Bunak, 1963; Davydova, 1963).

A few words should be added about recent expansion of anthropological research programs. This trend can be partly regarded as a revival of the long-standing tradition which was characteristic of the initial stages of the development of Soviet anthropology but was somewhat neglected after World War II, for example, blood type and dermatoglyphic studies. On the other hand, this trend is also a response to great advances in anthropological techniques which have made it possible to introduce into field anthropological work determination of odontological parameters, many physiological and blood type factors discovered during the latest period, and factors of proteins, serum, and anomalous hemoglobins. With further development of such studies, anthropology consolidates its union with human population genetics.

Progress in the above-mentioned fields has been so rapid that a by far greater part of collected information still remains unpublished. T. D. Gladkova and G. L. Khit' are distinguished for the preparation and publication of dermatoglyphic materials characteristic of peoples inhabiting the USSR; palm- and fingerprints were also accumulated by other scientists (Gladkova, 1966). Among isoserological studies particularly noteworthy are those of I. I. Gokhman, Zolotareva, M. G. Levin, and Rychkov on indigenous Siberian nationalities (Levin, 1959; Gokhman, 1963; Zolotareva, 1964; Rychkov, 1965b); Khit' on the highlanders of the Western Pamirs (Khit', 1961); and Gadzhiev on the peoples of Daghestan (Gadzhiev, 1964). The time lag between accumulation and publication of information on the structure of teeth variations among the peoples living in the USSR is particularly excessive. Till now, such publications are mostly restricted to odontological data obtained from paleoanthropological series; however, collections have been prepared for publication to present odontological results on the Kazakhs, Kets, Yakuts, Russian old-settlers of Siberia, and Russians living in the European Center of the USSR.

The above review is a vivid illustration of the broad front and rapid development of anthropological studies in the population of the USSR undertaken during the last few years; it demonstrates a much larger scope compared to the two preceding periods. Steady progress in this field is also seen in both a notable rise in the amount of publication and their wider coverage, a more thorough approach to interpretations of specifically anthropological problems, closer coordination with research programs carried on in history and ethnography, and selection of more specific problems of ethnogenesis for investigation from the anthropological angle.

THE ANTHROPOLOGICAL CLASSIFICATION OF THE PEOPLES OF THE USSR AND THEIR PLACE IN THE RACIAL SYSTEMATICS

Not a single general paper has yet been written on the anthropological composition of the entire USSR population. There is a review of the distinguished types in Debets's well-known summary of the paleoanthropology of the Soviet Union, but these types were segregated to be applied to paleoanthropological research, and this classification proceeds from primarily paleoanthropological analyses. As a rule, anthropological types found in the USSR are discussed in general papers dealing with the world's race structure, e.g., in the anthropology textbook edited by Bunak which appeared before World War II, in the anthropology manual by Ya. Ya. Roginskij and M. G. Levin, two editions of which appeared, in Cheboksarov's contribution to the collection entitled *Origin of Man and Spatial Distribution of Mankind in Ancient Times*, in Bunak's and Debets' articles on the principles underlying a classification of human races and their hierarchy, which aroused lively discussions. Thus it seems timely to sum up the major existing approaches to an anthropological classification of the peoples of the USSR and review the most interesting discussions devoted to specific problems involved in the genealogical relations between the anthropological types within given areas.

Using Cheboksarov's convenient terminology, we can refer to the inhabitants of the European North-West of the USSR including the West Finnish group, Komi, Lett-Lithuanians, and some Northern Russian groups to the White Sea as Baltic Sea or East Baltic group of anthropological types. This is the Eastern group of the Northern branch of Europoid peoples. For over a decade heated discussion has been going on about the origin of these types. The great majority of scientists including Aleksejeva, Aleksejev, Aul, Vitov, Debets, Denisova, E. V. Zhirov, M. G. Levin, Mark, Roginskij, and Cheboksarov support the idea of a small Mongoloid admixture among the members of the East Baltic group. All these authors proceed in their opinion from the morphological distinctions which separate the Scandinavians from the East Baltic areas and Northern East Europeans. They also appeal to facts proving the true nature of historic correlation between specific features, to paleoanthropological data, and to the results of analyses of archaeological findings. A basically different, in fact contrary, view was first voiced by K. Kuhn who denied differentiation of this set of features in his summary of European anthropology when he discussed the Lopar (Laplanders), whereas I. Schwidetsky advocates a similar view for the peoples of the East Baltic region and the Northern parts of Eastern Europe (Schwidetsky, 1959). In Soviet literature, this concept is shared by V. P. Jakimov, but his arguments more often than not rest on paleoanthropological materials and neglect the latest results of studies on the population of today (Jakimov, 1956, 1962; Debets, 1961).

It was in the first decade of the 20th century that the first objective concepts of anthropological composition of the population in Eastern Europe took shape with the appearance of E. M. Chepurkovskij's writings. He distinguished two anthropological types within the Russian nation: the Eastern Great Russian type and the Valdaj type differing in pigment intensity and cranial index. As studies went on, further differentiation of types resulted in a considerable rise in the number of types; however, even now the problem of their grouping and taxonomic hierarchy has not been satisfactorily solved. Almost all scientists unite these variants in the East European group of anthropological types, intermediate between the Northern and Southern brances of Europoids, supposedly formed as a result of the interbreeding of the two. There can hardly be any doubt that the very formation of these intermediate variants as a group might have been at least partly due to preservation of some integral, non-differentiated entities widespread throughout Eastern Europe during previous periods. Bunak traced the origin of these types back to the most ancient settlers of the Stone Age; some other authorities try to account for the role played by subsequent migrations and treat this group as a formation of later times, though they admit the existence of analogues for some types during the Bronze Age or even Neolithic times.

Bunak and Aleksejeva, the authors of the latest and most comprehensive and detailed surveys of the anthropology of the Russians, distinguish different numbers of local and regional types within the territory of the Russian habitat. Bunak distinguishes twenty local types within this area alone, whereas Aleksejeva outlines eight typological complexes throughout the whole of Eastern Europe, including Belorussia and the Ukraine. Djachenko divides the Ukrainian population into five spatial anthropological complexes of types, compared to the one suggested by Aleksejeva. Following Djachenko in his attempt to trace morphological similarity and genetic kinship between the Central Ukrainian type, distinguished by this author, and the Russian Valdaj and Eastern Great Russian types, one can diminish the number of the types; however, as stated in Aleksejeva's review of his book, these types are in fact different in many respects. If we compare all available classification patterns, we shall be able to see that they are dissimilar in the number and arrangements of separated variants, the ways of their groupings, their breaking, and their different levels of representing differentiation of races. Alongside the typological description of the anthropological peculiarities of the population of Eastern Europe, an attempt was made to prove the idea of the prevalence of local variability over typological variability within the Russian habitat (Aleksejeva, 1967). This attempt was based on craniological facts, and the idea still needs further development with the use of somatological data.

Whenever the Caucasian anthropological types come to the fore, the problem arises which has been actively discussed in Soviet anthropological literature — that of the role played by the Northern elements in the shaping of these types. As early as the late twenties, Bunak mentioned the Northern race in connection with his analysis of paleoanthropological finds obtained from burial places of the early Iron Age found in the vicinity of the Southern shore of Lake Sevan (Bunak, 1929). It is quite evident that if we admit contacts with the Northern race at the junction of the first and second millenia B.C., it would be difficult to eliminate effects caused by Northern elements in the formation of the peoples which inhabit the Caucasus today. Debets voiced sharp and well-founded objections to this theory in his review of Soviet paleoanthropology. His opinion was that some specific features of the proto-European type have been preserved in the body type of the Caucasian peoples. Later, Debets suggested that Caucasian nationalities are related to the peoples of Northern and Eastern Europe, not only morphologically, but also genetically (Debets, 1956b, 1960). His stand was supported by N. N. Miklashevskaja (1959, 1960). M. G. Abdushelishvili, A. G. Gadzhiev, and the author of this article advocate a theory stating that the Caucasian anthropological types characteristic of the peoples inhabiting the Central Caucasus (the Caucasionic type) were unaffected by any Northern elements in the process of their formation. They draw their arguments from the morphological uniqueness of these peoples and absence of analogues within Eastern Europe, the evident boundaries between their habitats, paleoanthropological analogues within the Caucasian region itself, and facts provided by history and ethnography which prove the originality and uniqueness of the ethnic history and cultures of the Caucasian peoples. Aleksejev advocates the idea of a protomorphous set of features preserved in the Caucasus since ancient times, probably since the Stone Age, due to isolation (Aleksejev, 1963), whereas the former two authors see the anthropologically peculiar features of modern Caucasian peoples primarily as a transformation of the ancient body type characterized by the gracility and narrow faces testified to by numerous paleoanthropological finds.

Most scientists agree on the number of anthropological types to be distinguished in the Caucasus: almost all classifications contain four: the Pontic type of the Western part of North Caucasus (the Abkhasian and Adygei group); the Caucasionic type of Central Caucasus (the Ossetians, Balkars, Karachevs, Georgian highland groups, Avars and Ando-Didoyan peoples); the Caspian type (the population of Azerbaidzan and South Daghestan — the Azerbaidzanians and part of Lezgins); the Armenoid type of South and, partly, Eastern Georgia (the Armenians and some Georgians). As for the arrangement of these types in the various classifications, no unanimity has been reached as yet. Bunak believes the Pontic type to be the most ancient in the Caucasus and traces its origin to Asia Minor. According to Abdushelishvili, all Caucasian anthropological types are about the same age, but belong to different classes of anthropological types: the Caspian type to the Indo-Pamirs group, or more precisely, to the Indo-Afghan class; the Pontic type to the Mediterranean class; the Caucasionic and the Armenoid types to that of Asia Minor. I agree with him on the taxonomic position of the Caucasionic and Armenoid types, but think differently about the arrangement of local elements distinguished within the populations of North and Central Caucasus — I believe the Pontic set of features to be the outcome of a transformation undergone by the more ancient Caucasionic type which unites both, as well as similar combinations, into the Balkan-Caucasian group of anthropological types, a subdivision coequal with the Asia Minor and Mediterranean groups of the Southern branch of Europoids.

The role of contacts with members of the Northern race is the central problem of Caucasian anthropology; the problem of the Mongoloid inter-breeding and of the significance and dating of this admixture is of similar importance for the anthropology of the peoples of Soviet Central Asia. The two Mongoloid peoples of Central Asia, the Kazakhs and Kirghizes, were united in a single South Siberian anthropological type the origin of which was discussed by M. G. Levin in a special paper (Levin, 1954). In his opinion, now supported by nearly every specialist in the field, this is a predominantly Mongoloid type with an European interbreeding which came into being as the Mongoloids of Central Asia mixed with the Europoids of the Andronovo culture. The other peoples of Soviet Central Asia are components in the Southern branch of Europoids though there is a Mongoloid admixture in them except, perhaps, the peoples living in the Western Pamirs. Since Oshanin's and Jarkho's papers made their appearance, two local types have been distinguished within the Southern branch of Europoids: the Transcaspian Turkmen type almost identical to the Caspian type of Azerbaidzanians (for the sake of uniform terminology, we shall refer to it as the Caspian type since a noticeable Mongoloid admixture among the Turkmenians is of relatively late origin), and the Pamirs-Ferghana type (Jarkho) or the race of the Central Asian Inter-fluve (Oshanin) among the Uzbeks and Tadziks.

The origin of the Pamirs-Ferghana type was given special, detailed consideration in Soviet anthropological literature. Debets believed the Pamirs-Ferghana type to have formed as brachicephalic features developed among the long-headed ancient settlers of the Mediterranean belt. Trofimova regards it as the outcome of interbreeding between the gracile type characteristic of Mediterranean population and the massive Andronovo (Trofimova, 1962). In his first papers on the origin of the Pamirs-Ferghana type, Ginzburg favored the idea of its direct genetical relation to the set of features represented among the people of the Andronov culture, but later he joined Trofimova in interpreting the origin of this type as a complex process involving brachicephalization of the Mediterranean and gracilization of the Andronov populations (Ginzburg, 1964, 1967).

Quite recently a basically new approach to the origin of the Pamirs-Ferghana type was formulated. Its typical representatives are seen in Tadzik highlanders, unaffected by any Mongoloid influences, in contrast to the Uzbeks. The type is treated in the entirety of its morphological features, including brachicephality, as an independent and fairly old formation component in the Southern branch of the Europoid race (Rychkov, 1964b). Finally, there exists a theory which regards only the Uzbeks and Tadziks of the plains as typical representatives of the Pamirs-Ferghana race, and classifies the Pamirs peoples and probably Tadzik highlanders as members of the Caspian type (Aleksejev, in print).

The anthropological type of the Volga Basin and the Urals zone are genetically closely related to those of Western Siberia. Within the Uralic group of anthropological types many scientists distinguish two local variants characteristic of the Finnish and Turkic peoples of the Volga Basin — the sub-Uralic and the sub-Laponoid types. The former differs from the "pure" members of the Uralic group in having a greater proportion of Europoid elements, i.e. being predominantly Europoid, while the latter differs by having a substantially higher cranial index, particularly characteristic of the Udmurts. Since these two types do not differ considerably in any other characteristic feature (the Udmurts possess neither a lower face nor any more expressed Mongoloid features), there is an opinion that the sub-Laponoid type is merely a local variety of the sub-Uralic type, hence it is unreasonable to promote it to an independent taxonomic rank of a unit of race classification. As far as the origin of the Uralic group of anthropological types is concerned, all scientists except Bunak treat this group as the product of ancient interbreeding between Europoid and Mongoloid formations dating as far back as Neolithic times (Aleksejev, 1961). This theory was first proposed by M. G. Levin, Trofimova, and Cheboksarov (Trofimova, Cheboksarov, 1941; Levin, 1941).

Of late the traditional genealogical tree of Siberian anthropological types which used to have three branches — the Paleo-Siberian or Baikalic type, the Central Asian type, and the Arctic type — has been somewhat amended. As new facts accumulated and were analyzed more thoroughly, the number of types distinguished among the Siberian Mongoloids grew, similar to what happened to the Uralic group of anthropological types where two types were singled out — Uralic type proper, and the Enisei type. M. G. Levin broke the Arctic group of anthropological types into two subgroups — the types of the Bering Sea and those of Kamchatka. The peculiar anthropological position of the Nivkhs among the peoples inhabiting the Amur Basin as regards their anthropological features, first mentioned by Debets in his book on the anthropology of the Kamchatka region, was confirmed by M. G. Levin who possessed more ample materials and accounted for their specificity by adding the Amur-Sakhalin type to the race classification of Siberian Mongoloids. Finally, the low-faced set of features singled out as an independent Khatanga type, which had been discovered by Debets along the Podkamennaja Tunguska River, was found by M. G. Levin in some other regions (the Eastern Tuvinians, Toffalars); thus its habitat was expanded considerably. In a paper on the anthropology of the Evenki, Rychkov tried to prove a wide spread of this Khatanga type beyond Central Siberia into Western and Eastern Siberia, and treated it as the most ancient of all Siberian types. His theory aroused strong objections (Levin, 1962).

Cheboksarov arranged all the above types into a single taxonomic system. He amalgamated the Arctic group of types with Eastern and Western Mongoloids into a Pacific branch distinct from the Continental branch represented by the Baikal and Central Asian types (Cheboksarov, 1947b). The Khatanga type may also belong here. This classification has been accepted by other scientists and is at present the most widespread in Soviet literature. Its author thinks that the set of features discovered by M. G. Levin among the Nivkhs and termed by him the "Amur-Sakhalin type", has developed as a result of ancient migrations of continental and Pacific elements. Morphology provides realistic proof in support of this theory.

Ample somatological information has been collected for practically every ethnic group living in the Soviet Union, though some of these data were provided by incompletely compatible programs. Generalization and synthesis of this information is on the agenda. The task can be broken into several more specific problems to be solved: the organization of all available, even unpublished, materials based on consistent and austere principles of selection; the development of connection techniques to enable comparisons of incompletely compatible data to be made, perhaps supplemented by sending out more parties to meet this need;

and the use of photographs in illustration of descriptive features, and perhaps, collection of additional necessary materials of this nature, particularly about the peoples inhabiting the East of the Baltic Region, the Volga Basin, the Urals, Central Asia, and Siberia. Even though collection of information about blood type factors, proteins, serum, and other physiological parameters, dermatoglyphic and odontological information, has been greatly increasing due to intense efforts by the staff of the expeditions sent by the Anthropology Department of the Institute of Ethnography of the USSR Academy of Sciences, by the Anthropology Chair and Anthropological Museum of Moscow University and by Republican anthropological centers, this work can hardly be completed within the next few years because the territory of the USSR is so large and the peoples inhabiting it are so numerous and diverse ethnically. Only by steadily accumulating information of these parameters will it become possible to describe the anthropological types characteristic of the population of the USSR with due thoroughness and detail, to reveal actual genetic links between them, and to supply additional information relevant to all critical issues of anthropological history and origin of the Soviet nations which cannot yet be solved at our present level of knowledge.

PART II

Ethnology

The Notion of "Ethnos" and Typology of Ethnic Communities

The Term Ethnos *and its Definition*

Yu. BROMLEY

The usage of the Greek word ἔθνος in international scientific literature was for a long time largely limited to two derivative terms, namely, ETHNOGRAPHY and ETHNOLOGY[1] actually denoting one and the same field of knowledge.[2] To denote the object of ethnographic-ethnological study, researches usually employed either general "generic" terms, used in everyday speech, such as the Russian *narod*, the German *das Volk*, the English *people*, the French *peuple*, etc., or "specific" terms differentiated in meaning by reference to the stage of social development, such as the Russian *natsija, narodnost'*, and *plemja*. Recently, the word ETHOS together with genetically associated specific terms, including as a necessary component the adjective 'ethnic' (e.g., *etnicheskaja obsjnost', etnicheskije protsesy*), has been increasingly used to denote the entire complex of such communities.

The works of P. I. Kushner, written at the beginning of the 1950's (Kushner, 1951), contributed in considerable degree to the introduction of these terms into scientific literature in the Russian language, especially in ethnographic literature.[3] The multi-volume series *Peoples of the World*

First published in the collection *Rasy i narody* (Moscow, 1971).

[1]   These terms gained currency already in the 19th century. As to the origin of the term 'ethnology' see Rohan Csermark, (1967: 170–84).

[2]   Sometimes West European authors regard ethnography as a descriptive subject and ethnology as a theoretical subject; however, this distinction is of a rather conditional character. In the USSR 'ethnology' has failed to gain currency, whereas 'ethnography' has united both descriptive and theoretical studies of the peoples of the world.

[3]   One of the first Russian works specially devoted to 'ethnos' was written by S. Shirokogorov and published in Shanghai in 1923 (Shirokogorov, 1923). The work remained unknown to Soviet readership for a long time, and that is why it could not have contributed to the introduction of 'ethnos' in ethnographic literature in the Russian language.

made a sizable contribution to the widespread use of 'ethnos' and 'ethnic community' (*etnicheskaja obsjnost'*). The preparation of this series has made imperative the use of terms which have denoted in generalized form the variety of the world's ethnic structure.[4] The growing interest of Soviet ethnographers in problems of ethnogenesis and ethnic history (Dolgikh, 1960; Pershits, 1961b; Cheboksarov, 1964; Bruk, 1964; Gurvich, 1966; Kozlova, 1968), and in present-day ethnic processes (Bruk and Cheboksarov, 1961; Zhdanko, 1964; Jefimov, 1964; Gantskaja and Terentjeva, 1965; Vasiljeva, 1968) in particular, has also exercised its influence on elaborating the terminology. As a result of this a series of special articles appeared devoted to 'ethnic community' and 'ethnos' and their typology (Tokarev, 1964a; Kozlov, 1967b; Lashuk, 1967b, 1968; Gumilev, 1967; Shelepov, 1968; Khomich, 1969).

In our opinion, the introduction of 'ethnos' and its derivatives in scientific usage to denote the category of human communities in question is fully justified, even if only because its conventional name is polysemantic in most European languages.[5] Our philosophical literature often uses a generic term such as 'historical community', but the latter conveys a much broader sense than the category we are concerned with, and offers little possibility of distinguishing it from numerous other varieties of historically-formed social communities, such as the state, the community, the family, etc. (Kozlov, 1969: 18). At the same time the prospects of international unification of the main nomenclature of terms used in ethnographic-ethnological research favor the introduction of specialized ethnic terminology. This in turn, it is hoped, will help bring the ideas about the subject of such researches closer together.

A number of new difficulties have arisen because of the introduction of specialized terms largely because the terms themselves have not been used with the same meaning. In most cases the terms ethnic community and ethnos have been used to mean 'people'. In such instances 'all kinds of ethnic communities — nations, nationalities, tribes (or groups of related tribes)' are usually meant (Bruk and Cheboksarov, 1961:76; Chislennost', 1962:29; Tokarev, 1964a:43; Kozlov, 1967b:117–18). A view is occasionally expressed that ethnos should be used to denote pre-

---

[4] Between 1956 and 1966 thirteen volumes (eighteen books) of this series appeared covering all the peoples of the world.

[5] For instance, the Russian *narod* 'people' sometimes loses its ethnic meaning and signifies 'working masses' or simply a 'group of people'. The German *das Volk* is also used in the meaning not only of 'people' or 'nation', but also of 'common folk' or 'the masses'. In English the word 'people' is similarly used. To some degree this is true also of 'nation' which appeared long before the community of people now denoted by the term (Kozlov, 1969: 19–20).

class formations only. However, in everyday Russian usage *narod* (just like the adequate terms in the other European languages) covers class structures as well. Since *narod* can be replaced by ethnos the use of the latter is justified with respect to all historical periods, including the present. It should be noted that ethnic community is interpreted as a broader conception than ethnos or people (Levin and Cheboksarov, 1962:29; Cheboksarov, 1967:100). This interpretation proceeds from the idea of ethnic communities existing at different taxonomic levels and orders. Ethnoses or peoples are "assumed to be the basic units in the ethnic classification of mankind, in addition to which it is possible to single out ethnic communities that are of a taxonomically higher or lower order" (Cheboksarov, 1967:96). Ethnolinguistic communities belong to one level, ethnoses or peoples belong to another, and so-called ethnographic groups belong to still another level. One and the same community of people may be a component part of several ethnic communities of different taxonomical levels thereby forming a peculiar sort of hierarchy (Bromley, 1968b:42).

It is quite obvious, however, that the amplitude of semantic divergencies in these cases is much smaller than in the case of the common usage of the word *narod* and its analogues in other West European languages. This fact once again points to the advisability of having a specialized ethnic terminology. In our view, however, a necessary antecedent condition to its introduction is the establishment of common characteristics that make possible the uniting in one category of all the communities that existed and continue to exist from the times of the early tribes to the nations of today. The problem is to establish the most typical intrinsic features, i.e., the essence of ethnos, people.

In solving this problem it would be incorrect to ignore completely the ideas which have taken shape both with respect to ethnos and to other terms denoting various kinds of ethnic communities. The question will inevitably arise: how can one take account of all the corresponding ideas? A simple, mechanical enumeration of existing definitions would hardly be effective because such an enumeration would not produce by itself the criteria for giving preference to one or another definition. In our view, it would be far more practical and important to establish beforehand some of the common and most characteristic features of the existing ideas about ethnos and ethnic communities. Such an approach may provide points of departure in judging the specific character of the phenomenon in question.

A more general point of departure would be the idea of ethnos as a community of people characterized by certain common features. In this case a confrontation of one community of people to other similar communities in the form of the "we-they" antithesis is meant (Porshnev, 1966:93 ff). The notion itself and the common usage of the existence of a special category of human communities, such as ethnical communities (irrespective of the words used to denote them — people, ethnos, nationality, nation, etc.), largely stems from the contraposition of one community to another. The opinion has been expressed that the question of distinguishing one ethnos from another is of secondary importance in establishing the essence and specificity of ethnic communities; however, this view overlooks the fact that it is precisely this contrasting of your community with another that helps in determining active consolidating of your own ethnic distinctions, and thus in cementing the community. Unless an ethnic community is distinguished from other similar communities, it is a fiction (Porshnev, 1966:95). The unity of external distinctive features of ethnos is an indication of its internal integrity to some degree, but the fundamental feature of ethnic communities which distinguishes them from other human communities is that they all possess a characteristic of sizable typological significance — mutual confrontation.[6]

This is turn determines the fact that a typical property of the differentiating features of ethnos is their distinct external manifestation. These features are established on the basis of data obtained through direct observation conducted through personal contacts of people belonging to different ethnic communities.

Not all communities characterized by the outwardly distinct "we-they" opposition can be regarded as ethnic communities. Cases of temporary, though obvious opposition of groups of people have nothing to do with the above (e.g., sports teams wearing different uniforms). It is not fortuitous that according to the current conception of ethnos considerable stability of the ethnos as a whole and of its basic differential features is regarded as one of its characteristic features.[7] Thus, among the numerous features characteristic of different communities of people, those that directly indicate stability should be included, in the first place, among ethnic features.

---

[6]   Two qualitatively different types of historical typology are known to exist. One of these performs the function of generalization by abstracting itself from the space-time conditions given directly, as conditions of existence of objects of historical research, whereas the other establishes the commonness and oneness of phenomena within a definite space-time continuum (Markarjan, 1969: 110). Quite obviously, it is the second type of historical typology that has a direct bearing on case distinction and specifically the version for which the existence of definite distinctions between the objects of typology is the main criterion.

[7]   It is significant that ethnoses — peoples — as a rule, survive several socio-economic structures.

This general definition does not dispense with the need to concretize the spheres in which these features manifest themselves most clearly. Although the above general criteria are implied in one degree or another in all the existing definitions of ethnos, this has not ruled out marked differences in the exact formulation of ethnic features. Thus, some of the Soviet researchers regard language and culture as fundamental features of this kind (Kushner, 1951:6); others add to these territory and ethnic self-consciousness (Cheboksarov, 1967:5); still others include in addition, the peculiarities of psychological makeup (Kozlov, 1967b:26); a fourth group, common origin and state affiliation (Tokarev, 1964a:44; Shelepov, 1968:65–73); and a fifth group sees the essence of ethnos only in specific psychological stereotypes (Gumilev, 1967). Foreign authors have given wide currency to the idea about ethnos as a group of families characterized by common origin and tradition.[8]

Wherein lies the source of this difference of opinion? In our view it is largely because both the essential and secondary features of ethnos are closely interconnected. Hence the difficulty in establishing the essence — the fundamental intrinsic features — and distinguishing it from the secondary features.

The primary object of a scientific analysis of ethnos is to establish precisely its essential features for "all science would be superfluous if the outward appearance and the essence of things directly coincided" (Marx, III:3 [1966], 817).

To solve this kind of problem in natural science the researcher, as a rule, conducts special experiments in the course of which he places the investigated system under unusual conditions to get an insight into its essence. In the case of the social sciences the possibilities for conducting mass experiments are rather limited. Some of the social sciences, like history, are almost totally deprived of such possibilities.[9] In their case experiment is replaced by the socio-historical experience of mankind. Therefore, to solve our problem we must turn to socio-historical experience with the object of establishing those of its "experiments" in which ethnic systems happened to be placed in conditions that considerably deviated from the normal conditions and caused the separation of the main features from the secondary ones. In our opinion, mankind conducted a large number of "experiments" of this kind in the course of its existence, e.g., the different forms of migration.

[8]   See, for instance, the word 'ethnos' in the book of Hirschberg (1965).
[9]   When nevertheless some experiments are conducted by historians they relate to the early periods in the development of mankind. Best known in this respect are those conducted by S. A. Semyonov to establish the productivity of labor of primitive people (S. Semenov, 1968).

It is generally known that when groups of people settle in a new place, not only they, but also their descendants preserve in greater or lesser degree their original distinctive, i.e., their ethnical features.[10] In our view it is the sum of these features, characterized by particular stability, that forms the essence of an ethnic community — ethnos in the narrow sense of the word. The features and elements of an ethnic community which are lost through migration should, consequently, be regarded as features of secondary importance. These represent, so to say, the outer shell for the nucleus of ethnos. A necessary preliminary condition for establishing the nucleus of ethnos is to remove the "shell".

When tackling this problem account should be taken, however, of the various "splitting" effects different forms of migration may have on ethnos. In a generalized form the different kinds of migration may be reduced to two fundamental types. In some cases these are migrations of large groups of people or even of whole peoples. A typical case in point is the Great Migration of Peoples, including the invasion of nomads into the European plains, which was accompanied by the settlement of some of their groups there (such as the Proto-Bulgars or Hungarians). Usually the consequence of such migrations for ethnic communities was the loss of their traditional natural environment and much of their cultivated landscape which usually was still poorly developed.

Another form of migration can be described as micromigration, i.e., migration of relatively small groups such as separate families. The form sometimes occurs within the framework of mass migration, which in this case is a gradual process extending over a long period of time.[11] Today micromigration is the main form of resettlement. It should be pointed out that such migrations on one scale or another have occurred throughout the history of mankind from the time of the peopling of the ecumene.[12] This is of particular interest to us because it is precisely micromigration that produces the greatest "splitting" effect on an ethnic system. In addition to the biosphere and cultivated landscape, micromigration usually removes a large part of the element of material culture and brings with it a complete change in economic ties as well as major social changes. In short, a study of ethnic systems through the prism of micromigrations shows that fundamental ethnic features are really the inherent

---

[10]   This circumstance should not be absolutized. Moreover, to ignore the fact that changing historical conditions, though gradually, inevitably transform ethnic features, may create the illusion that these features are immutable.

[11]   The settlement of Russians in Siberia is a case in point.

[12]   Although this peopling occurred in the form of group transmigrations, the groups, evidently, were often small (Bunak, 1968: 1–13; Khlopin, 1968: 99–100).

characteristics of people. That is why an ethnic community, or a part of it, will preserve its typical features for many generations, even though it may have been torn away from its traditional sociohistorical and natural environment.

It would be incorrect, however, to conclude (as is sometimes done) that ethnic features are eternal, that they do not depend on the environment. In reality it is the opposite. What is important here is that people in new conditions of existence reproduce in themselves some of their traditional ethnic features. This fact strikingly testifies to the relatively persistent character of such features in people.

What kind of features are there? We have established that they must be stable and externally explicit, and that they must also play a differentiating role. It would appear as though these requirements are fully met by the external physical features of people, i.e., racial characteristics such as color of the skin, hair, and eyes, type of hair, features of the face, height, form of skull, etc. It is significant that in common usage these external, visual, stable, and differentiating features often serve as a point of departure in deciding the question of the ethnic affiliation of an individual or group of people.

Soviet ethnographers have recently advanced the opinion that most peoples of the world are characterized by a relatively homogeneous racial composition (Tokarev, 1964a:44; Kozlov, 1967b:110). In contrast, Soviet physical anthropologists hold that the physical type of separate ethnical communities is not, as a rule, of a homogeneous character; accordingly, it is essential strictly to distinguish between races and ethnical communities.[13]

These diametrically opposed views proceed from anthropological units of different taxonomic levels. What is meant mainly in the former case are the major races and only sometimes the so-called small races, and in the latter case — the so-called anthropological type — the smallest classification unit. The layman will hardly notice the distinctions between close anthropological types. He, therefore, generally regards ethnic communities as an integral physical-anthropological unit. Despite the fact that in everyday usage it is the layman who determines the ethnic "we-they" opposition, racial distinctions in most cases are not essential ethnic features. This is not so much because there are no "pure" racially unmixed ethnoses, but because there are no clear-cut physical-anthropo-

[13]   In this case reference is made to the fact that Northern Italians are taller, more brachycephalic than Southern Italians, and that their eyes and hair are lighter; that Northern Frenchmen are taller, and their hair more fair, than that of the Southern Frenchmen (Roginskij and Levin, 1963: 321).

logical boundaries between adjacent ethnic communities belonging to one of the major races.[14] Such affiliation is rather typical of neighboring ethnic communities, for each major race has vast areas in which it prevails. The attempts to establish the ethnic origin of people on the basis of external anthropological distinctions alone, so often made in day-to-day life, are usually of an approximate nature. This also explains why cases when racial distinctions are used as the basic ethnic determinant are so exceptional. Such cases refer only to ethnoses surrounded by neighbors belonging to other big or small races.[15] Such ethnoses are known as "isolates" who have been surrounded by peoples of a different racial type.[16] Judging by everything, physical-anthropological characteristics are not used more frequently as one of the main ethnic features when combined, for instance, with language (Puchkov, 1968:93). Physical-anthropological characteristics play an important, though obviously auxiliary, role in distinguishing between ethnic communities that differ sharply from one, two, or more, though not all, of the adjacent communities (this occurs mainly on the boundaries of the main areas of habitation of the big races).[17]

In most cases when ethnic communities, though not identical at the level of anthropological types, are relatively homogeneous racially at the level of big and small races,[18] physical-anthropological distinctions

[14]   According to Soviet anthropologists there is, as a rule, a peculiar anthropological continuity between neighboring ethnic communities within the big races.

[15]   It is true that such a situation may arise as a result of the migration of a part of the ethnos in question, including individual members, to a different racial surrounding. For instance, it is easy to distinguish a Russian from a Buryat beyond Lake Baikal, or an Englishman from a Kaffir in South Africa, on the basis of their racial distinctions (Debets, 1938: 117). Such distinctions, however, are hardly characteristic of the aspect we are interested in for they cannot be applied to an ethnos as a whole (to the Russians and the English in this particular case).

[16]   Thus, all the Negritos of South-East Asia (the Andamans, Semangs, and Aetas) have, thanks to prolonged isolation that had protected them against mixing with other peoples, developed into stable ethnic communities (Bruck, Cheboksarov, and Chesnov, 1969: 93–94). Bearing in mind the present version of the race-ethnos relation, an interesting view has been advanced in the Marxist press to the effect that US Negroes are "a people within a nation" (Jackson, 1959).

[17]   In considering the role of physical-anthropological distinctions in ethnic differentiation we cannot ignore a rather widespread prejudice. According to this prejudice, recognition of the fact that these distinctions sometimes play a certain role in ethnic division opens the door to racialism. However, what is clearly overlooked here is that realism arises from the idea of inequality of races and not from recognition of racial distinctions which exist beyond dispute.

[18]   At the same time it would be incorrect to maintain that racial unity is indispensable distinction of any ethnic community, including the nation. For instance, C. A. Echanove Trujillo, a Mexican sociologist, writes that "a nation is a community of people united by common basic features, such as race, language, tradition, customs and trends"

play a differentiating role only if one or more such community is compared with ethnic units belonging to other territorially rather remote races. In other words, the reference is to situations that are by no means typical; thus racial characteristics, though plainly apparent, cannot serve as a sufficient basis for distinguishing ethnic communities.

Among the traits characterizing people, the group features of their activity are of far greater importance than their physical traits in establishing ethnic identity or ethnic division. Activity is the fundamental characteristic of people. To live man must first of all engage in practical work. In pointing out the active essence of people as doers, as subjects of the historical process, V. I. Lenin wrote: "... All history is made up of the actions of individuals, who are undoubtedly active figures." (V. I. Lenin, 1963:159). Human activity is extremely multifaceted. Although producing material values is a leading human activity, man's work is much broader in scope; for example, the arts and other aesthetic activities of society are highly specific, speech, both oral and written, represents special forms of activity, and human actions also include complex "internal" psychological processes.

The sum total of non-biological activities specific of human beings make up culture in the broadest sense of the word;[19] i.e., everything that is created by mankind as distinguished from the things created by nature (Frantsev, 1964:118; Sjepanskij, 1969:39; Markarjan, 1969:61 ff; Zvorykin, 1967:117). Culture includes the activity of people as expressed in their actions and deeds, and not only in materialized (indirect) labor.

It is necessary to distinguish between the personal culture of an individual and the culture of the community. The former functions within the framework of the latter; however, every society grants the individual a certain degree of freedom to be original, or to deviate from the generally accepted patterns. The culture of a community is not merely a sum of individual cultures of its members. "It is the sum of creative work, values and patterns of behavior accepted and recognized by the community, which have acquired meaning for its members, determining forms of behavior, regarded as 'obligatory', for instance, the rules of propriety, principles of social relations within a community, etc." (Sjepanskij, 1969:45).

(Echanove Trujillo, 1948: 182). This formula, if adopted even for big races, inevitably excludes from the list of nations all the ethnic communities that are not homogeneous in this respect, for example, the North Americans, Cubans, and Mexicans.

[19] The term 'culture' is extremely polysemantic. It has many meanings not only in everyday usage, but also in different sciences, including philosophy which uses it in different meanings (Sjepanskij, 1969: 38). The word 'culture' is defined in a variety of ways particularly in foreign literature (Shtaerman, 1967: 1).

The phenomenon of common culture is a vital condition for the performance of ethnic functions by culture, for if the culture of an individual is not characteristic of the entire ethnos, it cannot be regarded as a distinctive feature. A common culture is above all the "sum of living, current, and functioning works and models" (Sjepanskij, 1969:44–45), including those that have just emerged or have emerged in the relatively recent past. As we have already noted ethnic features must be characterized by stability; therefore, they should be sought first in those spheres of culture which are characterized by continuity and inheritance. These features are inherent in that part of a common culture which is passed on from one generation to another (Pimenov, 1967:3–14; Koleva, 1969:68–78; Baller, 1969) and which are known as traditional culture. Inheritability and stability of many components of culture alone is not enough for their performing of ethnic functions, for the traditional culture may include not only ethnically distinctive elements, but also national, international, and other elements common to the whole of mankind.

In short, only such cultural components may be called ethnic that not only are of universal significance to the given ethnos and are traditional, but that also are specific and distinctive of it, and explicitly evident. In most cases these features are seen in such spheres as language, material culture, folk art, folklore, customs, rites, etc. No wonder ethnic features are generally found in these spheres. It is the reproduction of such components of culture that helps the re-settlers to preserve their traditional ethnic features in the new zones. The process of reproduction itself calls for an explanation. Here we inevitably have to turn to human psychology and to social consciousness, for "everything that sets man acting must find its way through their brains" (Marx and Engels, 1970: 600). As Lenin put it, "man's consciousness not only reflects the objective world, but creates it." (Lenin, 38 [1963], 212).[20]

Unless account is taken of some of the qualities of human psychology in the broad meaning of the word it will not be possible to establish the mechanism that makes for stable common features in the activity and behavior of members of separate ethnic collectives and ensures their being passed on from one generation to another.

[20]   In investigating problems of social consciousness Soviet authors usually emphasize its reflective and cognitive function which enables man to find his bearings in the environment. The organizing function of the corresponding forms of social consciousness is equally important. It is this function that helps secure the integration and cohesion of a human collective and coordinate efforts by its members (Markarjan, 1969: 44, note 9), which are so important for the survival of society. Such an approach to consciousness as a factor of activity is known as a sociological approach (Kelle and Kovalzon, 1969: 280).

A peculiar but essential distinctive ethnic feature is ethnic consciousness, i.e., realization by members of a given ethnos of their affinity to it based on their opposition to other ethnoses and manifested first of all in a common ethnonym. A vital component of ethnic consciousness is the idea of a common origin. A common historical fate shared by the members of the ethnos and their ancestors throughout its existence forms the real basis of this common origin.[21] That consciousness is a fundamental feature characterizing an ethnic community is evident in particular from the fact that re-settlers lose it only after a long period of time. Practically, ethnos exists as long as its members preserve the idea about their affiliation to it.

Finally, an essential feature of an ethnos which in effect has until recently been left out of account by researchers is endogamy (Bromley, 1969b) in the literal sense of the word: couples mainly marry within their own community.[22] That endogamy was characteristic of the basic ethnic units of primitive communal society — the tribes — has long been generally recognized. It appears, however, that the overwhelming majority of modern ethnic communities — nations — follow endogamy to a similar extent — usually more than 90 per cent of the members enter into ethnically homogeneous marriages.[23] The significance of endogamy as a sort of "stabilizer" of the ethnos is connected with the special role played by the family in most societies in transmitting cultural information. Endogamy helps preserve the ethnic homogeneity of most of these units making up the ethnos, thus ensuring inheritance of traditional culture from one generation to another. At the same time marriage within an endogamous circle inevitably furthered cultural uniformity.

Various factors contribute to endogamous boundaries, including natural and socio-political barriers (language, state frontiers, etc.), and separate components of social consciousness such as religion and ethnic consciousness. As scientific and technological progress makes headway, accompanied by improvements in the means of communications, natural factors recede more into the background.

The boundaries of endogamy form a sort of genetic barrier for the ethnos concerned. As a result such a genetic unit as population becomes

---

[21] But not a common origin itself. The mixed racial composition of most ethnoses contradicts this.

[22] In its narrow specific interpretation endogamy is a custom which forbids marriage outside the given social group.

[23] A special survey has shown that among the Australian aborigines marriages concluded with other tribes averaged 15 per cent. In big modern ethnic communities, such as the Russians and Belorussians, mixed marriages between different nationals did not account for more than 10 per cent of the total number of marriages in the area of main habitation (data of 1925).

conjugated with ethnos.[24] In drawing attention to this circumstance it should be stressed that it would be incorrect to regard population as the essence and primary basis of ethnos (Gumilev, 1967:14–15). On the contrary, an ethnos performs the functions of population only thanks to endogamy which, as we have just seen, is itself derived from many factors including social and ideological factors in the first place.

Attention has long been drawn to the fact that none of the elements of ethnos such as language, customs, religion, etc., can be regarded as an indispensable differentiating ethnic feature. This is sometimes used as a reason for ignoring these elements as expressions of the essence of ethnos (Gumilev, 1967:5). Moreover in this case the fact that ethnos is not a mere sum of "features" and "common characteristics" but an integral system which is conscious of its integrity is overlooked. For instance, if language and ethnos, language and ethnic division, were always to coincide, distinguishing between the terms would apparently have been pointless.

At the same time it should be stressed that ethnoses are dynamic systems which have taken shape in the course of history. No ethnos is either eternal or immutable, but this does not contradict the fact that stability is a characteristic feature of ethnos, as we have noted more than once. What is meant here is a relative stability, changes occurring in ethnic phenomena at a rate which is slower than that in other components of social life. If we compare these with the biological changes taking place in populations conjugated with ethnoses, we will see that ethnic processes occur at a much higher rate.

Thus, ethnos in the narrow sense of the word and in the most general form may be defined as a historically formed community of people characterized by common, relatively stable cultural features, certain distinctive psychological traits, and the consciousness of their unity as distinguished from other similar communities.

In Russian the term *nationalnost* 'nationality', as applied to class society, is somewhat similar in meaning to ethnos when used to denote a people as distinguished from other peoples.[25] In this case the meaning

---

[24]   An example of the fact that the endogamous and genetic barriers are sometimes only conjugated, but not necessarily coincide, is that of the US Negroes. They are characterized by a high degree of endogamy (Negro-white marriages are an exception), though they are not rigidly isolated in the genetic sense (there is a high percentage of metis).

[25]   The term *nationalnost'* in the modern Russian language is used also to denote that one person or another belongs to a definite people (nation); besides, the adjective formed from it is used in the sense as 'state' since it was borrowed from the West European languages through direct translation: for instance, 'national income', 'national armed forces', etc.

implied in *nationalnost'* is much narrower than that of *natsija* 'nation'. Such terminological distinction[26] helps differentiate between close, though not identical, phenomena. Similarly, it is advisable to reflect in terminology also the distinction between the narrow and broad meaning of ethnos. The former will be expressed by the word ETHNIKOS (ἔθνικος) which is a derivative from the Greek ἔθνος. We should not forget, however, that "ethnikos" is by no means an isolated phenomenon. It is closely connected with its environment, made up both of social and natural factors which manifest themselves as necessary conditions governing the origin and existence of "ethnikos".

The role played by these factors in the origin of ethnos in general, and "ethnikos" in particular, is a complicated problem of a special type. It has several independent aspects of which the most important are the geographical, economic, and state-political aspects. Each of these may be the object of special research. We shall, therefore, in this connection confine ourselves to warning against a rather typical mistake that occurs under such circumstances: the confusing of the conditions of origin of ethnic systems with their cardinal components. The point is that factors that have played an important part in giving rise to phenomena afterward usually retain their significance only as auxiliary forms (Gulyga, 1965:7).

At the same time it is necessary to take account of the fact that ethnos in the narrow sense of the word, i.e., "ethnikos", is not connected with its environment unilaterally but interacts with it. Owing to their close interconnection "ethnikos" and environment constitute a complex formation of a peculiar kind. In addition to "ethnikos", two main spheres manifest themselves distinctly. The first could conditionally be called the "internal" sphere. It consists of all the "non-ethnic" social phenomena that are conjugated with ethnikos. The natural environment may in turn be regarded as an "external" sphere. "Ethnikos" is in effect a social phenomenon. As such it is particularly closely connected with its "internal" sphere with which it mutually penetrates one another, and by which in the final count, it is conditioned.

Generally speaking, it should not be forgotten that although both in the layman's mind and in some theoretical propositions ethnic characteristics proper may be divorced from other social phenomena, in objective reality the ethnos cannot exist outside social institutions of all levels, from the family to the state.

---

[26] It should be pointed out that in the stadial plane *nationalnost'* has a broader range of meanings covering not only capitalist and socialist nations, but also peoples of pre-capitalist class formations.

The way in which ethnic features proper are combined with the social (in the narrow sense of the word) depends to a certain degree on the space parameters of "ethnikos". What is meant is the homogeneous of heterogeneous (dispersed) distribution of the bearers of ethnic qualities within a given territory? In the USSR almost all the nationalities within their own republics are modern homogeneous ethnic formations. The people who do not belong to the indigenous population of the given republic and do not form compact groups there can be regarded as heterogeneous formations. No phenomenon, however, exists in pure form. Every modern homogeneous ethnic formation has alien ethnic inclusions which may be big or small. More than that, there exist so-called homogeneous-heterogeneous ethnic formations. They occur when one territorial unit is inhabited simultaneously by members of different ethnoses. In small territorial units, such as rural communities this is a rather frequent occurrence, but even within the boundaries of large political and territorial subdivisions one may encounter areas of inter-mixed settlements of two or even more large ethnoses (as, for instance, the settlements of the Russian and Kazakhs in Soviet Kazakhstan).

As to the connection between "ethnikos" and social institutions, a major role in its molding and reproduction is played by social formations that constitute the main units in the historical development of mankind. To denote these formations Soviet authors have recently proposed the term SOCIAL ORGANISM (Yu. Semenov, 1966b). Owing to the extremely broad meaning of "social", this term has become indefinite and poly-semantic. Experts have pointed out that this is also true of the use of "society" for the purpose (Porshnev, 1969:305). The proposal to use in this connection "country", a camouflaged synonym of state (Porshnev, 1969:306–08), is also an open question. It is still not clear why it is neces-sary to camouflage the social term "state" by the geographical word "country". It is true, "state" has more than one meaning. In Marxist litera-ture it means first of all the apparatus of class domination, but at the same time it is a political and territorial unit. With the origin of classes it is pre-cisely these units that have become the main social cell in the world-wide historical process. Since the reproduction of the internal social structure of these cells occurs, as a rule, in conditions of relative independence, they naturally may be regarded as independent organisms. This, in turn, enables us to denote the basic macro-unit in the socio-special division of mankind as a "social organism". For class society it would be more exact to call this unit a "political organism", but such a term is not applicable to primitive communal society for there was no state as a special organ of power divorced from the people. The basic independent unit of social development then was such a "non-political" formation as the tribe.

The special formations that originated as a result of the intersection of "ethnikos" and the social organism enjoyed relative independence which made possible reproduction. Such "synthetic" formations, which have been an important and widespread form of existence of "ethnikos", can, in our view, be defined as ETHNOSOCIAL ORGANISMS (or "ESO's"). In addition to ethnic oneness, such organisms are usually characterized by common economic, social, territorial, and political factors (the maximum version, so to speak). The socioeconomic factor is the most essential component of the "ESO". Socioeconomic factors which form the basis of all social phenomena, including ethnic phenomena, are more mobile than the latter. It is precisely this relative conservatism and certain independence of ethnic qualities that conditions the possibility to preserve basically the same "ethnikos" over a period of several socio-economic structures. For instance, the Ukrainian "ethnikos" existed under feudalism as well as under capitalism and socialism (that is why we refer to the Ukrainians in application to the feudal, capitalist, and socialist epochs).

The affiliation of the social components in an "ESO" to a certain socioeconomic structure usually exerts a definite influence on the structure of its ethnic qualities, especially on its homogeneity. Thus, the "ESO" of primitive communal society, the tribe, was socially homogeneous and simultaneously distinguished for its ethnic uniformity. Though class division in the "ethnosocial organisms" of antagonistic structures does not completely destroy their ethnic integrity, it is accompanied by the emergence of group (class, estate and caste) ethnic specificity in them.

Soviet experience has shown that the abolition of antagonistic classes in socialist society has sharply intensified the process of the so-called ethnic consolidation, i.e., the "ESO" is rapidly becoming more homogeneous ethnically.

In studying the typology of "ethnosocial organisms" in the historico-stadial plane it is necessary to mention the occurrence of transitional states. These may be conditioned by processes taking place both in the socioeconomic and ethnic spheres. In the former, we are confronted with transitional periods in social development. For instance, in the USSR in the transitional period between the Great October Socialist Revolution and the building of the foundations of socialism, the former bourgeois nations were gradually transformed into socialist nations. In speaking about the developing countries today (or "developing nations" as they are sometimes called), we could say that these "ESO's" are also in a transitional state.

As to transitional states of "ethnosocial organisms" arising from a change in their ethnic qualities, most illustrative are those cases when these changes end with a complete change in ethnic consciousness. Two cases in point are those of the French Canadians and Anglo-Australians who as "ESO's" were only recently in a transitional state of this kind. In the case of the Anglo-Australians, alien inclusions (German, Italian and other immigrants) played no small role in the qualitative change.

The intersection and the mutual penetration of "ethnikos" and the social organism have a spacial aspect, in addition to a historico-stadial aspect. In conditions of class society it is often observed that "ethnikos" and the social organism, as represented by a state formation, fail to coincide in territory. Depending on the character of this relationship it is possible conditionally to note three types of "ethnosocial organisms".

Type One ("ESO"-I). When outside the main common territory, the given "ethnikos" exists in heterogeneous form or in the form of small homogeneous groups that are not characterized by socioeconomic independence. Among the ethnic communities known today, the Italian nation belongs to Type One, since outside Italy the Italian ethnos exists in a dispersed state. The Slovaks are another example. The overwhelming majority of the Slovaks form the Slovak nation inside the Czechoslovak Socialist Republic (or the Slovak ethnosocial organism — the Slovak Socialist Republic). Only a small minority of the Slovaks live outside their country, either in a heterogeneous state, or in the form of small homogeneous groups (for instance, the Slovak settlements in the USSR, Hungary, Yugoslavia, and Rumania).

Type Two ("ESO"-II). The relation of the cardinal components is such that political formations mold several "ethnosocial organisms" out of one "ethnikos". A striking example is the Arab "ethnikos". The modern states have molded several "ethnosocial organisms" out of it: the Egyptian, Syrian, Iraqi, etc. Each of these is characterized by dialectal and cultural distinctions. In a certain sense the Spanish American "ethnikos" presents a similar picture, the only difference is that within separate political units it is not quite homogeneous. A graphic example of dismemberment of a single "ethnikos" into two separate "ethnosocial organisms" is the case of the two German states today — the German Democratic Republic and the Federal Republic of Germany. In this case we observe within one "ethnikos" at the same time two different historical types of "ethnosocial organisms" which belong to different socioeconomic structures.

Type Three ("ESO"-III). Within the framework of one political community (state) there are several homogeneous "ethnikos" with relative independence. The "ethnosocial organisms" which are thus formed should, perhaps, be regarded as bodies with structures that are not quite complete since they are deprived of their own statehood. A classical case of this variety are some of the nations within the framework of pre-revolutionary Russia: the Ukrainian, Lithuanian, Georgian, and a few other nations that acquired their own statehood only after the Great October Socialist Revolution.

A study of the different varieties of "ethnosocial organisms" in the historico-stadial and spacial (territorial) planes convincingly reveals a diversity of forms in the existence of "ethnikos". This diversity is by no means exhausted by the above types and varieties of "ESO's".

The ethnic picture of the world is considerably complicated by the hierarchical character of ethnic phenomena. This in particular has a direct bearing also on the structure of "ethnosocial organisms". In the ethnic hierarchy there are formations which not only rise above "ethnikos" and "ethnosocial organisms" (the so-called ethnolinguistic communities, for instance), but also enter them as ethnographic groups. Thus, the Russian nation, which together with the Ukrainian and Belorussian nations forms the East Slav ethnolinguistic community, only a short while ago had as component parts distinct ethnographic groups (the Pomors of the White Sea coast, the Kerzhaks, and the Don, Orenburg, Amur, and Ussuri Cossacks).

It is also necessary to take account of a vast number of small ethnic formations ("splinters" of "ethnikoses") both of a homogeneous and a heterogeneous character. They exist as inclusions (chiefly in the form of national minorities) in separate "ethnosocial organisms". As such they are distinguished one from the other by their basic structural components. It would be incorrect to ignore this circumstance in a detailed typological study of ethnic communities. Finally, it should be borne in mind that "ethnikos" forms certain systems not only with a social but also a natural environment. These systems are known as ETHNOSPHERES.

In a word, "ethnikos" is characterized by "polyvalence". This conditions the abundance of forms of its existence and correspondingly, the number of types and varieties of ethnic communities. To denote this diverse typology a rather limited number of terms are used. Often different researchers use the same term to denote typologically different ethnic phenomena. This, in particular, explains discrepancies between individual Soviet researchers in the field of social sciences, as was clearly shown by the discussions devoted to description of ethnic communities as a whole and to their separate types.[27]

---

[27] Particularly illustrative in this respect was the discussion on the term 'nation' held in 1966–1968 in the journal *Voprosy istorii*.

Misunderstandings frequently arise when one researcher uses ethnos in the narrow sense, i.e., in the sense of "ethnikos", and another, in the broad sense, i.e., in the sense of an "ethnosocial organism". The former will quite rightly say that community of economic ties is not characteristic of ethnos, whereas the latter, who regards ethnos as an "ethnosocial organism", will for good reasons of his own claim the opposite.

It therefore follows that it is urgently necessary to distinguish more clearly semantically between the terms that have been already formed. Maybe it will be better to use ethnos both in the narrow and in the broad sense, only to denote main ethnic formations (within the continuum tribe — nation); whereas ethnic community may be used to denote all stages of ethnic hierarchy. It will, nonetheless, not be possible wholly to overcome the somewhat polysemantic character of these terms which are of a broad general nature. Undoubtedly new terms are needed and should be introduced gradually. I have proposed to introduce only two new terms. One of these is "ethnikos" which has been used to denote ethnos in the narrow sense of the word, i.e., an ethnic phenomenon proper. The other term is "ethnosocial organism" ("ESO") which in general form reflects the main type of symbiosis of ethnic and macrosocial formations.

On the Concept of Ethnic Community

V. KOZLOV

The importance of the national question in the contemporary scene, the broadening of research into national, or in a wider sense ethnic, relations in various countries, and the features of the development of different peoples call for more thorough elaboration of the methodological basis of this research. An essential part of the work is to define more precisely the scientific concepts employed. The discussion that developed around the concept NATION in *Voprosy istorii* in 1966, fruitful as it was, could not result in a complete definition of the concept of nation. Though most important methodologically speaking, nation does not embrace all peoples or all forms of ETHNIC COMMUNITY.[1] The attempts at that discussion to differentiate the definition of nation by abstracting it from the concept of other communities of people was methodologically imperfect. Correct definition of a concept involves establishing, first, a generic criterion, i.e., an indication of the nearest, higher concept, and second, a narrower distinction — criteria appertaining only to the concept itself and differentiating it from other concepts of the same genus. "What does it mean to give a definition?" wrote Lenin. "It means first of all to describe a concept in terms of another, wider one" (Lenin, 1960:133). That means, as regards the concept of nation, first to establish the concept of ethnic

First published in *Sovetskaja etnografija*, N2 (1967).

[1] In place of the term ethnic community adopted by us, historical community is used as a rule in philosophical literature (Arkhangel'skij, 1961; Aleksejev, 1962; etc.). Historicism, however, is by no means a feature confined solely to tribes, nationalities, and nations. Many other forms of human community, from the family to the state, arise at definite stages of the historical development of society under the influence of various historical causes, and consequently can also be called "historical forms of human community".

community, and second to establish the difference between a nation and such related communities as, for example, nationalities (*narodnost'*) and tribes. Dzhunusov (1966) came closest to this of all the contributors to the discussion, but in our view was unable to resolve the task satisfactorily.

The establishment of the concept ethnic community is related to a number of most important problems of ethnography (of which it is the basic subject of investigation), but also presents considerable interest for related disciplines, viz., history, archaeology, sociology, linguistics, etc. For a long time it has not been given sufficient attention. The definitions of people or ethnic community that sometimes occurred in publications have been usually given as rather truncated, or on the contrary rather extended, versions of the well-known definition of a nation as an historical community of people developed on the basis of community of language, territory, economic life, and psychic traits expressed in a community of culture. Thus Levin and Cheboksarov defined a people as an historically formed group of human beings linked by community of language, culture, and the territory where it had taken shape (Levin and Cheboksarov, 1957:10). Djunusov characterized the ethnic community as a community of language, ethnic territory, economic ties, ethnic consciousness, and definite features of culture and character (Dzhunusov, 1966:22), without analyzing any one of these elements.

The sole attempt for many years to define the concept of ethnic community is that made by Tokarev in the first paragraph of his article "The Problem of Types of Ethnic Community" (Tokarev, 1964a). Tokarev's reasoning, it seems to us, is not free from errors of method. Thus, at the beginning of his article, he replaces the problem of the existence and specific character of an ethnic community by the secondary question of what distinguishes one people from another. After citing a number of such distinctions as "language, territory, common origin, economic ties, political unity, cultural features, religion, etc.", he calls them "features characterizing an ethnic community" and remarks that none of these features or attributes is indispensable. Then, substituting social links for "characteristic features", and contradicting his earlier statement about these features not being indispensable, Tokarev formulates the following definition: "An ethnic community is a community of people based on *one* [our italics — V. K.] or more of the following types of social link: community of origin, language, territory, state affiliation, economic links, tenor of cultural life, religion (where it is preserved)." He calls this definition "purely formal" and "very provisional", but a few pages later he writes that he is still unable to answer the question of "what it is that distinguishes an ethnic community from any other form of human community". That reservation, however, does not alter the essence of the matter; at the end of his article Tokarev repeats his "purely formal" definition in a somewhat abbreviated form as a final conclusion. We shall have occasion further on to allude to several of his propositions in more detail, the more so since they have not been subjected to critical analysis in spite of their methodological importance.

Elaboration of the problem of defining the concept of ethnic community, which is closely linked with that of establishing such principal types of this community as have evolved historically and exist at the present time, is a difficult task. Ethnic communities, especially in highly developed class societies, are complex, with a mass of individual peculiarities that put an almost insurmountable obstacle in the way of generalizing even narrow concepts like nation, for example. When we try to unite modern nations typologically with prehistoric tribes, generalization is even more difficult. In addition, human beings form a host of communities besides ethnic ones, which exist closely interwoven with one another. One group of people may simultaneously belong to a production organization, a social class, a political party, a religious body, a racial group, a people, and a state. The group is linked in a certain way with each of these communities, and in one set of conditions it will act as an inseparable part of one community and in other conditions as an indissoluble part of another community. To detach from this web ethnic interrelations and the characteristics appertaining only to an ethnic community is not easy.

Among the circumstances complicating this task, terminological difficulties are of no little importance not only to the special, narrow concepts like tribe or nation, but also to the general, wider "generic" concept. Because it seemed terminologically less vulnerable, we have given preference in this article to the concept of ethnic community, not identifying it in essence with the concept of people (*narod*).[2] Some scholars admit

---

[2] The word *narod* 'people' has several meanings in Russian (as in many other languages, for example, German *Volk* and French *peuple*). Occasionally, the ethnic sense is lessened and means 'the laboring masses' or simply 'a group of persons'. Its terminological relationship with such narrow concepts of the ethnic community as, for example, nation, has not been fully established. In our Soviet Press the use of *narod* most commonly met is as an equivalent for nation (*russkii narod* — 'Russian people or nation'; *ital'yanskii narod* — 'Italian people or nation', etc.). We also say and write *sovetskii narod* 'Soviet people', *indiiskii narod* 'Indian people', etc., the word covering a number of different ethnic communities. Not so long ago the expression "people constituting a component part of a nation" appeared in our Press and has since had a certain currency in ethnographic literature, where *narod* 'People' was used without adequate grounds for part of the nation (Jackson, 1959).

the possibility of employing ethnic community in a broader sense. Thus Levin and Cheboksarov, who were among the first to employ it in Soviet ethnographic literature, considered it a wider concept than *narod* because it could be used also for "a group of peoples related by language and culture", for example, all the Slav peoples, as well as for "a part of a people having certain specific linguistic and cultural features", for example, regional groups of Russians (the Pomors of the White Sea coast; the Don Cossacks, etc.) (Levin, Cheboksarov, 1957:11; Cheboksarov, 1964). In practice, however, ethnic community is almost never thus used since it could lead to undesirable confusion of concepts. In order to designate linguistically related groups of peoples it is customary to employ ETHNOLINGUISTIC GROUP, and for designating a part of a people, ETHNOGRAPHIC GROUP, RELIGIOUS GROUP, DIALECT GROUP, etc.

The poor development of our sociology, in particular the absence of a developed classification of various social forms that could help us define the place of the ethnic community among other social categories and its links with them, also complicates this problem. The term SOCIAL GROUP, employed by our sociologists which could also, it might seem, be applied to ethnic communities, is as a rule employed by them only for the class division of society.[3] Recently Semenov proposed the methodologically important category of SOCIAL ORGANISM, but unfortunately so limited his definition of the concept (as "a separate, individual society, as an independent unit of social development" [Semenov, 1966b:94]) that it is quite difficult to employ it for purposes of classification. Therefore, in order to define the concept of ethnic community we are driven, of necessity, briefly to examine certain general sociological questions.

We would begin by saying that the term SOCIAL should, in our view,

---

The term *natsional "nost"* in Russian is close in ethnic significance to the concept *narod; Soviet natsional "nostei"* 'Council of Nationalities' means the same as *Soviet narodov*, but *natsional "nost"* has a narrower scope than *narod* and is almost never employed with the significance of 'tribe'. In Soviet literature at present *natsional "nost"* is used most often with the meaning of ethnic (national) affiliation. In other countries (English 'nationality', French *nationalité*), the term is usually used in the political sense to signify membership of a certain state, i.e., citizenship; to express a concept close to the Russian, their literature sometimes uses 'ethnic nationality'.

[3] Thus G. V. Osipov, speaking of the principles of Marxist sociology, remarks: "A social group is a group of people united by a community of definite aims and interests and common efforts to achieve them; it is an element of the social structure of a definite socioeconomic formation. The variables which determine the affiliation of individuals with one group or another are primarily the function of the individuals in an historically determined system of social production, that is to say, their relation to the means of production, their role in the social organization of labor, and consequently the mode of obtaining and the scale of the share of social wealth that is available to them." (Osipov, 1964:215).

be applied to the diverse combinations and groupings of people that are based on actually existing links. The individuals belonging to them are conscious of their social membership, distinguish their group from others of the same kind by certain characteristics, and are capable in certain circumstances of acting as a single social whole. This qualification guards us against considering all the groupings of people encountered in scientific literature that are differentiated by researchers for one purpose or another (for example, the dolichocephalics and brachycephalics of anthropology; the cholerics and sanguines of psychology).

As to social formations proper, it is useful to differentiate them, first, into two groups according to origin: those consolidated in the course of mankind's historical development, irrespective of the will and consciousness of separate individuals, and those created at a definite time according to the wishes of the people joining them. There is no need here to demonstrate that the first group embraces ethnic communities, and that trade unions, for example, belong to the second category. For the next stage of classification it is pertinent to employ Semenov's category of social organism, with certain qualifications. In our view the term should only be used for social formations that can exist and evolve independently of others. This condition is linked above all with a definite minimum size of the social formation and is manifested in three principal processes: first, the production of the material values needed for the existence of the people constituting the social organism; second, the biological reproduction of the organism through the birth of a new generation; and third, the social reproduction through the passing on of certain social and cultural values and traditions to the new generation.

The concept of independent development helps to distinguish the initial form of ethnic community, the tribe, more clearly from other social formations of the same epoch. In our Soviet scientific literature, statements were found not so long ago, and still are found in popular philosophical writings, that originally there were only gens or clans (and even special clan languages), and that only after a long lapse of time with the development of the productive forces were clans succeeded by tribes (Arkhangel'skij, 1961:6). These statements are insufficiently substantiated. The clan as such from the beginning of its evolution could only exist in organic unity with other clans because its most important feature was exogamy, the banning of marriage relations within the clan. The establishment of marriage relations usually occurred, apparently, between clans stemming from one horde and speaking one language; marriage was inevitably combined with certain economic links and other types of relations. Wherever, "therefore", Engels wrote, "we discover the gens as the social unit of a people, we may also look for an organization of the tribe" (Engels, 1940b). The problem of the functions of clans is beyond the scope of this article, but it seems to us that the clan, based on blood relationships and forming part of the tribe, part of the social organism, must be classed not so much as an ethnic group as a marriage-family group. The widely held view that the tribe is also based on blood relationships cannot be accepted as quite correct, since such connections mainly determine the structure of the tribe only, and all the mutual relations between clans.

Some ethnographers, including Cheboksarov, consider the most typical forms of ethnic community in the primitive communal society to be not the tribe but a group of related tribes (Cheboksarov, 1964:6-7). Groups of tribes speaking related languages, or even dialects of a single language, were quite often encountered, but the co-existence of such tribes as an association of separate social organisms did not by any means always lead to their actual amalgamation. The life of an individual, or of a whole clan, in the tribal period was inseparably linked precisely with the existence of the tribe and did not depend directly on the existence or nonexistence of a group of tribes.

The problem of the ethnic correlation between the tribe and union of tribes deserves special consideration. It may be considered established that the amalgamation of kindred tribes into a group, and the development in their members of a feeling of belonging to that group as to a social whole, is more or less characteristic only of the final phase of primitive society, that is, of the period when it was already beginning to break up. As for the union of tribes (for example, the League of the Iroquois), it frequently originated not in the organic needs of the socioeconomic development of the various tribes, but in external causes, generally in joint war clashes with other tribes.

A number of other formations besides the ethnic community may be classed as social organisms, in particular the state (Semenov, 1966b:92-93). In order to clarify the specific features of the ethnic community, we must consider its basic characteristics and features.

The set of criteria usually employed by investigators trying to define the concept of ethnic community is quite large. It includes, as already said, the four "mandatory" elements of the definition of a nation — viz., community of language, territory, economic life, and psychical traits expressed in a common culture — but also a number of other essential elements such as ethnic self-consciousness, common origin or descent, religion, etc. Some of these elements, as will be shown later, cannot be considered basic criteria of an ethnic community because they either allow too many exceptions or are, in general, mainly characteristic of some other kind of community. In analyzing all these elements we should take into consideration that a factor conditioning the origin of a social phenomenon does not necessarily become a major characteristic feature of this phenomenon. Some of these elements, moreover, including language and territory, may underlie a definite form of social relationship; it is then methodologically vital to consider the relation of the ethnic community to corresponding types of community (linguistic, territorial, economic, etc.), each of which may evolve according to its own laws, so that its relation to the ethnic community may change in the course of historical development.

Language, the most important means of intercourse between people, is a precondition for the rise of many kinds of social organisms, including the ethnic community, for which it has special significance. Community of language is not, as such, inherent in either a state or, for example, in a religious community. Even in multinational states where there is usually some common language, that language ensures communication between people mainly in the economic and political fields and does not touch their spiritual life. For people who belong to a particular ethnic community, the mother tongue is not only a means of communication but also a means of developing the most important forms of their culture. Only the mother tongue, received and developed in early childhood, is capable of expressing the finest shades of the inner life of people, and enables them to understand each other by catching one another's meaning literally with half-a-word. Groups of people who change their language also change their ethnic affiliation in the course of time, usually in the second or third generation.

As for the incomplete coincidence of ethnic and linguistic communities, examples are most commonly adduced of several peoples speaking the same language. Spanish, for example, is spoken not only by Spaniards but also by Latin American peoples who owe their origin to the mixing of Spanish settlers with Indians and other ethnic components. These cases, however, do not detract from the efficacy of the criterion of community of language, since one understands by it a community of language within the people and not outside it; it is of no significance for the ethnic unity of Spaniards that Chileans or Nicaraguans also speak Spanish. A more basic case is that when sections of a people (*narod*) speak strongly differentiated dialects. This applies, for example, to the Germans, and especially to the Chinese, whose Northern, Eastern, and Southern groups do not understand one another. Sometimes sections of a people (*narod*) speak different languages. Among these exceptional cases are the Irish, for example, some of whom speak English and others a Celtic language. Despite Tokarev's opinion, these cases, too, do not disprove the importance of the criterion of community of language, but only require greater precision in its formulation. Many modern nations, especially in the Americas, have been formed from linguistically diverse groups of population, so that community of language, unlike community of territory, must be considered not only a pre-condition or basis for the formation of a people but also as a result of this process in the course of which language or dialect differences are levelled out through the effect of the educational system and the accepted norms of speech. Where this process has still not developed to its full, ethnic consolidation cannot be considered complete. An expression of linguistic community in such cases is the existence of a single written literary language and numerous groups of the population with transitional dialects. The Irish first took shape as a people having a Celtic language, Gaelic, in common; the later transition of the overwhelming majority to English, of course, disrupted their linguistic-cultural community, but for various reasons did not obliterate their ethnic unity. At present the linguistic community of the Irish is being restored by the spread of English among those who do not yet know it, and also through the revival of Gaelic and its spread among English-speaking Irish people.

Territory is primarily the pre-condition, the material base, for the formation of ethnic and of many other types of community since people must, as a rule, in order to associate, live close to one another. Territorial (i.e., neighborly) links, as such, have a rather narrow scope and usually do not go beyond the bounds of a settlement, the so-called village, neighborhood community, or a small district. Territory is basic, nonetheless, for the development of economic, linguistic, etc., links. Even groups of people differing in language and origin who live in the same territory can merge into a single nation in the course of time (such is the origin of many nations on the American continent, for example); on the contrary, the territorial dispersal of a formerly single people can lead to the formation of different ethnic communities among their parts. Being located on one territory over the course of many centuries, "settling" that territory, a people begins to consider it as their native land and to link their historical fate with it. The natural conditions of this territory find reflection in the accumulation of elements of culture and daily life, and the image of the "native land" plays a conspicuous role in the formation of ethnic self-consciousness.

Territory, furthermore, is not only an important condition for the rise of an ethnic community but also for its continued existence. Breach of the integrity of an ethnic territory, or territorial dispersion of the members of an ethnic community, and transformation of its separate groups into national minorities settled in the midst of other peoples, sooner or later ends in their assimilation, which implies that it is desirable to include territory among the features characterizing the ethnic community.

At the same time, it should be noted that territory does not itself, like language and culture, for example, have any ethnic connotations. The link with a territory, the country of habitation, is characteristic primarily of the concepts "compatrist" and "fatherland" (behind which, too, there are definite communities of people), but not of the concept people (*narod*). It may be good to cite a few examples of how quite different ethnic communities have taken shape at various times on one territory, or how certain peoples (Magyars, Kalmyks, etc.), having taken shape originally on one territory, migrated and lived in a quite different region.

The ethnic territory itself can be altered significantly; in some cases (Russians, Yakuts, etc.), it has been greatly extended through the settlement of new regions; in others (Mordvinians, Baskhirs, etc.), it has been reduced through the settlement of other national groups on it.

The development of humanity has gone hand in hand with the territorial mingling of peoples through migrations from rural to urban places, from one district of a country to another, from one country to another. In many parts of the world different peoples are intermingled and live in patches over a single area. Only those nations have an unbroken and clearly demarcated ethnic territory whose ethnic boundaries coincide with their state boundaries.

When one attempts to clarify the links between the members of an ethnic community, special attention is usually given to economic connections. This attention is only partially justified since economy, although a necessary condition in the final analysis for the existence of all kinds of communities, does not characterize the specific features of the ethnic community. Economic links only fully determine an economic community, i.e., those brought about by the division of labor in the course of producing the necessities of life. The ethnic and the economic community quite often coincide, but as a rule the link between them has an indirect character, primarily because of the community of territory and the sociopolitical organization connected with it. Community of territory is a necessary pre-condition for the rise of an economic community, and when the former is disrupted through territorial mingling of peoples so is the latter. Without dwelling on the problem of the hypothetical economic community of a nationality (*narodnost'*), we would note that the classic economic community, consolidated with the development of capitalism, is not the characteristic so much of the nation as of the state, since its main determining factors (division of labor between different districts and the establishment of transport links, etc., between them, a single monetary system, customs frontier, etc.) are directly linked with the state. A common economy coincides with the national community when the nation has its own state, and as a rule does not coincide with it, or does so only partially, in multinational states where several nations are linked in one economic system (Kozlov, 1967a). We, therefore, conclude that a common economy should not be included among the main criteria of the ethnic community.

The efforts of certain investigators to include common *psychological traits* or a *culture* held in common among the basic ethnic criteria seem to us to have little justification (Kaltakhchian, 1966). The psychological traits or the character of a people are determined, as is known, both by biological and social factors. The biological factors, primarily sex, age, and temperament, have no organic link with the ethnic community. Temperament is linked with climatic environment and with racial features rather than with ethnos. The fact that one temperament or another may predominate in a certain people does not contradict this general pattern. Among the social factors exerting a certain influence upon character is the ethnic environment; however, it is the class and occupational role of individuals that plays the leading part and this does not permit, especially in an antagonistic class society, the formation of a genuine community of psychological traits. Study based upon principles of social psychology clearly shows that the Russian peasant, merchant, civil servant, and worker had more differences of psychological traits than they had in common. Even to take only the Russian peasant, the Russian Pomor will be shown to be much closer in character to the Karelian than to the Russian peasant from Ryazan, and is still further from the Terek Cossack. When one speaks of the differences in psychological traits of definite peoples, for example the Norwegians and the Japanese, one has in mind a certain psychological stereotype of the one and the other abstracted from the differences within these peoples. Therefore, without glossing over the complexity of the problem, it would be much more correct to speak not of the existence of a community of psychological traits in a people, or of something called "national character", applicable, it would seem, only to peoples of pre-class societies, but rather of the existence of certain specific features of the psychological traits characterizing individual peoples, especially comparatively small ethnic communities, and the groups (class and occupational, regional, etc.) that make up each of those peoples.

The problem of community of culture is more complex because of the vastness and certain vagueness of the concept *culture*. If we narrow down this concept and turn, for example, to material culture, we are then faced with numerous cases of strong differentiation of its elements within any one people (especially within a numerous people who live under widely varying conditions), and, on the contrary, with strong resemblances of cultural elements between different peoples. Furthermore, material culture, being closely linked with the means of production, exhibits a tendency to the levelling of differences existing at any one time: there has never been a nation, it would seem, whose members have possessed only the "national" tools and implements appertaining to them, and dressed in the "national" costume, and ate only special "national" dishes. As for spiritual culture, there is no universal observed in all peoples. Capitalists and the proletariat have different spiritual cultures. Lenin more than once spoke of the existence of two cultures within the culture of each nation in the capitalist epoch and stressed that any attempt to demonstrate the community of its culture inevitably led to nationalism. Thus, in defining an ethnic community, one must lay stress not on "community of culture", which was inherent only in early forms of ethnic community, but on those specific elements of peoples' culture and way of life that, combined with their language, create a unique image of the main ethnographic groups of this community.

All social organisms have a definite self-awareness in the people constituting them; otherwise, they would cease to act as single social collectives and as subjects of historical development. The conditions of the material life of people can lead to one social phenomenon or another only through the consciousness of people being reflected in it in the form of definite conceptions or ideals. For man as a social being molded solely in organic connection with the formation of human society, consciousness of his membership of a wider circle of persons is not only a natural feeling but an inevitable one, giving him confidence in life, justifying his very existence on earth. This also fully applies to ethnic communities which arose earlier than many other communities at the dawn of human history as a necessary form of life and form of group struggle for existence. The attempts so far made to define the concept of ethnic community have proved unsuccessful, we think, usually because the investigators have mainly tried to compile a set of criteria for it with almost no consideration of the character of the connections between the people constituting the community and the reflection of those connections in their consciousness.

Ethnic self-consciousness — the awareness of belonging to a definite people (*narod*) — manifests itself concretely in that a people's use of a single name for themselves as a people arises in the course of living for a long time. A strong influence is exerted over this development by the social environment, by prevalent ideas of a common descent, and by common historical destinies, etc. Being one of the forms of social consciousness, ethnic self-awareness plays a leading role in the existence of the ethnic community; in this respect it differs sharply from the problematical community of psychological traits with which it is occasionally confused. At a certain stage of development, ethnic self-consciousness, like other ideological forms, can take on a relative independence. It can persist for a long time even when there is a territorial and economic-cultural rift between separate groups of a people and the main ethnic nucleus, and even when there is loss of the mother tongue. Cases of non-coincidence of language and ethnic affiliation make it necessary in practice to employ the criterion of ethnic (national) self-consciousness to determine nationality when taking a census. The criterion of language would take second place in these cases. Ethnic self-consciousness can have reverse impact on the factors generating it, which manifests itself, for example, in reviving of the mother tongue, in political and territorial unification, etc. Without attempting here to resolve fully the problem of the specific nature of ethnic self-consciousness, we would point out that it is distinguished from religious consciousness primarily by being directed towards the people (*narod*) and not to some other-world object, and from racial consciousness by centering its attention in distinguishing the kinship of people not upon external physical characteristics but on their linguistic and cultural peculiarities and features of their way of life.

In order to achieve stability and normal development, the ethnic community strives to take the form of a social organization. The tribe, as an ethnic community, is usually also a form of social organization. When class society evolves and the state takes the place of the clan-and-tribe organization, the ethnic community displays a tendency to take the form of a state structure; it is not without reason that nearly all national movements are directed toward the setting up of a national state or some form of autonomy within the framework of a multinational state. The difference between an ethnic community and a state community shows most clearly in multinational states where ethnic self-consciousness is linked with people's linguistic and cultural peculiarities and their way of life, and among oppressed national minorities with a struggle for national equality. In national states as such, ethnic (national) self-consciousness often merges with awareness of belonging to the state, and with a feeling of patriotism.

To conclude this brief analysis of the elements of the ethnic community, we would refer again to the definition suggested by Tokarev. His definition is particularly open to criticism where it says that the ethnic community may be based on one of the forms of social connection enumerated by him, viz., "community of origin, language, territory, state affiliation, economic links, cultural pattern, religion (where it is preserved)". We cannot accept this statement even apart from such strange "social connections" as "tenor of cultural life", since if the ethnic community may be based solely on linguistic links it becomes impossible to distinguish it from the linguistic community. In cases where the ethnic community is based solely on state affiliation it is unclear how it differs from the state community. It is particularly ill-advised to relate this condition to such "social connections" as community of origin (which in Tokarev's view is most clearly manifested in "identity of anthropological type") and religion. As an example of a people allegedly based on community of origin, Tokarev cites the Negroes of the USA, forgetting that the ancestors of the Negro population of the USA were brought from different regions of Africa, belonged to various peoples, and consequently had no common ethnic origin, although, of course, they had similar racial features and a definite common destiny linked with their new situation. In fact, this population is mulatto in its majority, with different degrees of racial mixture, i.e., there is no similarity of anthropological type, and furthermore, it is not a separate people (*narod*) at all but a special group within the American nation (Berzina, 1962:289). The imprecision of Tokarev's formula is the more regrettable since the relation of race and ethnos, race and ethnic community, is indeed an intricate one (Efimov, 1966). In Soviet science the view has become firmly established that there is no organic connection between race and language, that the process of race formation and that of ethnic formation did not in general coincide (Roginskii, Levin, 1955:330), although the fact that the majority of the peoples of the world have a comparatively uniform racial composition (as regards the major races, and in a number of cases, also as regards the smaller ones) is not a matter of change. Racial differences are clearly evidence of the heterogeneous origin and history of their bearers, and undoubtedly delay the development of a common ethnic self-consciousness. It has required a lengthy process of biological mixing with the formation of numerous transitional racial types for Caucasians, Mongoloids, and Negroids to form united peoples in Latin America (such as Cubans, Brazilians, etc.).

As for religion, common religious persuasion — religious community — can sometimes coincide with the ethnic community. As the history of mediaeval Europe and of Near Eastern countries shows, religious consciousness sometimes supplants ethnic self-consciousness, but religion of itself can neither establish nor preserve ethnic community, but can only contribute to it. Tokarev's example to demonstrate the strength of religious ties, the Jews, "scattered all over the world but not having lost their ethnic unit", is not very convincing. There is no doubt that Judaism, as a most clearly expressed "national" religion, has played and still plays an important role in the life of Jews, and is reflected in their self-consciousness and in certain features of their culture and way of life. The ancient Hebrew people, however, took shape several centuries before the Judaic religion, and the ethnic peculiarity of the Jews who settled originally in European countries is to be explained not simply by religious factors but also by socioeconomic ones. Judaism could not maintain the ethnic unity of the Jews. Even in the Middle Ages they were divided into two main streams — the Sephardim speaking Ladino, and the Ashkenazim speaking Yiddish. In the subsequent period the ethnic isolation of the group of Jews living in various countries became even more marked, and for some of them (especially the Jewish population of the USSR), Judaism has already lost its significance as an ethnic determinant. The Jews have long ceased to be a single people (*narod*), and many groups of them have nothing left in common except an identical self-name and certain, not infrequently vague, ideas about a common origin and history. The other examples given by Tokarev in this connection are also lacking in conviction.[4]

In conclusion, let us formulate a definition of ethnic community.

An ethnic community is a social organism consolidated on a definite territory from groups of people under the conditions — (already present, or achieved by them in the course of the development of economic and socio-cultural connections) — of a common language, common features of culture and way of life, a number of common social values and traditions, and a considerable intermingling of racial components sharply differentiated in the past. The basic characteristics of an ethnic community are ethnic self-consciousness and a common name for themselves (self-naming), a common language, territory, peculiarities of psychological traits, culture, way of life, and a definite form of social and territorial organization (or an aspiration to create such an organization). This brief formulation does not, of course, reflect the whole variety of reality, and

---

[4]   Without going into the details of these fairly complex cases we would remark that the Maronites mentioned by Tokarev are considered in Soviet ethnographic literature not as a special ethnic community, but as a part of the Lebanese people, the Yesidi, a religious sect within the Kurdish people, etc.

its concrete application calls for its supplementing in various ways as follows from the examples discussed above. It is quite clear, for example, that the criteria of community of language and territory can usually only be fully applied to the main ethnic nucleus of a particular people because of the marked territorial mixing of peoples and processes of linguistic assimilation.

A more complete unravelling of the essence of the main elements of the ethnic community could only be given in a number of specialized articles.

Contemporary Ethnic Processes in the USSR

Experience of a Socio-Ethnic Survey (Relating to the Tatar ASSR)

Yu. ARUTJUNJAN

CERTAIN THEORETICAL PREMISES

It is not possible in a modern, socially differentiated society to judge ethnic processes according to the ethnos as a whole. In particular, by comparing the ethnic and the social, the object of socio-ethnic research being undertaken today is to indicate what is peculiar to the ethnic processes taking place in various social environments and situations. This was the aim of a socio-ethnic survey undertaken by sociologists of the Institute of Ethnography of the USSR Academy of Sciences in the Tatar ASSR.

In embarking on the survey we had first to resolve several theoretical problems. It was of decisive importance to establish an adequate criterion of the social environment represented by classes, social strata, and social groups in Soviet society. The conception of the social structure of Soviet society that has dominated our literature for some time seemed too general and unsuitable for analysis. The category of collective farmer embraces both the chairmen of collective farms and unskilled rank and file members; employee embraces professors and bookkeepers. We came up against a need to develop a fuller, more detailed, and more varied classification. Taking a number of theoretical considerations as our premises, we based our classification on quality of labor, covering a continuum of "physical-mental labor" from simple labor to complex, from carrying out orders to giving them.[1]

In addition to the quality of labor, attention was also paid to the

First published in *Sovetskaja etnografija*, N4 (1968).

[1] The methodological principles for elaborating social structure have been developed by the writer in a number of works (*Problemy*, 1968: 102–107; Arutjunjan, 1966 a, b).

sphere of employment or performance of work. In this connection a distinction was made between town and country, and in the countryside between socio-economic spheres, i.e., between the state sector and the collective farm-cooperative sector. A distinction was also made between branches of the economy as between forms of industrial work, agriculture, services, etc. In as much as we were concerned with the social structure of the whole population and not just the working population, we also bore in mind the non-productive sphere: educational institutions, the army, housework, etc.

The working scheme of social structure that we employed is given in Table 1.

Table 1.   *Social Structure of Socialist Society*

Social group by type of work	Sphere of Activity				
	predominantly productive		non-productive		
	town	country			
	state sector	collective farm co-operative sector	school	army	housework
Intelligentsia (A) administrative creative (artistic) scientific productive mass (doctors, teachers)					
Employees (B) Skilled manual workers (C) Unskilled manual workers (D)					

Another theoretical problem was determination of the trend of ethnic processes in social spheres. How, and in what concrete way, do ethnic and social relations impinge on one another? What are the subjects to be studied in this field? In what do these processes manifest themselves? We distinguished the following:

1. changes in the ethnic composition of social groups;

2. the effect of the ethnic factor on social mobility, i.e., the influence of national affiliation on a person's social development;

3. changes in national interests, and their links with social interests

(the most general form of national interest is the striving to preserve the identity of one's own nation, culture, language, and statehood. National interests, however, always have their social epicenter and in essence serve as the national shell for social interests; different social groups within nations are consciously, but more often unconsciously, interested in preserving their culture and statehood to varying degrees, stemming from specific social drives and motives.);

4. the manifestation of a national psychology as a component part of the social psychology of various social groups, the expression of national self-consciousness in groups, occasionally overlapping with national prejudice and ethnocentrism;

5. changes in the proportion of the elements of national and international culture, traditions, and innovations in social groups.

Thus we were interested in the most varied ethnic characteristics of social groups as differentiated by quality of labor. Whereas the last of these subjects, the ratio between tradition and innovation in culture is common to ethnographers and has been treated by them in detail (although without linking it with socio-occupational groups based on quality of labor), the first four have not yet been given sufficient attention. Because we had set ourselves not so much traditional, historical, and reconstructive tasks as practical, regulative, and administrative tasks that are becoming more and more common in the social sciences, these trends were basic to our research.

PROCEDURE AND ORGANIZATION OF THE SURVEY

Simultaneously with these theoretical problems we also had to resolve practical ones connected with the organization of our research, including what was probably the most vital question of all — the choice of the field of investigation. Where and how should we make this test of the socio-ethnic fabric? After examining several possible areas, we settled on the Tatar ASSR as a republic that met our basic requirements for a field of study, and quite fully reflected the general socioeconomic conditions of the country. Tataria is an industrial-agrarian republic with a highly developed industry; agriculture occupies an important place in its economy. It is also close to the All-Union position in its socio-demographic characteristics as well as in its basic socioeconomic ones (see Table 2).

Thus Tataria was close to the general average for the USSR in all the main indices recorded in the census of 1959, although it has, in fact,

Table 2. *Comparative Social and Demographic Indices of the Population of Tataria*[a] (in percentages)

Parameters	USSR	Spread of the data (maximum and minimum) according to administrative divisions (regions, territories, and republics)		Tatar ASSR	Differ-ence
Urban population	52	92	(Murmansk Region)	42	−10
		18	(Mordvinian ASSR)		
Population engaged in mental labor	20.7			18.9	− 1.8
Sex composition					
male	45			43	− 2
female	55			57	+ 2
Population with higher education	1.8	3.1 (Magadan Region) 0.5 (Komi-Permyak Nat. Area)		1.4	− 0.4
incomplete higher, secondary, and in-complete secondary education	26.3	38.5 (Magadan Region) 16.8 (Tuva Region)		25.8	− 0.5
Social groups:					
workers	48.2	71.7 (Kemerovo Reg.) 21 (Moldavian SSR)		45.2	− 3
employees	20.1	32.6 (Chukchee Nat. Area.) 11.0 (Moldavian SSR)		18	− 2.1
collective farmers	31.4	67.5 (Moldavian SSR) 1.8 (Murmansk Region)		36.4	+ 5
individual peasants and non-cooperated artisans	0.3	1.0 (Chuvash ASSR) 0.0 (Murmansk Region)		0.4	+ 0.1
Population of work-ing age by source of income					
employed	74.4	84.9 (Chuvash ASSR) 64.8 (North Ossetian ASSR)		79.8	+ 5.4
self-employed in personal land holding	4.2	14.7 (Aginskij Buryat Nat. Area) 0.1 (Murmansk Region)		3.5	− 0.7
dependents	13.5	21.6 (Sakhalin Region) 7.4 (Evenk Nat. Area)		11.4	− 2.1
pensioners and students on grants	5.4	8.3 (Tomsk Region) 1.8 (Taimyr Nat. Area)		5.3	− 0.1

a rather more agrarian profile; it is also below average as regards the weight of the urban population, and in the proportion of people engaged in mental labor and relative numbers of workers, employees, and persons with higher or secondary education. In none of these instances was

[a] The table has been compiled from Itogi SSSR (1962: 13, 72, 81, 92, 93, 98, 130); Itogi RSFSR (1963: 24–25, 137, 140, 152, 153, 158–59, 160–61, 162–63); Narodnoje (1966:7).

the difference so great as to be vital; and (as regards scatter) Tataria fell within the limits of the average. It was to be expected that it would be even closer to the All-Union mean at the time of the survey since industrialization had continued between 1959 and 1967 and urbanization had proceeded at an accelerated pace.

While reflecting the social structure and social processes of the country as a whole to a considerable extent, Tataria was both a well developed social organism and typical of the country. All the socially advanced groups of the population, including the artistic, scientific, and technical intelligentsia, were represented there. Disposing of a large-scale industry, research institutes, a university and colleges, a conservatory, and an opera company, Tataria presented great possibilities for the most varied types of activity and quite broad opportunities for, and a high degree of, social mobility. In addition, ethnic processes were clearly expressed. The ethnic composition of the population was most varied, but at the same time there were large basic ethnic groups, Tatars and Russians who together constituted 90 per cent of the population, which made it a suitable field for studying the interaction of Russian and the local national culture. Tatars and Russians are different from one another both genetically and historically. If the effect of the process of mutual influence of cultures and languages and of assimilation has been tested here, so also has the stability of the ethnos.

The next step consisted in drawing up a questionnaire and verifying the sampling. The questionnaire was made in two variants, one urban, the other rural, with maximum unification of their main parts. The questionnaires asked for basic information on the living conditions of the people interviewed, their place of work, level of responsibility, education, and housing conditions. Points reflecting cultural habits and how informed the person was were recorded in some detail, and one group of questions dealt with attitudes toward international relations. On the rural poll papers (questionnaire and interview), we employed the principle of spreading questions over the stages of the person's life, which made questioning convenient and natural. The rural questionnaire was so drawn up that the answers could be recorded on a single punch card to facilitate and speed up processing. Questions were mainly closed-ended (i.e., several possible alternative answers were provided), which enabled the questionnaires to be completed on an average of fifteen minutes. For rural localities copies of the questionnaire were provided in Tatar. The alternative replies were coded in advance in a binary system suitable for processing on an M-20 computer and tabulator. In the end it was decided to correlate the objective data on the person interviewed with his national self-consciousness in order to obtain an idea of the significance of separate factors in educating internationalism. Special attention was paid to characterizing social and occupational mobility, and recording the job and education of the person interviewed not only at the time of questioning but also from the outset of his (or her) working life, as well as the jobs of his parents. It was hoped thus to clarify the correlation between social mobility, national affiliation, knowledge of languages, etc.

In studying the rural population we employed a tie-up of the questionnaire answers with an ecological description of the locality, which proved to be effective. At each populated point surveyed, we filled up a special form on which the main information about the settlement was recorded: the ethnic composition of the population (whether predominantly Tatar, predominantly Russian, or mixed), the number of inhabitants (under 100, 101–200, 201–500, etc.), the distance from towns, the distance to schools, clubs, etc. The data of these forms were also coded for processing and recorded on the punched cards together with the answers from the questionnaire. We were enabled to elucidate the dependence of social and ethnic processes on ecology; for example, the spread of the Russian language in Tatar villages and of Tatar in Russian villages, the effect of the size of settlement on the cultural level of the population, etc.

The questionnaires, both urban and rural, were preliminarily tested in enterprises in Kazan and in villages in the Lajshevo District of the Tatar ASSR where the work was done by a team led by M. N. Guboglo. This team had a double purpose, one methodological (to check the questionnaire and the sampling) and the other informative (collecting the information required on a scale sufficiently large for prior evaluation of the main problems of the survey). In the end five hundred questionnaires were completed on two collective farms and a state farm in quotas representative of the occupational groups in the farms studied.

Four months later, having checked the instrumentation and sampling, the Institute's Department of Concrete Sociological Research carried out a mass survey. During August and September 1967, ten thousand people were interviewed with the help of the Party and Komsomol organizations of Tataria. In the towns — Kazan, the new industrial center of Almetjevsk, and the small, old town of Menzelinsk — a one per cent sample of the working population was made. In the three rural districts linked with these towns, namely the Pestrinchin, Almetjevsk, and Menzelinsk Districts, the population of thirty-five villages was surveyed. The populated points were selected so as to reflect all the types of rural settlement in Tataria in proportions characteristic of the Republic.

The samples were broken down by occupational and technical groups differentiated according to quality of labor. The following groups were differentiated: the rural intelligentsia — leaders of the highest links (chairmen of collective farms, directors of state farms, directors of schools, directors of enterprises); leaders of middle links (departmental managers of state farms, team leaders, etc.); rural specialists of the highest link (agronomists, zoo technicians, engineers, and teachers with higher education); specialists of the middle link (predominantly those with secondary technical education); employees in the administrative apparatus (cashiers, bookkeepers, managers of day nurseries [crèches]); skilled industrial workers (tractor drivers, truck drivers, garage mechanics); skilled non-industrial manual workers (bricklayers, carpenters); permanently employed unskilled workers (mainly stockmen); and finally the large class of people in the country who are quite unskilled (mainly laborers working by the job).

The sampling was not proportional. The smallest categories in the village (intelligentsia and employee) were given a maximum quota of 50 percent, while only 10 per cent of the non-working population was sampled. The sampling was carried out according to the "Household Register", which was first checked at the village Soviet. The results of the count of questionnaires already made indicated that the quotas laid down were met in the main; in fact 45 per cent of leaders of the highest link were interviewed, 53 per cent of the specialists, 52 per cent of the employees, 45 per cent of the mechanics and drivers, 20 per cent of the general laborers, and 9.7 per cent of the non-working population. In order to establish the data for the general population it was proposed to weight these quantities, and by means of various correction factors to reduce them to a unit share of the representation.

As a result of such a significant sample of each socio-occupational group we obtained quite representative data. The calculations already made indicate that the actual error in the sample was not more than 1 per cent, even in the basic criterion of our survey (nationality). According to the returns of the 1959 census, the proportion of Russians in the rural Russo-Tatar population was 35 per cent; in our sample, Russians constituted 34.5 per cent, i.e., an actual sampling error of 0.5 per cent. In view of the fact that migration from the village is more marked among Russians than among Tatars and that the ratio is changing in favor of Tatars, it can be supposed that there were fewer Russians at the time of the survey than in 1959, i.e., the actual error in this criterion may be quite negligible.

The data of the survey of the rural population have already been processed by computer (the check sample fully, and the main survey to a significant extent), while the urban data are being processed by machine at the time of the writing of this article.

SOME RESULTS

We are attempting to summarize the preliminary results of the survey of the rural population, which permits us to assess how far the principal hypotheses of our survey have been substantiated.

In the program of the survey, relevancy of socioeconomic non-

Table 3.   *Social Groups and Socio-Ethnic Processes* (in percentages)

Groups by type of work	Unskilled workers and collective farmers	
	regular	se
	D_2	
Total number questioned	217	68
General criteria		
Nationality:		
Tatar	71	73
Russian	29	27
Education (higher or specialized secondary)	1	2
Party membership	5	7
With influence on decisions in production collectives	38	37
Monthly income per member of family in excess of 30 roubles		
(not counting income from holding on)	15	16
Culture and Language		
Fluent Russian (or Russian and Tatar)	34	36
At work using Russian more often, or both languages	35	29
Usually speaking at home Russian or both languages	24	25
Considering it useful for children to learn in a Russian school	78	74
Children studying in Russian schools	38	45
Reading fiction and belle lettres	44	47
usually in Russian	19	14
Reading newspapers	77	87
in Russian or both languages	34	32
Celebrating religious festivals (Ramadan, Easter, etc.)	37	37
Having a positive attitude toward baptism or circumcision	45	46
Attitude to national relations		
Considering nationality of the leadership not to affect		
the work of the collective	71	65
Having a positive attitude to nationally mixed marriages	74	78

homogeneity of labor was hypothesized as well as that this absence of homogeneity affected both the socioeconomic and ethnic criteria. The data of the survey indicate that the elimination of surviving traditional forms of culture and the spread of modern ones occurs unevenly in the various social groups. Modern forms of culture are most common among the relatively advanced social layers while traditional forms are most firmly entrenched among manual workers, though the sphere of employment has no essential significance here.

The socially advanced groups, especially the intelligentsia, are distinguished not only by higher income, a higher level of education, higher public and social activity, reflected in Party membership, and influence

	Mechanics	Employees	Specialists Leaders of middle rank		Specialists Leaders of the highest rank	
e	C	B	A_2		A_1	
	438	75	26	45	65	19
	63	64	54	69	66	68
	37	36	46	31	34	32
	1	16	42	20	83	79
	15	36	35	62	61	84
	50	68	70	85	90	100
	34	37	46	51	69	79
	52	60	69	55	69	79
	56	49	76	66	73	90
	35	37	38	35	47	42
	81	91	89	89	91	95
	54	50	47	45	69	77
	68	76	81	76	91	90
	47	65	61	67	84	84
	96	97	100	98	99	95
	62	57	73	71	92	69
	22	12	23	11	8	16
	26	24	15	17	14	5
	78	79	62	74	77	58
	79	81	73	75	68	68

on important decisions in production collectives, but also by cultured habits and customs (reading of fiction and belle lettres, knowledge of languages, etc.).

These features of the socially advanced groups are graphically reflected in Table 3 (for the male population). In addition, there is an almost complete elimination among these groups (as the Table shows) of certain survivals of the past, as shown for example in a negative attitude to religious festivals, ceremonies, and rites.

To evaluate the contentment of the various social groups with their social position, indices of social mobility are also extremely important. In the program of the survey the hypothesis was hazarded that "the national factor is not of essential importance in social mobility". The results have confirmed that hypothesis; in the data of the Lajshevo District we have interesting groupings characterizing mobility as between and within generations (see Tables 4 and 5).

Judging from these Tables, the Tatars in the countryside are more mobile than the Russians. A higher proportion of Tatars than of Russians have raised their status in comparison with their parents. Whereas the fathers of 84 per cent of the Tatar intellectuals belonged to the category of unskilled manual laborers, only 64 per cent of the

Table 4. *Intergeneration Mobility (Intermobility)* (in percentages)

Social group	Russians						
	Social origin (by father)						
	No. questioned	A	B	C	D_1	D_2	Total percentage of fathers occupied in manual labor
Intelligentsia (A)	30	13	23	—	29	35	64
Employees (B)	27	7	6	—	50	36	86
Mechanics (C)	39	16	8	15	5	56	76
Unskilled laborers							
regular (D_1)	43	—	3	6	26	65	97
seasonal (D_2)	67	5	6	6	6	77	90
	Tatars						
Intelligentsia (A)	24	8	8	—	34	50	84
Employees (B)	18	—	13	—	26	61	82
Mechanics (C)	32	9	—	9	20	62	91
Unskilled laborers							
regular (D_1)	89	3	1.6	6	43	46	95
seasonal (D_2)	40	4	—	—	23	73	96

Table 5. *Mobility Within Generations (Intramobility)* (in percentages)

Social group	Russians			Tatars		
	immo-bile (status lowered)	stable (status un-changed)	mobile (status raised)	immo-bile (status lowered)	stable (status un-changed)	mobile (status raised)
Intelligentsia (A)	—	69	31	—	41	59
Employees (B)	8	50	42	—	38	62
Mechanics (C)	—	23	77	—	19	81
General laborers and other unskilled manual workers	8	92	—	6	94	—
Total	4	58	38	2	48	50

Russian intelligentsia came from this sphere. Correspondingly, Tatars had raised their social position faster in the course of their work. Thus 50 per cent of the Tatars questioned had raised their status since the beginning of their working career, and only 38 per cent of the Russians had done so. This is explained by the fact that Tatars were more backward than Russians in both social position and education in the past; usually starting from a less favorable position, they had to cover a greater distance in social growth, encouraged by the Soviet national policy of liquidating actual inequality. On the other hand, Russians were more inclined to migrate and make their social and occupational advance outside the village.

As a result of the greater mobility of Tatars in the present generation, the representation of Tatars in the socially advanced groups in the village already corresponds, in the main, to that of Russians. Tatar men are equally represented among all the socio-occupational categories of the rural population.

The population of Tatar men among the categories of unskilled and skilled labor is identical in the main and corresponds to their proportion in the total population. As for Tatar women their representation in the groups of skilled workers is still rather backward (see Table 6).

Our research program also included the proposition "that a condition for rapid eradication of national prejudice is a high degree of social mobility". This proposition, as the preliminary results indicate for the bulk of those sampled, has not been confirmed by the survey. The socially more advanced and more mobile categories of the population, in spite of their successful and intensive acquisition of modern culture, their dropping of survivals of the traditional culture, and their knowledge of Russian, have basically the same attitude to national relations.

Table 6. *National Composition. Percentage of Tatars in Socio-occupational Groups*
(in percentages of the total number of groups members)

	Men	Women
Leaders of the highest rank	68.4	not available
Leaders of the middle rank	68.9	45.4
Specialists with high qualifications	66.1	64.6
Specialists with middle qualifications	53.8	40.2
Employees	64.0	49.6
Mechanics	63.0	—
Skilled, non-industrial manual workers	65.5	40.0
Unskilled workers, regularly employed	73.5	70.4
Unskilled seasonal workers	68.4	71.4

The attitude was recorded in various ways. The attitude of those questioned toward mixed marriages and toward joint work in collectives of mixed composition, and their preference for leaders of their own nationality was obtained in the survey of the main bulk. The replies revealed a high degree of internationalization, practically identical for all groups (see Table 7). To the question on choice of direct leadership, an absolute majority of all groups of the population answered that "the nationality of the leaders has no significance". To the question, "do you approve of marriages between Tatars and Russians?", the reply, "nationality has no significance, the main thing is the personal qualities of the person, and love for each other", also received an absolute majority of votes.[3] Nevertheless, the preliminary results of the survey show that there is no marked positive connection between the replies to these questions and social mobility, social position, material prosperity, public activity, education, or knowledge of Russian. Thus, attitude toward relations between nationalities remains almost unchanged from the less socially advanced groups to the more advanced ones, while at the same time we observe an unbroken sequence of growth of all indices concerning culture and knowledge of Russian.

An insignificant positive link between attitude to relations between nationalities and objective factors of cultural development is traceable only in one case, that of fluent mastery of Russian. Tatars in the various socio-occupational groups who knew Russian often had higher indices in the attitudes studied (Table 7).

We found the same tendency of an absence of any positive link between attitudes and social position in the data from the experimental survey from which the stereotypes of Russian and Tatar were obtained. Those

---

[3]   This question was put into the questionnaire by L. M. Drobizheva. The material obtained by her from a survey of Belorussian villages and villages in other national districts gave results analogous to ours (Drobizheva, 1967).

Table 7. *Knowledge of Russian and Attitudes*

	Tatar Men				Tatar Women			
	Positive attitude to leadership of another nationality		Positive attitude to mixed marriages		Positive attitude to leadership of another nationality		Positive attitude to mixed marriages	
	1	2	1	2	1	2	1	2
A₁	73	54	56	59	85	59	73	57
A₂	76	61	88	48	67	63	76	78
B	70	77	65	83	91	57	68	51
C	85	69	70	68	—	—	—	—
D	69	65	71	67	77	45	77	54

Notes: 1. Tatars speaking Russian fluently or speaking both Russian and Tatar;
2. Tatars speaking only Tatar fluently.

interviewed were asked: "Which of the following attributes is character-istic of Tatars and which of Russians?" Then followed a list of various positive qualities — kindness, hospitality, industriousness, enterprise, and talent. These qualities are not as objective and definite, of course, as hair color, height or weight; their attribution to a whole nation reflects the subjective attitude of the person questioned to representa-tives of another nationality, i.e., his evaluation of a nation. The test indicated that all groups of the population, Tatars and Russians alike, esteemed their own nationality higher. The Russians, belonging to the larger and more numerous nation, as was to be expected, revealed a comparatively slight difference between their self-appraisal and the appraisal of the other nationality. As for social groups, the difference between the two evaluations was almost the same among the intelli-gentsia as among the general laborers.

The system of facts characterizing national attitudes given here is evidence that education in internationalism depends on other variables with little connection with culture and language, and determined, it would seem, by a complex set of socioeconomic factors. We hope, in the course of a further survey to throw additional light on this problem.

In this article we have tried to give the reader only a general im-pression of the character of the socioeconomic investigations being made. It is a promising direction, broadening our knowledge of the essentials of socioethnic processes and of the concretization and extension of the subject matter of ethnosociological research. Together with purely ethnographic studies it should find an important place in the arsenal of our social sciences.

Contemporary Ethnocultural Processes in Udmurtia
(Program and Method of Investigation)

E. VASILJEVA, V. PIMENOV, L. KHRISTOLJUBOVA

In the broad spectrum of research into the ethnic processes taking place in the Soviet Union, problems of how far traditional ways of life and culture are preserved or eroded in any particular people occupy a special place. In 1967–68 the present writers attempted to collect data that would throw light on these problems, by taking the example of a single people, the Udmurts.[1] The main programmatic principles adopted in the survey are outlined here and the techniques, organization, and procedures employed described.

I. A systematic approach to the analysis of social phenomena is being more and more widely adopted in modern science. In this connection it seems desirable to treat the basic object of ethnographic research, the ethnos or ethnic community, as a certain, relatively separate, dynamic social system with its own inner structure. Unfortunately, the structure of the ethnos at this level has still not been worked out, but if we base ourselves on the concepts of ethnic community traditional to Soviet ethnography, we can single out a set of essential characters that are typical of an important aspect of the ethnos. These include for example, mother tongue, spiritual and material culture, family life, and certain forms of ethnic self-consciousness. Each of these aspects can also be taken as a system of a lower order.

Two aspects of studying and describing the ethnos are possible:

First published in *Sovetskaja etnografija*, N2 (1970).
[1] The Udmurts were formerly know as Votiaks and many Western writers still use the old name. In this article, the modern Soviet usage will be adhered to. — Ed.

(a) within its own framework as a system, with the aim of studying its inherent properties, relations, and tendencies (in which case we abstract it from outside influences); and (b) in a broader system, in the group of ethnic communities in which the ethnos studied is organically included as a subsystem. In our case investigation preference was given to the first aspect, but it was necessary to take a number of outside influences into consideration. For that purpose the concept of social-ethnic situation was introduced to describe the position of the ethnos studied in the general context of its internal and external connections and influences and to determine the probable trend of these connections at the 'comment' the investigation was carried out.

Several different ways of penetrating the ethnos are possible. We studied the individual whom we treated as a representative of the ethnos and the bearer of that ethnic feature, the ETHNOPHOR. The justification for this approach is, on the one hand, the well-known Marxist definition of personality as an aggregate of social relations (including, consequently, ethnic relations), and on the other hand, the view of social processes (i.e., ethnic ones as well) as mass processes, the laws governing which are expressed as probabilities or statistical tendencies.

Taking these as our programmatic premises, let us define the field of our research, the ethnographic situation, and formulate our main problems and hypotheses.

The survey concerned one people, the Udmurts, living in the Udmurt ASSR. Our field of view necessarily included all the social classes, strata, and groups of this people (workers, peasants, and intellectuals — more detailed stratification), their composition by sex, age, family or marital status, place of residence (rural or urban settlements), and ethnographic group (Southern, Northern, Central Udmurts, and Besermans).

According to the data available, the social-ethnic situation had the following features. The Udmurts are a Soviet socialist nation. They have state autonomy (since 1920). Their numbers within the boundaries of the Udmurt ASSR (according to the 1959 census) are 475,900. Apart from Udmurts (35.59 per cent), the ethnic composition of the Republic includes Russians (56.75 per cent), Tatars (5.48 per cent), and other nationalities (2.18 per cent) among whom the Udmurts are interspersed. There has been a migration of population from village to town, and from Udmurtia to neighboring regions and republics, as well as in the opposite direction. Although the general growth of towns is quite high, the degree of urbanization of Udmurts is not high, and the Udmurt population of the various towns of the Republic is between 7 and 30 per cent. On average 18.5 per cent of Udmurts in the Udmurt ASSR are town-

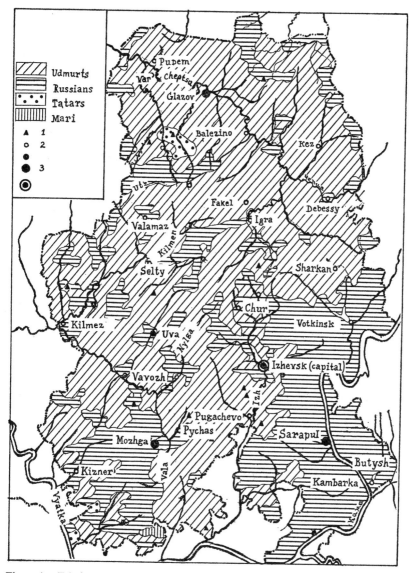

Figure 1. Ethnic composition of the population of Udmurtia and settlements, covered by fieldwork in 1968.

1. rural settlements
2. other settlements
3. urban settlements

dwellers (1959); it should be noted that townsmen constituted only 7.5 per cent of the Udmurt population of the Republic in 1939.

The social structure of the Udmurt nation is the same in principle as that of the other Soviet socialist nations, but the numbers of the working class and intelligentsia are lower than the average for the RSFSR.

The Udmurt language belongs to the Permian group of the Finno-Ugrian branch of the Uralic family. The overwhelming majority of Udmurts in the Republic consider it their mother tongue, but (in 1959) 6.72 per cent gave Russian as their mother tongue. In the South of the Republic some Udmurts also speak Tatar as well as Russian, and some consider it their mother tongue. An absolute majority of Udmurts speak Russian fluently, which was important to take into account when working out the plan of our survey. Traditional forms of material culture are well preserved in rural houses and certain farm buildings, but much less so in women's dress (the men have long since not worn national costume); national types of utensils, farm tools, etc., are even less preserved. The folklore stratum of spiritual culture is appreciable but has a tendency to decrease. The professional stratum of the national culture, on the contrary, was created only in Soviet times and is increasing in scope and scale. Its development has been fostered by the founding of organizations of writers and journalists, a national (Udmurt) theater, a song and dance ensemble, and by means of mass communication (i.e., radio broadcasting and television in Udmurt, an Udmurt magazine, two republican and several district newspapers, and a publishing house, etc.). The observance of religious and calendar customs and festivals is much reduced among Udmurts, but family rituals are preserved.

Long links with the Russian and Tatar peoples have left a marked impression on all components of the Udmurt ethnos, and this is evident in the language, the material and spiritual culture, etc. The constant close community has also had the effect that there is no place in Udmurt consciousness for anti-Russian and anti-Tatar prejudices. Among the features of the ethnic psychology, attention needed to be given to the marked shyness of the Udmurts. Finally, as was known earlier, there is a notable difference in all ethnographic characteristics between the North and South of Udmurtia; these characteristics are most strongly expressed in the South and less so in the Center and North.

On the basis of our general view of the social-ethnic situation in Udmurtia, we formulated three main questions for our investigation.

1. How far are national forms of life and culture preserved among various social strata of Udmurts?
2. What components of the ethnos are most (or least) stable?
3. What are the general trends in the development of the Udmurts as an ethnos?

The posing of these aims was dictated by their scientific and practical urgency, by the requirement of a more exact delineation of the factors affecting the course of the ethnocultural process, and by the desirability of making a more or less reliable forecast and obtaining means of guiding the process, i.e., of optimizing it.

In the course of the investigation three main hypotheses were to be tested:

1. The raising of the social status of an Udmurt leads on the whole in Udmurtia to a weakening of adherence to national values.
2. The relative stability of the different elements of the ethnos (in diminishing order) was (1) language, (2) ethnopsychological qualities, (3) spiritual culture of the professional layer, (4) customs and rituals, (5) spiritual culture of the folklore layer, and (6) material culture.
3. There is an increasing tendency for close assimilation of Udmurts to Russians, but the possibility of their independent ethnic development has not yet been exhausted.

II. The posing of the problem called for the solution of another two tasks: (1) the choice of a suitable method for the investigation, and (2) the development of appropriate techniques. It became clear at the beginning that it was only possible to check our hypotheses by mass representative material that lent itself to a statistical treatment. (The statistical procedures for the collection of information were worked out by E. K. Vasiljeva.) We decided on the method of standard interviewing, considering that it gave the highest assurance in this case that the information would be credible, full, and reliable. It also combined the possibility of recording information verbally and expressing it numerically.

The main working instrument of the investigation, the "ethnographic questionnaire" compiled by V. V. Pimenov, was worked out in accordance with the programmatic setting, the character of the tasks, and the method selected. A first variant was tested in the summer of 1967 in Southern Udmurtia, in the Highland-Mary District of the Mary ASSR, and in the Laishev District of Tataria (altogether around 200 persons were interviewed in villages and towns). As a result questions "which worked badly" or which were not directly related to the problem were excluded, and the formulation of several others was improved. With the remainder it was possible to obtain a comparatively clear set of variants of the answers.

The questionnaire was drawn up in accordance with our views on the essential features of the ethnos. Six groups of questions were distinguished which defined the ethnographic specifics of our research: (1) language; (2) material culture; (3) customs; (4) folklore; (5) professional spiritual culture; and (6) ethnic psychology. Each group or set of questions (each block) covered six attributes (parameters). They were intentionally made equal in a number of questions because this made it possible to measure the relative weight of each of them in the system of the ethnos.

We encountered great difficulty in defining the concrete characteristics that should be included and measured in a group. Here we were guided by the experience of ethnographic studies and our own experience and the date of test inquiries, but intuition played no little role. In the end the structure of the groups acquired the following form:

1. the language — questions about mother tongue and degree of mastery of it, about the language of the family, the language at work, and in social life; and about knowledge of other Soviet languages;
2. the material culture — questions about dress, food, and utensils;
3. the customs — questions about weddings, birth rites, and funerals;
4. the folklore — questions about traditions, folk tales, folk songs, and dances;
5. the professional culture — questions about knowledge of national (Udmurt) writers, reading of national literature and press, knowledge of composers and their works;
6. the ethno-psychological — questions about ethnic preferences, national self-consciousness, degree of consciousness of belonging to one's nationality, etc.

In a special group of questions (No. 7) three control questions were put, not to the informant but to the interviewer, about the attitude of the informant to the interview, the themes that aroused his interest, and the questions that he had difficulty in answering.

In the biggest section (No. 8) there were nineteen questions, which included a number relating to social and demographic indices (sex, age, education, social position, etc.); certain questions were especially important — those about the ethnic composition of the main reference groups, i.e., the family, the primary work group, neighbors, and friends.

The questions were varied in character. Some were oriented toward elucidating the existence of a character or attribute, others towards determining how far the person interviewed was informed about the attribute, and still others toward discovering his attitude to the attribute. For example, in asking about customs, we began by asking the informant to describe the birth and christening customs, and then we inquired how, in his view, the birth of a baby should be marked, whether by observing the traditional folk customs or without it. Questions were also classified by other features. There were some that were intended to stimulate anamnesis or recollections in the informant ("How were you dressed at your wedding?"). The technique of posing a hypothetical situation encouraged anamnesis ("If you could begin your life over again, what kind of wedding would you choose when you married?"). This combination of questions diverse in style and character was designed to obtain quite varied and authentic information.

There are no natural units for measuring ethnographic attributes. Since from the start it was proposed to process the information obtained quantitatively, and as far as possible by mechanical means, the working out of the method of measurement was looked upon as a priority task. We decided to combine verbal recording of information with an approximate evaluation of the expressiveness of the attribute according to a four-point scale (for example, "does not know", "does not know very well", "has a clear idea", "knows very well"). Consequently the intensity of an attribute was marked within the range 01 to 04. In certain cases we were able to introduce a more definite numerical criterion (for example, the number of national dishes known to the informant). The evaluation was made by the interviewer, but the existence of the verbal record enabled it to be checked.

III.   The collection of material for a far-reaching investigation of contemporary ethno-cultural processes is so laborious that it can only be done by a method of patchy coverage and random sampling.

The subjects of our research were adult Udmurts (17 years of age and above) permanently resident in the territory of the Udmurt ASSR. Their numbers in 1968 were a little more than 300,000. In the light of the actual conditions and possibilities of our survey, the availability of personnel, the material and technical provisions, and times for performing the work, the size of the sample was limited to not more than 2000 to 2500 persons, which constituted 0.7 to 0.8 per cent of the general total.

It was necessary first to establish whether a sample of 2000–2500 persons would provide representative data from which judgements about the aggregate could be drawn. The first condition for the authenticity and reliability of the sample data was that the sampled part should be sufficiently large to bring out the objective patterns of the process being studied. The proposed size of the sample satisfied that condition (see Table 1); it would ensure the singling out and analysis of the decisive trends although certain interconnections would not be disclosed with comprehensive fullness.

Sampled data would be reliable if the numerical size of the sample is large enough so that mistakes in its representative character do not exceed permissible limits. The probable maximum error in the representative nature of a sample of 2000 persons was calculated to be 0.954 per cent. The calculations showed that with such an index as the proportion of women among adult Udmurts, which was around 63 per cent for the general aggregate, the limit of representative error was 2 per cent. The maximum size of the sampling error for the proportion of the elderly (aged 60 and over) among Udmurts and the proportion of persons considering Udmurt their mother tongue was 1.5 per cent and 0.7 per cent respectively. Thus a sample of 2000 persons would yield data representative of the Republic as a whole.

Table 1. *Theoretical and Actual Sampling Error in the* 1968 *Survey*

Indices of the adult population of the Udmurt ASSR	Value of index from data		Sampling Error	
	Census	Sample	Theoretical	Actual
Percentage of women	63.0	64.4	2.0	1.4
Percentage of persons aged 60 and over	13.2	14.8	1.5	1.6
Percentage of persons whose mother tongue was Udmurt				
(A) in urban population	86.0	77.7	0.7	9.0
(b) in rural population	97.5	96.5		1.0

The size of the sample decided on for the project survey was 2300, i.e., the necessary minimum was raised by 15 per cent. Thus, a reserve was created in case of a shortage of data or of low-quality completion of questionnaires.

The survey was based on the method of random sampling in which all units have an equal chance of being selected. This ensured proportional representation in the sample of all types and categories of units of the aggregate. In two cases this technique was complicated by the employment of special means of selection. The principle of proportional sampling was convenient for obtaining representative data on the aggregate as a whole, but at the same time it sacrificed the possibility of studying certain parts of the aggregate, small in numbers but important for the pattern being investigated. In our survey it was necessary to increase representation of the group of creative intellectuals, who might be too small in the general total. Therefore it was decided to complete another 100 questionnaires, in addition to the 2300, for persons of this social and professional group, in order to process them subsequently as an independent section.

To preserve the actual proportions in the sampled aggregate it would have been necessary to take 1425 persons from the rural population and 875 townsfolk. This ratio was corrected by increasing the proportion of the urban population because a greater variation of characteristics has been noted among the inhabitants of towns. In addition it proved necessary to increase the volume of the town sample to a size permitting processing of the results in two groups for the urban and the rural populations. It was decided to sample 1300 persons in the rural population and 1000 in the towns. To restore the real ratio of rural and urban population in the Republic as a whole a correction would be introduced in the processing.

In order to determine the optimal principle for organizing the work in the conditions of this survey, we were forced to check several variants of the sampling experimentally. The checks showed that it would be impossible to obtain full identification of the sampling procedure in town and country. The urban population of the Udmurt ASSR is concentrated in a limited number of populated points while the rural population is scattered over a considerable territory and a large number of inhabited places. In addition, the lists of units of the general aggregate needed a basis from which the sample would be made different in town and country.

In the towns a zoned choice of units (disperse sample) was made. The urban population itself was divided in several groups (characteristic types) according to the size of the population and the proportion of Udmurts in it, the level of economic development, and the function of the town as a cultural and administrative center. A proportionate number of the population in each typical group was sampled. As a rule the sampled aggregate was taken at random from all the units comprising the typical group, but we were twice forced to depart from this procedure. The sheer number of settlements of urban type and sma towns (under 16,000 inhabitants) turned out to be too labor-consuming because of their great territorial dispersion, while their significance in the total population was comparatively small. Therefore, they were represented in the sample by a single point, the settlement of Uva. In addition, in order to reduce the volume of work, the town of Votkinsk was excluded from the number of towns surveyed and it was represented in the sample by another town of similar type. In the final analysis the towns of Izhevsk, Glazov, Sarapul, and Mozhga, and the workers' settlement of Uva were surveyed.

As units of the sample we took the units of the aggregate, i.e., individual persons among adult Udmurts who were permanent residents of the town. For that purpose it is convenient to employ voters' lists or census lists if a survey is made soon after an election or the taking of a census. Because that possibility frequently did not exist, it was preferable to base ourselves mainly on data of the current population count. We employed the card indexes of the address bureaux. The fullness and authenticity were sufficiently reliable for the sampling in our survey, and in addition made it possible to distribute the units of the sampling aggregate over the territory of the town. If the sampling had been clustered, i.e., if we had taken city blocks, or households, or other large units, it would have proved difficult to maintain the representative character of the data, given the smallness of the sample and the considerable differentiation of the structure of the population in the different parts of a town.

Whereas with a cluster sample one can base oneself on a stable list of clusters, with a list (or card index) of the population this is out of the question. Population, especially urban population, is mobile; any count material proves more or less out-of-date. Several reasons can be advanced for the partial discrepancy between the data of address bureaux and the actual composition of the population. The documentation of such events as death or change of residence takes place with a certain delay. It was necessary to make an empirical estimate of the size of the discrepancy between the data available and the actual situation. For our survey, sampling was carried out with a necessary reserve (up to 40 per cent of the size of the sampling aggregate). The technique of mechanical selection was employed.

While the high density and concentration characteristic of towns enable sampling to be made by units, that method is inapplicable to the village. In rural localities and zones, two-stage cluster sampling was carried out. Administrative districts (four districts in which the proportion of the Udmurt population was under 4 per cent were not taken into account) were united into typical groups on the basis of a complex evaluation of ethnic and economic-geographical characteristics. The first stage of the sampling — the mechanical choice of cluster — was carried out in each of the four typical groups delineated.

In this case the sampling units could also have been administrative subdivisions like the rural soviet or populated point, but rural soviets are significantly bigger than the clusters that were optimal for our survey. It was also inexpedient to take populated points as units since their total number was large and the work would be complicated by the host of tiny populated points. The most convenient system proved to be the system of clusters compiled by the state statistical services for sample surveys. These clusters were drawn up in such a way that they had roughly the same size and consisted of compactly located populated points. Since it was necessary to select a small number of clusters, repeated mechanical selection was made with change of starting point. As a result the most appropriate variant was found to be the one that gave results closest to the mean for typical groups. When the clusters selected had been plotted on the map it proved that districts with different natural and climatic conditions and geographical locations were represented in the sample (the Yukama, Balezino, Selty, Syumsin, Igra, Zavyala, Mozhga, Nalopurga, and Alnash Districts). The sample included eighteen clusters embracing forty settlements (see map).

The second stage of the sampling was the mechanical selection of households within the clusters. On the basis of Form No. 1 for Household Accounts (the "Household Register") at the rural soviets, families were selected that were of Udmurt or mixed national composition in which there were adult Udmurts. The course of the choice was differentially established according to the number of Udmurt households in the cluster and the number of persons required to be selected in accordance with the proportional distribution of the sampling aggregate of typical groups. For selecting the exact member of the family to be interviewed a special scheme was worked out (see below).

The choice of urban and rural populated points was made in accordance with the procedure settled on for the organization of the sample. There was a shortfall in rural localities of 80 persons and in urban localities of 79. This nevertheless raised the required minimum number since its initial volume had been calculated with a reserve. Consequently, from the proposed aggregate of 2300 units we succeeded in questioning 2141 persons. The main reasons for the shortfall were either the temporary absence of persons falling within the sample, or the impossibility of finding the required person because of inaccuracies in the lists. We surveyed various categories of the population so that the shortfall did not lead to any essential increase in the sampling error.

The indices calculated for the sampling aggregate compare with the corresponding data of the census of 1959.

As a rule the sampling data did not deviate essentially from the indices characterizing the whole adult Udmurt population, but it had to be remembered in making this comparison that the census data could be out-of-date. It is this that most likely explains the big deviation from the theoretical error of the proportion of the urban population who consider Udmurt as their mother tongue.

Thus for the given volume of the sample we ensured obtaining sufficiently representative data on the Udmurt population of the Republic as a whole and for the following basic categories: (a) urban and rural population; (b) men and women; and (c) augmented social and professional groups.

It is possible to form groups by combining these attributes and others, but in doing so it is necessary to avoid excessive division of the data. Where necessary the limited possibilities of dividing the sampling aggregate can be compensated by means of mathematical methods of processing (standardization, etc.).

The comparatively small volume of the sample limits only the number of typical groups. The system of indices, including the whole complex of special ethnic characteristics calculated for each separate category of the population, does not suffer from this limitation.

IV.   Great significance was attached to the organizational and procedural aspects of the survey. With full support from the Udmurt Regional Committee of the CPSU, the Council of Ministers of the Republic, the Udmurt Research Institute for History, Economics, and Literature under the Council of Ministers of the Udmurt ASSR, higher educational institutions and teacher training colleges, and other institutions, we succeeded in carrying through the organizational work without essential blunders, which ensured comparatively favorable conditions for gathering the primary information.

The survey was carried out on an expedition basis. In the first stage in the summer (July–August) the rural population was surveyed, and in the second stage (November–December), Udmurts living in the towns and workers' settlements of the Republic.

We considered it essential to inform the population in advance of the main aims and character of our work. For that purpose the head of the expedition made broadcasts over the regional radio and television. Reports were published in the republican newspaper at the beginning of the expedition's work. In each town radio broadcasts or press announcements were arranged. This informing of residents facilitated the work of the interviewers and enabled them to establish contact more quickly and easily.

The backbone of the expedition was the Udmurt research team of the Institute of Ethnography of the USSR Academy of Sciences, which varied in number from four to six persons (one scientific worker, one postgraduate student, and the remainder technical workers and assistants); in addition, there was a total of 220 voluntary temporary workers for carrying out the survey.

In the summer period the staff of the expedition included twenty-seven second-year students from the history faculty of the Udmurt State Pedagogical Institute, for whom this involvement counted as fieldwork practice. They were divided into three subgroups, each of which was "in the field" for sixteen days.

The expedition was divided into two teams which worked simultaneously. In forty days 1220 people were interviewed. Each interview required around two hours on average.

In the second stage 1013 urban residents were surveyed (including ninety-four members of the creative intelligentsia). The organization of work in urban conditions proved much more complicated than in the villages. The contingent of interviewers in each town changed; in Izhevsk it consisted mainly of students of the history faculty of the Udmurt State Pedagogical Institute (some of whom had already had practical experience in the summer), and in Glazov of students from the local pedagogical institute. In Sarapul and Mozhga students of the teacher training college were used, while in the workers' settlements of Uva, where there is no specialized educational institution, the teachers of the local schools acted as interviewers.

The interviewers did their work on a voluntary basis. None were released from their studies so that the tempo of the survey proved much slower in the towns than in the country, apart from the complications caused by the large number of incorrect addresses, the shift working of informants, and several other factors.

We considered the task of training members of the expedition to be most important and gave it the maximum care and attention. The basis for their training was the "Instructions for Completing Ethnographic Questionnaires" drawn up by V. V. Pimenov. All interviewers received instruction according to a six-hour program, in the course of which

the general problems of the survey were explained, the role of the interviewer in the "interviewer-informant" system was elucidated, and concrete examples of work with the questionnaires were gone into. Each
question was read over, the best way of putting it to the informant was
discussed, and the information required explained. Possible versions of
replies were indicated with ways of recording them. On individual
questions, instruction was given directly on the spot (for example, the
types of houses). Interviewers were also given general information on
the ethnography of Udmurts (national folk costume, dishes, and foods,
family customs, and so on). Special attention was paid to the shyness
and sensitivity peculiar to Udmurts; ways of overcoming this obstacle
were suggested with the aim of obtaining the fullest possible information
on each question.

To test how far the technique of interviewing was grasped, the interview situation was imitated at the end of each lesson. Later, during the
testing of the questionnaires and at conferences for exchanging experience
of the work, each member of the expedition was individually given the
pointers required. In all stages of the survey we tried to communicate
to the interviewers the importance of the work they had undertaken and
their responsibility for the quality of its fulfillment. In addition interviewers were informed that their work in the sampling procedure would
be checked by means of control visits. Special attention was paid to
ensuring that all members of the expedition had the same criteria for
evaluating the expressiveness (force) of the attributes (parameters) included in the questionnaires.

An important stage in the survey was the compiling of lists of persons
to be interviewed. These lists were drawn up directly by visits to the
locality, and in rural populated points the data of the "Household
Register" was employed, as already mentioned. Each family (household)
was represented in the lists by a single adult member. Families were
classified according to the number of generations (children under 16.5
years of age were excluded from all calculations and processing), families
of one, two, and three generations being distinguished. The procedure
for compiling a list was as follows. The "Household Register" was gone
through and the composition of each Udmurt family (or family containing Udmurts) established first of all according to the number of
generations in it. When we encountered a family consisting of two
members of the same generation (a man and a woman), the woman of
that family was put on the list, and then the man from the next similar
family. When a family consisted of members of two generations, a woman
of the younger generation was taken from the first such family, a woman

of the older generation from the second family, a man of the younger generation from the third family, and a man of the older generation from the fourth. When there were two, three, or more persons of the same generation and sex in a family, first the youngest was put on the list, and then the others. Families with three generations were treated in a similar way, youngest, middle, and oldest generations being distinguished. For those who did this job a work matrix, on which the alternation of persons according to generation, age, and sex was recorded, was compiled for self-checking.

When the generation in the next family in order was represented by a single person, this person was entered on the list and a plus sign (+) entered on the matrix (it was not necessary in this case to distinguish the person's sex, since he or she was the only one to be included). In other cases women were indicated by F (woman) and men by M (man).

In the end we obtained lists on which each person represented one family. Later, in accordance with the representative quota previously determined for each cluster, and at a certain stage in the survey, only those were left on the list whom it was proposed to interview. The people excluded from the lists served as a reserve for replacing missing informants. Then individual address cards were completed which were distributed to the interviewers for their work. To facilitate control the serial number of a person on the list was recorded on his address card and questionnaire. On the first day of work in the field the interviewers were divided up into pairs. Later (in towns) we abandoned this procedure because it did not stimulate individual responsibility. Each interviewer was given an address card. If the person concerned was absent, the card was returned to the leader of the team and exchanged for another one (from the reserve). Filled-in questionnaires were immediately checked by the team leader and subjected to logical and quality control. Only after they had been checked and the necessary corrections made were the questionnaires considered completed.

The work showed that it was best to distribute all the address cards for a given settlement on the first day. That enabled the team to establish the presence of all informants and, if anyone was absent or not available, to explain the reason and the period of absence and decide whether to substitute someone else for his or her 'portrait'. Cards were distributed in accordance with the interviewer's mastery of Udmurt and the informants' knowledge of Russian. Persons of the older generation who had little or no Russian were questioned as a rule by Udmurts.

V. Such were the programmatic, methodological, organizational, and procedural principles and techniques employed in the course of the ethnographic survey of Udmurts. It is too early yet to speak of the results as the data are still being processed at the time of writing. Certain conclusions, however, can already be drawn, three of which are the most essential.

First, we succeeded in experimentally testing the feasibility of organizing and carrying out a sufficiently extensive survey in strict accordance with the rules and requirements dictated by statistical procedures, utilizing an extremely thorough questionnaire, and employing a large number of volunteer interviewers.

Second, from the results of the fieldwork, we are convinced of the usefulness of the forms and procedures employed. The questionnaire, as explained, required only slight editing and technical correction.

Third, preliminary analysis of the data obtained permits us to consider them adequate in quantity and good in quality. As a result of the survey we have obtained an abundance of ethnographic information on a whole people.

Table 2. *Control Matrix for Classification of Families*

Families of One Generation consisting of			Families of Two Generations					
			Younger Generation consisting of			Older Generation consisting of		
one person	two persons	three or more persons	one person	two persons	three or more persons	one person	two persons	three or more persons
+	—	—	—	F	—	—	—	—
—	F	—	—	—	—	—	F	—
—	M	—	—	M	—	—	—	—
—	—	F (youngest)	—	—	—	—	M	—

Families of Three Generations

Younger Generation consisting of			Middle Generation consisting of			Oldest Generation consisting of		
one person	two persons	three or more persons	one person	two persons	three or more persons	one person	two persons	three or more persons
+	—	—	—	—	—	—	—	—
—	—	—	+	—	—	—	—	—
—	—	—	—	—	—	+	—	—
—	F	—	—	—	—	—	—	—

Social Organization

Early Forms of Family and Marriage in the Light of Soviet Ethnography

A. PERSHITS

The outstanding U.S. ethnographer, Lewis H. Morgan, proposed the first scientific periodization in the development of the forms of marriage and the family. The conceptual part of this periodization has largely remained meaningful even today. Before going on to deal with these problems in Soviet ethnography, let us take a brief look at Morgan's basic propositions.

Morgan, opposing the assertions prevalent in his day about the individual family being an everlasting form, proposed that relations in marriage and the family evolved through a succession of historical forms. He singled out five forms which had successively developed from the primordial sexual promiscuity: the consanguine group family barring persons of different generations from marital intercourse; the punaluan group family, additionally excluding brothers and sisters from such intercourse; the pairing family; the patriarchal family; and finally, the monogamous family of class society which emerged with the development of private property.

Morgan drew up this scheme of the development of the family and marriage on the basis of the ethnographic material available at the time, the most important of which was information about the systems of kinship terminologies reflecting, as Morgan was the first to show, preceding forms of family and marital relations. In particular, the consanguine and the punaluan families were reconstructed through an analysis of the classificatory systems of kinship terminologies, among which Morgan brought out two successive stages, the so-called Hawaiian or Malayan

First published in *Voprosy istorii*, N2 (1967).

and the Turano-Ganowanian. In both these systems the kinship nomenclature, and consequently also the marital and familial relations on which they rest are of a group (classifying) character, that is, definite groups of persons are at one and the same time in marital relations with each other. The Malayan system, however, makes a distinction between groups of kinsmen only horizontally by generation, which, Morgan held, corresponds to relations which had existed in the consanguine family, whereas the Turano-Ganowanian system also draws a vertical distinction between the patrilateral and matrilateral kinship, which corresponds to the relations in the punaluan family. The distinction between the patrilateral and matrilateral kinship is evidence of the emergence of the clan society.

The existence of the punaluan and the pairing family has been proved not only by an analysis of the systems of kinship terminologies, but also by the direct ethnographic data on the marital customs of some peoples of the world which Morgan had at his disposal. According to the reports of missionaries, the Hawaiians, which were at one time considered to be among the most backward peoples, still retained the punaluan family founded upon group marriage of several sisters including the first, second, and more remote female cousins, to each other's husbands or of several brothers including the first, second, and more remote male cousins to each other's wives. There were also numerous data (mainly relating to the Indians of North America) on the pairing family, which enabled Morgan to characterize it as deprived of internal economic bonds, an unstable social form under which relations between the spouses were broadly combined with survivals of group marriage.

This coherent and logical periodization in the development of the family and marriage, based on solid factual material and at the same time aimed against the reactionary idea that the individual family of class society had existed from time immemorial, was in the main accepted by Friedrich Engels. Engels, however, has not overestimated certain parts of Morgan's theory but has repeatedly stressed that the various specific conclusions he had drawn depended on the accumulation of new ethnographic facts. Thus, in the first edition of his *The Origin of the Family, Private Property and the State*, Engels accepted Morgan's idea that the consanguine family had been a necessary stage in the development of family and marital relations. In the fourth edition, which appeared after the publication of L. Fyson's and A. Howitt's studies of Australian aborigines, he accepted in principle that in Australia the dual-phratral group marriage, i.e., the state of mutual matrimony between two phratries, could have emerged directly from primordial promiscuity.

At the same time, Engels came out resolutely against the view of the punaluan family as a necessary stage in the development of family and marriage (Vinnikov, 1936). Engels warned that Morgan's general periodization of primitive history would remain in force only "unless important additional material necessitates alterations" (Marx and Engels, 1970 : 204).

Soon new data were obtained which cast doubt on the historical reality of some of the familial and marital forms suggested by Morgan. The studies begun by W. Rivers, G. Frazer, and L. Sternberg, and continued by Soviet scientists S. Tokarev, A. Zolotaryov, and D. Olderogge showed that Morgan was wrong in his view of the place occupied in history by the Malayan system of kinship terminologies which he took as the basis for reconstructing the consanguine family. It turned out that the merger of the patrilateral and matrilateral line of kinship, characteristic of this system, was not a reflection of the earliest (preclan) state of marital and family relations but, on the contrary, a relatively later simplification of the Turano-Ganowanian system, resulting from the disintegration of the clan society. In other words, the Malayan system was not older but younger than the Turano-Ganowanian system of kinship terminologies (Tokarev, 1929; Zolotarev 1940, 1964; Olderogge, 1951).

Morgan was wrong on yet another point: studies carried out by ethnographers specializing in Oceania, including the Soviet ethnographer D. Tumarkin, established that reports of punaluan marriage had been an invention of the missionaries who had either honestly erred or had tried to present the pagans of Hawaii as immoral savages. In effect, by the time the Hawaiian Islands were colonized, the state had already been taking shape and pairing marriage combined with polygyny (and rarely with polyandry) in the high life was developing into monogamy (Tumarkin, 1954). Thus, the punaluan family turned out to be not merely an exception to the rule but a figment of the imagination. Finally, studies carried out by foreign and Soviet students have shown that because Morgan had limited factual material, he had failed to devote sufficient attention to the connection between the initial forms of familial and marital relations and the dual organization.

All of this quite naturally required that Morgan's scheme should be given greater precision. In Soviet science the work on these problems is still far from complete. Views concerning the development of the primitive family differ; for one thing, there is no consensus about the initial forms of regulation of marital and familial relations. Some Soviet specialists in the history of primitive society, while accepting the modern view of the Malayan system of kinship terminologies, believe that this system was not the only basis for the reconstruction of the consanguine family. Thus Olderogge who did much to bring out the later origin of the Malayan system, found it necessary to add the reservation that the latter constituted no more than partial evidence of the existence of the consanguine family (Olderogge, 1951: 31–32).

M. Kosven (1957 : 25) and P. Boriskovskij (1957 : 139–40) have made more definite statements on this score, and referred to Engels' remark that it is not only the Malayan system of kinship terminologies, but all the subsequent development of the family, implying the existence of this form as a necessary initial stage, which provides evidence in favor of the existence of the consanguine family. The reference to Engels on this point, however, is hardly justified. We have already seen that the facts dating from the 1870's and 1880's, which had made it possible to place the stage of the punaluan family in the development of familial and marital relations, can now no longer be taken into the account. Moreover, as A. Zolotarev has shown, the hypothesis of the consanguine family clashes with the marriages, widespread among some backward peoples, between representatives of different generations, including father and daughter (Zolotarev 1940 : 157). In one of his works, Kosven himself drew attention to similar marriages mainly between uncles and nieces or nephews and aunts (Kosven, 1946). It is true that in the recent period attention has been drawn to the fact that because of the short span of life among paleolithic peoples (Vallois has estimated that most women died under the age of thirty years) the shared period of life of successive generations was short, and this could have resulted in the actual impossibility and later in a prohibition of this kind of marriage (Vallois, 1961; Semenov, 1963; Boriskovskij, 1970). The consanguine family implies the exclusion from the marital circle not only of mothers but also fathers; this is not borne out either by palaeodemographic calculations, or, as we have seen, by ethnographic data. Consequently, at the present time there appear to be no factual or logical arguments in favor of reconstruction of the consanguine family.

On the strength of this, most Soviet researchers believe that the exogamous dual-clan group marriage was the first historical form of social regulation of relations between the sexes which developed directly from the primordial promiscuity. In other words it is assumed that the earliest form of marriage included: first, prohibition of marriage with clan members; second, the intermarriage age of two specified clans; third, the marital community of members of both clans (Zolotarev, 1940; Tokarev, 1946; Tolstov, 1947a; Semenov, 1966b).

The mechanism behind the emergence of exogamy is one of the most complex problems of ethnography. Let us recall that Morgan explained its appearance by the urge to avoid the biologically injurious consequences of incest. This explanation was already partially corrected by Engels who observed that such an urge could have been no more than spontaneous without clear consciousness of purpose (Marx and Engels, 1970 : 223). The latest data makes it possible to draw the conclusion that, given sufficiently large biological populations, the idea of incestuous marriages being injurious was doubtful. What is more, in primitive society such forms of relatives-marriage, as cross-cousin marriages (with the daughter of the mother's brother or with the daughter of the father's sister), had not been merely allowed but had even been prescriptive. Another fact that had been brought out was that primitive men, like the Australians, the Trobrianders or the Avuna, may not have been aware of the connection between copulation and conception.

Most Soviet scientists have now abandoned the purely biological theory of the origin of exogamy and seek to find an intrinsic connection between this form of regulation of marital relations and the general course of the regulation of productive activity in the primitive human horde. The view advanced by Taylor and Lévi-Strauss has been fairly widely accepted — that exogamy was designed to fix the economic or social bonds between neighboring collectives (Zolotarev, 1931; Olderogge, 1947; Tokarev, 1968a). Another hypothesis was put forward by S. Tolstov (basing himself on some propositions expressed by A. Crowley, M. Kovalevsky, and M. Zhakov, 1933) among Soviet scientists; he linked the appearance of exogamous taboos with the regulation of internal economic life of the early primitive collectives. According to this hypothesis, sexual relations not being socially regulated must have been accompanied by ceaseless clashes on grounds of jealousy, thereby undermining the human horde as a production cell. In combating this, mankind gradually introduced various taboos which increasingly limited, and ultimately made altogether impossible, sexual intercourse within one's group. The result was exogamy, and at the same time the duty organization in the form of a combination of two exogamous clans into a single marital connubium (Tolstov, 1935a). This view is accepted by A. Zolotarev in his latest work (Zolotarev, 1964), and in the recent period by Yu. Semenov who has sought to trace the origin of the dual (dual-horde) exogamy at the latest stages of the existence of the primitive human horde (Semenov, 1966a).

There has also been inadequate study of the mechanism behind the emergence of the dual organization. The question of how the dual structure of early clan society arose — was it through the division of one collective or through the merger of two isolated groups — is now being essentially considered arbitrarily. This question may subsequently be answered when considerable palaeoanthropological data are at hand about the mutability of local groups of earliest mankind. Nonetheless, the fact that the dual organization had existed as a primary form in the regulation of marital relations is generally accepted. The survival of the dual organization or its echoes in the clan, tribal or political structure, mythology or religion, has been recorded among most peoples of the world (Tolstov, 1948; Zolotarev, 1939; Pershits, 1956). It is true that alongside this, another ancient form of interclan mutual marriage — the asymmetric connubium (Olderogge, 1946 a; b) — has been discovered, but it was less widespread and must have appeared later.

The group character of early marital relations is reconstructed, on the one hand, on the strength of the above-mentioned features of the Turano-Ganowanian system of kinship terminologies, and on the other — and this is especially important — through an analysis of some remaining survivals. Such, for instance, are the marriage classes of the Australian aborigines and the piraungaru-type customs discovered among some Australian tribes, where both men and women had, in addition to their "principal" wives or husbands, several "additional" ones. Such, too, are the diverse survivals of freedom of extramarital sexual intercourse, evidence of which has been found in historical and ethnographic material among many backward, and now and again, even among fairly developed peoples of the world. Some of these materials were already used by Bachofen and Morgan or by the followers of the latter, while others are reflected in the works of numerous foreign and Soviet students. Nevertheless, there are many controversial issues here, too; of primary importance is the problem of localizing the marital residence of the spouses.

The conception of the exogamous group marriage inevitably had to pose the question of where the marital intercourse of the spouses was actually realized. Ethnographic data allow two answers to this question: unilocal (joint) and dislocal (separate) marital residence. In the first instance, under the practice of matrilocal residence (that is, settlement with the women), the group husbands had to resettle to their group wives; under the practice of patrilocal residence, which succeeded the former, the wives had to resettle to their husbands. We find survivals of this unilocal group marriage in its patrilocal variant, for instance, among the Arabana of Australia and the Semangs of Malacca. In the latter instance, as W. Schmidt and W. Koppers and the Soviet researcher

Kosven (Schmidt and Koppers, 1924; Kosven, 1932) suggested, both groups of spouses had to remain in their clan collectives, undertaking sexual intercourse only during short nocturnal visits or even outside the boundaries of the settlements, for instance, in the forest. The hypothesis of the dislocal character of group marriage is confirmed not only by numerous folklore subjects but also by the marital customs of some peoples, including relatively primitive ones like some Papuan tribes of New Guinea. Evidence in favor of this hypothesis also seems to come from the widespread custom of the dislocal settlement of the spouses until the birth of their first child. This hypothesis has been supported by various other Soviet researchers (Tolstov 1935b; Zolotarev, ms, b) and was given its logical completion in Semyonov's proposition that group marriage should be considered as a socially regulated relationship between collectives, but not between individual men and women (Semenov, 1964). Yet, we cannot consider this to have been proved.

A special problem which, let me say, has also not been adequately studied, is about the reasons for the transition from group marriage to pairing marriage. Those who favor the biological explanation of exogamy connect the emergence of pairing marriage with the further gradual taboo on marriages between relatives, which steadily narrowed down the circle of marital partners and ultimately made group marriage impossible (Nikolskij, 1950). According to another view expressed in Soviet writings, the transition to the pairing family took place when, with the emergence of the surplus product and the incipient disintegration of primitive communism, the first family cells, initially on a consumer and then on a production basis, began to emerge within the clan collectives (Semenov, 1965a). Finally, there is another answer which logically flows from Tolstov's proposal to explain the emergence of exogamy in terms of production: dual exogamy had carried marital relations beyond the boundaries of the clan but necessarily left a room for rivalry between group husbands or wives. Thus, the new bans continued to narrow down the circle of group spouses, as a result of which pairing marriage took shape through some intermediate but not necessarily similar forms.

Soviet ethnographers have devoted more attention to the subsequent forms of familial-marital organization — the extended and monogamous family. It was Kosven who did most in this sphere. He believes that the extended family appeared as early as the epoch of the developed matriarchate in the form of the so-called maternal extended family, which constitutes a group of the nearest kinsmen living and keeping house together, a group which is differentiated within the matri-clan. The Iroquoian *ovachira* is the best example of such a cell. Subsequently, with the disintegration of the matri-clan system, this family gives way to the patriarchal extended family of the "democratic" type, and the latter, as private property develops, either becomes a late ("despotic" or "paternal") extended family, or gives way to the small family organization (Kosven, 1940, 1963). Kosven's scheme for the development of the extended family has been broadly but not generally accepted. Many ethnographers, on good grounds, have pointed to the fact that the maternal family, insofar as it did not include affines, cannot be regarded as a form of family organization, so that it is impossible to speak about the prepatriarchal forms of the extended family. In the recent period, a substantial specification in the periodization of the extended family was introduced by Yu. Bromley who showed that the patriarchal forms of the extended family were preceded not by a maternal but by a fraternal family community (Bromley, 1968c).

However great the difference between views concerning the existence of the consanguine family, the origins of exogamy, the reasons for the transition to pairing marriage, and the period in which the extended family organization originated, all the Soviet researchers mentioned above are working to elaborate the problem of the evolution in the early forms of the family and marriage from standpoints that are close to each other in principle. They assume that present-day ethnographical data make it possible to bring substantial precision to the various theses set out by Morgan, and fully confirm his proposition that the group, collective forms of familial, and marital relations inevitably preceded the pairing and subsequent forms of the family. There is, however, another view which is quite new in our historical science and, for that reason alone, calls for special attention.

As I have said, the group forms of family and marriage are a historical reconstruction based on the study and scientific interpretation of various survival phenomena. When living familial and marital institutions are directly observed, even among the most backward peoples of the world, like the Australian aborigines, the Aeta, the Semangs, the forest Vedda, the Bushmen, the peoples of Tierra del Fuego, and so on, it is the prevalence of the pairing and not of the group family that is discovered. Now and again, especially when marriage is unilocal, some kind of internal economic bonds have already emerged in such a family. On the strength of these facts, many ethnographers abroad continue to hold the view that the individual family has been there from time immemorial. In particular, much factual material designed to confirm this idea, and so to refute the idea of the historical development of familial forms, has been generalized in the works of prominent bourgeois ethnographers, including E. Westermarck, B. Malinowski, P. Lowie, G. Murdock, and others.

Until recently, the material these researchers used was either ignored in our writings or declared to be false. What is false is not the facts themselves but their interpretation and the theoretical constructions based on them; they make no distinction between two fundamentally distinct types of family — the pairing and the monogamous family. In this context, some interest is attached to the views expressed by Soviet ethnographers N. Butinov and V. Kabo. On the strength of the ethnography of the Australians and the Papuans of New Guinea, they, too, refuse to reconstruct the group forms of family and marriage, and begin the history of familial and marital relations with the living forms they have directly observed. According to Butinov, the pairing family was already in existence in the primitive human horde and produced an acute antagonism between the horde and the family. Gaining independence from time to time, the family hampered the cohesion of the collective. In order to ease this contradiction, there arose the custom of exogamy which produced some alienation between the spouses and so weakened the family. In this weakened state, the pairing family passed from the stage of the primitive human horde to the stage of the communal-clan system: it had had definite economic functions but was merely the lowest economic cell within the basic economic collective, the clan community. This kind of family, Butinov says, in considering the family organization of the Papuans, is incapable of carrying on economic operations on its own; the husband and the wife own their property separately, they cannot inherit from each other, they belong to different clans, and even frequently live in different huts — the husband in the male house, with other adult men of the clan community, and the wife in the family hut with the minor children (Butinov, 1962, 1968; Kabo, 1968).

This view does not appear to be convincing because it is based only on information relating to the pairing family, and completely ignores the sum total of the data on the group forms of family and marriage. The deliberate refusal to consider all the facts known to science, interconnection, and historical succession inevitably leads to one-sided and flimsy conclusions. In another sense, the idea expressed by Butinov and Kabo is indicative. It shows that if we take only the observations on which the above-mentioned bourgeois ethnographers had based themselves, and, in contrast to them, if we take an unbiased view of these facts, little ground will be left for the assertions that the individual family has always been there as the basic economic cell of society. It is this that constitutes the conceptual nucleus of the doctrine of the development of familial and marital relations developed by Morgan and Engels.

The problem of the evolution of familial and marital relations is not only of importance as an element of one's world outlook; it is also of great cognitive importance. In the recent period, its elaboration in Soviet ethnographical writings has been invigorated and, what is especially important, this is being done on a common methodological basis from different research angles. The possibility for extensive polemics is thus created and should help to clarify our ideas about the development of familial and marital forms.

"Military Democracy" and the Epoch of Class Formation

A. KHAZANOV

It is well known that many institutions of early class society did not newly arise but had their roots in the preceding epoch of disintegration of primitive society. With the split of society into classes these institutions appear to us in a markedly transformed shape adapted to the conditions of class existence. The various forms of political organization, which gradually and covertly take shape in the entrails of a primitive society approaching destruction, do not constitute any exception. The exact forms of this shaping political organization, the extent to which they are antithetical to society in which class contradictions have not yet reached the level entailing the emergence of the state in the proper sense of the word, and finally the very mechanism of their development remain little investigated and debatable. As a result, the existence of many institutions which have the character essentially of pre-state institutions is now and again taken as evidence of the existence of the state in this or that society. This, for its part, leads to an artificial merger of two qualitatively distinct epochs in mankind's history — the epoch of class formation, and the early class epoch. In this way, the dialectically intricate process of emergence of the state is now and again oversimplified with the state itself acquiring some supra-class features (because the society where it is said to exist still lacks antagonistic classes). At the same time, precisely in consequence of an inadequate distinction between the concept of "the epoch of class formation" and "the stage of early class society", we occasionally find the reserve approach, so that the society in which antagonistic classes have already appeared is presented

First published in *Voprosy istorii*, N12 (1968).

as a preclass society at the stage of its disintegration.

In this context, special importance attaches to the meaning of the MILITARY DEMOCRACY concept (Morgan, 1877: 132, 193, 221, 256, 259, 272, 288, 317, 325), which Lewis H. Morgan first brought out, and to its place in mankind's history, a question that Soviet ethnographers and historians have already repeatedly dealt with. Morgan himself failed to give a clear-cut definition of his military democracy, but laid emphasis on two of its features: the military state of society, and the system of administration consisting of an elective and removable supreme chief, a council of elders and a popular assembly. Attention was particularly drawn to the democratic character of this system which left the decisive say to the free people. Morgan saw military democracy not so much as a definite stage in the development of human society but rather as a specific form of its organization and administration.

In one of his early works, S. Tolstov expressed the view that military democracy was a special period of transition from preclass to class society: "The society of the epoch of military democracy is both pre-class and class — to be more precise, it is simultaneously a slave-holding society" (Tolstov, 1935a: 206). Subsequently, Tolstov virtually abandoned this view and defined military democracy as the final stage of primitive society (Tolstov, 1946). This view is shared by other ethnographers (Pershits, 1953; Kosven, 1957 : 220; 1960 : 250). In a recent article, Yu. Semenov once again expressed the idea that military democracy corresponds to a specific transition stage in the transformation of clan society into class society (Semenov, 1965a: 79, 80, 93). In the recent period, the military democracy concept has been criticized by some Soviet and foreign historians. In its place, they have suggested the "Asian mode of production", a concept which in this case means either a special period of transition from the classless to the class society, or the final stage in the history of primitive society (Suret-Canale, 1965: 101–2; Godelier, 1965 : 102–4; Berzin, Vitkin, Andrejev, 1966). The substance of this criticism, however, does not consist of any new period-ization of primitive history — there is nothing new in this or in a simple substitution of one term for another — but in a different view of the essence of the stage being defined.

Below I shall consider this in greater detail, but at this point I should like to observe that some ethnographers have already pointed out that the term introduced by Morgan was unsatisfactory and inadequate for the content of the epoch it defined (Potekhin, 1951 : 235–36; Kosven, 1960 : 245). I shall have to confine myself to the briefest possible historiographical review of some of the debatable matters connected with the "military democracy" concept so as to go on to a consideration of the problem itself.

Over ninety years have passed since the publication of Morgan's book, a period in which ethnography, history, and archaeology have amassed vast quantities of new data on the concluding stages of primitive society and the emergence of the state. Many of these data are at variance with those science had at its disposal in the second half of the 19th century. Morgan's view was necessarily restricted by the data bearing on Ancient Greece and Rome, two instances that he used to trace the direct transformation of the organs of administration in disintegrating primitive society into state organs. He failed to understand and did not give full due to the extent to which Aztec society developed. Our present-day knowledge of the subject is much fuller. Oceania and Africa have been yielding much new and fundamentally important material. Some success has been achieved in the study of the early state formations on the American continent. New information has been obtained on the emergence of the world's most ancient states in the East, although there are many points still controversial and obscure. There is a lively discussion of the specific emergence of the state in nomad societies. At the same time many problems of the early history of Greece and Italy now appear in a different light. All this has made it possible to take a fresh look at some of the questions bearing on the final period in the history of primitive society and the emergence of the state.

Morgan correctly remarked on the role of the military factor in the life of the societies he classified as military democracies. He was also right about the influence this factor had on their social institutions, but I think he overestimated the democratic character of these societies. This happened primarily because Morgan was able to trace the substitution of tribal society by "political" society, that is, the emergence of the state only, as I have said, on the strength of data bearing on Athens and Rome. The regularity he derived on the strength of this limited material, expressed in a gradual transformation of fundamentally democratic clan institutions into state institutions, was presented as a universal one. Considering the institutions of Athens and Rome before the emergence of the state there through the prism of the Iroquois clan, Morgan saw them as being a direct continuation and development of the social system which lay at the basis of the Iroquois confederation. Behind these features of outward similarity he failed to discern the fundamental distinctions separating the Greek *genos* and the Roman *gens* from the Iroquois clan.

It is impossible to see the Athenian state as arising directly from tribal institutions. The earliest states on the territory of Greece — the Achaean kingdoms — appeared not later than the 16th century B.C. (Blavatskaja, 1966 : 66), and their existence left a strong imprint on the subsequent historical development of Greece, not excluding Athens itself which had existed in Achaean times as well (Blegen, 1940 : 1–9). The discovery of the Achaean kingdoms complicated the question of the period to which Homer's epos belonged, but it was the latter on which scientists from Morgan to Kosven based their description of the military demo-cracy of the Greeks. Today, more and more researchers seem to accept the view that this epos had taken shape in Achaean times, that is, some-where between the 16th and the 13th centuries B.C.; the fall of Troy, which is now dated at 1260 B.C. (Blegen, 1963 : 163), gave an impetus not to the production of the epic tale but to its final formulation (Nilsson, 1932 : 11–34; 1933; Blavatskaja, 1966 : 7–14). The *Basileus* was, after all, a king, if not in Homer's poems, at any rate in actual reality. In the *Iliad* and the *Odyssey* socioeconomic relations were presented as considerably more archaic and idealized as is generally characteristic of epic tales. It is just as dangerous to be directly guided by them in reconstructing Greek society as it is to try to restore the social system of the peoples concerned on the basis of Popol-Wuch, Nartes and the Nibelungs, or the bylinas of the Vladimirian cycle. As for Attica, in the epoch examined by Morgan its social system cannot be called military-demociatic. On the contrary, it was the scene of a long and bitter struggle for democracy, already characteristic of the slave-holding polis, a struggle in which the broad masses of free people were con-fronted by the eupatrids, who used the survivals of tribal institutions to safeguard their own privileges.

We find a similar picture in Rome. Archaeological evidence on the disintegration of the primitive communal system in Italy dates it from the end of the second and early first millenium B.C. R. Gunter writes: "The first settlers on the hills already lived, as the spade shows, in conditions of a relatively developed social differentiation. In the period when the names we now know of the *Curiae* and the three most ancient gens had been determined, these were not harmoniously developed clan institutions, but already bore the mark of state formation." The state in Rome arose in the regal period, not later than the 6th century B.C., which, like the shaping of some political institutions, was strongly promoted by Etruscan influence (at one time Rome was ruled by the Etruscan Tarquinian dynasty) (Günter, 1959 : 79–82; Yelnitskij, 1958 : 143; Nemirovskij, 1962 : 212, 239; Gjerstad, 1963 : 44; Grenier, 1912 : 78; Ryberg, 1940 : 5). Thus, the early political structures in Rome were already of a state character even if a highly primitive one, and are burdened with considerable survivals of earlier, prestate relations. As in Greece, these survivals suited the patricians, the descendants of the gens aristocracy, and can be traced in Rome almost back to the Punic Wars. The centuriate reform, which, according to Morgan, inaugurates the Roman state, now turns out to date from a period not earlier than 443 B.C. (Nemirovskij, 1959 : 162). Both in Rome and Greece at the dawn of their authentic history we find a much greater social and proprietary differentiation of society than Morgan had realized. The organs of power which he had held to be clans, appear to us from the outset in a strongly modified form adapted to conditions of a state existence however primitive, and expressing for the most part the eupatrids and the patricians. The descendants of the aristocratic clans contrasted themselves with the strata of the free part of the population which had fewer rights, and fought to retain their privileges. The term democracy, even if it is a military one, is hardly adequate to such a state of society.

Turning to the history of other countries and peoples, we find a considerable diversity of social institutions in the various societies at the final stage of the primitive society undergoing transition to the state. For the most part, these institutions do not fit into the procrustean bed of the triad characteristic of the military democracy: the supreme chief, the council of elders, the popular assembly — nor is this at all surprising. Although the emergence of the state is everywhere determined by the same regularities, in each concrete instance this process is influenced by an aggregation of different factors. The level of development of the productive forces, the forms of the economy, the role of exchange, the extent of disintegration of tribal institutions, the character of external relations, etc., has an influence on the forms of the emergent political structures of society, which can far from always be characterized as military democracy.

In this context, considerable interest is attached to the Polynesian society, which on the eve of the colonial period (19th century) was at the stage of the disintegration of the primitive society and the emergence of the state, although on some of the islands and archipelagoes the process ran an uneven course (*Narody*, 1956a; Tokarev, 1958c; Williamson, 1924; Best, 1924; Hogbin, 1934 : 235–60; Sahlins, 1958). In Polynesia the extended family was the main cell of society, and affinity gave way to territorial ties. Exchange did not develop to any great extent, but the handicrafts, already separated from agriculture, were considerably developed. The importance of slavery was on the whole not great. In these conditions, a special part fell to social differentiations which largely

determined proprietary distinctions within society. The main characteristics of Polynesia were undeviating practice of the genealogical principle
of seniority, the separation of the nobility, and the tendency to the
formation of closed hereditary caste groups. So even before the emergence of the state a sharp social stratification had occurred and the bulk
of the still free members of the society had been barred from the
administration of social affairs. It is true that all the adult members of
the commune were entitled to attend the communal councils — the *fono*
of Samoa and Tonga — and even take part in discussing affairs, but for
all practical purposes things were discussed by the heads of the extended
families, and the decisions were taken by a handful of the senior chiefs.
In fact, only the chiefs took part in the councils which brought together
several neighboring villages.

Even among the Maoris of New Zealand who were at a relatively
lower stage of social development in comparison with Tahiti and Tonga,
the tribal chiefs were restricted in their action by a council of elders
representing the individual *hapu* (groups of kindred families), but never
by ordinary, free members of the communes. Administration of the
larger territorial and tribal associations rested on a hierarchy of chiefs
belonging to the same estate of the nobility — *alii* (*ariki*). We find
nothing resembling a popular assembly in Polynesia. It is therefore not
at all accidental that, although all Soviet researchers are unanimous in
their evaluation of the level of development attained by Polynesian
society, none of them uses the term military democracy to describe it.
Otherwise, the facts would clearly stand as incongruous.

We find something similar in Africa, which reveals a diversity of
forms of social administration in the transition period. Alongside the
military-democratic forms (among the Fulbe, Azande, and Southern
Bantu) there existed other forms based on greater social differentiation.
In the Indenie "kingdom" (Ivory Coast) a whole superstructure of variously ranking chiefs headed by a supreme chief rose over the demo-
cratically ruled communes in which the extended families were banded.
No trace of any popular assemblies can be found above the level of one
village (Suret-Canale, 1958 : 91). The Mandingo-speaking Africans had
popular assemblies only on the level of the settlement or district, but
these were rather of a gerontocratic character and consisted only of the
chiefs of extended families (Labouret, 1934 : 46). Among the Bemba in
North-Eastern Zambia, although each man was armed, there were no
regular detachments and no trace of any popular assembly; nonetheless,
there was clear evidence of a ruling elite consisting of representatives of the
supreme "crocodile clan". A council of elders merely was in charge of

religious affairs and considered disputes over the succession to the throne (Fortes and Evans-Pritchard, 1940 : 85–112).

The available material gives ground to assume that the formation of classes frequently ran through the formation of hierarchic caste groups which emerged and were considerably developed as early as the final stage of primitive society. The emergence of such groups could be promoted by conquests which transformed ethnical distinctions into caste and then into class distinctions (as in fact happened in the Mbau "kingdom" in Fiji, and in Ruanda, Urundi, and other countries of tropical Africa). An example of this type of development is offered by the social organization of the Lan Shan group of the Yih people in China where the whole of society was divided into a number of hereditary endogamic stratas, the boundaries between which were highly clear-cut, and absolutely insurmountable between the highest stratum, Nosu, and the rest which it maintained in semi-feudal bondage. Let us add, however, that among the Yih the state never in fact took shape, and the social system of the Nosu closely resembled the form characteristic of military democracy with the difference, however, that it was a democracy for 7 per cent of the population (Its, 1964; Its, Yakovlev, 1967).

Castes and strata could also emerge without conquest within primitive society itself as it was disintegrating. These emerge on the basis of the emergent hierarchy of clans, communes and extended families, compounded by the social division of labor and the emergence of professional castes.[1] What this led to is clearly seen from the example of the Micronesians of the Marianna and Marshall Islands, who had, alongside their matrilineal clans, sharp hierarchical distinctions within society. Representatives of the noble clans, which had been converted into endogamic castes, monopolized the right to the land and to the administration of society. Subsequent social stratification led to the emergence of different social groups enjoying various rights even within the dominant aristocratic caste (Thompson, 1945 : 11–20; Erdland, 1914 : 99–114). Similar phenomena will be found among some mountain peoples of Assam. From the existing hierarchy of clans among the Lushu and the Konyak Naga, one tribe developed which monopolized all the senior offices and became an endogamic caste gradually taking shape as a feudal

---

[1] The tendency to form these closed stratas existed both in Athens and in Rome, and its vehicles were representatives of "noble" clans, the eupatrids and the patricians. Eventually another tendency became uppermost there: the establishment of a single class of slave-holders, in contrast to Sparta where the early class society assumed the form of a clearly expressed caste character.

class. Around the chiefs there took shape a peculiar aristocracy which marked the division of society into estates (Maretina, 1967). How the ruling clan or extended family could grow in these conditions will be seen from the example of Dahomey where the royal house numbered 12,000 persons. It is hardly possible to speak here about a military democracy because most free members of the society were removed from administration before the hierarchic caste distinctions assumed a class character and the state itself emerged.

I have sought to show that the disintegration of the primitive society did not necessarily lead to the establishment of a military democracy and that there were other ways based on greater social differentiation. There is yet another aspect to this question of military democracy. Can it be assumed that military democracy as a stadial concept corresponded to the whole epoch of transition from primitive society to class society, at least among the peoples where we in fact find it in existence? Above I remarked on the difficulties which the researcher into the early history of Greece and Rome inevitably faces when taking such a view of military democracy — on the one hand, the level of social differentiation in pre-Solonic Athens, as in Rome of the early royal period, clashes with the idea of the people being free under a military democracy; on the other hand, no more than an intensive process of class formation, but never the existence of fully fledged classes, can be assumed. As a corollary of this, state power both in Greece and in Rome in the specified period was embryonic, and it is precisely the initial stages of class formation in Athens and in Rome that are most obscure.

There is much more material on a similar period among the ancient Germans, where it is quite obvious that military democracy did not immediately precede the emergence of the state. The military democracy epoch among the ancient Germans as a whole ranges over the period from the 1st century B.C. to the 4th century A.D. The royal power emerging in the period from the 1st century B.C. to the 2nd century A.D. was elective and unstable, and for the time expressed the interests of the tribe as a whole, and not only of the tribal nobility (Neusykhin, 1929; 1967 : 79). In the 3rd and the 4th centuries when the military alliances of the German tribes occupied definite territories, more or less stable formations arose with a more complex social and political structure. At the end of the 5th and during the 6th and 7th centuries the states were formed which were usually called "barbarian", though not long ago they were characterized as early feudal states (Vsemirnaja, 1957 : 140–41, 189, 204). Today, more students incline to the idea that these were not yet states in the full sense of the word because they were not the product of a division of society into antagonistic classes but constituted a form of social organization at the stage of transition from a preclass to a class structure (Neusykhin, 1956 : 31; 1967 : 81; Korsunskij, 1963 : 20, 160–62; Gurevich, 1967 : 12–23). In these societies there was already a pronounced tendency towards the transformation of social distinctions into class contradictions; however, as Neusykhin observed, "this social system, being a communal one without being primitive, and simultaneously including within itself elements of social inequality, was not yet a feudal class society, even in the sense in which very early feudalism itself was such". A term introduced into scientific usage is the stadial concept of the "prefeudal period", which, in Neusykhin's opinion, begins with the disintegration of the tribal system (Neusykhin, 1956 : 76, 82), in application to the Germans of the early centuries of our own era, and lasts until the formation of the basic classes of the feudal society and the emergence of the state as an expression of the interests of the ruling class. Consequently, the "prefeudal period" is regarded as a transitional one between two social formations — the preclass and class formations — while military democracy corresponds only to its beginning.

Similar views were developed even earlier by B. Grekov on the strength of his study of the history of the Slavs. He dated the epoch of military democracy among the Eastern Slavs to the period from the 4th to the 6th centuries, and regarded the period from the 6th to the 8th centuries as a transitional one from the primitive society at the final stage of its development to class society, from the military democracy to the early feudal state (Grekov, 1953 : 533; 1948 : 94).

On the whole, such conclusions appear to be highly convincing. In the period of transition from the primitive system to the class system political structures with a tendency to set themselves above society could arise. These would not yet be in final contrast to society because of the embryonic social contradictions and the incompleteness of the process of the class formation, and therefore they would not yet be states in the true sense of the word. This accords well with the information we have about the emergence of classes and the state among many peoples. Not long ago, L. Kubbel stated that there are no grounds for classifying the Ghana of the 8th–11th centuries as belonging to the first few nearly class states in Western Africa, as had been done till recently. In that period Ghana had not yet crossed the line separating primitive society from class society: there was no exploitation of the rank-and-file members of society, slave labor was not used inside the country, and the principal means of production were still not concentrated in the hands of a minority. The embryonic forms of statehood arose there largely under the influence of the needs of the trans-Sahara trade, which hastened the disintegration of tribal relations. Kubbel showed Ghana society to be "preclass" and drew a parallel with the "prefeudal society" of early medieval Europe (Kubbel, 1967). Similar "barbarian states" are also to be found in Eastern Africa. There is good reason for the British scientist, A. W. Southall, to compare the "segmentary states" (as he calls the early state formations in Africa) with state formations in Europe in the early Middle Ages. Suret-Canale also wrote about the "embryonic state formations" in Africa, which appeared before the emergence of class antagonism (Southall, 1953 : 235–56; Suret-Canale, 1958 : 104).

Present-day researchers into the precolonial history of Latin America note the existence of similar prestate forms among Indians. S. Sozina says that the society of the Chibcha-Muisque (South America) was a "barbarian state" where in the mid-16th century the privileged stratum had not yet developed into a class, although the owners of the means of production had already separated themselves from the mass of ordinary members of the commune (Sozina, 1967).

Similar-type structures are also to be found among the Aztecs, although it should be remembered that their development was accelerated and stimulated by the highly developed culture which they found on the Mexican plateau, and by their ceaseless wars of conquest. There is one point in the Aztec tradition, dating to between 1427 and 1430, when as the result of a conflict between the military nobility and the ordinary members of the commune, the popular assembly ceased to exist. This, however, did not make Aztec society a class society. The land was still held by the communes, and the privileges of the nobility had not yet become hereditary (Katz, 1958 : 15–23). The "barbarian state" concept best accords with the form of political organization of Aztec society in that period.

The "barbarian state" concept also helps in the study of nomad society, in particular of the ancient nomads. There has been endless controversy over what the Scythian society of the 6th–4th centuries B.C., or the Hun society of the period immediately preceding the enthronement of Mode-shanyui, looked like — was it a military democracy or a fully-fledged state? They cannot be classed as the former because of the existence of a marked social differentiation and a fairly strong central power; they cannot be ranked with the second because there is no noticeable exploitation of ordinary members of society, and the share of slave labor is insignificant. It may well be that the Scythians and the Huns of the said period were going through the completion of the process of class formation. Their society was not yet a class one, but political structures with definite state institutions had already appeared (Lashuk, 1967c : 112–13, 114–15).

Recent studies make it increasingly clear that despotism was not the initial form of statehood in the countries of the East, as was until quite recently assumed; rather it was preceded by other, more democratic forms of political organization characterized by the existence of a council of nobles and a popular assembly. This is sometimes used as a basis for the conclusion that military democracy had at one time also existed in the East. In no way denying this possibility, I must draw attention to the need to have more specific evidence of this proposition. We find traces in the Ancient East of the existence of institutions typologically similar to military-democratic ones only where the state has already either emerged or was in the final stages of its formation. We have no authentic sources on the epoch preceding this. As we have seen, military democracy is not the only possible form of political organization of society going through the disintegration of primitive communal relations. The formal similarity of social institutions does not tell us much. The *posadnik*, the *boyar* council, and the *veche* of medieval Novgorod outwardly appeared to be similar to the supreme chief, the council of elders, and the popular assembly typical of military democracy. Almost no one will assert on this ground that the Novgorod of the 13th–14th centuries was a military democracy, or that its state institutions directly go back to it.

There arises this question: what were the early state formations of the countries of the East? With regard to Mesopotamia, I think I. Djakonov has a strong case when he characterizes the Jemdet-Nasr period as the time of formation of tribal alliances, and the first early dynastic period as the epoch of the shaping of the state in Sumer (Djakonov, 1959: 156). What he calls "nome" states of this period correspond, in stadial terms, to the already described "barbarian states" in other parts of the world, whose emergence marks the moment when the process of class formation in society has already gone far enough to have brought to life some state institutions, but has not yet gone to the extent of splitting society into antagonistic classes. In any comparison it is necessary to reckon with the specific features of ancient Mesopotamia where the requirements of irrigation farming under relatively undeveloped productive forces had to determine an especially early emergence of embryonic state power.

The final period in the history of primitive society was much more complex and diverse than that of the 19th century, although it was everywhere given the same content: transition from preclass to class society. As a form of emergent political organization of society, military democracy was not universal; it does not cover the whole period as a stadial concept. I think this period is better designated as an "epoch of class formation", which gives a clearer idea of the significance of the transition period. In the broad sense of the word, an epoch of class formation applies to every stage of disintegration of the primitive society from the emergence of a regular surplus product. Since the emergent proprietary inequality and the social differentiation do not at once reach the level at which they grow into class distinctions and contradictions, in the narrow sense of the word it could be taken to mean the epoch in the course of which the classes are shaped. The "prefeudal period" concept appears to be unsatisfactory because it has a negative aspect; the "Asian mode of production" concept appears to be unacceptable as a designation for the period of transition from the preclass to the class society because it is imprecise, regional, and vague. Used in this sense, it artificially brings together two fundamentally distinct epochs: the epoch of class formation and the epoch of early class society. The end of the epoch of class formation marks the emergence of the state. It is much more difficult to determine the beginning of this epoch. Intensive disintegration of the primitive society begins only from the point at which it attains a sufficiently high level in the development of its productive forces. It is the task of the researcher himself to establish this point for each given society, and no general recipes will do here. Semenov is, therefore, hardly right when he suggests that we should consider the emergence of slavery a universal criterion marking the beginning, according to his terminology, of the "epoch of the transformation of clan society into class society" (Semenov, 1965a: 9). The role and significance of the institution of slavery is known to have been dissimilar for the process of class formation in different societies.

It is my view that the initial stage of the epoch of class formation should be connected not so much with the emergence of new forms of the emergent political organization of society as with the transformation and modification of the old organs of administration which are of tribal origin, and their adaptation to the more complex social structure. Such, too, is military democracy, one of the existing forms, but not the only form, of administration of society, which on the whole corresponded to the period in which large inter-tribal alliances were established. Military democracy as a form of social administration is contradictory, as is the whole epoch. The supreme chief and the council of elders quite naturally express primarily the interests of the tribal elite, but it would be an oversimplification to assume that they did not also express the interests of the whole of society. Hence, there was a two-fold importance to the plunderous wars and campaigns whose role increased especially at this historical stage. The wars helped the tribal elite to increase its power, wealth, and influence, and temporarily ironed out the contradictions within society by carrying them outside and resolving them at the expense of neighbors.

While war did constitute an integral factor in the process of class formation, its role in different societies varied with local conditions. Thus in Polynesia it had a smaller part to play than in Western Europe. I should imagine that some of the societies in which war had become a regular function of popular life, and where a majority of the population were drawn into campaigns, conquests and migrations, were those which in fact had passed through a military democracy stage. The ordinary free member of the commune, in possession of weapons and skilled in their use, was not an ideal object for exploitation. For these reasons, military democracy could not be directly transformed into the state. It had to give way to, or rather be transformed into, other political structures more in line with the character of society at the subsequent stage of its development.

The gradual substitution of territorial for tribal bonds, the growing proprietary inequality, the spreading social stratification of society, and the emergence of the ruling stratum of the population (partially consisting of descendants of the tribal aristocracy and partially of men rising to positions of importance during the tempestuous events of the initial stage of the epoch of class formation) all led to the emergence of embryonic state formations, "barbarian states". These in the strict sense were "prestates", that is, political structures which already contained some elements of the future statehood, even if in a very undeveloped form.[2] In barbarian society the process of class formation was not yet complete, so that contradictions had not yet assumed their antogonistic character: the free commoners continued to constitute the majority which was not exploited to any considerable extent. Thus we designate the final period in the epoch of class formation as a prestate period. It is characterized by the removal of the majority of still free members of society from the administration, the emergence of embryonic, primitive state formations expressing mainly the interests of the social elite acting as a peculiar catalyst in the process of class formation, and promoting its completion. Therein lay their principal function. Only with the division of society into opposite classes did these "prestates"

---

[2] The term "barbarian state" appears to be most apt for designating such political structures because the concept of "barbarians" has been strongly fixed for the peoples which had gone through the epoch of class formation.

give way to state political structures in the true sense of the word.

What is the place of the epoch of class formation in the history of mankind? A great deal depends on one's approach. For the historian of class societies, it may indeed appear to be transitional from preclass to class society because there he first finds the phenomena which are subsequently developed in societies based on exploitation. For the historian of primitive society, this is the final epoch of the primitive communal system because only with the emergence of the state and the appearance of antagonistic classes did primitive society finally cease to exist.

A Description of Systems
of Kinship Terminology

Yu. LEVIN

1. INTRODUCTORY

1.1   As early as 1958 S. A. Tokarev wrote: "It goes without saying that kinship notation systems used by various peoples ... are an invaluable source enabling one to reconstruct diverse early forms of family marital and clan relations. However, the techniques applied in studying kinship nomenclatures... are still poorly developed" (Tokarev, 1958b: 4). The situation has considerably improved lately due to efforts by the American school of componential analysis,[1] but we can hardly feel content with either the descriptive methods or, particularly, the way of denoting kinship relations used by the Americans. In this paper I attempt to introduce a language convenient to denote kinship relations, and propose some techniques for descriptions of kinship notation systems, including coordinate systems, tables, and graphs. These tools are used to describe two such systems: the Russian and the Iroquois (Seneca). Our discussion will be restricted to the notations of consanguineal relations alone; however, the apparatus proposed herein can well be used (with corresponding supplements) to describe systems beyond consanguinity.

This brief communication is meant to suggest a formal description of a kinship system and aims at developing a corresponding formal apparatus. No contentual aspects involved in kinship systems (of historical, social, etc., nature) will be discussed; these can be found in the extensive literature published since L. H. Morgan's time. In Soviet specialist literature this problem is primarily dealt with by D. A. Olderogge (Olderogge, 1951, 1958, 1959, 1960a).

---

[1]   See, for instance, contributions to *American Anthropologist*, 67: 5 (1965), part 2.
First published in *Sovetskaja etnografija*, N4 (1970).

1.2.   Two basic symbols will be used to denote kinship relations: C for 'child' and P for 'parent'. Anybody's status as a relative can be recorded as a sequence of symbols, e.g., CPP (decoded, 'child of the parents of the parents of Ego' — 'aunt/uncle', or *djadja/tjotka* in the Russian system). Thus our record proceeds from *Alter* to *Ego*. Let P following C denote parents (both) and a single parent in all other positions; let CP denote child of the parents of Ego other than Ego, that is, the sibling; thus the sequence $CCPP$ will be decoded as 'child of the sibling of the parent' — a 'male or female cousin', or *dvojurodnyj brat/sestra* in the Russian system.

Not every sequence of C and P is admissible in the sense that it may represent actual kinship relations. Thus excluded are sequences where P is followed by C. All allowable sequences can be determined based on Table 1.

Table 1.

	P	C
P	$+$	$-$
C	$+$	$+$

where $(+)$ stands for an admissible sequence of the left and upper symbols whereas $(-)$ eliminates such a sequence.

Hence all admissible sequences have the form $\underbrace{CCC \ldots C}_{k \text{ times}} \underbrace{PPP \ldots P}_{l \text{ times}}$ or in short, $C^k P^l$ where k and l may be equal to 0, 1, 2..., etc. For instance, with $k = 0$ or $l = 0$ our sequences will assume the form $PP \ldots P$ or $CC \ldots C$ which represent lineal consanguineal relations.

Note that the sequence $C^k P^l$ is equivalent to the genealogical tree of the form shown in Fig. 1 which follows:

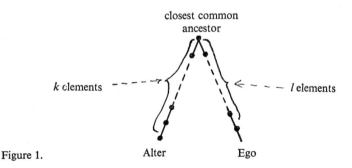

Figure 1.   Alter   Ego

Thus, irrespective of sex, seniority, etc., each consanguineal relation has as its counterpart a couple of k and l values: for instance, the Russian *syn/doch* corresponds to $(1,0)$ $(C^1P^0 = C)$; *ded/babka* to $(0,2)$, *dvojurodnyj brat* to $(2,2)$, *vnuchatyj plemjannik* to $(3,1)$, etc.

1.3. Let us now introduce additional symbols m and f as sex indices to be attributed to our basic symbols C and P, e.g., C_mCP for *plemjannik*.

It is seen that the level of the *Alter's* generation relative to *Ego*, p, is easy to find either by tracing the sequence or by taking the difference between the values of l and k; namely, $p = l - k = $ (the number of P symbols subtracted that of C symbols).

Let us also introduce two more values: $m = \min(k, l)$, that is, the lesser of the two numbers; $M = \max(k, l)$. Thus, for C^1P^3 (*dvojurodnyj ded*) $m = 1$ and $M = 3$.

Let r denote the *rank* of a sequence, that is, the number of symbols in a sequence other than diacritics. For instance, for C_mC_fPP, $r = 4$. Evidently, $r = k + l$.

2. THE RUSSIAN SYSTEM

2.1. Assume that the Russian system of terms denoting consanguineal relations includes the following terms: *otets* (P_m), *syn* (C_m), *ded* (P_mP), *vnuk* (C_mC), *praded* (P_mPP), *pravnuk* (C_mCC), *brat* (C_mP), *djadja* (C_mPP), *plemjannik* (C_mCP), *dvojurodnyj brat* (C_mCPP), *trojurodnyj brat* $(C_mCC\text{-}PPP)$, *dvojurodnyj djadja* (C_mCPPP), *dvojurodnyj plemjannik* (C_mCCPPP), *dvojurodnyj ded* (C_mPPP), *vnuchatyj plemjannik* (C_mCCP) and their female analogues denoted by the same sequences in which the initial symbol is supplied with the female index, f. In describing the Russian system it is advisable, in addition to the above terms which we shall refer to as *actual*, to consider *potential* terms like *prapraded* (great-grandfather) or *trojurodnyj plemjannik* (2nd cousin's son) which, though almost never used in fact, can be easily constructed ad hoc in accordance with well-known models, though a strict border between the two kinds of terms can hardly be drawn. Further we shall consider the entire system of terms, including potential ones, unless otherwise stated specifically.

2.2. First, let us emphasize the major feature of the Russian system: sequences like $\underbrace{C \ldots C}_{k \text{ times}} \underbrace{P \ldots P}_{l \text{ times}}$, where k and l are *any* integers, $(0, 1, 2\ldots)$, and the initial symbols bear a sex index, each corresponds to a single relationship term, in other words, a sequence of this type has only one counterpart among the terms, and each term among the sequences.

Thus, factors which define a term to make it unique include:

(1) *alter*'s sex ($S(a)$, for short);
(2) the value of k;
(3) the value of l.

2.3. To scrutinize the Russian system in more detail, let us make use of the fact that each sequence (disregarding the diacritics) corresponds to a pair of k and l values; this enables one to represent kinship relations as integer points in a coordinate system with the two axes for k and l values (see Fig. 2). The entire set of these points, or, otherwise stated, the totality of diacriticless $C^k P^l$ sequences will be referred to as *the space of kinship relations*. Each point of this space corresponds to two terms, depending on $S(a)$ (male terms alone are cited in Fig. 2). We shall assume this space to be divided into two layers based on the meaning of $S(a)$. Indeed, one can well imagine two parallel planes (layers) corresponding to male and female terms, respectively, instead of one plane (only one layer is represented in Fig. 2).

Note that the points corresponding to lineal kinship relations are found on the coordinate axes (that is, where $k = 0$ or $l = 0$); the lines of generation levels (those all points of which correspond to relations characterized by the same value of p) are the bisectrix and lines parallel to it (represented by the equation: $l - k = p$); the lines of rank level are straight lines at right angle to the bisectrix ($l + k = r$). Points corresponding to conversion relations[2] are symmetrical relative to the bisectrix.

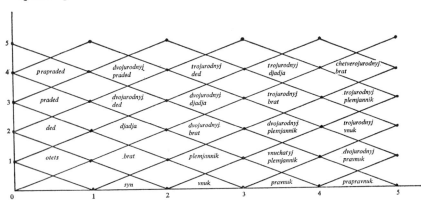

Figure 2.

[2] A relation *conversional* to a given one is that formed if *Ego* and *Alter* change places.

2.4. In addition to the above system, we shall use another system of coordinates with the m and p axes, where $m = \min(k, l)$, $p = l - k$ (see Fig. 3 where only one of two layers [male] is shown again). Here lineal relationship points are located along the p-axis (where $m = 0$); the generation level lines are horizontal straight lines; and conversion points are symmetrical relative to the m-axis.[3]

P			
praded	*dvojurodnyj praded*		
+3			
ded	*dvojurodnyj ded*	*trojurodnyj ded*	
+2			
otets	*djadja*	*dvojurodnyj djadja*	
+1			
	brat	*dvojurodnyj brat*	*trojurodnyj brat*
0			
syn	*plemjannik*	*dvojurodnyj plemjannik*	
−1			
vnuk	*vnuchatyj plemjannik*	*trojurodnyj vnuk*	
−2			
pravnuk	*dvojurodnyj pravnuk*		
−3			

Figuur 3.

2.5. Besides the rank r (genealogical distance), let us introduce some other types of distances between *Ego* and *Alter*, namely:

$$p^2 = k^2 + l^2, \text{ and } M = \max(k, l).$$

These three dimensions can be used (r, p^2, and M) to construct three classifications of kinship relations in which we shall record only male terms and present potential terms in brackets (see Table 2).

Note that the distance denoted by M provides the least fractional but most natural classification for the Russian system (more precisely, for one of its modern varieties): $M = 1$ covers members of the same family; $M = 2$, close relatives.

---

[3] Some other coordinate systems can also be used, e.g., (r, p) or (M, p) where $r = k + 1$ (rank), and $M = \max(k, l)$. Note that any couple of numbers: (m, p), (r, p) or (M, p) defines kinship relations precisely (excluding sex); hence in Section II, two factors k and l could be replaced by any other couple.

Table 2.

r	Relations	p^2	Relations	M	Relations
1	*Otets, syn*	1	*Otets, syn*	1	*Otets, syn, brat*
2	*Brat, ded, vnuk*	2	*Brat*	2	*Ded, vnuk, djadja*
3	*Djadja, plemjannik,*	4	*Ded, vnuk*		*plemjannik, dvo-*
	praded, pravnuk	5	*Djadja, plenjan-*		*jurodnyj brat*
4	*Dvojurodnyj brat,*		*nik*	3	*Praded, pravnuk,*
	dvojurodnyj ded,	8	*Dvojurodnyj brat*		*dvojurodnyj*
	vnuchatyj plemjan-	9	*Praded, pravnuk*		*ded, vnuchatyj*
	nik (prapraded,	10	*Dvojurodnyj ded,*		*plemjannik,*
	prapravnuk)		*vnuchatyj plemjan-*		*dvojurodnyj*
5	*Dvojurodnyj djadja,*		*nik*		*djadja, dvojurod-*
	dvojurodnyj plem-	13	*Dvojurodnyj djadja*		*nyj plemjannik,*
	jannik (dvojurodnyj		*dvojurodnyj plem-*		*trojurodnyj*
	praded, dvojurodnyj	16	*jannik (prapraded,*		*brat*
	pravnuk, praprapra-		*prapravnuk)*	4	*(chetverojurodnyj*
	ded, praprapra-	17	*(dvojurodnyj pra-*		*brat, etc.)*
	vnuk)		*ded, dvojurodnyj*		
6	*Trojurodnyj brat*		*pravnuk)*		
	(trojurodnyj ded,	18	*Trojurodnyj brat*		
	etc.)	20	*(trojurodnyj ded,*		
			etc.)		

The above statement (Section 2.2) concerning denotation of kinship relations with specific terms needs further development: it is the value M that acts as the factor determining actual terminology, namely, those relations are denoted with actual terms for which $M \leqslant 3$ — in the (k, l) system this area is represented by the square defined as:

$$\begin{cases} 0 \leqslant k \leqslant 3 \\ 0 \leqslant l \leqslant 3 \end{cases}$$

2.6.   Let us now consider the interactions between kinship relations and the linguistic structure of respective terms. The Russian system is noteworthy for the fact that from a finite number of linguistic elements (both, full words and stems, such as *ded, brat, plemja[nnik]*, etc.; prefixes such as *pra-;* adjectives like *dvojurodnyj*, etc.) an infinite set of various terms can be constructed.

2.7.   Let us start by distinguishing simple terms (consisting of prefixless single words: *otets, syn, ded, vnuk, brat, djadja, plemyannik*, and their female analogues), and then proceed to complex ones (the rest).

The value p^2 can be thought of as the factor determining simplicity of terms, namely, simple terms represent all (and exclusively those) relations for which $\rho^2 \leqslant 5$ (see Table 2).

2.8.   Let us now introduce the following definitions. We shall speak of a factor (e.g., *Alter*'s sex or generation level, etc.) as being *relevant* to the nature of term usage provided the change of this factor (all other factors remaining the same) involves the use of another term. So, factor $S(a)$ is always relevant for the Russian system because the change of *Alter*'s sex involves the change of term: *brat-sestra, vnuk-vnuchka;* the same can be said about any couple of independent integer indices, as $(k, l) : (1,1)$ — *brat,* $(2,1)$ — *plemjannik,* etc. (see Fig. 2), or $(m, p) : m = 1, p = O$ — *brat; m = 2, p = O* — *dvojurodnyj brat,* etc. (see Fig. 3).

We shall refer to the nature of relevancy as lexical if this change is of a root nature (e.g., *brat/sestra*) and as structural if the change is effected by means of affixes (e.g., *ded — praded; plemjannik — plemjannitsa*) or by the addition of an adjective (*brat — dvojurodnyj brat*).

2.9.   Lexically relevant factors are the easiest to reveal if one resorts to the (m, p) coordinate system (see Fig. 4 [cf. Fig. 3]): all space of kinship relations is broken into seven areas where each term has one and the same root (within the areas of *vnuk* and *plemjannik*) or two roots, depending on $S(a)$ in the other five areas. Fig. 4 shows that the *Alter*'s sex is lexically relevant at $p \geqslant O$; moreover, at $m = O, p = 1$ (*syn/doch*). Thus, male and female terms are asymmetrical in their correlation relative to the sign of the generation: for non-negative generations the terms are better differentiated.

A more detailed picture of all lexically relevant factors can be conveniently shown by a graph (Fig. 5) in which three lexically relevant factors are distinguishable: I — generation level, p — five values: $\geqslant +2 + 10, -1,$ $\leqslant -2$; II — the value $m = \min (k, l)$ — two values: $O, > O$; III — *Alter*'s sex, $S(a)$ — two values: m and f. In some cases Factors II or III may be redundant, namely, Factor II operates only at $|p| = 1$, whereas at other values it is redundant; Factor III is redundant at $p \leqslant - 2$ and at $p = 1$ provided $m > O$.

A simplification was made in Fig. 5: at $m = 1, p = -2$ the term *vnuchatyj plemjannik* is used in place of *dvojurodnyj vnuk* required by the logic of the system.

2.10.   Again, p, m, and $S(a)$ are structurally relevant factors, the latter being relevant where it is irrelevant lexically, that is, at $p < 0$ (except the point corresponding to the *syn/doch*).

The presence of the adjective n-*jurodnyj* (n = 2, 3...) and the value of '*jurodnost*'[4] in this adjective are determined by the values of $|p|$ and m, as seen from Table 3 (cf. Fig. 3).

Table 3.

m / $|p|$	0	1	>1
>1	—	$(m+1)$-*jurodnyj*	
⩽1		—	m-*jurodnyj*

The presence and 'length' of the prefix *pra-* is determined by the value $|p|$, namely, if $|p| > 2$, the prefix $\underbrace{pra \ldots pra}_{|p|-2 \text{ times}}$ takes place.[5]

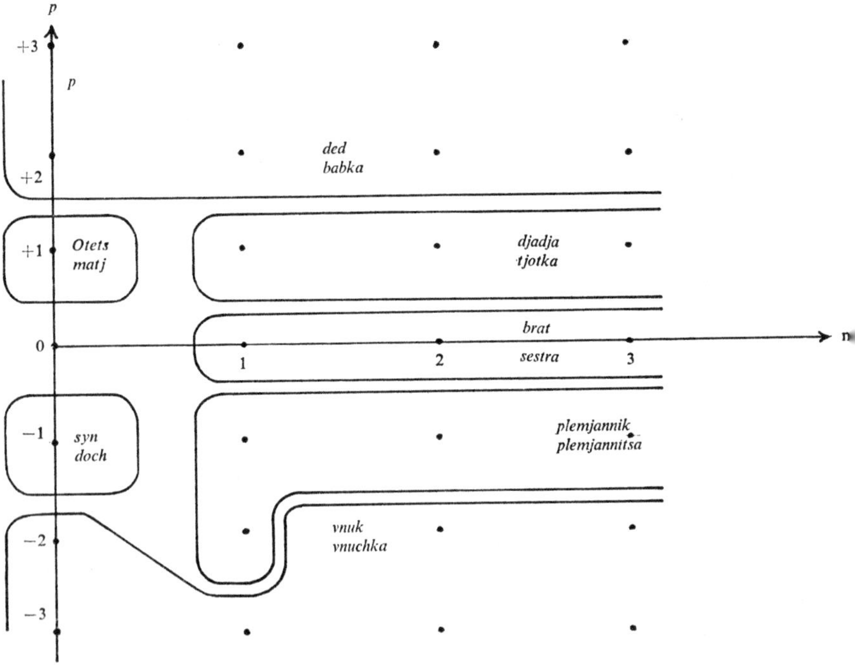

Figure 4.

<hr/>

[4] '*jurodnost*' — a substantive formed of the adjective *jurodnyj*, something like "jurodnity" — Ed.

[5] The Russian prefix *pra-* corresponds to German *Ur-* in words like *Urgrossvater* — Ed.

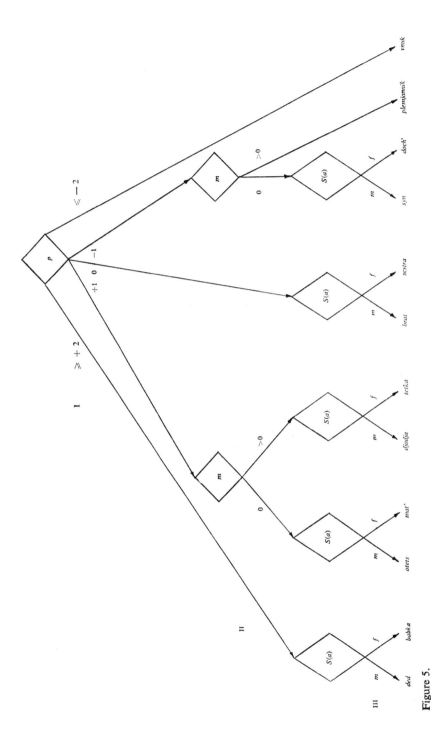

Figure 5.

Table 4 sums up everything stated in 2.9.–2.10. This table enables one to define a term with the sequence C^kP^l, find $p = l - k$ and $m = \min(k, l)$ and see the term in the corresponding place of the table. Thus, C^5P^6 gives $k = 5$; $l = 6$; $p = 6 - 5 = 1$, $m = \min(5, 6) = 5$ which yields *pjatijurodnyj djadja*.

Table 4.

p	Type of sequence	$S(a)$	m	
			0	$\geqslant 1$
0	C^mP^m	m	—	brat
		f		sestra
+1	C^mP^{m+1}	m	Otets	m-*jurodnyj(aya)** djadja
		f	Matj	tjotka
−1	$C^{m+1}P^m$	m	Syn	plemjanni k
		f	Doch	tsa
$\geqslant +2$	C^mP^{m+p}	m		ded
		f		babka
$\leqslant -2$	$C^{m+}\,|p|P^m$	m	$(m+1)$-*jurodnyj(aja)* pra ... pra $|p|$-2 times	k^{**} vnu
		f		chka

* Assume that *odnojurdonyj* is the 'zero word'.
** The only exception (*vnuchatyj plemjannik*) has been mentioned.

The same table can be used to construct a sequence from a known term. Thus, take *trojurodnyj prapravnuk*; the corresponding term is found in the lowest cell; $m + 1 = 3$, $|p| - 2 = 2$ with a negative p; find $m = 2$, $p = -4$. According to our formulas, $k = \max(m, m - p)$, $l = \max(m, m + p)$, find $k = \max(2, 2 + 4) = 6$, $1 = \max(2, 2 - 4) = 2$. Hence the sequence sought is $C^6P^2 = CCCCCCPP$.

3.   THE SENECA SYSTEM

3.1.   L. H. Morgan (Morgan, 1871) collected information on the Seneca kinship system a structural analysis of which was carried out by F. Lounsbury (Lounsbury, 1964: 1073). In fact, our results will be similar to the latter's but they are obtained with considerably less effort because of a more convenient kinship notation.

First, let us introduce some new symbols unnecessary when analyzing the Russian system. It will be allowed to supplement every sequence with the symbol e (*Ego*) which can be indexed for sex, like C and P: e.g., $C_m CPe_f$ for nephew (of a female *Ego*). Further, seniority will be denoted by above-lined and juniority by underlined symbols, e.g., $\bar{C}_m P\underline{e}$ (elder brother) or $\underline{C}_f P\bar{e}$ (younger sister).

Further, we shall need the following denotations: $v(x)$ for x's age: $S(2)$ — the sex of the second member of the sequence, and $S(n)$ — that of its last member.

3.2.   Let us now draw a table (Table 5) of Seneca kinship terminology provided with respective sequences for each term. We shall use Lounsbury's table of these terms; his sequences have been translated into the language of C and P terms applied by us, which makes it possible to greatly reduce the number of sequences to be cited (see Column A). Column B contains generalized formulas (with dots) of those from column A. Column C contains general formulas ($C^k P^l$) for classified terms as well as the features (factors) underlying the grouping of these terms and enabling a term to be distinguished within its group. These can be easily seen if we scrutinize Column B with sufficient care. Note that p and m in Column B have the same meanings as in Section II, that is, p is the generation level ($= l - k$), $m = \min (k, l)$.

3.3.   The results obtained from Column B, Table 5, can be conveniently represented by a graph (tree) (see Fig. 6 which, among other things, proves that the factors distinguished are sufficient to identify each term). These factors are broken into four types (according to the maximum possible number of tree levels); some of these can prove redundant, namely:

(a)   Generation level, p, at values $\leqslant -2$ $-1, 0, +1, \geqslant +2$.
(b)   Correlation between the sexes of two members of the sequence, namely, 2 and e (at $p = -1$), 2 and n (at $p = 0$), a and n (at $p = +1$); for $p \geqslant 2$ this factor is redundant. Its values are $=$ and $\neq$.[6]
(c)   *Alter*'s sex $S(a)$, is redundant, only at $p = 0$; $S(2) \neq S(n)$. Its values are m and f.
(d)   Miscellaneous, including: (1) *Ego*'s sex, $S(e)$, at $p = -1$, $S(2) \neq S(e)$; m or f; (2) *Alter*'s relative age ($v(a) \sim v(e)$) at $p = 0$, $S(2) = S(n)$. Its values are $>$, $<$.

---

[6]   Lounsbury terms this factor 'bifurcation', and its values 'parallel' and 'cross'.

Table 5.

NN	Term	A. List of sequences
1	hakso:t	P_mP, C_mPPP, C_mCPPPP etc.; P_mPP, C_mPPPP etc.
2	akso.t	P_fP, C_fPPP, C_fCPPPP etc.; P_fPP, C_fPPPP etc.
3	ha?nih	P_m, C_mPP_m, C_mCPPP_m, $C_mCCPPPP_m$ etc.
4	no?yèh	P_f, C_fPP_f, C_fCPPP_f, $C_fCCPPPP_f$ etc.
5	hakhno?sèh	C_mPP_f, C_mCPPP_f, $C_mCCPPPP_f$ etc.
6	ake:hak	C_fPP_m, C_fCPPP_m, $C_fCCPPPP_m$ etc.
7	hahtsi?	C_mP, $C_mC_fPP_f$, $C_mC_mPP_m$, $C_mC_fCPPP_f$, $C_mC_mCPPP_m$ etc.; $v(a)>v(e)$
8	he?kè:?	the same $v(a)>v(e)$
9	ahtsi?	C_fP, $C_fC_fPP_f$, $C_fC_mPP_m$, $C_fC_fCPPP_f$, $C_fC_mCPPP_m$ etc.; $v(a)>v(e)$
10	khe?kè:?	the same $v(a)>v(e)$
11	akyä:?se:?	CC_mPP_f, CC_fPP_m, CC_mCPPP_f, CC_fCPPP_m etc.
12	he:awak	C_m, $C_mC_mPe_m$, $C_mC_fPe_f$, $C_mC_mCPPe_mD_m$, $C_mC_fCPPe_f$, $C_mC_mCCPPPe_m$ etc.
13	khe:awak	C_f, $C_fC_mPe_m$, $C_fC_fPe_f$, $C_fC_mCPPe_m$, $C_fC_fCPPe_f$, $C_fC_mCCPPPe_m$ etc.
14	heyẽ:wõ:tẽ?	$C_mC_fPe_m$, $C_mC_fCPPe_m$, $C_mC_fCCPPPe_m$ etc.
15	hehsõ?neh	$C_mC_mPe_f$, $C_mC_mCPPe_f$, $C_mC_mCCPPPe_f$ etc.
16	kheyẽ:wõ:tẽ?	$C_fC_fPe_m$, $C_fC_fCPPe_m$, $C_fC_fCCPPPe_m$ etc.
17	khehsõ?neh	$C_fC_mPe_f$, $C_fC_mCPPe_f$, $C_fC_mCCPPPe_f$ etc.
18	heya:te?	C_mC, C_mCCP, C_mCCCPP etc.; C_mCC etc.
19	kheya:te?	C_fC, C_fCCP, C_fCCCPP etc; C_fCC etc.

* – x – any sex index
** – xy – different sex indexes

B. General form of sequences	C. Clustering
$\underbrace{_mP...P}_{j}, \underbrace{C_mC...C}_{i} \underbrace{P...P}_{j+i}$ $(i=1,2...; j=2,3,...)$	
$\underbrace{_fP...P}_{j}, \underbrace{C_fC...C}_{i} \underbrace{P...P}_{j+i}$ $(i=1,2...; j=2,3,...)$	C^mP^{m+p} $\quad$ $\dfrac{S(a)=m}{S(a)=f}$ $\qquad$ $p\geqslant +2$
$_m, \underbrace{C_mC...C}_{i} \underbrace{P...PP_m}_{i+1}$ $(i=1,2...; j=2,3,...)$	
$_f, \underbrace{C_fC...C}_{i} \underbrace{P...PP_f}_{i+1}$ $(i=1,2...; j=2,3,...)$	$S(a)=S(n)$ $\quad$ $\dfrac{S(a)=m}{S(a)=f}$
$\underbrace{_mC...C}_{i} \underbrace{P...PP_f}_{i+1}$ $(i=1,2...)$	C^mP^{m+1}
$\underbrace{_fC...C}_{i} \underbrace{P...PP_m}_{i+1}$ $(i=1,2...)$	$p=+1$ $\quad S(a)\neq S(n)$ $\quad$ $\dfrac{S(a)=m}{S(a)=f}$
$_mP\underline{e}\ \underbrace{\bar{C}_mC_xC...C}_{i} \underbrace{P...PP_x\underline{e}}_{i}$* $(i=2,3...)$	
$_mP\bar{e}, \underbrace{\underline{C}_mC_xC...C}_{i} \underbrace{P...PP_x\,\bar{e}}_{i}$ $(i=1,2...)$	$S(a)=m\dfrac{v(a)>v(e)}{v(a)<v(e)}$
$_fP\underline{e}, \underbrace{\bar{C}_fC_xC...C}_{i} \underbrace{P...PP_x\,\underline{e}}_{i}$ $(i=1,2...)$	C^mP^m $\quad$ $S(2)=S(n)$
$_fP\bar{e}, \underbrace{C_fC_xC...C}_{i} \underbrace{P...PP_x\,\bar{e}}_{i}$ $(i=1,2...)$	$p=0$ $\qquad$ $S(a)=f\dfrac{v(a)>v(e)}{v(a)<v(e)}$
$\underbrace{C_xC...C}_{i} \underbrace{P...PP_y}_{i}$** $(i=1,2...)$	$S(2)\neq S(n)$
$_m, \underbrace{C_mC_xC...C}_{i+1} \underbrace{P...P\,e_x}_{i}$ $(i=1,2,...)$	$S(2)=S(e)$ $\dfrac{S(a)=m}{S(a)=f}$
$_f, \underbrace{C_fC_xC...C}_{i+1} \underbrace{P...P\,e_x}_{i}$ $(i=1,2,...)$	
$_m\underbrace{C_fC...C}_{i+1} \underbrace{P...P\,e_m}_{i}$ $(i=1,2,...)$	$C^{m+1}P^m$
$m\underbrace{C_mC...C}_{i+1} \underbrace{P...P\,e_f}_{i}$ $(i=1,2,...)$	$p=-1$ $\qquad S(a)=m\dfrac{S(e)=m}{S(e)=f}$
$_f\underbrace{C_fC...C}_{i+1} \underbrace{P...P\,e_m}_{i}$ $(i=1,2,...)$	$S(2)\neq S(e)$
$_f\underbrace{C_mC...C}_{i+1} \underbrace{P...P\,e_f}_{i}$ $(i=1,2,...)$	$S(a)=f\dfrac{S(e)=m}{S(e)=f}$
$\underbrace{_mC...C}_{i+j} \underbrace{P...P}_{i}$ $(i=0,1,...; j=2,3,...)$	$C^{m+|p|}P^m$ $\quad$ $\dfrac{S(a)=m}{S(a)=f}$
$\underbrace{_fC...C}_{i+j} \underbrace{P...P}_{i}$ $(i=0,1,...; j=2,3,...)$	$p\leqslant -2$

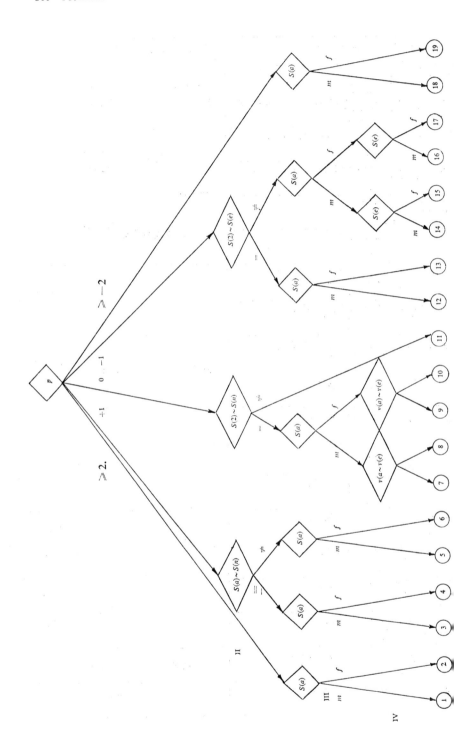

By assigning specific values to each of these factors we shall unambiguously define a term (some of these values may be redundant). Thus if Factor (a) has the value $+1$, Factor (b) $--=$, Factor (c) $-f$, then we obtain term 4.

3.4. It is worth mentioning that with all the apparent diversity of meanings for different generations (sex correlation between a and n, 2 and n, 2 and e), factor (b) is indeed uniform which can be easily seen from Fig. 7: the asterisk is used to denote the elements of the sequences for which correlation of sexes is relevant. These are terms belonging to a generation one level higher than that of p', the junior of the sequence, be it *Ego* or *Alter*.[7]

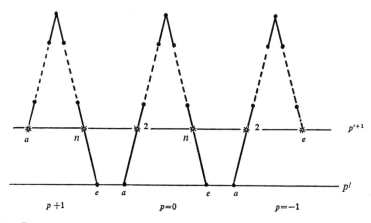

Figure 7.

3.5. In view of improved illustrativeness and subsequent comparison with the Russian system, let us use the coordinates m, p introduced in 2.4. — see Fig. 8 (cf. Fig. 4) — to represent the Seneca system. The entire space of relations is broken into five terminological areas, each, in its turn, being layered; thus each point of the space has more than one

---

[7] Let each element of the sequence $C...CP...Pe$ be attributed the number of its generation relative to *Ego*. Namely, e will be attributed the number 0, and, further, right to left, each next P will be given a number larger by unity, while each consecutive C — a unity smaller (e.g., $C_1 C_2 C_3 P_3 P_2 P_{1e0}$). Let p be *Alter's* generation, that is the generation of the initial element of our sequence. Assume $p' = \min (p, 0) + 1$ (in our example $p=1$, $p'=\min (1, 0)+1=0+1=1$). Now, Factor II can be formulated as follows: coincidence (non-coincidence) in sex between the elements of the sequence of generation p'.

terminological counterpart ranging between two and six (a more detailed discussion see Section 4).

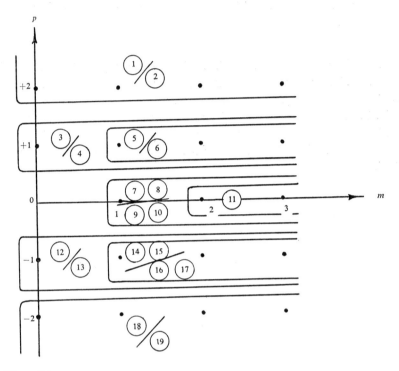

Figure 8.

3.6.   In conclusion, note that of all the three factors mentioned in 3.3., $S(a)$ alone is structurally relevant. Namely for the junior generations $(p \leqslant -1)$ and the 'junior terms' of the zero generation $(v(a) < v(e))$ transition from m to f involves the addition of the element k—; for the senior generations $(p \geqslant +2)$ and 'senior terms' of the zero generation $(v(a) > v(e))$ transition from f to m involved the addition of the element h—. At $p = +1$, $S(a)$ is relevant lexically, not structurally.

4.   COMPARISON OF THE TWO SYSTEMS

4.1.   For the sake of brevity, let us denote the Russian system as RS, and the Seneca system as SS. From a comparison of Figs. 5 and 6, Figs. 4 and 8, and Tables 4 and 5, it is seen that the two systems under consideration possess many more structural similarities than are apparent at first sight. The same may probably be true of many other different-type systems. In view of the peculiar feature of RS discussed in 2.6. (infinity of terms), similarity becomes evident if we compare SS not with RS as a whole, but with the root system of Russian terms (represented by the graph in Fig. 5), or, which is almost the same, with that of Russian simple terms (see 2.7.) from which the entire Russian terminological system is constructed by adding prefixes and adjectives (see Fig. 4).

4.2. Relevancy of the generation level, p, is the most important feature of similarity common for the two systems. This fact determines general and evident stratification of the term space in either system (cf. Figs. 4 and 8, 5 and 6).

Further, the relevance of $S(a)$ is another common feature; it is universal in RS and has but one exception in SS (Term 11). Either system reveals a trend towards structural relevance of $S(a)$ for junior generations and lexical relevance for senior generations (cf. 2.10. and 3.6.).

When comparing Figs. 5 and 6 we see that similar roles in the discussed systems are played by m in RS (at values 0 and > 0) and sex correlation $S(x) \sim S(y)$ in SS (at values $=$ and $\neq$). This similarity raises the problem of dissimilar but functionally equivalent factors in different systems — an issue of critical significance in constructing a typology of kinship systems.

4.3. Let us now discuss the dissimilarities of the two systems.

4.3.1. DISSIMILARITIES IN SPECIFIC FACTORS:

(a) The quantity m (or rank, r) is relevant in RS and irrelevant in SS. Namely, each new value of m in RS involves an unavoidable change of the term, whereas in SS a CP element can be introduced into or removed from any sequence in a proper place[8] without changing the term, provided the factors (b) — (d) remain the same (see 3.2.).[9]

(b) $S(e)$ is irrelevant in RS but relevant in SS (at $p = -1$).

(c) The relative age of *Ego* and *Alter* is irrelevant in RS and relevant in SS (at $p = 0$).

(d) The correlation of sexes is irrelevant in RS and relevant in SS (at $p \leqslant 1$).

---

[8] Namely, for sequences of the form $C...CP...P$ at the junction of C and P, for $C...C$ at their termination, and for $P...P$ at the beginning.

[9] This provides a rule enabling one to perform evolution or convolution of sequences, particularly to reduce them to the shortest possible form. This rule is easy to formulate in an explicit way.

Thus, SS has a richer set of relevant factors: here account is taken of sex and age parameters meaningless in the Russian system; but irrelevancy of m is SS results in the use of the same term to denote both "close" and "distant" relatives (in the Russian understanding of these notions). One can say that qualitative distinctions alone are of importance in SS, whereas RS also takes into consideration quantitative distinctions, while the diversity of meaningful quantitative distinctions is narrower.

4.3.2. DISSIMILARITIES IN THE OVERALL STRUCTURE:

(a)   The Russian system (of basic simple terms) divides the entire space of relations into seven areas, whereas their number in SS is only five (see Figs. 4 and 8). The two "extra" areas available in RS are single-pointed and correspond to closest lineal kinship relations in either direction (P and C sequences). In SS there are no single-pointed areas of this kind: each area may, in principle, contain an infinity of points.

(b)   In either system each area within the space of relations is layered (see 2.3.), thus each point corresponds to more than one kinship term. In RS all areas are divided into two layers, according to $S(a)$ (see Fig. 9a); whereas in SS areas may be divided into different numbers of layers ranging between 2 and 6. Two areas (for $p \geqslant +2$ and $p \leqslant -2$) are layered in the same manner as in RS; it is not as simple for the others. There exist two layering levels in each of these areas: the first level incorporates all points within the area and consists of two layers for $p = \pm 1$, according to $S(a)$, whereas for $p = 0$ the number of layers is four, according to $S(a)$ and relative age; the second level covers points starting with $m = 1$ (at $p = +1$) or with $m = 2$ (at $p = 0$) and consists of two layers; for $p = +1$, of four levels for $p = -1$ and is single-layered for $p = 0$ (see Fig. 9, [b] — [d]), which provides kind of a "side view" at the respective areas in Fig. 8.

Thus, in SS the points which correspond to the 'specific points' of P and C in the Russian system (also the point of CP) are also somehow peculiar; they are covered by fewer layers (that is, have fewer terms for counterparts) than the other points of the same generation.

(c)   Within each layer of an area all points correspond to one term in SS, whereas in RS they possess only a common nucleus, the terms proper (eing different in all points.

bd)   Hence, RS has an infinite set of terms while SS has a finite number of such terms.

(e)   In contrast to RS where senior (non-negative) generations are

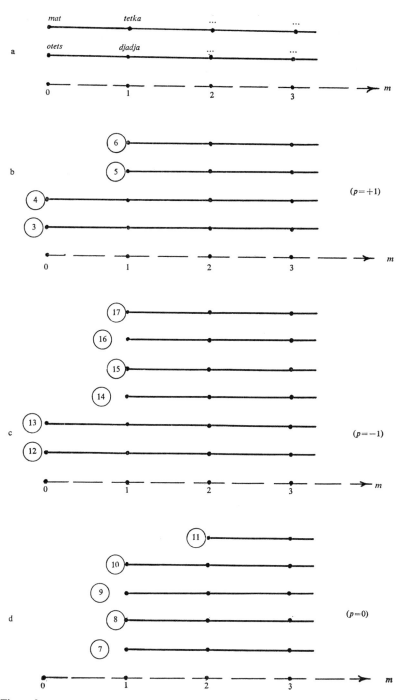

Figure 9.

better differentiated as far as the terminology is concerned (due to different roots of male and female terms), better terminological differentiation in SS is characteristic of non-positive generations, namely the zero and (—1)st generations in particular (for $p = +1$ there exist four terms, there are five for $p = 0$ and six for $p = -1$).

Problems of Culture Studies

Review of "Ocherki teorii kultury" (Essays on the Theory of Culture) (Yerevan, 1969)

E. MARKARJAN

The book is devoted to the initial and main questions of theory of culture which we consider as part of the more general theory of social systems. These questions are grouped around two central problems: the problem of culture as a specific phenomenon of reality and the problem of historical typology.

The essence of the solution of the first problem suggested in this book lies in treating culture as a specific function of the social life of people. In contrast to the majority of other existing meanings of the term "function" ("functional"), the stress in this case should be laid not on the components of the system (their mutual relations, their role in the functioning of the system, etc.), but on the characteristics of the system on the whole, and be directed to accenting its special and extremely important aspect of consideration connected with the study of the ways of human action and behavior. This aspect acquires its meaning only as compared to another aspect of consideration of the social system — the one expressing its structure (morphology). To give the functional characteristics of a system is to express the specific ways of human action, the complex of the means and mechanisms due to which a social system functions and develops. This very aspect of consideration of social life, the aspect of its functional characteristics, expresses, from our point of view, the concept of culture.

In order to define the concept of culture in a proper way, it is first necessary to clear up its relation to the concepts of human action. These concepts are often wrongly identified. Culture is not the human action and behavior itself, but is the way of their realization. The direct identification of culture with human action imperceptibly leads to a great confusion, the result of blending two qualitatively different methods of approaching social life.

Action (*dejatel'nost'*) is an activity expressed in the behavior of a system as the subject of action. The system arises on the basis of its relation to the environment with the view to satisfying its requirements. The concept of action (and accordingly the concept of behavior) is applied not only to the individual subjects of action, but naturally to the collective ones as well, to the social system as a collective body in particular. In this connection the concept of human action in its broader sense expresses an abstraction involving the socially directed activity of human beings as a whole. This abstraction, in spite of all its importance, is not enough for understanding the social life of people as a real functioning and developing system.

To solve this problem it is necessary to express the social system structurally in two other aspects as well. These aspects are formed as a result of dismemberment of *the socially directed activity* of human beings on the whole from the point of view of *its social structure* (the relations between human beings and the groups which they comprise) and *the way of its realization.*[1]

The concepts of human action and the way of realization of human action are aimed at expressing the correlation between socially directed activity applied to the solution of the most different problems which arise in the process of historical practice, and on the other hand, the system of specific means and mechanisms due to which the realization of this directed activity of human beings (social institutions, implements, symbolic systems, etc., i.e., the whole system of culture) becomes possible.

The comprehension of the phenomenon of culture as a specific way of realizing human action has a rather precisely formulated criterion, which gives a potential possibility for revealing all many-sided forms of its manifestation and bringing them to inner unity. The presence of such a criterion is the most important premise of creating the methodologically effective concept of culture, capable of avoiding the danger of an extremely narrow understanding of the phenomenon expressed by it, as

---

[1] So the sphere of social life, as we understand, can be structurally expressed from three main points of view: from the point of view of social organization, i.e., the system of mutual relations which is established between human beings and groups into which they are united in the process of their life activity; from the point of view of organizing culture, i.e., those specific human, non-biologically worked out means and mechanisms due to which human beings act; and lastly, from the point of view of organizing the action itself which comprises various socially coordinated efforts of human beings directed to the solution of the problems necessary for supporting their social life. We think that the above-mentioned ways of approaching social life express three relatively independent directions of modern sociological investigation.

well as the danger of an extremely broader interpretation which dissolves this phenomenon in the whole sphere of human life activity and is unable to answer the question, what is not culture after all?

The elaboration of such criterion in this case is attained because of the distinctly and definitely expressed point of view from which the social system is considered. This point of view of the functional characteristics of the social system, enables us to make the specific means and mechanisms by which the directed activity of human beings is realized the subject of a special scientific study.

The first part of the book deals with the general sociological characteristics of culture, and the second part is devoted to the methodological problems of cultural and historical study (particularly the logical differentiation of the main types of historical generalization), to the analysis of the initial system of concepts used while studying cultural systems, and the elucidation of the central problems and aspects of the comparative study of these systems.

One of the main tasks of the second part of the book is to attempt to solve those logical contradictions which arise when one accepts the non-axiological interpretation of the concept of culture in the study of history. It would not be exaggeration to say that the problem, which scholars were confronted with in their attempts to successively apply the new non-axiological interpretation of the concept of culture to the sphere of historical study, may be considered as one of the most difficult problems to solve in 20th century social science.

The essence of the axiological point of view in culturology is the division of different ways of human existence into cultural and non-cultural and higher and lower according to some value orientation. The acceptance of this or that cultural practice as a pattern for the comprehension and classification of other historically worked out cultures inevitably led to their axiological interpretation and to the construction of false egocentric schemes of history.

It would seem that the only way which was dictated by the acceptance of the non-axiological interpretation of culture should be the levelling of all the historically given ways of human existence, and considering them as something quite equivalent! In criticizing traditional Eurocentrism, many representatives of Western culturology of the 20th century followed such a way. It is erroneous to divide cultures into higher and lower, for they represent historically worked out modes of life, equivalent in their alternativeness: such is the fundamental thesis on which is based the general trend in the Western culturology of the

20th century formed as a result of the criticism of the Eurocentric
system of views. We will call this trend the concept of equivalent cultures
(civilizations).

By putting this thesis into practice, the representatives of the conception of equivalent cultures (R. Benedict, M. Herskovitz, F. Northrop,
O. Spengler, A. Toynbee, and others) tried to do away with the optical
illusion which created the domination of the Eurocentric point of
view, and to bring to conformity the violated proportions of history.
However, the consistent application of this principle of equivalence of cultures meant the inevitable acceptance of the position of anti-evolutionism
and extreme relativism inadmissible for historical science, for, as a
result, the cultures of paleolithic and modern societies could be found in
one parallel line. For such inferences the representatives of the conception of equivalent cultures more and more often received great criticism in Western literature itself, where this conception predominated for
almost the first half of the 20th century. To make this critique effective it is
necessary not simply to reject the inferences which the representatives of
the conception of equivalent cultures arrive at, but also to understand
the problem which gave rise to this conception and to thoroughly analyze
its conceptual apparatus with the view of clearing up to what degree it is
able to express historical reality.

An attempt of this kind is made in the first two chapters of the second
part of the book. In our opinion the contradiction to which the representatives of the conception of equivalent cultures come is conditioned
by the fact that they do not take into consideration one extremely important point — a historically given culture represents a complicated
formation and it may be logically built up in qualitatively different ways.
The concept of culture may express, on the one hand, the local form
of the historical practice of people, and on the other hand, its general type.

The essence of the problem in this case lies in the fact that only the
first of these two elements (the local form of cultures) is rightfully to be
considered as equivalent (in that sense this concept has been used up
to now) in the comparative study of different cultural systems. As for the
second element (the general type of cultures), it cannot be defined as
equivalent in this sense and requires quite a different consideration.

The confusion of these two elements, existing in any historically given
sociocultural system, inevitably led and is leading the representatives of
the conception of equivalent cultures to irresistible contradictions.

The main concept which the representatives of the conception under
consideration use is the concept of local culture. At the same time other
terms for this concept are given in their works. Spengler, in particular,

uses the concept of culture without the adjective local. Toynbee uses the term civilization in much the same way. In American cultural anthropology a pattern of culture is mostly used in this connection.

In the book we specially introduce the term local culture (civilization) to stress that the representatives of the conception of equivalent cultures have in view just local systems of culture and that the concept of historically given culture (civilization) can be built logically in a qualitatively different way, and thus express not the local form of cultural systems but their corresponding general types.

In the book an attempt is made to analyze and define the logical structure of the local culture concept. We regard it as a proper historical concept. The category of these concepts is termed in the work a "local historical type". The most characteristic logical feature of this kind of concept is that the generalization which is realized by them involves the cases included in the limits of a definite space and time continuum.

The concept of local culture, accenting the attention of the scholars on the peculiarity of the historical practice of a definite group of people, leaves out of view the features common with the practice of other people. These features cannot be brought to light without introducing other (in its logical structure and cognitive functions) kinds of concepts, directed this time not to the reconstruction of the peculiarity of the objects under consideration, but to bringing out their similarity. We consider that concepts of this kind are conveniently termed "general historical types" which, in contrast to the "local historical types", fulfil their generalizing function, abstracting from the directly given space and time conditions of the system under analysis. In the work we give a detailed analysis of the Marxist concept of the social economic formation as an example of a concept of this kind.

In this instance we come across two qualitatively different kinds of generalization whose distinct, logical differentiation is of paramount significance for historical knowledge. At the same time, we did not find attempts at such differentiation even in the literature specially devoted to the questions under consideration.

In this summary we dwelt only on a few problems considered in the work. The spectrum of questions raised is much wider. The conceptions of A. Kroeber, R. MacIver, T. Parsons, A. Radcliffe-Brown, J. Steward, O. Spengler, A. Toynbee, A. Weber, M. Weber, L. White, and other representatives of Western culturology and sociology all receive critical analysis in the book.

Methods of Ethnographic Research into Material Culture

S. TOKAREV

1. Ethnography took to the study of material culture later than it did that of folklore, beliefs, common law, family, and marriage customs: the systematic research of material culture began only at the end of the 19th century. That Russian and Soviet ethnographers especially scored remarkable successes in this field is a fact recognized by many foreign colleagues (Leroi-Gourhan, 1964: 210). Most important is that our ethnographers (V.V. Bogdanov, B. A. Kuftin, N. I. Lebedeva, E. E. Blomkvist, G. S. Maslova, and others) found a correct approach to phenomena of material culture: an ethnographer is interested not so much in the objects themselves as in their relation to people. Ethnography is a science about people, not about things.

Indeed, though the researcher must know how to fully and accurately describe the objects of material culture (dwellings, clothing, ornaments, household articles, etc.), and how to supplement his description with graphic portrayals, plans, drawings, sketches, photographs, how to describe equally fully and accurately the technology of the production of such objects and their utilization, descriptions have still only been auxiliary methods and have never been the aim of ethnographic study. If it were otherwise, such study of the material culture would soon lose its specific features: the study of clothes would become a manual for tailoring, the study of food, a cookbook, and the study of dwellings a section in a textbook on architecture.

To an ethnographer "an object does not exist (except perhaps purely physically) outside of its importance to man", as the French ethnog-

First published in *Sovetskaja etnografija*, N4 (1970).

rapher Marcel Maget aptly remarked. In studying objects, he said we must also consider all those people who "have the ability, right, duty, exclusive or otherwise, to produce, distribute, sell, and use that object" (Maget, 1953: 15–16). Material objects present no interest to an ethnographer outside of their social use and relation to man, their producer and consumer.

Moreover, it is not so much the relations between the object and man, or man and object, as the relations between people with respect to the object that is of importance to us. We find here a close analogy with the economic category of property. From a Marxist point of view property is not the relation of man to a thing but it is the relation between people with respect to definite things. An ethnographer must approach the study of all objects and products of material culture in a similar way, as all serious ethnographers are well aware.

At the same time it would seem that while recognizing in principle such an approach to the study of material culture, Soviet and foreign ethnographers do not draw all possible conclusions from that approach. The tasks and possibilities of studying material culture are far from being exhausted by the range of questions by which researchers of native dwellings, clothing, food, means of transport, etc., limit themselves.

A glance at the comparatively voluminous writings (candidates and doctors' theses, articles) dedicated to the material culture of various peoples shows that they generally confine themselves to the same range of problems, which thus becomes, as it were, the theoretical basis of all research. These problems most frequently are:

(1)   the dependence of the objects of material culture (food, dwellings, clothing, etc.) on the natural environment and economic activity;

(2)   the dependence on ethnic traditions, the manifestation of ethnic peculiarities, similarities and distinctions in material culture, and, hence, the use of objects of material culture as a source of studies on ethnogenesis, the ethnic history of a people, the cultural ties between peoples;

(3)   the belonging of definite forms of material culture to some historico-ethnographic province, irrespective of the differences in origins of the peoples having this form of culture;

(4)   the connection between the forms of material culture and distinctions in family status, sex, and age of their bearers (this pertains particularly to clothes and ornaments, and less to food and dwellings);

(5)   dependence of the element of material culture on the social system and on class distinctions;

(6)   the connection between the forms of material culture and religious

beliefs and rites; in particular, the study of ritual food, ritual clothing, and less often the ritual purpose of edifices or their parts;

(7) the links with art: the artistic aspect of native architecture and clothes — architectural ornaments, embroidery and ornamental patterns in clothes, ornamental styles, etc.;

(8) changes in the material culture of a people under capitalism owing to the penetration of commercial commodity relations, the urban way of life, the erosion of traditional ethnic specifics;

(9) changes in the form of the material way of life in our time in connection with socialist transformations.

This enumeration of the main problems embraces the theoretical (problematic) aspect of practically all Soviet writings dealing with the material culture of various peoples both in the USSR and outside. Some works concentrate on individual problems. In others the author divides his attention among several aspects of the study of material culture; sometimes, not a single problem is clearly framed. Attempts at different approaches which are not limited to the above enumerated range of problems are rare. A few authors try, for example, to reconstruct the morphological changes of the types of the objects being studied (buildings, clothing) — their inner evolution; occasionally attention is paid to socially preconditioned taboos and limitations on the utilization of certain household articles, but these are rare deviations from the standard range.

There can be no doubt as to the actuality of the questions listed above. It is always important for us to know to what extent the type and form of some costume or building, etc., are determined by ethnic traditions, the influence of neighboring peoples, the impact of natural conditions, and the class allegiance of their user. It is particularly important to discover the interaction of all these factors, which often work in opposite directions: changes in the natural environment give an impetus to the improvement or replacement of the form of traditional clothing or some form of structure, while ethnic traditions tend to preserve them.

Yet, while recognizing the importance of the usual range of problems in the study of material culture, we want to stress again that it does not exhaust all the aspects of interest from the ethnographic point of view. I should like to draw attention to those aspects of material culture which have up to now remained in the shade or have been passed over altogether in silence as objects of ethnographic study.

As we have already mentioned, a material object per se does not interest the ethnographer, it interests him only in its relationship to people, or in the relationship of people to that object. What is even more important to the ethnographer is the relation between people with respect to that object, or in a broader sense, the social relations mediated by material objects. Let us try to clarify the meaning of this by a few examples.

2.   In studying the food of a particular people, we must proceed first of all from the fact that food plays many different functions in any human society. Food and drink serve not only the purpose of purely physiological satiation, that is, not only to satisfy the elementary biological need for nourishment as in the organic world, both among animals and plants. Food is also a form mediating social contacts between people, and as such has numerous and variegated manifestations. Joint repasts have at all stages of historical development been an important form of social intercourse between people. Starting from the collective devouring of the hunted down animal during the early Stone Age to the traditional etiquette of dividing game, from the joint feasts of hunters down to the periodic "bratchina" of the Slavonic peoples, to the ceremonial family dinners in English aristocratic and bourgeois circles, to diplomatic luncheons and breakfasts, the receptions where important questions of world politics are discussed, we could probably mention hundreds of different occasions political and private in the social life of people when it is considered essential to eat or drink jointly. In most cases the elementary biological purposes of food and drink are pushed far to the background, or disappear completely.

Moreover, the joint partaking of food or drink is often not only a manifestation of friendship or kinship between people, but serves to produce relations of friendship or kinship. In ethnographic and historical writings one frequently comes across descriptions of the custom of fraternization through the joint partaking of food. To eat in the house of one's enemy means to put an end to enmity and to restore peace; the joint partaking of food by the bridegroom and the bride (*confarreatio*) is an essential part of the marriage ceremony.

The ritual significance of joint eating is emphasized in some cases by special ritual dishes. Ethnographers always give due attention to them, but do not always see in them the manifestation of the same general law: ritual food is but a means of strengthening the symbolic significance of joint meals as a form of social intercourse, in which case the deity, the guardian spirit of the family, or the ghost of the ancestor also participate in the ritual meal.

These facts underlie Robertson Smith's theory, according to which initially the sacrificed object was the deity itself, the totem of the clan, whose meat was solemnly eaten as a symbol to strengthen the unity of the kin (Robertson Smith, 1907: 345). This has given rise to the system of "god-eating" rites, including the Christian Holy Communion — the partaking of the flesh and blood of Jesus Christ.

Thus, so-called ritual dishes become such not because of their material contents, but because of the social role assigned to them.

Food not only unites people, it also segregates them. Along with the function of social integration, food fulfils also the reverse function, that of social segregation.

Among all peoples of the world there were customs banning or limiting the joint partaking of food by a certain person with some other person. Maybe the most ancient form of such a separation based on food was the sex segregation in food linked partly with the division of labor according to age and sex. A man predominantly ate the meat of the beasts he killed, while the women did not always receive some. Later this food segregation of the sexes grew stronger, and was linked partly with marital and sex relations. R. and L. Makarius, two modern French researchers, disclosed and analyzed the characteristic customs of "food exogamy" — the incompatibility of nuptial and food intercourse — "we do not marry those with whom we eat together, we marry those with whom we do not eat together." An expression of this were the widespread bans prohibiting women to eat together with men, notably of wives with their husbands. These bans assumed a particularly rigid form among the peoples of Oceania, milder forms in North America and Africa. Vestiges of this ban remained until recently among the peoples of the Caucasus, the Balkan Peninsula, and other countries: the women in the family eat after the men and separately from them (Makarius, 1961: 105–18.

Social segregation in food embraces also estate, caste, and class distinctions. In India, for example, the ban took strict forms. "One faith will neither drink or eat, nor marry with people of another faith", wrote Afanasy Nikitin in the 15th century. The connection of food segregation with religious differences is rare nowadays, however, the Russian Old Believers still refuse to eat from plates and dishes that have been used by the "mundane". Even in the modern developed European and American countries the luncheon table is a place where class segregation is best preserved: the masters will not sit at the same table with the servants, the factory owner with the workers, the beau monde with the common people.

All bans and limitations in food and drink — permanent (religious asceticism, Nazaretism, monasticism) and temporary (fasts) — should be regarded from this point of view. At first sight it may seem that a temporary or lifelong interdiction on some food expresses man's attitude towards that food, i.e., an attitude towards a material object, one that has nothing to do with social relations. Actually, however, just a property is not a relation of man towards things, but a relation between people mediated by things, a ban on food is a symbol of definite social relations.

A person observing a definite ban on foods sets himself up against those who do not observe that ban. Moslems who do not eat pork confront themselves as Moslems to all non-Moslems. Conversely, for a Russian peasant to eat horse meat means to be a *basurman*, a non-Christian. Monks, who abstain from milk, meat, wine, etc., dissociate themselves thereby (as also by their other vows) from laymen who do not observe these vows. The faithful, who strictly observe fasts, confront themselves to free-thinkers who refuse to fast. This applies even to purely individual food prohibitions and limitations. A Judean Nazarite, who has taken a life-long vow not to drink wine, use vinegar, or eat anything made of grapes, thereby sets himself apart from all the people around him. The moment he infringes upon his vow, he stops being a Nazarite, and becomes one of the crowd.

From the above it is clear that food bans, fasts, monastic vows, etc., are nothing but symbols or manifestations of some human relations and confrontations which may be based on national, religious, professional, or class distinctions.

Food bans and limitations, especially if they extend to a whole ethnic or groups of ethnics, can also be regarded as an expression of definite internal links welding that people together as a definite ethnic mark. This negative feature has a positive equivalent well-known to all ethnographers, namely, ethnic specifics in food, national dishes. We do not eat some certain foods, but we like certain other dishes. National kinds of food is one of the favorite subjects for ethnographers and quite a bit has been accomplished in this field (*Etnologia*, 1971; 1972). One should not forget, however, that an ethnographer does not care as much about the way in which some national dishes are cooked or about their material composition, as he does about the form in which that dish occurs, its social function. Allegiance to a traditional national food is an ethnic feature, a social phenomenon, just as are taboos or limitations applying to other kinds of food. Both are cementing the members of the given ethnic group and at the same time confronting them to other groups.

Thus, the topic of national food, national dishes, i.e., ethnic specifics in food, should be regarded as part of a larger topic — the study of the social functions of food, and ultimately, as the problem of food that on the one hand integrates people, and on the other segregates them.

The various customs linked with food and with the methods used for its preparation and consumption, the beliefs or rites concerning food, and their reflections in folklore are caused not by the material properties of food, but by its symbolic meaning as a form of intercourse between people, or as a form keeping them apart.

All this gives rise to another, relatively broad problem, one that is of cognitive, theoretical, and practical importance: if the main and prime — physiological — function of food had always existed and will always do so, what will be the further state of its secondary function, its social function, which is, as we just saw, also highly important? Will food and drink, in say one hundred years, play the same integrating and segregating role they are playing today? Will that function change or disappear completely? What are the present development trends, especially in the socialist countries standing on the threshold of communism? Without going into details, I want to mention in passing that there are many weighty arguments speaking in favor of the first assumption, and no less serious ones in favor of the second one. The question is one of principle, even though it has not yet been posed by science.

3. Let us see if we can apply the same line of reasoning to an ethnographic study of clothing.

Clothes, just as food, have different functions to fulfil. Their main and primary function in cold zones is to protect the body against cold and other unfavorable environmental influences. In hot zones clothes serve mainly to decorate the body. These two initial purposes of clothes, even though their roots do not reach back to pre-human history, have their analogies in the animal kingdom, for animals, too, have a protective covering of the body and an attractive coloring. Clothes have long since also had a secondary function — the establishing of a division between the sexes and social positions; the latter includes, as a particular case, the ritual and the religious role of clothes. We shall have to dwell on this derivate, but important function of clothes at some length; we shall discover much that has not been studied before.

First of all, we have as yet no clear idea as to the role of clothing in the relations between the sexes, especially in the early stages of the development of clothing. It would seem that clothes had from the very beginning a dual role to play: on the one hand, they were a means of preserving the sex taboo by concealing the sex organs; on the other, they were a means of enhancing sexual attraction by ornamentation and emphasizing those parts of the body. Ethnographic material contains many examples of both functions, and it would be difficult to say which of them emerged earlier — concealment or exposure (Grosse, 1894; Westermarck, 1901: 186–201, 206–12). Probably they are just two aspects of a single phenomenon, of the ambivalence in the relations between the sexes — attraction and repulsion.

With the cultural development of mankind, the sex-dividing function of clothes displays a peculiar trend: it first increases and then begins to wane.

Beginning with the "barbarian" period and right up to precapitalist class society and partly also under capitalism, people gradually begin to wear more and more clothes, covering their bodies with ever greater care. Partly this proceeds independently of the climate, and we therefore cannot say that the increase in the amount of clothes worn had the aim of affording better protection for the body against cold. The main aim was different: a stricter preservation of the sex taboo, a stricter segregation of the sexes by their clothes, (the same happened with respect to food, dwellings, etc.). This is undoubtedly linked with the transition from group to pair, then to polygamous and monogamous marriage, with the strengthening of the patriarchal principle in the family and society. In some places this striving to cover the body with clothes took on exaggerated and even barbaric forms — for example, the ugly *paranja* Moslem women had to wear, a dress that hid the body together with the head and face. Secondly, in parallel with it there proceeded under the influence of the same factors an intensification of the sexual dimorphism in clothes and in the role of sexual attraction by clothes, especially of the female, the development of ever finer forms which stressed the wearer's form and accentuated and revealed the most attractive contours of the body.

Under capitalism, as the social system and the way of life in the European countries began to become more democratic, and as technology advanced and worked out more rational forms of clothes, the tendency opposed to the above grew stronger. Clothes became simpler and more standardized. Gradually, especially in later years, we observe a waning of the sexual dimorphism in clothing. It practically disappears in some forms of professional costumes — among pilots, tractor operators, steeplejacks, etc. — there is practically no difference between men's and women's clothes. In everyday life, too, the wearing of slacks, jackets, men's hats, etc., by women tends to erase the distinction between men's and women's dress (unisex). Yet it is difficult to say how that trend will develop.

On the other hand, the striving to cover the body because of a feeling of sexual shame is also growing weaker. Miniskirts, the evolution of bathing and sports suits which have been reduced in some cases to a minimum and create only the semblance of covering, and the growing nudist movement in a number of countries among people who maintain that no clothes are needed on beaches, in sports, etc., show that the tendency to link clothes with the preservation of the sex taboo is losing ground.

The sex-dividing function of clothing is, however, only a manifestation of the more general social segregating function. Clothing is a social sign, a mark showing a person's place in the social system.

Probably already during the Upper Palaeolithic age, and in any case in the Neolithic age, the first signs of a division appeared in the primeval commune. At first these were scars on the body and other signs of age group initiations which may have also been an identification of the clan, totem, and tribal allegiance of the bearer. These irremovable ornaments later gave way to removable ones — simple ornaments became primitive forms of clothing. This process was an external manifestation of growing internal disintegration in the community. The ruling elite in Oceania, America, and Africa, the chieftains and the aristocracy wore more clothes than their subjects. As the social system grew more complex, the clothes worn by the different estates became more diversified. In the old and new Eastern despotisms, and in the feudal age in Europe, the differences between the dress of the noble and the rank-and-file, the aristocracy, the urban dwellers and peasants, reached a maximum. In medieval Europe the peasants often walked about in rags while the feudal lords wore expensive luxurious costumes. Special clothes were ascribed to every one: a bourgeois, to say nothing of a peasant, would not dare wear the clothes of a nobleman. The clergy and the military had their specific costumes. Naturally there were also national and regional distinctions in clothes. Quite recently still in Brittany in France alone there were over twenty different national women's dresses. Among Moravian Slovak women, too, recently still there were dozens of local costumes. Nonetheless, the national and regional distinctions were unimportant in comparison with sharp social distinctions.

When the distinguishing function of clothes was at its highest in Europe, the costume tied a man to his estate, his profession, his birthplace, his nationality. It was not only an external mark of all these social and territorial links of the individual. It evolved and strengthened the subjective feeling of belonging. Dressed in the clothes befitting his estate, a French nobleman of the 17th century felt precisely a French nobleman, and not a Spanish one, let alone a French bourgeois. Clothes then played an important role in building up the estate as well as national self-consciousness.

The social segregating function of clothing has a reverse side: clothes unite people on the same social (also ethnic) status, and this serves as an integrating factor within a given group, and simultaneously confronts it to other groups.

It is easy to see that ritual or religious clothes also serve to segregate the group of people or even the individual that dresses differently from others. This may not apply subjectively. A shaman's costume, differing sharply from the everyday clothes worn by the common people can subjectively, i.e., in the minds of the shaman himself and the people around him, be understood as a means of attracting spirits or of scaring them off. Objectively, however, the shaman's costume is but an external means of singling him out from the others, of showing his special position. The costume is needed by people, not by spirits. Just as the dress of the priest, bishop, Buddhist lama, and Moslem mullah and hadji may subjectively be a means by which the wearers of these costumes seek to draw closer to the deity; actually it is a means to dissociate them from the crowd, to place them above it. On the other hand, by separating the clergy from laymen, the ritual vestments emphasize also the allegiance to his estate, to his order, to his profession.

All these examples show that so-called ritual and religious clothes also play the role of a social sign or mark, signifying the allegiance of a person to a definite corporation and confronting him to all those not belonging to it.

All these distinctions in clothing, dividing people into groups by profession, estate, region, nationality, etc., reached their peak under feudalism. The reason for it is not hard to understand: the typical feature of feudalism was a corporativism, a hierarchic subordination of estates and traditional regionalism.

In the capitalist epoch, and especially in the past few decades, a process of levelling is at work in clothing. One of the main factors of this levelling is the penetration of manufactured fabrics and, later, of ready-made clothes not only into the towns but also into rural areas where purchased clothes have ousted home-spun ones. The growth of the commercial economy alongside the general democratization of the whole way of life played the greatest role in smoothing out the former contrasts in clothes.

Now it is not always possible to distinguish in the streets of a European town between a rich banker or factory owner and a worker or petty employee. There are somewhat more pronounced distinctions in women's clothes, but here they depend to a higher degree on fashion than on the social position of the wearer, and fashions tend to make dresses more uniform rather than more varied. Only the clergy, the military, and the police, and sometimes artists, the judiciary, and the professoriate continue to wear professional costumes. National distinctions in clothes are gradually disappearing and are preserved in part only in a few countries (Leroi-Gourhan, 1965: 186–95).

In short, dress gradually stops fulfilling a social segregating function. It grows ever more difficult to establish by the clothing the allegiance of a person to a definite class, profession, religion, or nationality. This is but a manifestation of the general principle of social mobility typical of modern society.

The ethnographer studying national (ethnic) specifics in clothing must not lose sight of the more general problem of which this topic forms part. The ethnic distinctions in clothes are only one of the manifestations of the general function of clothes as a social segregating factor. That is why a student interested in the ethnic specifics of clothes must not confine himself to a study of their importance, to the problem of the ethnogenesis and interethnic links, as many scholars do. He must show a more diverse interest, for his subject touches upon the general question of the forms taken by the intercourse and the segregation of people, the question of the development trends exhibited by these forms, and of the future patterns of people's social life.

Finally, one more general and essentially practical question concerns social forecasting: will there be a time when the types and forms of our clothes will be determined only by practical expediency and the laws of aesthetics? How is such an advent to be accelerated? When will people stop submitting to the whims of fashion[1] and to philistine prejudices? The attempts that are being made at present to reform our clothing, hesitant and sporadic attempts, often frustrated by the fear of departing from European standards, will lead to nothing unless ethnographers are drawn into this work in future, or, to be more exact, unless they assume the initiative in this matter. Ethnography has amassed an enormous body of facts about the spontaneous experience of all peoples: as a result of age-long experience clothes were worked out which were well adapted to geographical conditions and people's labor activity. Alongside with outdated and irrational ones, there are also rational ones which are well

---

[1] The question of so-called fashion as a social phenomenon and an evaluation of its role in society and everyday life in the past and present is an important subject which has, unfortunately, as yet hardly been dealt with in ethnographic studies.

adapted to the climate and people's way of life, and are simple and beautiful. The ousting of such national types of clothes by European factory-made suits and modern dresses is not always progressive. This area offers a vast field for research and practical work by ethnographers.

4.   The third phenomenon of a folk material culture ethnographers frequently have to deal with are dwellings. Russian and especially Soviet ethnographers have given much time to the study of peasants' houses and auxiliary buildings. In the other European countries there are also abundant materials on that matter. Here again, ethnographers, notably Soviet scholars, have always tried not to confine themselves to a formal description of structures, but to look at their social aspect: the cooperation and division of labor during their building, the hired labor used, the class distinctions reflected in the dwelling, the purpose of the various parts of the building in its relation to family life, superstitions connected with the dwelling, the ritual purposes of its various parts, and, most important, the ethnic distinctions. All these are important ethnographic questions,[2] still they do not exhaust all the aspects of the ethnographic approach to this subject.

Man's dwelling, like his clothes, fulfils the elementary function of protecting him from the external environment. This is similar and even identical with the parallel phenomena in the animal world: the palaeolithic cave, windshelter, mud hut, and tent of ancient men did not differ in their primary function from the den or lair of the beast, or the bird's nest. However, the social consequences arising from this commonly-known and elementary fact transform human dwellings into a historical category with an inexhaustible and extraordinarily changeable content.

First and foremost, even the most primitive human dwelling exerts a strong impact on man's psychology, on his perception of the world around him. The singling out of microspace, the interior of his dwelling, from the endless universe is the first step towards the formation of the concept of space in man's consciousness. This is quite correctly noted by André Leroi-Gourhan, who first posed the question about the domestication or the humanization of space, as the first step in man's

---

[2]   Lewis Henry Morgan was the first to give weighty scientific arguments in favor of a sociological study of native dwellings. In his last and little known work, *Houses and House Life of American Aborigines*, he studied the types of dwellings and public structures built by the Indians in various parts of America as a reflection of the forms of their social life, notably as a reflection of their traditions of "communism in domestic life", and of the customs of hospitality (Morgan, 1881).

cognition of the ambient world.[3] This humanization of space within the limits of the dwelling as a perimeter of safety was a fact of social and not of individual consciousness, and not only of consciousness but, primarily, of social life: it immediately led to the practical organization of that microspace — man's dwelling. In the earliest remnants of dwelling, for example, in the Maltan palaeolithic camp site studied by M. M. Gerasimov, we see traces of a definite purposeful distribution of its parts: the male and female furnishings are in different parts of the dwelling (Gerasimov, 1937).

The entire following history of human dwellings can be regarded as the development of two primary relations or two antitheses: (1) the correlation, or to be more exact, the opposition between home and everything outside of home, and (2) the distribution of the parts of the dwelling among its inhabitants. These are two aspects of purely social relations, an opposition of "we" to "not we", and a distribution of relations and functions within the collective "we" (Porshnev, 1966: 78–84). In other words, like food and clothing, the dwelling fulfils a dual, purely social function: it unites some and segregates others. Let us look briefly at both aspects of the sociology of dwellings.

The very opposition of domestic microspace, i.e., the interior of the dwelling to the entire external world, even though it extends in all stages of human history, varies historically within broad limits. These variations are subordinated to strict regularities, which are by no means simple and, what is more, have as yet not been studied.

It would seem that the sharpness of this opposition is the function of a certain coefficient that expresses the correlation between the time spent by man in his home and that spent outside of it. This coefficient depends, in its turn, on climatic conditions, on the form of activity, on the way of life, and on various social factors. In warm and hot countries, especially where people lead a nomadic life, man often only sleeps in his dwelling, and even that not always. He carries on practically all his activity and spends most of his leisure outside the home; a fire is lit outside the dwelling and food is prepared there. Naturally, here the opposition between "home — outside of home" is reduced to a minimum. An example are the Australian tribes and other hunting people in the tropical and subtropical countries. They have practically no customs, beliefs, rites, taboos, limitations concerning the dwelling, and there are

---

[3] Naturally, this development of microspace was paralleled by the reconnaissance by the primeval hunter of the big world around him — the "itinerary" perception of space, as Leroi-Gourhan calls it (Leroi-Gourhan, 1965: 139–57).

no beliefs or rites relating to the hearth, and no family or clan "fire-cult".

Things were different in the North where the dwelling played a more important role in the lives of people, where, even when the forms of hunting, fishing, and reindeer-breeding were still undeveloped, the dwelling was the essential focus of all family life. Here dwellings (various tents of skins or bark — *chum, yaranga, iglu*), and also the homefire, hearth, and oil lamp were objects linked with various beliefs, bans, and customs. A typical example is the *yaranga*, the Chukchee dwelling. V. G. Bogoraz observed that all parts of the *yaranga* — the supporting poles, the covering, curtains, etc. — form a single and sacred whole. When a new *yaranga* is built, sacrifices are made to the supporting poles; they are smeared with the blood of sacrificial reindeers, and a new smearing is applied every year. No part of a strange dwelling is to be brought into the *yaranga* under any circumstances. Everything linked with the hearth (oil lamp) is considered holy: to borrow fire from a neighbor is a major sin, it is also a sin to put on the fire a pot that has previously been in contact with a stranger's fire or to heat a cold piece of meat that has been cooked on somebody else's fire (Bogoraz-Tan, 1939: 54–55, 62–63). Similar customs and bans can be observed also among the Koryaks, Eskimos, etc.

At the time of the class formation, dwellings became the object of superstitious rites and beliefs not only among settled peoples who lived in strong permanent dwellings, but also in the tropical countries; for example, the Polynesians and Micronesians assign sacred purposes to some parts of their huts.

At higher stages of historical development the customs and beliefs linked with the dwelling became more complex. It is interesting to note that in some measure there were distinctions between these customs of Southern and Northern peoples even on the European continent. The inhabitants of Southern Italy and Greece spend most of their time outside of home. In the villages and towns, the population, at least the male population, spends a minimum of time at home; they not only work outside their home, but also eat in cafes, restaurants, or simply in the street and spend their leisure and recreation time outside of home. Even the architecture of the houses, with their open doors, windows, balconies, and external staircases is such that there is no distinct border between the interior of the house and the ambient environment. Conversely, in the North European countries, in England and Scandinavia, a dwelling is sharply separated from the outer world; it is locked materially and spiritually, the life of the inhabitants proceeds behind its walls and no outsiders are admitted. "My home is my castle", says the Englishman.

The law on the inviolability of one's home was drafted in England and is strictly observed to this day.

Alongside the geographic factor there are naturally also other, sometimes even stronger, factors like religious traditions. In many Moslem countries the tradition of sealing off the dwelling from the outer world was long-lived and continues in part to this day. Many streets and alleys in old Moslem towns and villages are lined by high walls of houses without windows or doors, or by fences behind which stand houses with windows and doors facing an inner courtyard which is linked with the street only by a small gate.

We should not, however, exaggerate these distinctions; in some measure the opposition "home — outside of home" applies to all peoples, as can be seen from various customs, legal norms, beliefs, and rites.

Even the unwritten laws of etiquette makes man behave differently at home and outside of it. At home one dresses as he pleases, different from the way one does when "seeing people", and acts as one would not do outside of home. Even in our days many behave at home unceremoniously (unfortunately!), to put it mildly; on the other hand, one often discovers in a person unexpected traits of character when meeting him in the family circle; it is the psychological "at home" atmosphere that influences him. Sometimes even religion makes such distinctions, for example, according to the Talmudic laws of Judaism one is not allowed to carry things from one place to the other on Saturdays — that would be work — but one is allowed to do so within the home.

Another aspect of the same ethics of the dwelling is the custom of hospitality. It exists in different forms among various peoples and ascribes a special place of honor to the guest entering the home, affording special rights and privileges to him. Among peoples where hospitality is highly developed on the level of the patriarchal clan and early class system, for example, among the peoples of the Caucasus and the Balkan Peninsula, the guest crossing the threshold of the dwelling enjoys the special protection of the host and his family and even of the domestic guardian spirit. His person is considered holy and the host is obliged to protect him even at the cost of his own life, even if the guest is his mortal enemy. He has to indulge him in every way, to treat him, to let him have the best of everything, to give him presents; among some people this went as far as hospitable hetaerism. However, as soon as the guest left the house he was deprived of these privileges and of the host's protection. In the Caucasus cases were known of a host following his former guest on his way home and killing him.

Even in the modern developed countries where old customs have withered, a guest still enjoys special rights in the host's house; he is under the protection of special norms — to insult a guest or to evict him from one's home would be a gross violation of generally recognized moral norms.

The opposition "home — outside of home" is often emphasized by the use of additional, non-material means of fencing off the dwelling as a "perimeter of security". In addition to bolts, locks, bars, grates, shutters, etc., intended to keep out uninvited visitors, people attach all sorts of superstitious symbols and magic signs to the windows, doors, doorstep (or near the entrance to the barn or stable), carve or draw crosses or use the smoke of Easter candles on the lintels, nail horseshoes to the entrance, paint magic pentagrams on the threshold, or use platbands for windows which are ornamented with apotropaeic motives. All of these are to transform the dwelling into a bulwark that is inaccessible not only to thieves and robbers but also to evil powers and evil magic.

The defence of the dwelling by superstitious means from real or imaginary dangers is expressed not only in the external measures protecting the dwelling directly: this role is essentially played also by the various cults of the domestic guardian spirit. The history of religion abounds in examples of such cults: from the worship of the hearth as the "fire goddess" with the Siberian peoples to the Roman cult of domestic household gods, Lares and Penates, to the Russian *domovoi*, a sort of "grandad Brownie" who cared for the safety and welfare of the home. Various family rites, domestic holidays, etc., also belong to this category.

Do all these customs, rules, and beliefs concerning the dwelling pertain to the dwelling itself as a material structure or to the people inhabiting it? They pertain to both. To an ethnographer a dwelling is a dwelling only insofar as somebody lives in it (or at least lived or intended to do so). A dwelling, like any other object of material culture, does not exist to an ethnographer outside its social occurrence.

What is the social equivalent of a dwelling? What human collective dwells in it? In class societies it was generally a family. The house, the household, the family are synonymous. A family is also the economic cell of society, sometimes a productive cell and almost always a consumer cell; hence, the opposition "home — outside the home" is equivalent to a counterpositioning of the family to the whole ambient world. The more clearly the family cell stands out in the system of national economy, the more noticeable is also the counterpositioning "home — outside of home". The manifestations of this casual relationship are a subject worthy of special study.

In ethnographic descriptions of various non-European peoples who still preserve features of primeval society, one often comes across the following: if one of the inhabitants of the village is hungry he can enter any hut and take anything edible without asking the owner for permission. In other words, the absence of a sharp separation of the family as an economic cell weakens also the inviolability of the dwelling by outsiders; all houses are to some extent a common house.

Still, the family, and hence also its dwelling, are to some degree, and sometimes sharply, counterposed to the environment. To what family do we refer? In addition to the pair family, which originated already in primeval society and has now practically universally turned into the nuclear monogamous family, there existed and often predominated for many ages in history an extended family (a family community), which was preceded, apparently, by the clan community. Numerous ethnographic examples of the extended family are known: the Iroquois *ovachira*, the Sumatran *sabuah parui* (or *jurai*), the Southern Slavonic *zadruga*, etc. The idea that the type, or to be more exact, the size of the dwelling occupied by the family must correspond to the form and the size of the family seems logical: a small family has a small dwelling, a large family has a large dwelling. Factual materials show that in some cases this correspondence really did exist. The Iroquois *ovachira* lived in a "long house", the *jurai* among the Minangkabao people, in one communal home; the huge huts in Northern Russia are also obviously adapted for big families. This correspondence is not always observed: among some peoples the whole community (clan, village) lives in one big house in which the separate families have their sleeping places. This is observed in some remote areas in New Guinea and in South America. Large structures of the Lower Saxon or Alpine type in Europe, and big houses of the Basques on the contrary are inhabited only by small families at present, and the free part of the house is rented out. It can only be assumed that these houses were built for big families, although this, in our opinion, has not been clearly proved. Among the Moldavians and some other peoples the social ambition was to possess a big house, much bigger than the family needed. The motives for building a big house may not necessarily have been linked with the size of the family. This question demands a further study. On the other hand, the Southern Slavonic *zadruga* frequently lived in several small structures, that is, each wedded couple lived separately. They were grouped around the central house with the common hearth of the homestead. The same applies to the Khasi tribes in Assam. The conclusion of some archaeologists, who make judgements about the nature of the family from the size of the remains of structures, is not always warranted.[4]

No matter whether it was a family or some other collective that lived in the dwelling, this group always had its own structure which was invariably reflected, sometimes even very much so, by the type of the dwelling, the correlation of its parts, the distribution of the furnishing in the house, and the functions of the separate premises, rooms, and corners.

This aspect of the study of dwellings is well known to both Russian and foreign ethnographers. Detailed studies have been made of the characteristics of the distribution and purpose of the various parts of peasant dwellings, but as yet no sweeping generalizations have been made of them, and general regularities have not been established.

First and foremost, even common habitation, which unites a group of people or family, at the same time serves to segregate them. We have already mentioned that traces of a division of dwellings into a female half and a male half were discovered already in the dwellings of the early Stone Age. This sex-dividing tradition later grew stronger, just as the sex-dividing function of clothes and food. Among many non-European peoples there were even separate male and female houses, and sometimes there were no family houses at all. This was the case, for example, among the Marind-anim of New Guinea (Wirz, 1922: 41, 79, 92; 1925: 178) and the islanders of Palau in Micronesia (Semper, 1873: 51, 75, 318). The nomadic peoples of Northern and Central Asia almost always strictly observed the division of their pelt yurtas or teepee-like *chums* into the woman's half, which was to the right of the entrance, and the men's half, that was to the left. At later stages of historical development, we frequently find a strict division of the dwelling into two halves, one of which, the internal, is intended exclusively for woman and children — the *gynaikeion* in ancient Greece, the *ichkari, harem*, etc., in the Moslem East. In Russia before Peter the Great, women of nobility and merchant families lived in special tower chambers *terem* or the special women's section of the house (*svetlitsa*). Among the peasants in Russia, as also in West Europe, there was no such sharp segregation of the sexes in the dwelling, but there was a sharp demarcation between the various parts and the corners of the hut: the *babii kut* (the woman's corner near the stove), the *chulan* (pantry) in the North Russian huts, etc., were sometimes isolated by a curtain or a partition.

---

[4]   I do not go into the various forms of men's houses and other public structures of the communal-clan epoch which are beyond the scope of the article.

Still another sex-dividing feature that existed among many peoples was that the dwelling itself was considered a place for women rather than for men. The latter, who were more mobile, spent a large part of their time outside the home, at work, on trips and voyages, etc.; they spent their leisure hours at public places — cafes, taverns, pubs, clubs, etc. — while the women and children remained at home. The *Gemütlichkeit* 'coziness' at home has always been a concern where women could apply their taste.

Alongside these sex-dividing purposes of the different parts of the dwelling, the distribution of its part also reflects another aspect of the family structure and social relations. There is always a place of honor for the head of the family and for guests of honor. In the *yurta* of the nomads this place is generally opposite the entrance and slightly to the left; in a Yakut *yurta* there is the *bilirik*, a part of the plank-bed near the wall, diagonally opposite the fireplace; in the Russian, Belorussian and Ukrainian huts it is the sacred ("red") corner diagonally opposite the stove. Among many peoples, for example, in the dwellings of the Central Asian and Siberian nomads, the degree of honor attached to the place was measured by the distance from the entrance: the most honorable place was opposite the entrance, while servants and poor people were placed near the threshold. Among some Caucasian peoples the most honorable place was the chair opposite the stove built into a wall. In the architecturally complicated houses in the European countries which are divided into rooms, their distribution also corresponds with the social status (hierarchy) of its occupants: the room of the husband, of the wife, of the young couple, of the servants, etc.

A comparative ethnographic study of native dwellings must pursue the main aim of tracing the general regularities of historical changes in the functions of dwellings and their separate parts, and their general trend of development. Undoubtedly, it will be found that this general trend corresponds not only to the progress made by technology and urbanization (new building materials, mechanization, and electrification of domestic chores), but also to the general historical process and, notably, to the current and future changes of the family form.[5]

It would seem that, as in the case of food and clothing, and perhaps

---

[5] Here I have considered only separate dwellings. Naturally, dwellings are hardly ever isolated from each other and it is essential to study all forms of groupings of houses, single houses, *zaimka*, farmsteads, villages, etc. Sometimes the border between the separate dwelling and the set of dwellings is difficult to establish, for instance, with the Pueblo Indians in the South-Western part of the USA. This question demands special study.

even to a higher degree, the evolution of dwelling corresponds first to the increase and then the wane of social distinctions in everyday life. The latter takes the form of revolutionary cataclysms or gradual democratization, but this, too, is a problem of a special concern. In the past, up to a certain moment, there was a gradual intensification of the sex-dividing and social-segregating function of the dwelling. From a definite moment onwards, say, from the beginning of capitalism and the emergence of broad democratic movements, both functions began to wane. This was particularly noticeable in the case of the sex-dividing function of dwellings. All that is left of it now is separate bedrooms in some families. Naturally, the class distinctions in dwellings, as in clothing and food, remain and will continue to exist so long as there are classes. In fact, they are even more pronounced in dwellings than they are in clothes and other objects of material culture: the luxurious castles of multimillionaires and the slums of Harlem are two poles of the phenomenon.

Speaking of future trends in dwellings, a matter extremely important to urban development and the planning of new towns and villages, we must rely on forecasts about the future development of the family. Even now in laying out new houses and blocks of houses, attention is given, especially in the socialist countries, to the fact that a number of the former functions of the family are disappearing. The growth of public catering, the spread of various communal and welfare service establishments especially in tenement houses, the spread of children's pre-school institutions, the development of collective forms of sports and entertainment, youth and other clubs, etc., are gradually eroding the traditional family-domestic way of life and, at the same time, weakening the "perimeter of security" which is (or was) the dwelling. It seems likely that with the evolution of the family, future dwellings will resemble but little, if at all, the traditional family nest, the bulwark based on a family life rooted in private property.

Modernization in Non-European Urbicultures

S. ARUTJUNOV

In their everyday domestic material culture, the developing countries in Asia and Africa are undergoing rapid changes which in the main boil down to various *forms of interaction of the local "ethnic" culture with the European culture*, that is to say, with the modern world urbanistic cultural pattern. Japan is the best model of the analogous-extrapolative prognostication of these processes which have been going on there for over one hundred years. All objects and complexes are classifed into two cultural spheres in the contemporary Japanese cultural medium: "Japanese" (*washiki*) and "Western" (*yoshiki*), but usually one sees a combination of both.

In studies of culture, like in art, ethnic (non-authorial) phenomena should be distinguished from authorial phenomena which do not necessarily have any ethnic features.

The process of technical modernization must be treated separately from the process of cultural incorporation.

Radios can be attributed neither to *yoshiki* nor to *washiki*, just as plastic plates and dishes in the traditional Japanese form cannot be regarded as Europeanization, but modernization. However, apart from this the interpenetration of *washiki* and *yoshiki* is observed today in the entire Japanese life. In the most general form, the nature of this interpenetration is made up of three variants. First, it is the *mechanical supplement* of one cultural tradition by another one, for instance, *ryokan* is a hotel in the Japanese style, yet, it is equipped not with Japanese bathtubs (*furo*), but with a European type of bathtubs. Another example is Japanese ornamen-

First published in *Problemas teoricos de la etnografia* (Moscow, 1971).

tation on European types of plates and dishes. Second, it is *the synthesis of the features of both cultures in one object* (the raincoat, *amagoto*, worn over the kimono, is partly *washiki* and partly *yoshiki* in cut). Third, it is *the adaptation of the borrowed object to traditional practices*. Moreover, the object may either not undergo any changes, or may be modified: for instance, the chair, *zaisu*, is a European one, but without legs.

This begs the question: what are the structural specifics of the laws which determine in one sphere of everyday life or another the choice of the Western, traditional, mixed, or synthetic forms, and the type and balance of combination?

There are four main factors which condition these laws: the role of habit, the structural pattern of the given sphere of life in the traditional cultural model and its fate in the process of acculturation, the conformity or non-conformity of the ethnic tradition's structural principles to the borrowed models' structural principles and the attitude to a domestic object as a sign of social prestige.

Zaisu is an example of the action of the factor of habit. In the sphere of trade we can observe a case where the borrowing of a cultural complex depends on the degree of development of its analog in the traditional culture. Despite the generally high level of wholesale and retail specialization of trade, Japan did not have an institute of universal trade before European penetration. Therefore, although petty specialized trade preserved many traditional features, everything concerning universal trade was borrowed in the complex, and no attempts were made somehow to "Japanize" it.

The bath practice in Japan, for instance, which was well developed earlier as well, largely maintained its traditional features. Later, when the hot springs bathing (*onsen*) began to develop under European influence, they adopted many features of the traditional bath practice.

At times the borrowed cultural complex takes root easily and soundly because its structure is sufficiently parallel to the functionally similar traditional complex's structure. Thus in Japan the ceremonial complex of a black cutaway and striped trousers with a white chemisete, now out of date in most European countries, is still quite popular. Japan long had a national costume (*reifuku*) for ceremonious occasions. The borrowed complex went well with the usual strict black-and-white tone of the *reifuku* and the mind quickly absorbed the structural parallelism of the costume's details: *kimono*—shirt, *hakama*—trousers, *haori*—cutaway, *himo*—tie.

The costume serves as an example of the prestige considerations in the balance of *washiki* — *yoshiki*. The costume's structural model can be defined as the balance of two components: basis and accessories. The basis is the possible costume's minimum, and the accessories are everything else. The basis as a minimum is possible without accessories, but the accessories are impossible without the basis. In the European case the accessories would be the shirt, tie, frock coat, or blouse. In the Japanese case, they would be the *hakama* and *haori*, and in all cases the footwear and headdress. The trousers and skirt (Europe), and the *kimono* (Japan), would be the basis. The accessory may be replaced by another, more smart-looking one while preserving the basis, but not vice versa.

As for the complexes, the European costume was naturally more ornamental and prestigious when acculturation began. In the 1920's it was possible to combine the Japanese basis (*kimono*) with European accessories (hat, shoes, and so on) in Japan. Incidentally, this is now true of India and Malaya where European accessories, even the jacket, could supplement the basis (*dhoti* and *sarong*).

In the 1940's and 1950's the European costume became popular in Japan owing to the war and occupation; the national costume became a sign of prestige. Today the *kimono* is more expensive and ornamental than the equivalent European clothes. European accessories are now incompatible with the *kimono*, while national accessories (*haori*, *happi*, and footwear) go with the European basic costume.

This is also true of architecture. Its basis would obviously be a building's main functional, utilitarian component, i.e., its interior, while its accessories would be its facade and external appearance. One may notice an interesting law: the features of *yoshiki* grow and the features of *washiki* diminish from the center to the periphery, from the building's interior to its passages, stair, facade, and fences. This concentric structure, with the growth of the Western from the internal to the external, is reflected in the entire Japanese life: the more intimate and domestic it is, the more pronounced are its traditional features, and, conversely, the more official and businesslike is the sphere of activities, the more powerful is its organization in the spirit of *yoshiki*.

The costume structure in the South-East Asian countries, as in Japan at the turn of the century, consists as a rule of a European accessory and a traditional basis. As the Europeanization of the costume reaches its peak there, usually at the highest official level, the need arises for a mark to indicate ethnic self-assertion. This mark is an individual standardized national detail in a generally European costume and is usually the headdress. The architecture of official buildings, which on the whole keeps to the European style, likewise often has an ethnic mark that is strictly external in nature in the shape of a roof or some other element of decor.

This ethnic mark is seen in the architecture of many Japanese official buildings of the first half of the 20th century. In these cases it becomes possible to observe the manifestation of certain universal structural laws which pass a similar stage-by-stage development.

In Japan the borrowed cultural elements are spreading and being assimilated in the same way as the specifically Japanese cultural phenomena spread earlier in many respects corresponding to G. Naumann's concept of "reduced culture". This is how, for instance, such main components of the Japanese interior as the *tokonoma* and *tatami* spread. Having first entered the life of the upper sections of the aristocracy, they became signs of prestige and passed down to the *samurai*. It was only later, in the 19th century, that they passed to the peasants, becoming a general ethnic standard and, accordingly, loosing prestigious importance. This was also true of European food, clothing, and houses in the 20th century.

As a result of this brief analysis of some individual features pointed out from an extremely wide range of the interaction of the traditional and the Western in modern Japanese life, the laws of this process could now be presented in the form of some geometric concepts, above all the concept of parallelism. According to this concept the elements of a complex are, in a way, arranged in a line: for instance, in *reifuku* it is *hakama-kimono-haori-bow*. In nourishment it is the pair *shushoku* (starchy substance, rice and noodles) and *fukushoku* (flavoring substance). In perceiving the borrowed features, the ethnic consciousness performs a substitution, breaking up the borrowed complex into the same linear elements. Bread is thus equated with *shushoku*, rice in particular; *haori* and *happi* are equated with the jacket, blouse, frock coat, and so forth. It is something of an equation in which both halves, or individual corresponding members in the halves, may be rearranged.

The second concept is that of concentricity. According to it, the basic, the main, the functional, and the intimate are situated at the center, and the supplementary, the formal, the ostentatious, and the official are situated at the periphery. One variant is a sector of this concentric circle giving a graphic of the vertical and hierarchical structure. In essence both concepts express the same law in the most diverse spheres of life. The movement proceeds from the periphery to the center which is quite natural, that is to say, from the external layers subject to influences, to the inner layers (this is evident from the structure of the house and from the general structure of the spheres of life). It goes from the "top to the bottom", from the cap to the basic element of clothing, from the upper sections of society to the lower ones. At the same time the traditional element not ousted yet from the basis may once more turn out to be in the upper, external part of the graph if it again becomes a sign of prestige. This, in particular, explains the enormous Europeanization of the life of the middle sections of the population in several Asian countries.

This vertical graph also reflects the statics of society or the given complex of the domestic culture and its dynamics. It must be noted that in various spheres of life influences are not replaced with the same rapidity, and therefore the diagrams of the various spheres of life may somewhat differ at a given moment. Moreover, a fact of decisive importance is that in passing the graph from the top to the bottom the layers and waves of influence do not merely oust one another, as we have already seen, but a diffusion, a cultural synthesis, takes place between them. Therefore, this acculturation's extrapolative, foreseen ultimate result is a strongly Europeanized (but not simply European) synthetic basic part of the domestic culture with many decorative, external, accessorial traditional features. One half of the traditional part also consists of borrowed elements, but these innovations were made so long ago that no one in life would ever think of separating them from the traditional. Generally these are mainland (Korean-Chinese) borrowings made in the limited period from the 6th to the 9th centuries A.D.

Thus, the Japanese ethnic community, known to us historically, has twice passed through the epoch of mass borrowings: in the early Middle Ages and in the 19th and 20th centuries. An interesting fact is that both these times coincided with the social system's revolutionary transformations; in the first instance it coincided with the formation of the early feudal state, and in the second instance, with the transition from the feudal system to the bourgeois one. Japanese society assimilated cultural innovations in the first instance generally according to the aforementioned graph. In the domestic culture the Chinese and Korean adoptions likewise first became the property of the upper sections of society, and then became public cultural property. This was followed by the trend to revive the traditional. For the medieval times it would be difficult to see this from the strictly domestic objects, but the trend becomes apparent from the facts of language. In the two instances the assimilation of foreign borrowings by the Japanese language seems to coincide structurally with the aforementioned graph for the domestic culture.

The Chinese lexical borrowings of *kango* first began to penetrate into the educated elite's speech in the 6th and 7th centuries. They then gradually became a public linguistic factor and were no longer regarded as borrowed. The Japanese language began to assimilate the European vocabulary (*gairaigo*) on a large scale in the 19th century. *Gairaigo* at first figured prominently only in the elite's speech, but later it greatly penetrated into common speech as well, and in several instances it was even no longer regarded as borrowed. As a result a trend arose in the speech of the "high style", especially the intellectuals' written speech, to use *wago* and *kango* in places where the *gairaigo* figured prominently in oral speech.

This general law, according to which the cultural innovations alien to the ethnic tradition first penetrate largely into the ordinary life of the upper sections of society, and then make their way from the "top to the bottom", acquiring connections of the synthetic interrelations with the traditional culture as they pass, presupposes as a component part of its mechanism the repetitive bringing of the "age-old" traditional elements of culture to the top of the social prestige scale. This historical rotation apparently greatly helped the Japanese and other cultures to digest and assimilate all the repeated cultural borrowings, and to preserve continuity and originality of their own culture over the centuries despite the intensity of foreign influences.

Ethnology and Adjoining Sciences

Atlas of the World Population (Basic Problems of Demographic-Ethnographic Cartography)

S. BRUK

Mapping of phenomena is the most visual method of expressing the results of their study. At the same time it is a source of cognizing laws which have previously escaped the attention of scholars: maps link up geographical phenomena with socioeconomic and historical factors and help to bring out their correlational ties. This particularly applies to maps which furnish a comprehensive view of population characteristics. During the mapping of population, materials from a number of related sciences are utilized: ethnography, archaeology, linguistics, demography, geography, and so on. Moreover, extensive use of mass statistics is highly characteristic of population mapping: it is impossible to compile population maps on an even relatively small scale without collecting detailed information on populated localities or small administrative units.

A detailed examination of changes in different objects and phenomena in space and time, which is done when making maps for different historical periods, and also consideration of the quantitative factor on these maps, actually represent an introduction of the mathematic-statistical method in science, which is particularly fruitful in characterizing phenomena changing from place to place. Comparison of a number of maps enables the researcher to bring out the facts and the causal connections that are insufficiently disclosed by the usual methods of study. These facts and causal connections may, in turn, be reflected on composite maps whose scientific merits are indisputable.

Cartographic studies hold a considerable place in the research plans of the Institute of Ethnography of the USSR Academy of Sciences. They

First published in *Sovetskaja etnografija*, N1 (1970).

follow two directions: (1) historico-ethnographic (compilation of historico-ethnographic atlases for large regions of the Soviet Union), and (2) demographic-ethnographic (compilation of maps and atlases of the present-day national composition of the population, and the mapping of the location of the population and of different demographic and ethnic phenomena).

Historico-ethnographic cartography developed in the USSR immediately after the end of the Second World War. Two large scientific bodies were set up to collect materials for historico-ethnographic atlases devoted to the indigenous peoples of Siberia and the Russian population in the European part of the USSR.

The *Atlas of Siberia* was published in 1961. It reflected such important elements of the people's culture as dwellings, clothing, headwear, ornaments, transport by reindeer, dog-breeding for sleighing, the tambourines of shamans, and so on. Three sections of the historico-ethnographical atlas *The Russians* were published in 1966. They deal with agricultural implements, dwellings, and traditional folk costumes. Work is under way on regional historico-ethnographical atlases of the Ukraine, Belorussia, Moldavia, the Baltic area, the Caucasus, Middle Asia, and Kazakhstan. The first two atlases are being prepared according to a program which is close to that of the atlas *The Russians* but with due consideration for all the peoples inhabiting these regions. The atlases of the Caucasus, Middle Asia, and Kazakhstan deal primarily with farming, irrigation, and cattle-breeding; they will also reflect settlement and dwellings, clothing and ornaments, the crafts, and so on.

Two aims are usually pursued in preparing historico-ethnographic atlases. The first is to fix diverse elements of the traditional culture of the peoples, and the second is to sum up and systematize the accumulated materials for solving important problems related to the ethnogenesis, ethnic history, and reciprocal influences of peoples. Special methods have been elaborated for coping with all these tasks in compiling atlases. All phenomena must be shown in their dynamics, in historical development. For this purpose maps are designed for several chronological dates. The presentation of phenomena in their dynamics is supplemented by their quantitative characteristics. Alongside separate elements of culture, synthetic maps also bring out the types of phenomena. The methods of collecting materials and of map-making have been elaborated in detail.

In this article we shall discuss the basic problems of demographic-ethnographic cartography.

For more than twenty years scientists of the Institute of Ethnography of the USSR Academy of Sciences, have been compiling ethnographic maps of different areas of the world. In 1951, the Institute published a map of the peoples of the USSR for students. Subsequently, beginning in 1956, the Institute issued maps of the peoples of the Indian subcontinent, the peoples of China, the Mongolian People's Republic and Korea, Western Asia, Indonesia, Malaya and the Philippines, the peoples of Africa, and, lastly, a general map of the peoples of the world.

All these maps were made with a new method developed in the Institute, namely, the method of the simultaneous presentation of the national composition and the density of population. *The Atlas of the Peoples of the World*, published in 1964, summed up the results of studies over many years. In preparing all these works a number of methodological problems had to be solved. It was necessary to formulate the principles of singling out and classifying ethnic communities, to improve the methods of ascertaining ethnic territories and boundaries, to substantiate the methods of compiling ethnic maps, and to define the possibility of utilizing diverse data and indices (including indirect ones), and to elaborate methods of presentation, and so on.

Extensive materials on related branches characterizing some or other aspects of the population of the world were accumulated in this process. *The Atlas of the Peoples of the World* had many maps showing population density, the concentration of population in cities, and maps of the linguistic and racial composition of the world population.

The Laboratory of Ethnic Statistics and Cartography of the Institute of Ethnography plans in the next few years to prepare an *Atlas of the World Population*, a summary work which would give comprehensive characteristics of the population. So far no scientists of any country have attempted to give comprehensive cartographic characteristics of the world population. The preparation of such atlas is a new, qualitatively higher stage in demographic-ethnographic cartography. The scientific and political value of such an atlas is determined by the sharp changes in the nature of ethnic and demographic processes after the Second World War. The ethnic consolidation and shaping of big nations have started at a swift pace in Asian and African countries which have recently won their independence. What is known as the "demographic revolution" has been under way in the world during the recent two decades. It is marked by a swift growth of population which can be explained by many reasons: in the first place, sharp shifts in natural movement (birth and deaths) and changes in the sex and age composition of the population; these have been influenced by many ethnic factors. Only by applying the new research methods is it possible to understand with sufficient profundity all these processes. The *Atlas* is conceived as a comprehensive cartographic work designed to sum up in the form of maps, charts, diagrams, tables, and texts, a wide range of phenomena and processes related to population. There will be two hundred multicolored maps (not counting inset maps). The text will describe the mapped phenomena and processes, and provide explanations to the maps and thus facilitate their reading.

The content of the *Atlas* will be highly diverse. The introductory section will carry a series of historical maps showing the gradual development of ecumene throughout man's history, the growth of population by continents and countries. A large group of demographic maps will illustrate the natural movement of the population, its sex and age composition and also migration processes. Another section of the *Atlas* will be given-over to the distribution of the population (density and cities) and also to the forms and types of settlement. Ethnic maps in the broad sense of the word (maps of the national, linguistic, racial, and religious composition of the world population) will make up a separate group. They will help in understanding major events of socio-political life and reveal the essence of contemporary ethnic and national processes. The last section of the *Atlas*, consisting of a relatively small number of maps, will offer socioeconomic, cultural, and medico-geographical characteristics of population (maps of the class and professional composition and employment, distribution of manpower resources, literacy, educational levels, medico-sanitary conditions, cultural, and everyday services, and so on).

In contrast to the *Atlas of the Peoples of the World* where one method of mapping was chiefly used (the method of colored surfaces), here the most diverse methods are to be used. A big part of the demographic and sociocultural maps is to be made by the method of cartograms and cartodiagrams, and others by the method of colored surfaces and other ways. Countries will form the cartographic units; in a number of cases primary administrative units within countries will be used (republics and regions of the USSR, states of the USA and India, and so on).

One of the major purposes of the *Atlas* is to reflect wherever possible all phenomena and processes in their dynamics. In some cases the mapped phenomenon will be shown over a long historical period (many decades and even centuries); in other cases, over a much shorter period. The authors of the *Atlas* will strive to show, if the respective materials are available, the state of the mapped phenomena at the following dates: 1900 (beginning of the century), 1913 (eve of the First World War), 1920 (end of the First World War and the initial period in the life of the world's first socialist state), 1937 (eve of the Second World War), 1950 (postwar period and the formation of the world socialist system), and lastly, the last three or five years for which data are available. Apparently, most often maps will be made for 1900 and the present period. It is planned to utilize materials of the 1970 population censuses which are conducted in most countries of the world. Naturally, the more remote the mapped period, the more schematic will be the maps. It is already now clear that in the absence of data in a number of fields the dynamics will not be reflected in all cases.

Special attention will be paid to compiling so-called synthetic maps by comparing elementary maps. Synthetic maps will make it possible to reveal the laws which so far have escaped the attention of scholars. Highly promising, in our opinion, are general maps which trace the links between the natural movement of population and its sex and age composition, or even simpler maps which connect the high birthrate with the spread of early marriages, and so on. The *Atlas* will enable scholars to study in greater detail the causes affecting the fluctuations of the birthrate in different socioeconomic epochs and among different peoples. Let us recall that ethnic and ethnopsychological factors hold quite an important place among these causes.

The introductory section of the *Atlas* will consist of two parts. The first will include maps which, although they are not directly related to the subject matter of the *Atlas*, give some general information about the world, and the history of its settlement — maps of the political division of the world (for 1900 and the latest date, and on a smaller scale also for a number of intermediate dates), physico-geographical (terrain and landscape geographical zones) and a number of maps on the development of the ecumene. These maps will facilitate better understanding of some demographic and ethnic regularities. The second part will consist of the most diverse maps characterizing the dynamics of the world population. The dynamics of the population of continents in ancient epochs will be shown with the help of simple schematic maps; more detailed cartograms will reflect the growth of population in the Middle Ages. The population dynamics of European and North American countries will be specified in detail; there is also comparatively detailed information on the dynamics of the population of some Asian countries (China and India). For the world as a whole and for all continents the population dynamics can be shown with a sufficient degree of authenticity approximately since the mid 17th century, and for all countries only since the beginning of the 20th century. The introductory section will be rounded out by maps showing the present state of demographic studies of the world, offering data on the latest censuses and the degree of their completeness.

The first section of the *Atlas* ("Demography") illustrates the natural movement of population, its sex-age composition, and mechanical movement of population (migration processes). Migration processes exert such an essential influence on the distribution of population that they are often considered a section of population geography and not of demography. Let us recall that the swift growth of the world population is determined by sharp changes in the postwar structure of the natural movement of the population in developing countries where more than two-thirds of all mankind is concentrated. A comprehensive study of the structure of the natural population movement and its causes is of tremendous practical significance and is almost the central task of demographic science.

The birth and death rates and the natural increment are the main indices of the natural movement of population. The most commonly used crude birth and death indices are obtained by comparing the total annual number of births (deaths) with the average population. The difference between births and deaths provides an index of the natural population increase and their ratio, the general reproduction index. Maps for all these indices will be compiled for different years beginning with 1900. The birthrate will be characterized more precisely by maps giving the fertility rate (the ratio of the number of children born to the average number of woman of a fertile age), and fertility rates by ages and marriages. Maps giving the percentage of married women in different age groups will help bring out the causes for the different levels of births (it is especially interesting to ascertain the peoples among whom early marriages are widespread). The deathrate by age is usually employed for a detailed characteristic of mortality; of special significance is infant mortality obtained by comparing the number of infants who died under one year of age and the total number of children born alive.

The *Atlas* will reflect the main historical changes (as far as information is available) in the character of natural population movements for the world as a whole, for continents, countries, as well as for individual selected parts of countries and the emergent types of natural reproduction, and reveal differences in the natural movement between the urban and rural population. A comparison of the maps of the natural movement with the maps of the dynamics of total population will give an idea of the role of migration processes. Maps of manpower losses in the First and Second World Wars will also be of great interest.

Establishment of a complex of factors influencing the birth and death rates is a major question of demographic science which had not been fully ascertained to this day. The deathrate, to a much greater extent than the birthrate, depends on the level of a country's socioeconomic development, the welfare of the population, and the public health system. At the same time it would be an oversimplification to perceive full conformity between mortality indices and indices in these spheres. The point is that as the deathrate decreases the share of people of ages with the highest mortality, namely, of persons of advanced age, rises in the total population; as a result after a certain time the mortality index rises slightly.

The birthrate is determined by more complex factors and does not show a close dependence on the welfare of the population. In some specific social conditions the birthrate may rise as the well-being of the population improves, or, on the contrary, drops. The assertion often found in the literature that a high birthrate supposedly is a result of improved well-being of the population in one or another country is not confirmed by facts; the reverse assertion (the poorer the population, the higher the birthrate) also does not reveal the mechanism of this phenomenon and reflects the unjustified generalization of a limited number of facts. A definite link has been established between the birthrate and the distinctions in the age-sex composition of the population, the average marriageable age, the educational level of the spouses, and some other, including ethnic and psychological, factors. In towns the birthrate, as a rule, is lower than in rural localities. Religion, too, exerts a noticeable influence on the birthrate. Islam, for example, prompts families to rear many children and, therefore, the birthrate in Moslem countries, as a rule, is high. It is also characteristic of countries with a preponderance of Catholics, since the Catholic Church condemns the use of contraceptives and abortions and prohibits divorces. Account should be taken of the influence of state measures aimed at encouraging or retarding an increase in births (for more details on these problems see Kozlov, 1969).

The mapping of at least some of these indices will help establish their actual role in the population reproduction processes. Possibly, new dependences which have not so far attracted the attention of scholars will be found.

The connection between the sex-age composition and the ethnic origin of the population is highly complex. The total number of men in the world slightly exceeds the number of women, but there is considerable unevenness in the distribution of sexes by continents and countries. The general tendency is as follows: in economically developed countries there is usually a bigger proportion of women because of the higher mortality of men; in less developed countries where the women do the hard work and often are in a subordinate position, there is a bigger proportion of men. In many European countries and in the USSR the number of women greatly exceeds the number of men because of the big losses of the male population during the two world wars. There are countries with approximately equal living conditions but with a different ratio between the sexes. Thus, in India, Pakistan, and Ceylon women make up altogether 48 per cent of the total population, and in neighboring Afghanistan, Iran, Burma, Thailand, Vietnam, and Indonesia, about 50 per cent. If we take countries of tropical and Eastern Africa, there are more women than men. No doubt, the ratio of sexes depends on many historical and ethnic factors. Detailed maps and cartograms will make it easier to reveal them.

An analysis of the age composition of the population will show considerable fluctuations in the proportion of young (up to fifteen years) and old (above sixty years) ages in different countries. Developing countries with a high birthrate, considerable mortality, and short longevity have a higher share of children (in many Asian, African, and Latin American countries the number of children is only 20 to 30 per cent below the number of persons of productive age), and a low share of persons in older ages (3 to 6 per cent). In the industrially developed countries the number of children is less than half the number of persons of working age. On the other hand, the share of old people is two or three times higher than in the developing countries.

The *Atlas* will include a series of cartograms of the sex composition of the population as a whole with a breakdown by age groups separately for the urban and rural population. Cartograms of the age composition and cartograms of the percentage of persons of different ages in the total population (children, persons of working age, elderly people, and so on) will be compiled. Special maps will show the average age of the population of different countries, the life expectancy at birth, the share of persons above the age of 90 or 100, the average age of marriage, the average size of the family, and so on.

Migration processes have played an important part in populating some parts of the world and in shaping their population. They exert a considerable impact on population dynamics in different countries. In some countries the influence of migration on population dynamics in certain periods is even greater than the influence of the natural movement of the population. The demographic consequences of migrations are determined both by the number of migrants and the specific of their age-sex composition, that is, by the noticeable preponderance of young and middle-aged people, and of men among the settlers.

It is difficult to overestimate the influence of migrations on ethnic processes. A continuous mixing of the population belonging to different ethnic groups has been going on throughout mankind's long history, beginning with the primitive communal system and continuing up to our days. Any contemporary nation or nationality has arisen from diverse ethnic elements. The nature of the interaction of these elements has depended on the proximity of language, religion, and traditions, the features of their settlement, economic development level, and many other factors.

The ethnic map of the world has been tremendously influenced by big population shifts like the great migration of the peoples in Europe (4th to 7th centuries), the invasion of the Arabs (7th to 8th centuries) who reached the African Atlantic coast in the West and the Indus River in the East, and the expansion of the Turko-Mongols (11th to 17th centuries) who captured a considerable part of Asia and South-Eastern Europe. Lastly, the age of the great geographical discoveries (end of the 15th to 17th centuries) initiated the wide development of intercontinental migrations, chiefly from Europe to other parts of the world. In the 20th century the pace of migration has not slackened although it has acquired a different aspect in a number of cases: resettlement for reasons of a non-economic nature steeply increased (huge migrations of the population caused by the two world wars, the movement of more than sixteen million people for religious reasons caused by the division of British India into two independent states, India and Pakistan, and so on).

The subject "Migration Processes" will be covered by a series of world and regional maps of major migrations from ancient times up to the beginning of the 19th century, cartodiagrams of big world migrations and major internal migrations in the 19th and 20th centuries, cartodiagrams of migrations between countries in the interwar period and after the Second World War, and world cartograms showing the role of migrations in the increase or decrease of population in the 19th and 20th centuries. Maps will be prepared to show how the Eastern territories of the USSR and the Western areas of the USA were populated; they will also demonstrate seasonal migrations in Russia prior to the First World War, the migrations between India and Pakistan during the division of British India, the settlement of virgin lands in the USSR, and so on. The *Atlas* will also describe special types of migrations — from villages to towns, seasonal migrations for work, temporary importation of manpower, and so on.

The next section of the *Atlas* ("Territorial Distribution of Population") will consist of two parts: the first will show the distribution of population, and the second, the forms and types of settlement.

The population is distributed unevenly throughout the world. In some countries (the Netherlands and Belgium) the average population density reaches 300 to 400 persons per square kilometer; in others, it drops to one person per square kilometer and even less (Mongolian People's Republic, Libya, and Mauritania). About 10 per cent of the entire land surface (polar regions, deserts, and high mountain districts) has not been developed by man at all; at the same time there are vast densely populated areas of intensive irrigation farming (the valleys of big rivers in Southern and Central China, the valleys of the Mekong, Red, Ganges, and Lower Brahmaputra rivers, the island of Java and the Nile Delta) where the density of the rural population reaches 1,000 to 1,500 per square kilometer. Half of all mankind lives in the most populated areas of the world which take up only five per cent of the land surface. Population density depends on many factors: the natural conditions, development level of the productive forces, type of economy, historical conditions in which the given area was populated, and differentiation of population growth determined by the natural increase and migration. It should be stressed that all these factors are closely interconnected and that the natural conditions influence settlement always in an indirect way — through the connections of these conditions with a historically shaped type of the economy.

The distribution of population is largely determined by the location of cities in which more than one-third of the world population is now concentrated: in Asia (excluding the Asian part of the USSR) and Africa about 20 per cent of the population live in cities, while in all other regions the share of urban dwellers is considerably above 50 per cent. Notwithstanding the swift growth of world population, the density of the rural population in many countries is not increasing because the entire accretion is absorbed by the cities.

The ever accelerating urbanization is exerting a tremendous impact on demographic and ethnic processes. In particular, the birthrate and the natural population increase in the cities is, as a rule, decreasing, which leads to a change in the age composition (the proportion of children in the total population declines). The cities are growing largely through immigration (men in the first place) and the ratio of sexes is gradually changing. In India, for example, according to the population census of 1961, there were 941 women per 1,000 men, while in the cities there were only 845 women (in the bigger cities even less — in Calcutta 612, Bombay

663, and New Delhi 777). The same tendency is also displayed in other countries which suffered big losses of the male population as a result of the two wars.

Cities are noted for a highly diverse national composition of the population, which may be explained by the influx of people to the cities not only from nearby rural districts, but also from remote areas of a country which often differ ethnically. Most of the emigrants to new countries settle in cities. The processes of ethnic mixing in urban centers is accelerated, particularly if we consider the closer mingling of urban dwellers and their greater social mobility.

Comprehensive maps of the distribution of the population are to be prepared for different periods. The population of cities will be indicated on such maps by circles of different size, and the density of the rural population, including the inhabitants of small towns and settlements, will be shown by colored surfaces. A world map of population density and the population of cities on a scale of 1 : 15 million was published in 1970, prepared by the Laboratory of Ethnic Statistics and Cartography, Institute of Ethnography, USSR Academy of Sciences, and the Scientific Mapping Section of the Central Geodesy and Cartography Administration. Its materials will be utilized for the maps of the *Atlas*. Cartograms will reflect the level of urbanization in different periods, the ratios between the urban and rural population in some of the biggest cities, and the percentage of inhabitants in towns of different size. Since in various countries there are different criteria for defining cities, a special map will deal with the problem of distinguishing urban settlements.

The forms and types of settlement are most intimately linked with the distribution of population and with its socioeconomic and cultural distinctions, inasmuch as the forms and types of settlement are ultimately determined by production and the way of life of people. The settlement of peoples also substantially affects the intensity of ethnic processes. The very concept "settlement" is rather broad and includes the most diverse subjects, only some of which will be considered in the *Atlas*. Thus, attention will be paid to the typology of settlements, the dependence of settlement on the physical-geographical conditions, and the problem of suburbanization and city agglomerates. Even with such a relatively narrowed interpretation of the content of this subject, it is possible to deduce a number of new, formerly undiscerned regularities, because until recently the types and forms of settlement, particularly for large regions of the world, have been hardly subjected to mapping.

An attempt will be made to compile maps showing the classification of populated localities for the size of population, features of their layout, and the forms of settlements in different landscape zones. Other maps will indicate the distribution of population by altitude zones: there will be maps of the economic types of agricultural settlement, maps of nomads with a reflection of their settlement on land, cartograms of the dynamics of the growth of cities in the world, world maps of the types of urban city layouts and construction, maps of suburbanization processes, maps of population distribution in highly urbanized areas of the world, and plans of the biggest cities and their environs.

The third section of the *Atlas*, dealing with the ethnic, linguistic, religious, and anthropological composition of the world population, may in a certain sense be described as generally ethnic.

We pointed out earlier that the ethnic composition of the world population had been reflected in great detail in maps and atlases published in recent years; in our *Atlas* the presentation of the ethnic composition is to be only one aspect of the comprehensive analysis of population. It is abundantly clear that the number of maps on this subject should not be as many as in the special *Atlas of the Peoples of the World* and the methods of representation must intrinsically blend with the general structure of the contemplated work. This means that besides ethnic maps compiled by the method of colored surfaces, the new *Atlas* should have various cartograms and cartodiagrams and numerous inset maps which will make it possible to tie the ethnic subjects up with the subjects of other sections.

It is planned to compile maps of the peoples of the world as a whole, for the USSR, and for separate parts of the world (Asia, apparently, will be divided into several regions). Territories with a mixed ethnic composition will be indicated by alternating color stripes, with the width of the stripes showing the share of different peoples in the total population. Sparsely populated areas will be singled out by a special method. The genetic proximity of peoples will be conveyed by a specially selected range of colors. For the same regions cartograms will show through diagrams the percentage proportion of the biggest people in each country's total population. Special maps will be made showing the peoples settled in many countries: Russians, Ukrainians, Poles, Britons, Germans, Frenchmen, Italians, Greeks, Indian peoples, Chinese, Japanese, Armenians, Arabs, Gypsies, and so on. Maps will also describe the ethnic composition of the population of cities with more than one million people.

Quite close to the ethnic maps are the maps of the linguistic composition. It should be noted that until now in mapping languages account has been taken mainly of their genetic proximity which is important for the classification of peoples, but almost no attention has been paid to other aspects characterizing the languages of the world. We expect to give in the new atlas the following linguistic maps: language families, branches and groups; a morphological classification of languages; state and official languages of the world; bilingualism; and written languages. There will also be tables of the graphic systems of written languages.

To give the full ethnographic characteristics of a people, or of a group within a people, it is necessary to ascertain their religious affiliation. Religion has played, and continues to play, an important part in the life of many countries. In a number of cases it exerts a noticeable influence on ethnic processes — accelerating them if peoples professing one religion are in the process of ethnic interaction, or, retarding them if the con-tacting peoples have different religions. Many demographic indices (early marriages, the birthrate), some types of migration processes, and even the nature of settlement (blocks of houses in cities according to religion) directly or indirectly depend on religious affiliation.

It is planned to draw up maps of religions indicating their main trends and denominations for the world as a whole, and for separate parts of the world, cartodiagrams of the religious composition by countries and cartograms of the spread of the biggest religions (Catholicism, Protestant-ism, Greek Orthodoxy, Islam, Buddhism, and Judaism).

The absence of massive data on the basic anthropological indices for most peoples has restricted the possibilities of extending anthropological cartography. Until now primarily maps of racial types and primitive charts of the ways of their settlement have appeared in different anthro-pological and ethnographic works. Some prospects in this field have been opened only recently owing to the great successes in the most diverse sectors of anthropological science. The *Atlas* is to have maps with anthropological indices which are of interest from the angle of ethnic anthropology or ethnogenetic problems.

The main subjects in this part of the *Atlas* will be the contemporary spread of the main anthropological types, centers of race formation and the approximate ways of the settlement of the human races, territorial distribution of the varied lengths of the human body at the end of the last century and at present, territorial distribution of the variations in weight, biacromial diameter, thorax circumference, and so on (for the two indicated dates), territorial distribution of the variations of facial di-mensions, territorial distribution of variations of the facial profile (hor-izontal flatness and vertical), color of hair, eyes, skin, growth of beard, and territorial distribution of blood groups (distribution of the frequency of genes).

The title of the last section of the *Atlas* — "Socioeconomic, Cultural, and Medical-Geographical Characteristics of Population" — points to its composite nature. At first glance it might seem that these subjects offer little for the ethnodemographic characteristics of population, but such is not the case at all. This section of the Atlas will show the complexity and many aspects of population, the diversity and interdependence of the social, economic, demographic, and ethnic elements. It is important to select maps carefully — to include only those which will supplement all other sections. The inclusion of any map should be logically justified. It is still possible that maps will be included in the *Atlas* which have no direct bearing on the main subject — a comprehensive ethnodemographic characteristic of population — but there will be some of interest to a wide readership (for example, maps of centers of international and national tourist travel, maps of international fairs or maps of "holy places", and routes of pilgrimages). The composition of the maps in the last section is outlined only preliminarily: it is intended to give cartograms showing the share of the economically active population in the total population, the structure of employment of the economically active population in industry, agriculture, forestry and fishing, the transport system, the social services, and non-material types of activity; cartograms of the literacy and educational levels of the population and the provision of the population with educational establishments of different types; maps and cartograms of the provision of the population with medical service, maps of the areas where diseases are spread by natural carriers, and maps of diseases determined by social causes; and world and regional maps characterizing some features of the way of life (mobility of population, territorial distribution of diets, the spread of different kinds of sports, and so on).

We have described the main tasks of the comprehensive *Atlas of the Population of the World* which is to be compiled in the next few years. We have also enumerated the subjects and groups of maps which are to be prepared for the *Atlas*. Even a cursory review of these subjects makes it clear that the authors will encounter major difficulties, in the first place because of the absence of the necessary information. To compile a map and a cartogram for one or another phenomenon or object, it is necessary to have data for most states of the world. Unfortunately, the level of demographic and ethnic studies in many countries, notwithstanding the substantial achievements registered in recent years, leaves much room for improvement. Suffice to say that up to now no general census of the population has ever been made in Afghanistan,

Ethiopia, some Arab states, and other regions. It is even more difficult to reflect the dynamics of phenomena on maps. We have authentic data for the beginning of the 20th century only for the main countries of Europe and North America. Thus, some subjects cannot be worked out in sufficient detail owing to the lack of the necessary data.

Moreover, so far we have accumulated experience in compiling maps and have carried through the relevant methodological work only for one section of the *Atlas* — the ethnical (in the broad sense). As for other sections, much preliminary work is to be accomplished and many methodological questions have to be solved.

Toponymy and Language
(On the Problem of Differentiating
the Substratum of Geographical
Place-Name Areas)

M. CHLENOV and D. DEOPIK

Language is accepted as one of the most important characteristics of the ethnos. The value of linguistic data for the ethnographic characterization of existing peoples is unquestioned, but they are no less important for studies in the field of ethnogenesis. In that connection two cases may be distinguished: (1) when the language of an extinct people is preserved for us in written memorials; and (2) when such memorials have not been preserved or did not in fact exist.

In the second case, to which our research relates, a number of sources can be found for elucidating the linguistic affiliations of the extinct linguistic community: a foreign linguistic substratum in the vocabulary of the contemporary population and individual words preserved in the written sources of other peoples; but mainly place names.

Study of a linguistic complex according to toponymic[1] data can again be divided into two main streams: (1) when representatives survive of the linguistic family to which the extinct people belonged, in which case the use of etymological studies is justifiable (this is the position with researchers concerned with the ethnogenesis of the population of the North European part of the USSR, where a rich Finno-Ugric substratum has been preserved in place names); and (2) when there is no possibility of forming any substantiated hypothesis about the origin of the extinct peoples. There are also other, more complicated cases when no information has been preserved on the nature (ethnic or linguistic)

First published in *Sovetskaja etnografija*, N3 (1970).
[1]   In Russian usage, the term toponymy (*toponimija*) means the whole of the place names of a certain territory, whereas the term toponymics (*toponimika*) indicates the science that deals with toponyms — Ed.

of the substratum population except the fact of their having been settled in that territory in the past.

In the last case results of no little value can be obtained by means of formant-series analysis of place names, i.e., the establishing and mapping of stable sound combinations characteristic of the particular toponymic area. The most complicated problems arise when it is difficult or impossible to restore this kind of toponymic formant, at least at an early stage of the investigation. In such a situation, it seems to us that the only real characteristic of the extinct language will be the frequency of the distribution of phonemes and their combinations. When there is a concentration of quite numerous frequency characteristics systematically deviating from the modern language, it can be hazarded that some linguistic community existed on that given territory within certain limits or boundaries.

In studying the course of ethnogenesis in Indonesia one frequently comes across this last possibility. The writers have therefore directed their attention to making a detailed analysis of this problem.

Theoretically it can be supposed, when an area of systematic deviation of frequency characteristics has been established, that it reflects the influence of an extinct substratum language or a specific distribution of phonemes in the place names that may be due to various factors, or that this area reflects both the first and the second possibilities. The problem can only be resolved with any certainty by comparing the phoneme frequency structure of the concrete living language and of geographical names undoubtedly created by the speakers of that language. As an hypothesis it can be suggested that the phoneme frequency structure in both cases will be identical. This paper is devoted to testing that assumption. If it is confirmed it would be possible to say that a stable deviation from the phoneme frequency in a definite area is a consequence of the influence of a substratum language, whose sphere of distribution is thus established approximately. Evidence for this hypothesis would enable certain linguistic characteristics of a completely extinct language to be reconstructed. The possible influence of the proto-substratum language is assumed to be slight. After individual areas of systematic deviation had been revealed, they could be taken as the basis for confrontations and comparative analysis.

The testing of the hypothesis of the unity of phoneme structure of language and place names calls for a quite different technique than etymological or formant-series analysis which still predominate in works on toponymics. Studies of the type proposed, employing massive material (ideally everything available), would of necessity rely on statistical methods. The technique itself is especially important for countries where etymological analysis is complicated by the existence of unwritten and consequently little-studied languages, such as in the countries of South-East Asia, Africa, and Latin America.

It must be mentioned here that we come up against the problem of phonetic adaption in work on substratum place names, i.e., the remolding or repronounciation of the sounds of the place names of a foreign linguistic substratum by the modern population. This makes it practically impossible to reconstruct the phoneme structure of the substratum completely since the process of phonetic adaptation is irreversible. Some of the phonemes characteristic of place names of the substratum are adopted by the winning language; the existence of the remainder (but not the nature of their sounds) can be established by means of statistical analysis of place names and is found as a deviation in the frequency of the phonemes concerned from their frequency in the winning language.

To test the hypothesis suggested above, we set up an experiment using material from modern Malay (including both its existing literary forms, Malaysian and Indonesian) and place names of the territories inhabited by Malay-speaking peoples. In choosing Malay from all the languages of the islands of South-East Asia we were guided by the following considerations.

1.   Malay is the most widely distributed language of this region, having already become established in the Middle Ages as the language of communication between the various peoples of Indonesia and since then constantly extended its sphere of influence.

2.   The oldest districts of compact settlement of a monolingual population (of those of a similar kind whose antiquity of settlement can be traced historically) correspond to Malay. It is more realistic to suppose that the difficulties created by a substratum would be minimal in precisely such districts, and correspondingly, there would be the greatest probability of delineating a toponymic substratum area by stable deviations of frequency characteristics in districts of comparatively recent settlement.

3.   An extensive, easily accessible Malay literature exists.

The choice of language also conditioned our choice of the territory from which we took our toponymic material. These were districts inhabited by peoples who considered Malay or one of its dialects their mother tongue, i.e., the Malacca Peninsula, the East coast of Sumatra from Medan to Palembang, Central Sumatra, the Riouw-Lingga archipelago, the islands of Bangka and Billiton, the Anambas and Natuna islands, and the Malay districts of Kalimantan including the territory of the former sultanates of Pontianak, Kotawaringin, Kutai, and Bulungan. The inclusion of the region of Minangkabau in this territory may be considered debatable since some investigators are inclined to consider Minangkabau a separate language, but there is no doubt that it is the closest to Malay of all the Sumatran group languages and is on the vague and blurred boundary between a language and a dialect. In this connection, we considered it permissible to regard Minangkabau provisionally as a dialect of Malay, taking into account that any differences between these two languages would come out in the course of the experiment.

At that stage of our research we avoided analysis of the dialectical differences within Malay since the most important frequency characteristics of the language should also be common to its dialects within the limits of the accepted zone of distribution of Malay.

We processed 721 place names from the territory selected employing the maps of an atlas (*Atlas untuk sekolah landjutan* [Djakarta, 1957]) and 857 words from texts taken from three extracts from the following books:

(1) a passage from H. B. Jasin's *Kesusasteraan Indonesia dimasa Djepang* (Djakarta, 1954), pp. 19–20;

(2) a passage from the novel *Lajar terkembang* by the well-known Indonesian writer T. S. Alisjahabana (cited in *Obraztsy sovremennoj indoneziiskoj prozy* [*Examples of Modern Indonesia Prose*] [Leningrad, 1964], pp. 24–25);

(3) a passage from the fairy tale *Kanchil dan anak-anak memerang* kindly given to us by E. V. Kochanov (this passage was published in the Malaysian literary form of Malay).

These three texts reflect the most important genres of literature (scientific, fiction, and folklore) and can therefore be considered as a rough sampling of language adequate in volume for a phonological investigation and approximately the same size as the place names sample selected.

The sampling of place names from all the available geographical names was made according to the usual requirements for statistical studies of this kind. The problem of whether the sample was representative, i.e., of whether it was sufficiently characteristic of the population, consisted first in determining whether it was of the necessary size and secondly in ensuring that it was a random sampling.

Around 4000 phonemic segments in the place names and approximately as many in the texts were a large enough sample for statistical analysis. We would recall that the classification of a sample as large or small is determined not by its ratio of the size of the population but by its absolute size. In our analysis of the data for districts we worked with small samples, the theory of which is quite well developed. In that connection we would remind readers that the data obtained from samples even of the order of twenty place names would be suitable to characterize the population if the percentage values for various phonemes were sufficiently high.

Since it is assumed in most work on frequency analysis of phoneme structure in various languages that the distribution of the values of the experimentally observed frequencies of any one phoneme around a certain constant frequency (probability) is a normal one, we assumed a normal distribution also for Malay. The phonetic composition of place names is a linguistic phenomenon and the standard for the distribution of probability around the mean should be analogous. The large volume of the samples and the fact that only relatively frequent phonemes were utilized for conclusions enabled us to employ prepared tables of confidence limits for binomial distribution (Bolshov and Smirnov, 1965: 5,2), which considerably lightened the calculations. The legitimacy of the use of a binomial distribution is its approximation to the normal for sufficiently large numbers. For our quite rough calculations it could be taken that frequency approximated probability, since corrections for deviations are only required in a stricter approach. It is intended, of course, to test their approximation on a number of supplementary samples.

As will be seen later, the statistical treatment of the material carried out demonstrated the adequacy of the material adopted as evidence of a correlation of phoneme frequency in the language and its place names. At the same time the need for such an investigation was evident since it gives the possibility of determining the substratum area of place names linked with languages of other families, and it can serve as the basis for reconstructing the phoneme system of the substratum, and it can be employed to analyze languages, like Javanese, for example, that are related to Malay but are quite distinctly different.

The phonological analysis of place names faced us with a problem common to many onomastic exercises — that of recording the place names by some generally accepted system of transcription. Since most place names in Indonesia have found their way on to modern maps through the modern Indonesian and Malaysian variants of Malay, and since these variants are extraordinarily close, we considered it feasible to record the place names we had selected by means of a special transliteration system developed by us (applicable to the graphemes of our sources), approximately the same in character as the phonemic system.

Later we provisionally treated our transliteration units (graphemes) as phonemes of the language, fully realizing that this approach gave no possibility of judging the sound (phonetic character) of the given phonemes. Nevertheless, that did not hamper the work since their acoustic substance was not the subject of our research. Justification of provisional identification of graphemes and phonemes was the sign character of the languages as a whole and the semiotic (phonological) character of the phonemes in particular. It should be noted that phonological analysis on the basis of a study of graphemes is nothing new either in linguistics or toponomy (Lekomtsev, 1964). When working with unwritten or newly written languages (like the majority of those of Indonesia), this approach is legitimate and fruitful.

For the statistical treatment of the material of our samples we employed 80-column punched cards, which were processed on punch card machines (a T-5-M tabulator, a sorter, and a punch) because the indeterminate character of the task itself complicated modelling of it for processing on an electronic computer. The phonemes, syllables,[2] and intersyllabic biphonemic junctions were subjected to statistical analysis. Each was analyzed according to the type of place name, the district in which the place name was found, the possibility of a given place name having been borrowed from a non-Indonesian language, the length of words, and the position of a given element in them. Dependence on one or more of these factors was also investigated. This method enabled an analysis of the main indices interesting us to be made both in relation to each other and in relation to non-linguistic factors. From the results obtained the following model of a punched card was made on which all information about place names was recorded in a digital code.[3]

Columns 1 and 2 were used for coding the number of the district. We split the whole area up into 19 districts according to the historical and administrative divisions of the region. The code numbers increased from north to south.

01	Perlis	10	Johore
02	Penang	11	Central Sumatra

---

[2] The results of the analysis of syllables are omitted since the method of processing them did not differ in principle from the work on phonemes and space does not permit us to set out the concrete results.

[3] The columns of a punched card can carry information written in a digital code (from 0 to 9). The choice of the number of columns is determined by the number of digits needed to code a given element, thus, for example, since the number of phonemes exceeded ten, each one was recorded by a two-digit code number ('a'=03) occupying two columns.

03 Perak
04 Trengganu
05 Kelantan
06 Pahang
07 Selangor
08 Negri Sembilan
09 Malacca

12 Kutai-Bulungan
13 West Kalimantan
14 Bangka-Biliton
15 Palembang
16 Djambi
17 North Sumatra
18 Riouw
19 Kedah

In columns 3 to 5 — the numbers of the place names — the numbering was sequential within each district (for example, Palembang, Bajunglintjir, would be coded as 15001, where 15 is the number of the district [Palembang] and 001 is the number of the place name [Bajunglintjir] in order within that district).

Column 6 is the type of place name. In view of the object of the investigation we did not propose to use a fractional classification of types in it and also decided not to use place names signifying large toponymical objects. The following list of types was used:

1 names of settlements
2 names of islands
3 hydronymy (excluding marine objects)
4 oronymy
5 names of capes
6 names of straits and bays

In columns 7 and 8 — the number of phonemes in a place name — the code number corresponded to the number of phonemes (thus 07 meant seven phonemes, 12 twelve).

Column 9 was for the number of syllables in a place name.

Column 10 was used for the number of root and service morphs in a place name, as follows:

1 one root morph (rm)
2 2 rm
3 3 rm
4 4 rm
5 1 rm and 1 sm (service morph)
6 1 rm and 2 sm
7 2 rm and 1 sm
8 2 rm and 2 sm

9 3 rm and 1 sm
0 3 rm and 2 sm

Column 11 was for the borrowing of a given place name (assigning the word to one linguistic complex or another) as follows:

0 unborrowed place name
1 one element Malay and one Indian
2 one element Malay and one from another Indonesian language
3 borrowed from other Indonesian languages
4 one element Malay and one from some other language (e.g., Khmer, Arabic, European, Persian)
5 one element from some other Indonesian language and one element Indian
6 borrowed from Indian languages (Indo-European or Dravidian)
7 borrowed from a non-Indonesian, non-Indian, and non-European language
8 borrowed from a European language
9 others and unknown

It became clear in the course of the work that such a gradation of borrowings was not justified and that its further employment was pointless. First of all, it is often difficult to distinguish purely Malay place names from those that might belong to other Indonesian languages. Futhermore, some separate forms of borrowing were usually represented by too few place names for statistical analysis. And finally, analysis of the phonetic structure of each of the separate types of borrowing was not one of the projects of the exercise. The best means of recording borrowings for such purposes is probably a dichotomous record in which place names belonging to other Indonesian languages would be included among the unborrowed names.

Columns 12 to 31 were used to record the two phonemes at the junction of two syllables in the order in which the syllables occurred (for example, Bajunglintjir — *Bajuŋ-lint'ir*: its intersyllabic junction will be coded as follows: *a — j* by 03–93 where 03 is *a* and 93 is *j*; then *ŋ — l* by 77–10 where 77 is *ŋ* and 10 is *l*, etc.).

Columns 32 to 55 were employed to code the first word of the place name by syllables: six columns were allotted to each syllable and a system of coding syllables was used by which each syllable independent of its length began in a certain column; in the rare case of a syllable with four phonemes the first two phonemes were coded by a special code number.

For example the syllable *slim* was arbitrarily broken up not into four elements but into three, the phonemes *s* and *l* being coded separately by one code number, *s* as 22 and *l* as 10, and together as *sl* as 98.

Column 56 was a spare.

Columns 57 to 80 were used to code the second word of two-word place names which are widely met in Indonesia. The not very numerous five-syllable undivided place names forming a single word were coded as follows: the fifth syllable was written in the column reserved for the first syllable of the second word.

The following coding can serve as an example:

150011111420039377100299000000000060300933077101202991211000000000

... 0, which is read thus: 15 — Palembang; 001 — the number of the place name in that district; 1 — a settlement; 11 — the number of phonemes in the place name; 4 — the number of syllables in the place name; 2 — two root morphs; 0 — unborrowed; 0393 — the first intersyllabic junction *a — j*; 7710 — the second intersyllabic junction *ŋ — l*; 0299 — the third intersyllabic junction *ŋ — t*; 00000000 are spare places for the intersyllabic junctions of longer place names; 06 is *b*, 03 *a*; 00 are spare places for a third phoneme in the first syllable; 93 is *j*, 30 *u*, 77 *ŋ*, 10 *l*, 12 *i*, 02 *n*, 99 *t*, 12 *i*, 11 *r*; 0000000...0 are spare columns for a second word where it exists (not present in this case). As a result we read the place name, the town of Bajunglintjir (*Bajuŋlint'ir*).

The punched card model for the words of the text was drawn up on the same principles. In columns 1 and 2 instead of the district, the name of the text was coded, and in column 6 instead of the type of place name, the membership of the given word in a definite syntactical category was recorded.

Each place name and each word of the text was coded on a separate card.

To begin with the whole stack of cards was processed on a sorter for each concrete task. For example, the task was posed of sorting out all unborrowed place names and putting them into a definite order (for technical convenience not corresponding with alphabetical order) according to the first phoneme and according to the type of place name. This whole operation took a minute and a half to two minutes on the sorter for a stack of 721 punched cards. As a result the material was grouped according to three criteria for a set of around 800 place names that would have taken much longer by hand, and the correlational link between them was established. A quantitative evaluation of this link was obtained after the sorted cards had been processed on the tabulator, an operation which took another six or seven minutes. The answers obtained (for example, a predominance of certain phonemes in unborrowed place names in a particular district or group of districts) were printed out by the tabulator in tabular form, so that subtotals could be taken simultaneously for several criteria. The printed table was a standard list of phonemes with indications of their numbers in the whole territory, their occurrence in certain regions, their number in a given region, their membership of a particular type of place name and their number by types of place name. By resorting to other types of sorting and commutating on the tabulator we can also obtain other characteristics, e.g., the number of syllables, territories, and length of words.

The number of numerical characteristics obtained cannot by itself serve as the basis for any kind of interpretation since the number of place names varied in the different districts and the statistical reliability of the quantitative data was thus not uniform.

For collation it was necessary to employ relationships (in our case percentages) and not absolute figures, but percentages by themselves have no statistical significance since 50 per cent has a quite different degree of reliability in a sample of four place names and in one of 200 as regards evaluation of the total universe of place names in a designated territory.

It therefore proved necessary to introduce the concept of confidence interval. The confidence interval is an interval within which there is a given probability that it contains a given population parameter as the mean. For example, in our sample for Central Sumatra, 17.6 per cent of the place names turned out to begin with an initial b. For all the place names of this district (no matter how many there were), the confidence interval indicated that the lower limit was 11.3 per cent and the upper 23.3 per cent (with a probability of 0.95).

To determine confidence intervals we employed Bolshov and Smirnov's tables of the confidence intervals of binomial distribution already referred to.

By comparing the confidence intervals of the percentages of one phoneme in the same position in various combinations, we found a significant difference both between the place names and texts as a whole, and between the place names of the various districts and groups of districts.

When the largest (upper) confidence limit of one of the groups compared proved to be less than the least (lower) limit of another group, we assumed that the percentage of that phoneme in the group was significantly higher than its percentage in the second group (and vice versa), indicated by + + (or ——).

When confidence intervals partially coincided, but the observed significance of one group was less than the lower confidence limit of the other group, *the difference was noted but was not considered significant* until the statistical base was augmented, and the difference was marked by a single + or — sign. Such findings have significance for further investigations and can also be employed when grouping districts.

When there was no such difference, the compared percentages were considered practically identical, and were marked by a zero.

The significant deviations and coincidences thus revealed are also material the interpretation of which can give reliable conclusions for constructions of one kind or another in the fields of toponymics, history, ethnography, and linguistics. It may be recalled that no conclusions were drawn from rarely encountered phonemes.

In relation to our task this meant determining whether there were differences in the distribution of phonemes, syllables, and intersyllabic junctions in the Malay place names and text in order, as remarked above, to have a reliable basis for reconstructing the pre-Malay phonetic complexes on the territory now occupied by Malays. This meant distinguishing groups that had no essential differences and those that did. As regards the second group it was also necessary to distinguish whether the cause of the differences lay in the specifics of the place names or in certain non-phonetic regularities which, if taken into account, would eliminate the differences.

By compiling a table of the appropriate frequencies (Table 1), we tried to check our suggestion that the specifics of the text and of the place names complicated comparison of the phoneme composition of the one or the other. As will be seen, frequency by initial phoneme showed significant differences, although even here twelve of the twenty-five phonemes did not display any difference, three gave an insignificant difference, and only ten showed essential differences and among these there were phonemes of both high and low frequency of occurrence. This is quite natural since both the place names and the text have certain specific elements whose frequency is higher than the frequency of employment of root morphs. Comparison of the total frequency of concrete phonemes from place names and text became possible after taking these elements into account. Strict differentiation of these elements requires further treatment on a general theoretical level; as regards our task, the problem was decided on the following grounds.

1. Indonesian place names often include designations of the character of the geographical object ('water', 'river', 'mountain', etc.) and words

characterizing its quality ('new', 'old', 'high', 'favorite', etc.). We call both of these categories toponymical *determinative* when they had a quite high frequency in the names taken as a sample (five cases as a preposition and three as a postposition). The difference in frequency is the consequence of the features of Indonesian place names in which postpositions are seldom encountered.

2. For the text we considered it necessary to take account of the various service morphs and other phenomena that are not encountered in practice in place names. They include, above all, verb and substantive affixes, phonetic changes of stem in conjunction with an affix (place names do not employ affixes as a rule), pronouns, and prepositions.

Both of these prepositions have a distinguishing sense only when there is a considerable frequency that could influence the outcome of the experiment we had undertaken. The singling out of the elements concerned from the texts and place names facilitated their reduction to a comparable form and the formation of comparable phoneme-frequency complexes, which (lacking their specific features in each case) were most amenable to comparison.

Both complexes were reduced to comparative form by means of the procedure just outlined. The results obtained are given in Table 2, from which it will be seen that the frequencies of the majority of phonemes of the toponymic complex and the text either coincide (11 out of 21) or differ only slightly (seven out of 21); only three of the original list of non-coincident phonemes in Table 1 remained (h, k, o).

Initial phonemes were taken for comparison; lack of space prevents presentation of the data on the other phonemes, although it is technically feasible to compare them. Initial phonemes, which are the least affected by the laws of phonetic combinations in languages and which are not assimilated by preceding phonemes, seemed the most representative group for our first experiment. According to the preliminary data, comparison of the phonemes in the second position in a syllable, which are mainly rare vowels, gives fewer differences between place names and text than initials. The same was also true of final syllables whose phoneme structure is subject to definite phonetic limitations, the essence of which will be outlined below. In addition, our choice of initials as a first example was also influenced by the fact that they are often linked with definite morphological elements (prefixes, etc.), which at first glance should cause a quite large divergence in comparisons of the two complexes studied. This possibly also explains the discrepancies preserved, as already mentioned, after processing of the complexes (Table 2), although the results of the processing to date has shown the procedure used to be productive and gives us grounds for hoping that its refinement will also remove these discrepancies. Perhaps the discrepancies can be explained in part by defects in the initial transcription, and in particular by mistaken determination of whether a given word or place name was indigenous or borrowed;[4] it is not excluded that they may also be interpretable on the basis of the specific features of one district or another.

It was also considered advisable to analyze the composition of biphonemic intersyllabic junctions,[5] since it has been suggested that they are less affected by phonetic assimilation than intrasyllabic combinations and that a greater preservation of substratum elements could therefore be expected in them. In that case, when the discrepancy is not significant, there would be a real possibility of reconstructing elements of the phonetics of the substratum from the data of toponymic survivals.

The experiment carried out showed that the frequency of the distribution of intersyllabic junctions did not form a system (Table 3). Not only in the comparison of place names and text was no correspondence observed in the frequency of definite junctions but also even in comparison of those in the words of the text (between the first and second syllables on the one hand, and between the second and third syllables on the other hand) within the limits of a single stack. Without going into the possible interpretations, which are outside our terms of reference, we would say that these frequency characteristics could not be used within the framework of our experiment because junctions, while more numerous than phonemes, have a low frequency in our material. The junctions themselves could be the object of a qualitative comparison and as such present definite interest. The set of junctions itself has already proved to be uniform and stable both for place names and for texts, which is evidence that in this case both place names and language reflect existing linguistic patterns in equal degree. In addition lists of junctions specific to place names and to the texts were compiled. Further work may reduce them by eliminating junctions still seldomly met; at the same time the specific character of the appurtenance of certain of them is obvious. A means of comparing the junctions it is suggested, could be to evaluate them by the "valency" of the syllable's auslaut. By valency we mean the capacity of the auslaut of a syllable to combine with definite anlauts in the syllable that follows. Both complexes display a significant similarity as regards valency, and this similarity shows up above all in

---

[4]   This arose from the absence of specialized etymological dictionaries of the Malay language and Malay place names.
[5]   In debatable cases the division of syllables was made in accordance with the scheme proposed by A. P. Pavlenko in his paper (Pavlenko, 1967: 117–25).

a comparatively small set of phonemes in the first position of the inter-syllabic junction. The limited size of the set is a consequence of the known laws of language; it is of importance that these laws operate in the same degree both in the language and in the place names. As an example we cite the list of phonemes that cannot be final in a syllable either in Malay itself or in Malay place names: *k, b, p, l, d, w, t', *d', *ń, f,* and *j.*

The appearance of one of these phonemes in the place names of any district can only be the consequence of the effect of a substratum or a later borrowing.

The experiment outlined was carried out with the aim of clarifying the degree of correspondence in the frequencies of phonological indices in Malay language place names and Malay literary texts. The statistical treatment of the mass material on punch card machines had made it possible to affirm the following:

1. the frequency of individual phonemes (according to their position in a syllable and a word) coincides in general outline in place names and language;

2. the frequencies of intersyllabic junctions are not stable and are variously expressed both in the complexes compared and within each complex itself;

3. the set of junctions itself is relatively stable in both place names and text;

4. discrepancies in the frequency of different phonemes and differences in the choice of intersyllabic junctions between a concretely studied language and place names compel one to suppose a foreign origin for those place names;

5. where it is impossible to relate the given difference to any factor except a substratum (i.e., when the existence of direct borrowings, ad-stratum, or superstratum language is excluded), it becomes possible roughly to determine the geographical area of distribution of the language concerned (which is particularly important for vanished languages), and to give a certain approximate evaluation of its phonetic structure.

Since a similarity of phoneme frequency in place names and the language of their creation adequate to our purpose can be considered established, it will be sufficient in future to compare the place names of any closed monolingual area with a part of the same toponymic complex, taking it that average frequency indices of a certain area reliably reflect the language of the area, and considering concrete regional, or simply marked, divergences from the average as traces of a substratum.[6] The results of the present work make it possible to affirm that the phonetic peculiarities discovered in any toponymic complex by this means cannot be explained away at the cost of the phonetic specificity of place names within the language forming them, and are the consequence of the influence of another language.

Table 1. *Frequency of Initial Phonemes in Place Names and Texts* (ignoring the specific features of each group)

Phoneme	Place Names			Texts			Evaluation
	Min	%	Max	Min	%	Max	
b	12.8	15.6	18.2	6.2	8.1	10.0	+ +
s	11.7	14.4	16.9	8.8	10.9	13.0	+
k	10.5	13.2	15.5	5.4	7.2	9.0	+ +
t	9.5	11.9	14.3	5.9	7.7	9.5	+ +
m	8.9	11.2	13.5	10.3	12.6	14.9	0
p	7.5	9.7	11.9	7.6	9.6	11.6	0
l	3.8	5.5	7.2	1.8	2.9	4.0	+
a	3.5	5.1	6.7	4.7	6.4	8.1	0
r	2.2	3.6	4.8	0.1	0.5	1.0	+ +
g	0.8	1.8	2.8	0.1	0.4	0.7	+ +
d'	0.8	1.8	2.8	0.6	1.4	2.2	0
d	0.7	1.7	2.7	10.9	13.2	15.5	− −
n	0.3	1.0	1.7	0.1	0.7	1.3	0
i	0.1	0.8	1.5	5.0	6.7	8.4	− −
t'	0.1	0.8	1.5	0.1	0.6	1.1	0
u	0.1	0.6	1.2	0.1	0.5	1.0	0
w	0	0.3	0.7	0	0.2	0.5	0
ə	0	0.3	0.7	0.1	0.6	1.1	0
ń	0	0.1	0.3	0	—	0.2	0
o	0	0.1	0.3	0.6	1.4	2.2	− −
h	0	0.1	0.3	2.6	3.8	5.1	− −
ŋ	0	0.1	0.3	0	—	0.2	0
j	0	—	0.2	3.0	4.4	5.8	− −
e	0	—	0.2	0	0.2	0.5	−
f	0	—	0.2	0	0.1	0.3	0

[6]   By means of a similar procedure the area of an ethnic substratum has been delineated in the Central Moluccas (Chlenov, 1969: 17–20).

Table 2. *Frequency of Initial Phonemes in Place Names and Texts* (taking the specific features of each group into account)

Phoneme	Place Names				Texts				Evaluation
	n	Min	%	Max	n	Min	%	Max	
b	54	10.6	14.2	17.8	31	9.5	14.2	17.8	0
s	53	10.4	13.9	17.4	18	4.5	8.2	11.9	+
k	50	9.8	13.1	16.4	12	2.4	5.5	8.6	++
t	49	9.5	12.9	16.3	24	6.8	11.0	15.2	0
m	40	7.4	10.5	13.6	11	2.1	5.0	7.9	+
p	42	7.8	11.0	14.2	18	4.5	8.2	11.9	0
l	23	3.6	6.0	8.4	16	3.8	7.3	10.8	0
a	11	1.2	2.9	4.6	13	2.7	5.9	9.1	0
r	15	1.9	3.9	5.9	3	0	1.4	3.0	+
g	7	0.4	1.8	3.2	3	0	1.4	3.0	0
d'	9	0.8	2.4	4.0	2	0	0.9	2.2	+
d	11	1.2	2.9	4.6	14	3.1	6.4	9.7	−
n	5	0.1	1.3	2.5	1	0	0.5	1.5	0
i	1	0	0.3	0.9	5	0.3	2.3	4.3	−
t'	3	0	0.8	1.7	2	0	0.9	2.2	0
u	4	0	1.0	2.0	4	0	1.8	3.6	0
w	—	0	—	0.6	—	0	—	0.9	0
n	1	0	0.3	0.9	—	0	—	0.9	0
o	—	0	—	0.6	10	1.8	4.6	7.4	−−
h	1	0	0.3	0.9	26	7.5	11.8	16.1	−−
j	—	0	—	0.6	—	0	—	0.9	0
e	—	0	—	0.6	2	0	0.9	2.2	−
f	—	0	—	0.6	—	0	—	0.9	0
ŋ	—	0	—	0.6	—	0	—	0.9	0
ə	2	0	0.5	1.2	—	0	—	0.9	0
Σ381					Σ219				

Table 3. *Frequency of First Intersyllabic Junction in Place Names and Texts**

Junction**	Place Names			Texts	Evaluation	Junction	Place Names			Texts	Evaluation
	Min	%	Max	%			Min	%	Max	%	
m–p	2.2	4.0	5.8	1.2	+	i–a	0	0.7	1.5	1.8	—
a–b	0.7	2.0	3.3	0.8	0	i–d	0	0.2	0.4	3.9	—
a–k	0	0.9	1.8	2.0	—	i–n	0	0.2	0.4	1.4	—
a–t	3.2	5.3	7.4	3.2	0	i–j	0	0.4	1.0	4.3	—
a–p	0.2	1.3	2.4	2.0	0	u–b	0.8	2.2	3.6	0.8	0
a–l	1.4	3.1	4.8	3.7	0	u–m	0.1	1.1	2.1	—	—
a–r	1.4	3.1	4.8	1.8	0	u–l	0.7	2.0	3.3	1.2	0
a–d	0.5	1.7	2.9	2.4	0	u–a	5.0	7.5	10.0	1.6	+
a–n	0.1	1.1	2.1	3.0	—	u–d'	0	0.6	1.3	1.2	0
a–i	1.8	3.5	5.2	—	+	ʉ–h	0	—	0.6	1.0	—
a–w	0.1	1.1	2.1	—	+	u–ŋ	1.6	3.3	5.0	—	+
a–ń	0	—	0.6	1.2	—	o–r	0	—	0.6	1.6	—
a–h	0	0.6	1.3	1.0	0	ŋ–k	1.9	3.7	5.5	0.2	+
a–j	0.3	1.5	2.7	—	+	ə–b	0.5	1.8	3.1	2.2	0
a–mb	0.1	1.1	2.1	—	+	ə–s	0	0.9	1.8	1.4	0
r–s	0	—	0.6	1.4	—	ə–k	0.2	1.3	2.4	1.8	0
r–t	0	—	0.6	1.6	—	ə–t	0	0.6	1.3	1.0	0
n–t	1.3	2.9	4.5	0.4	+	ə–m	0.1	1.1	2.1	3.4	—
n–d'	1.3	2.9	4.5	0.4	+	ə–l	2.6	4.6	6.6	2.2	+
n–d	1.6	3.3	5.0	2.6	0	ə–r	2.4	4.4	6.4	1.4	+
i–s	0	—	0.6	1.0	—	ə–n	0.1	1.1	2.1	2.2	—
i–k	0	0.4	1.0	1.2	—	ə–n'	0	—	0.6	2.2	—
i–t	0	—	0.6	6.7	—	ə–n'	0	0.6	1.3	4.1	—
i–l	0.5	1.7	2.9	1.0	0	ə–mb	0.3	1.5	2.7	—	+

* For considerations of space only those intersyllabic junctions are given in the table whose frequency in one of the complexes compared is not less than 1 per cent.
** Differences are only given when the confidence interval of the percentage for place names does not overlap the observed value of the percentage for the text.

PART III

ANTHROPOLOGY

Problems of Anthropogenesis
and General Questions of Anthropology

Patterns in the Links between Characteristics in Anthropology

Ya. ROGINSKIJ

The theme of my communication cannot, of course, be said to be close to the interests of D. N. Anuchin, but some justification can be found for its choice in the intense treatment of the subject by anthropologists belonging in some degree or another to Anuchin's school. The broad significance of the theme, moreover, could not but affect the thinking of Anuchin himself. It is no accident that V. V. Vorobjev, in an article in one of the first numbers of *Russkij antropologicheskij zhurnal* on the ratio of the main dimensions of the human head and face to height, named Anuchin among the authors who had established the natural lag of the relative size of the circumference of the chest with increase of stature, and in particular his well-known work on the geographical distribution of height among the male population of Russia (1889). Anuchin himself, in one of his program articles, wrote about knowledge of the interconnection between the bodily and spiritual varieties of human kind (Anuchin, 1900).

It is hardly necessary to say that I must restrict myself to only a small fraction of the vast subject matter of my theme. I shall therefore speak mainly about Russian and Soviet works and shall begin with a short excursion into the history of the problem of links in human and animal morphology.

First published in *Sovetskaja etnografija*, N5 (1962).
This paper was originally read on 20 December, 1961, at a memorial session of the Moscow University Institute and Museum of Anthropology devoted to the work of Academician D. I. Anuchin.

CORRELATIONS IN GENERAL MORPHOLOGY

Geoffry St. Hilaire, in his search for evidence of the unity of the animal kingdom, advanced four rules or principles: (1) the theory of analogues; (2) the principle of connections; (3) the principle of the selective likeness of organic elements; and (4) the principle of the compensation of organs. The second and fourth of these principles have direct bearing on our theme. The principle of connections consists of this: the criterion of the identity of organs in various groups of animals cannot be either their form or function which are extraordinarily variable, but their disposition, relationship, and interconnection. The principle of equilibrium is that no organ increases or diminishes in volume without a proportionate change in some other organ belonging to the same system or connected with the first organ. As Amlinsky has rightly said, it is a matter which in evolutionary morphology came later to be called 'morphogenetic correlations' (Amlinskij, 1955).

Much greater fame, however, is enjoyed in the history of science by the theory of correlation of St. Hilaire's contemporary and opponent Georges Cuvier, who took his stand on the "principle of conditions of existence", i.e., on the need for the parts of a creature to serve the good of the whole. From this principle flowed Cuvier's statement that all the organs of an animal form a single system, the parts of which are connected and act together and against each other, and that no change in any part could come about without its leading to corresponding changes in all the others (cit. after Shmalgauzen, 1939). The positive value of his view was that it indicated the vital significance of the adaptability of the organism to its environment, which constituted, as it were, a single whole with it. Cuvier's denial of the idea of evolution could only lead to confusing the various types of connection. Not admitting the possibility of historically evolved interdependencies between organisms or characters, he considered all correlations to be functional. Since that is not so, Cuvier, by deferring the possibility of understanding the functional, inner, necessary connection of the parts of an organism, was bound in fact to be satisfied with empirically obtained facts of the simple existence of the properties of the separate parts within an organ or within the organism as a whole.

We find a different conception of correlation in Darwin. He examined this question in great detail in Chapter XXV of his work *The Variation of Animals and Plants under Domestication* (1900) in which he specially analyzed the laws of coordinated or correlative variability. Darwin had already fully realized that the essence of the connections between the parts of an organism was profoundly varied. Thus, at the beginning of the chapter he wrote: "... in large groups of animals certain structures always coexist, for instance, a peculiar form of stomach with teeth of peculiar form, and such structures may in one sense be said to be correlated. But these cases have no necessary connection with the law to be discussed in the present chapter; for we do not know that the initial or primary variations of the several parts were in any way related: slight modifications or individual differences may have been preserved, first in one and then in another part, until the final and perfectly co-adapted structure was acquired" (Darwin, v. II, 1900: 301).

Here the correlations within and between groups are quite obviously opposed to one another. As regards *intragroup* correlations, Darwin spoke in detail about certain laws governing them. He pointed out the influence exercised on other organs by an organ that had been altered at an early embryonal period, the connection between adjacent parts, the determining influence of the whole mass of the body on its different parts, the tendency of homologous parts to change in the same direction when they develop in similar conditions, the correlated variation of skin and its appendages, and so on. His views on the relationship between evolution and correlative variation are well known. He suggested that useless characters might be reinforced in the structure of a species if they were correlatively related to another useful one, "encouraged" by natural selection.

A distinction between physiological and individual correlation on the one hand and phyletic correlation on the other hand was introduced by Plate (Plate, 1910), to whom we also owe the differentiation between functional and idioplasmic correlations. The work of A. N. Severtsov was of great significance in developing the problem further. In his theory of monophyletic evolution, Severtsov substantiated and developed the proposition that parallel with the evolution of primary adaptive variations there is an evolution of correlative characteristics functionally linked with them, of which some are useful and others may be indifferent (Severtsov, 1939).

It is quite understandable that Severtsov's interests were concentrated on elucidating those correlations that had been called phyletic. Instead of 'phyletic correlation' he proposed 'coordination' with the aim of introducing order into the system of terms for the various types of connection, which had become complicated by the different meanings given to the word 'correlation' in the works of Beher, Dürken, and Dombrovsky. Severtsov divided coordinations into two kinds, (a) morphological and (b) topographic, saying that the relation between morphologically and topographically coordinated organs, i.e., "between the two links of the coordination chain, could vary in different ways in the course of evolution" (Severtsov, 1939: 447).

Whereas Severtsov was interested in the problem of phyletic correlations, analysis of the links between parts within a separate individual became the object of investigations in other fields, mainly in experimental embryology, biometry, and genetics. The brilliant work of the embryologists threw light on the formative processes in the development of the eye in vertebrates, and the organogenesis of the otocyst and periotic capsule, and demonstrated the mutual effect of their laying down on the development of the axial organs. The role of Russian embryologists, headed by D. P. Filatov, in studying and proving the existence of an interaction of the parts in organogenesis should be specially noted, and in particular their bringing out of the fact that a "passive" part is not inert in the determinant process but influences the determining part.

A quite different approach to the study of the internal connections between characteristics, both in method and in aims, was adopted in biometry. It was much less suitable than the experimental approach for understanding the direct causes of form derivation but enabled one to judge the quantitative extent of the interconnections between dimensional and descriptive characters within a homogeneous population. As an example of this research I would cite the work of V. V. Alpatov on insects, fish, and birds.

Finally, in genetics the link between characteristics has been mainly studied in the phenomenon of pleiotropy, but also in those of linkage and crossing over.

From 1935 on, J. J. Shmalgauzen devoted a major place in a number of researches to the problem of the significance of correlation in the evolution of animals. To him belongs the credit for the synthesis in the problem we are surveying; he played a major role in developing the general theory of connections in which he based himself on both the experimental and the historical approach. Shmalgauzen considered it necessary to stress that biological thinking has only a dynamic understanding of correlation; he assigned importance to statistics only as a method of research and not as a concept of theoretical biology. By 'correlation' Shmalgauzen understood only those relationships that existed between the organs of a developing individual. Relationships between organs of an evolutionary type he called 'coordinations' (following A. N. Severtsov). 'Correlations' he divided into genomic, morphogenetic, and ergontic, in accordance with the factors of ontogenesis: the first were directly conditioned by inherited factors, the second were the interdependences determined by internal factors of development and created the general structural plan of the organism, and the third type consisted of dependencies called into being by functional relationships — they mainly regulated the coordinated development of the finer structures in the post-embryonal period. 'Coordinations' were divided according to the character of the connections between the parts and organs into topographic (after A. N. Severtsov), dynamic, and biological. The first were expressed in the spatial relations between organs that had no direct functional relationship; dynamic 'coordinations', on the contrary, were expressed in dependent changes in the relations, magnitude, and forms of functionally linked parts or organs. Biological coordinations were expressed in relationships depending on the environment and not directly on one another; they were easily disturbed by leaving a given environment.

All forms of interdependence were established, in Shmalgauzen's view, by the effect of natural selection and coordinations were exclusively established through it. They all had significance in the course of evolution, their significance being qualitatively varied. Topographic coordinations operated to some extent as a conservative basis; dynamic ones ensured the viability of form in the sense of "harmony of the parts", while biological coordinations expressed the correlation of organs with respect to the external environment.

Shmalgauzen considered that new dynamic coordinations had the greatest significance in the process of aromorphic evolution, and biological coordination played a decisive role in adaption (Shmalgauzen, 1939). It should be noted that Shmalgauzen recognized only a limited significance for the correlations studied in biometry, which in our view play an important role in anthropology.

CORRELATION IN ANTHROPOLOGY

I shall not dwell on individual works on the calculation of correlations between the dimensions of the human body although their theoretical and applied value is great. The scale of the research of this kind at the Moscow University Institute of Anthropology is particularly great in the field of anthropological standardization. Here, however, we are solely concerned with research in which light has been thrown on the more theoretical problems relating to the connection between characters. First let me mention the work of E. M. Chepurkovskij on the geographical distribution of head shape (Chepurkovskij, 1913).

In his work Chepurkovskij (1902) wrote of the need to differentiate interracial correlations strictly from intraracial ones. Because of the importance of this proposition regarding evaluation of the significance of systematic characters, let me cite Chepurkovskij's own words: "There is a certain possibility of judging the relative significance of characters through comparing their interracial and intraracial correlation, without posing the question of their physiological significance. And when, we suggest, there is a relationship between characters 'a' and 'b' in a member of a race such that 'a' increases at the same time as 'b', and if the same is observed in other members of other races, that is an *intraracial* correlation, perhaps a simple anatomical, physiological dependence. But suppose we have determined the average values of 'a' and 'b' in a significant number of separate groups of humanity. Then, by determining the relationship between these average values of the groups, we may find that 'a' increases simultaneously with 'b', or diminishes, or remains unchanged. In the first case the interracial correlation coincides with the intraracial one, but in the other two the processes that formed the race destroyed it (the correlation — Ja. R.) or even completely distorted it.

"I suggest that we should consider as real racial characteristics only those in which the two correlations do not coincide, because when they do we then have a simple interracial relation extended, so to speak, between races, and when they do not, then these relationships have been outrun by the processes that formed the race." (Chepurkovskij, 1913: 3).

The work of V. V. Bunak occupies a major place in the further development of the problem of correlation between anthropological characters. In 1924 he suggested distinguishing between types as combinations of independent properties and types representing internally connected phenomena of a single common type of physique (Bunak, 1924b). The most characteristic complexes of the first type, i.e., the combinative type, are races. Types of the second complex are characterized by an aggregate of characteristics, inseparably linked together, the source of whose coexistence flows from physiology, and each of which is a partial phenomenon of a single whole. Such constitutions are functional. Bunak developed the fundamental differences between physique and races in greater detail in a work of 1928 (Bunak, 1928a) in which he distinguished nine types according to muscular tonus and fat deposition. In 1940 he again returned to this division in work (Bunak, 1940) in which with even greater clarity and precision both of the content of the concepts analyzed and of the terminology employed, he distinguished between historical correlation on the one hand and mechanical, ontogenetic correlation on the other. Historical correlations develop between 'daughter' groups descended from a group of bearers of the given properties which had arisen in them at a definite historical moment through the combination of mutually independent mutations. These links, according to Bunak, can be called racial-systematic or historical. They show up in intergroup comparisons and express no physiological relationships. One can therefore only speak of them as constitutional. True constitutional connections between characters are marked, in Bunak's view, by having a single trend within the most varied groups and by preserving a single sign of correlation. An example is the relationship between the mass and length (weight and height) of the body.

In the kind of uniform, intragroup connection conditioned by the mechanics of the development and inevitable in character, habitus complexes can be distinguished, according to Bunak. From an analysis of the techniques of constitutional typology and extensive material, Bunak formulated many patterns of intragroup connections, of which we shall cite the most important: individuals differing in absolute height also differ in bodily proportions; an increase in the vertical dimension of the body also shows in an increase in those of the face and nose and in the length of the longitudinal axis of the head; fat deposition and musculature strongly affect a whole complex of descriptive characters, viz. shape of the back, belly, and chest, carriage, etc.; there is little connection between these two characters (fat deposition and musculature); individuals differing in fat deposition or musculature are almost indistinguishable as regards bodily proportions (a thesis that rests, in particular, on the special research of P. N. Bashkirov [1937]); increase of the fat layer is linked with a reduction of stature and an increase of the muscle layer with an increase in stature; three characters determine habitus (i.e., the morphological component of constitution), viz. fat deposition, musculature and absolute height; twenty-seven different combinations can be distinguished according to their permutations, but nine when the secondary significance of height is taken into account; functional features most common for the organism as a whole are linked with metabolism in particular with carbohydrate-fat metabolism on the one hand and water-salt (mineral) metabolism on the other; nine diathetic types are obtained corresponding to the nine habitus types; their correspondence also permits one to speak of types of constitution. I would note that Zenkevich's works (Zenkevich, 1937; 1940) are of great significance for an understanding of water-mineral metabolism and its links with bone structure. The relationship between increase of the general dimensions of the body and uneven growth of its parts, formulated in the last century by Hiss and subsequently studied in detail by Huxley (1932), was the subject of Bunak's special research into the postnatal onto-genesis of man. He surveyed the relative growth of the organs of the various systems, the relative growth of the longitudinal dimensions of the body and of the structural elements of the various organs, including their histostructure (Bunak, 1958). Bunak classed variations of hetero-geneous growth in the human constitution as simply subsidiary cha-racters.

A. A. Malinovskij, whose research was an important contribution to the subject under consideration, assigned a much greater role to hetero-geneous growth as a constitutional property. He first published his views in 1935 in his candidate's dissertation on the theme of the significance of correlations in the theory of physique. His main publications on the subject belong to the late 1940's (Malinovskij, 1945, 1948).

Malinovskij's contribution consisted above all in the depth, precision, and diversity of his analysis of statistical correlations in connection with the problem of constitution. It was he who threw light on the essence of statistical correlations in regard to this problem, contrasted multibase and elementary correlations, and showed that the permanence and stabi-lity of typical correlations in all populations were characteristic precisely of elementary correlations. In the more complex forms of connection the permanence of correlations was easily disturbed. Malinovskij con-vincingly demonstrated that it was impossible to account for correlations through linkages, and that linkages cannot ensure permanent correlation of characters because the distributions of genes, however large the gene linkage, even in the limited case of crossing over, and with it also of the characters within the range, would tend towards an independent dis-tribution, i.e., to abrogation of the correlation. Malinovskij also ad-vanced interesting considerations against the hypothesis that the corre-lation of characters in typical build could be accounted for by an original pleiotropy of inherited features. It was much sounder to ascribe a purely physiological character to this correlation, including physiological devel-opment in the concept as well. Malinovskij singled out the following variations (suggesting that there might be more) as the two fundamental coordinates: a leptosome-eurysomatic coordinate (the same as the as-thenic-pyknic) and a cerebral-athletic coordinate. A dissimilation-as-similation ratio underlies the first and phenomena of heterogeneous growth the second. Both coordinates were independent of one another. Malinovskij summarized the data of a great many authors who had characterized the types distinguished by them from a morphological or a functional aspect. In his factual substantiation of the independence of variations of both basic coordinates, Malinovskij was helped in some measure by my researches covering more than 500 persons and carried out in 1929–30 at the Central Psychophysiological Laboratory of the Red Army.[1] It should be noted that Malinovskij did not in the least deny the existence, in addition to the two main ones, of various other coordinates calling for special research.

CERTAIN PROBLEMS OF THE STUDY OF CORRELATIONS IN ANTHROPOLOGY

From our short survey of the history of study of the laws of the connections between characters one gets the impression that there is a main line, running from Darwin's passing remarks to the research of present-day morphologists, that divides correlations into the historical and the morphophysiological. The significance of this division is great and is seen of various fields of anthropology. Thus, in racial studies, it is obviously important to be able to distinguish race as a complex of many different independent features from physiques as phenomena of one or two definite properties. It is also quite essential in problems of anthropogenesis to be guided by analogous principles when characterizing stages. An example of the mistakes made by some anthropologists is the demarcation of the man of the late paleolithic as an independent stage of morphological evolution sharply differentiated from humanity as it now exists, on the grounds that he possessed a rather lower cranial vault. This feature, which in fact is characteristic of certain varieties of man at the beginning of the late paleolithic, is revealed in several indices (height/longitudinal; height/cross-section; cranial height index; the bregmatic angle, etc.), but because of that the relative height of the vault does not in fact cease to be a characteristic; in no case can it be evaluated from the point of view of its stadial significance as something coinciding

---

[1] In 1921 the writer read a paper to the Student Anthropological Circle of Moscow University on "Adults Who Resemble Children", in which he attempted to draw a connection between morphological types and psychic traits. Ernst Kretschmer's *Body Physique and Character* also appeared in 1921. The problem obviously arose of how far both lines of variation coincided, i.e., the line from "childish" type of "adult" described by me and the line from asthenic type of pyknic described by Kretschmer. My research of 1929–1930 at the Red Army Laboratory showed that the two lines were mutually independent. I only managed to publish my results in 1937, i.e., six years after my departure from the Laboratory. I had not concerned myself then or since with the theory of physique. The credit for constructing and substantiating the theory of the two main coordinates of the human physique is Malinovskij's alone. My attention in those years was exclusively centered on the problem of the links between body structure and character.

with the whole complex distinguishing modern man from *Palaeoanthropus*.

On the other hand, knowledge of the intragroup correlation saves one from needless quests for special adaptive significance in the properties of a certain organ when the latter may have arisen simply as a side effect of the adaptive reconstructions of some other organ. So, I suggest, the view expressed by V. P. Alexeev presents methodological interest (without prejudging the correctness of his conclusions about the essence of the problem of the evolution of the hand), namely, his idea that the hand of *Palaeoanthropus* became extremely broad not because its width was useful to its possesser but because of the functional morphogenetic correlation with the foot; the hand became broad after the foot, and the foot became broad in consequence of the need to acquire stability of upright posture (Aleksejev, 1960).

In addition to these conclusions, however, which follow from the principle of the division of correlations into historical and functional, there are many other general and partial laws relating to the connections between characters that are of great value in anthropology. In what follows, I shall speak mainly about intragroup correlations.

One must first of all point out the great value attaching to the development of methods of studying correlations as such. Not being a specialist in this field I can only remind you that these methods were rigorously developed at the Moscow University Institute of Anthropology by M. V. Ignatjev and his co-workers A. V. Pugacheva and E. I. Fortunatova, and are being developed at present by the young researchers Yu. S. Kurshakova and V. P. Chtetsov. I shall refer briefly to a comparatively recent example of the study of connections, namely what is called factor analysis and analysis of the calculation of vector correlations in Ignatjev's special article (Ignatjev, 1957).

Let me cite several examples illustrating the value of the investigation of correlations for evolutionary human morphology.

In the anthropological literature the following problem is discussed: how far does the closeness of coefficients of correlations in various populations and races go? It is found that their resemblance as a whole is great between the same characters in various groups, provided that the groups are not mechanical mixtures of various components. Vlastovskij obtained extensive material from his research, which indicated that the pattern of connections is similar among vertebrates even in distant systematic units (Vlastovskij, 1958). The various characters, however, behave not quite identically in this respect. Thus the correlation between the lengths of the long bones proves much more constant than that between the diameters of the skull. Analysis of this kind of phenomenon enables one to explain when we are dealing with elementary correlations and when with multibase ones.

There is no doubt that the magnitude of the link between morphological characters depends on the properties of one sort or another of the characters themselves. Vlastovskij's research showed that this dependence is governed by several laws, which are still, incidentally, far from being adequately elucidated.

Above all attention is drawn to the circumstance that the stature or overall height of the body is more strongly correlated with the major longitudinal dimensions of the body than with the minor ones, which also applies to dimensions that are not components of the total length (height) of the body. In other words, this relationship also occurs without involving the 'false correlation'.

Examples are the coefficients of the correlations between stature and the length of the upper limbs (G. A. Chistjakov's data on Ukrainians), between stature and the longitudinal dimensions of the body that are not constituents of stature (Bunak's data on Russians), and between length of the trunk and the longitudinal dimensions of the body (Bunak's data on Russians). In the skull a distinct picture of a fall in the value of the correlation coefficient as the contrasted dimensions diminish is given by the frontal index, i.e., by the relation between bimastoid width and the transverse diameter of the skull (Miklashevskaja's data on the Kirghizes) and between the transverse diameter of the skull and its width (M. G. Levin's data on the Khanti).

The exceptions to this rule are so numerous that one must conclude that other conditions of some kind affect the correlation coefficient apart from span.

Thus the index of the correlation between the lengths of the hand and foot (0.739) (from P. I. Zenkevich's data on Russians) is higher than that for the lengths of the hand and 'sitting vertex height' (0.511). Similar results were obtained in Bunak's studies of Russians (hand/foot index 0.470; hand/trunk index 0.245; hand/stem index 0.274), and in Ya. Ya. Roginskij's studies of Buryats (hand/foot index 0.640; hand/trunk index 0.369; hand/stem index 0.409).

It would seem that as homologous organs, the hand and foot, experience the effect of general factors of some sort influencing their longitudinal dimensions. The high arm/leg indices (r) have the same origin. According to Bunak's data relating to the Russian population r for the length of the leg and stem is 0.283, for the length of the arm and stem 0.360, while the limb coefficient (r for arm and leg) is 0.760.

Does the adjacent position of the measured organs or skeletal elements play a role? Matters would seem to differ in various cases. Thus, the hand is rather better correlated with the forearm than with the upper arm, and the foot with the lower leg than with the thigh (Roginskij's research on the Buryats). For the six series of skeletons studied by the British biometrist Warren it was found that coefficients of non-related and non-homologous long bones of the extremities, i.e., of the femur and radius and of the humerus and tibia, were rather less than those of homologous or related bones. The lowest coefficient (0.57) proved to be the comparison of the clavicle and humerus. In contrast to all these coefficients, high and very high (0.57 to 0.86) variations of the length of the parietal, occipital, and frontal arcs of the skull including the adjacent arcs, prove to be almost mutually independent (Schreiner, v. I, 1939).

Has the morphogenetic community of the bones comprising the skull, i.e., their appurtenance to the covering membrane or the preformed cartilage, any significance? The indices calculated for the small series of Kirghiz skulls measured by Miklashevskaja showed that the topographical relationship in many cases had much more influence on the value of the coefficient than the appurtenance of the bones to a type (i.e., membranous or cartilaginous).

Attention has been drawn to the rather higher correlation between cerebral dimensions and the foot, rather than the leg, although the foot is much shorter than the leg and further from the head. The position is well illustrated, for example, by the figures in the following table.

Coefficient r of the Correlation between the Transverse Diameter of the Head and Length of Leg and Foot

Group	Author	Ratio of transverse diameter of the head	
		and length of leg	and length of foot
Buryats	Ya. Ya. Roginskij	0.195 ± 0.070	0.244 ± 0.066
Russians	P. O. Zenkevich	0.195 ± 0.043	0.269 ± 0.041
Russians	V. V. Bunak	0.087 ± 0.038	—

The same correlations have been obtained by calculating the index for children of three, four, and five years of age:

Age of children	Ratio of transverse diameter of head	
	and length of leg	and length of foot
3 years	0.210	0.287
4 years	0.167	0.316
5 years	0.218	0.254

With children aged six and seven *r* for leg length proved rather higher than for the foot; *r* of the circumference of the head gives a bias toward the foot in both adult groups and in three-, four-, five-, and six year-old children. In seven year-olds only was *r* for the foot 0.407 and for leg length 0.438. Considering the small size of the foot and its topographical distance from the head, one is justified in concluding that there is some special factor slightly heightening the connection between the cerebral part of the head and the foot.

In 1952 in an unpublished paper "On the Correlation of Characters in Adults and their Relation with Ontogenesis", I drew attention to the fact that characters found to be more or less closely linked in adult populations proved similar in that both grew fast during at least some one period of ontogenesis, while characters that had little correlation with one another usually grew strongly, on the contrary, at different periods. Thus it is known that the hands (feet) and cerebral part of the head are large in the foetus at the end of the first and beginning of the second month; consequently they grew more strongly in the preceding period. On the other hand the hips and shoulders continue to grow intensively for several years after both the longitudinal and transverse dimensions of the head have almost ceased to increase.

What here is cause and what consequence? For the present writer it has long been unclear whether it stems from the similarity of the processes of ontogenesis of the two characters or from the value of the correlation between them. How are we to explain that the highest coefficients are those between the characters that simultaneously grow intensively over a long period during ontogenetic development? Do not the length of the skull and width of the nose correlate a little better than facial height and width of the nose because the length of the head and width of the nose are greater in the foetus at a certain period? And are the circumference of the head and length of the foot not more closely linked than the circumference of the head and length of the leg because the brain and the distal links of the limbs grow intensely in the foetus at an early stage? Why is leg length more closely correlated with facial height than with the diameters of the cerebral part of the head? Is it not because the face and legs continue to grow after growth of the brain has ceased? The answer to all these questions, however, is quite different. Coefficients are higher where the morphogenetic connections are closer. And the common periods of higher rates of growth in ontogenesis are a consequence of these connections. The common rate of growth is not the cause of the high correlation but rather its consequence.

Thus, I suggest, we must take as the main phenomenon not the *path* of ontogenetic development but the *mechanism* of the correlation between organs and their constituent elements, dimensions, etc., i.e., everything that Shmalgauzen included in the concept of morphogenetic correlation. The grounds for this conclusion are as follows. Quite different organs, independent of one another and their dimensions, may have similar growth rates during one and the same interval of time. Their dimensions simultaneously grow fast because of historically-conditioned forms of ontogenesis and not in consequence of any common morphophysiological necessity. The existence of a more or less significant correlation, on the contrary, is evidence of an inner connection between the dimensions that must imperatively show up in ontogenesis, although it may sometimes appear with less force in consequence of the effect of other factors that are not common to the given dimensions. Thus the link disclosed by the coefficient cannot help not being detected in some degree in ontogenesis. If there is something in common in the nature of the two properties, in particular of two dimensions, this common element will also have a certain effect in the sense that the course of their ontogenetic variation will be similar. Thus a similarity of the tempos and periods of development of two characters can be considered, albeit partially, as a consequence of their mutual morphogenetic connection. Such a similarity of itself, as we have said above, is not generally necessarily a reflection of morphological community.

As an example let us recall the correlation of size of head, hand, and foot. Complex connections of sorts have been noted between the brain and the distal elements of the extremities (hands and feet) as a result of work in the field of experimental embryology. With abnormal development of the centers of the mid-brain, caused by removal of a front limb or an eye (e.g., in amphibians), the rear limb turns out to be deformed and underdeveloped and develops four, or even three, toes instead of five.

One must also bear in mind the great area in the fourth field of the cerebral cortex of the sectors linked with the distal elements of the limbs (especially the hands).

It can be said, furthermore, that the foot (longitudinal axis) is generally closely linked with all the main sections of the body and with stature. The many exceptions to the rule about the increase of r in major dimensions as compared with minor ones are due to the hand and foot.

Thus, at bottom, there is apparently a correlation expressing a stable inner connection. Ontogenesis then is a path laid down both by the dynamics of development and by the history of the formation of the species. The value of the biometric method of analyzing correlations here is that it functions as a kind of experiment disclosing connections between 'fluctuating phenomena' (in this case variations), unlike embryology when the latter preserves a purely descriptive character and describes only the sequence of events.

The conclusions to be drawn from study of the influence exerted by the closeness of the link between dimensions on the stability of coefficients embracing those dimensions are also not without significance for evolutionary morphology, for example, the influence of the connection between length of leg and arm on the stability or permanence of the relation between their lengths. This stability has been established in two different spheres of phenomena. It has been shown, first of all, that the proportion of the parts of the body (coefficients) that are of vital significance for the species are usually characterized by small coefficients of variation and that this comes about in particular through the coordinated variability of both the components of these coefficients (Roginskij, 1959). A similar pattern is observed in human ontogenesis. It has been shown that if any two dimensions are closely interlinked (as regards intragroup correlations), the index calculated from them changes little with growth, provided that their rates of growth do not differ too sharply (Roginskij, 1959). This dependency is of interest as concerns the problem of the relation between ontogenesis and phylogenesis. It indicates that it is unlikely that a new value of the index arises in evolution through the action of an internal factor of some kind when both dimensions used in the index are closely interlinked.

Furthermore the elucidation of what features characterize individuals is of interest, that is, dimensions or characters that are combined in an untypical way, either in a direction contrary to the normal correlation or not corresponding well with it, such as for example, the combination of dark eyes and light hair or light eyes and dark hair. Deviations of this kind are particularly important in types of physique or constitution, although they cannot depart far from the typical correlation because of the very nature of physique.

CERTAIN PROBLEMS OF GENERAL THEORETICAL INTEREST

In conclusion I should like to touch on that field of the study of connections between characters in anthropology that bears closely on the philosophical problem of the rise of qualitatively new forms of the motion of matter.

Hitherto we have been speaking of the two types of connection between the properties of an organism, namely the historical and the morphophysiological. In essence, the first type is evidence of a complete absence of inner connection between the characters, while the second expresses the existence of such a connection, although it may not be very apparent in the separate individual. If we consider just how little a correlative connection is obligatory for any single individual (the statistical regularity), the idea of a third type of willy-nilly connection arises, i.e., of a kind that consists in the absolute inevitability of the occurrence of one event in the presence of another in any single separate case (dynamic regularity).

When connections of this last sort are counterposed to correlations we enter the realm of problems widely discussed at present in natural science and the philosophy of science, namely, problems of the relationship and role of dynamic and statistical laws.

From the formal aspect all connections can be called correlative since the absolute value of a coefficient of correlation varies from zero to unity and so embraces all possible degrees of closeness of connections from full mutual independence of the phenomena to complete absence of freedom within the limits of the pair of phenomena studied. If, however, we bear in mind the great qualitative peculiarity of the two extreme types and their immense theoretical significance, we must divide them, at least provisionally, into special types of relationship and all three types must be distributed in a series from historical connections through statistical ones to dynamic links.

In what follows, I begin from the proposition that, microphysics apart, we are concerned with statistical laws in the social sciences, meteorology, biology, etc. (Anisimov, 1955).

The question may arise whether, in general, there is any significance in the absence of a connection between phenomena and whether this negative circumstance merits being made the subject of study.

Theoretical work in general biology that bears closely on this question, and the interests of the anthropologist, is Malinovskij's important research into types of control system distinguished according to the interrelations between their constituent links which may be processes, organs, nerves, or hormonal connections, etc. Malinovskij concluded in particular that "adaptation to a medium constantly changing in any direction, both in the course of evolution and in the course of developing optimal forms of behaviour, is ensured through discrete ('corpuscular') systems, namely, in the form of separate genetic units as regards evolution, and as regards behaviour in the form of reflex reactions that are capable of combining comparatively freely and forming various combinations responding adequately to any new combination of environmental conditions. Adaptation to permanent conditions, or to a limited, regular succession of conditions, is attained through the development of correlation systems in which certain links (organs, functions) are in permanent close connection with others" (Malinovskij, 1960: 178).

Clearly, the sharpest contrast between the two types of biological system will be where full mutual independence of the elements of one system is contradicted by a close connection between the elements, i.e., a connection that is expressed by coefficients (indices) of correlation equal to unity. Although the vast number of systems in an organism has a less close connection and the morphologist in particular is concerned as a rule with coefficients less than unity. The most important role in the vital activity of an organism, however, is played by qualitative dependences in which changes of one factor invariably lead to strictly defined changes in another.

While I am fully in accord with Malinovskij that the basic form of adaptation to an undetermined, different type of changing environment is discreteness, fragmentation, and a capacity to create free combinations of the units through which adaptation to the environment is realized (Malinovskij, 1960), I suggest that this discreteness has great significance in a field that is specially important to anthropology, namely the problems of man as a creature governed simultaneously by two different systems of laws, the one biological and the other social.

There is no department of anthropology in which the problem of the relationship between biological and social laws does not arise. It also exists in the field of the study of physique. It inevitably arises in study of the specific character of human races compared with subspecies of animals. Finally, at the basis of the theory of anthropogenesis we again meet these problems of the relation between nature and society, in particular in studying the role of natural selection in the process of the formation of man and the process of the rise of social patterns, which lead, at a definite level of the development of society, to an abrupt change in the role of selection and to its attenuation.

In conclusion, I should like to say that the interaction of the phenomena of qualitatively different laws of the motion of matter, in this case of social and biological laws, is mainly possible precisely in the realm of statistical regularities and not in that of dynamic patterns. This idea can hardly claim to be original, if only because when formulated more simply it becomes almost self-evident.

There can only be outside interference of any kind or outside influence on any process where there is some degree of independence of the separate parts of the process. In the case of law as a kind of chain of closely connected links of cause and effect, there is no place, and cannot be any, for the application of forces from another field, forces transforming the old connections and themselves determining new relationships. On the contrary, only there, where phenomena are combined by the laws of probability and not by laws permitting reliable prognosis, where there are consequences of the absence of predeterminancy in the sequence of phenomena, only there could the pattern of a different, new form of movement encroach, as it were, on a sphere of phenomena foreign to it and transform their combinations. Let us take examples from several fields of anthropology.

The conductor of the influence of social laws and patterns on the behavior of man could only be the cerebral cortex, i.e., that region of the central nervous system whose elements have the property of vast plasticity of interconnections and which can serve as the basis for the elaboration of an endless number of conditioned connections. On the contrary, the stem part of the brain, for example, was and remains almost impenetrable to outside reconstructing influences, including social ones, if we consider not its connections with the cortex but its internal, intrinsic, automatic, fixed connections between the link of the processes going on in it.

The principle of systems embracing independent elements has been employed by man himself in the history of his culture. It is easily recognized in articulated speech, i.e., in the system of a vast number of combinations of a limited number of phonemes, in alphabetical scripts, and in keyboards in which only the system 'keys/sources of sound' is built on the principle of dynamic connections, and the separate keys are independent of one another. These properties also make these systems satisfactory means of intercourse, thinking, music, etc.

The same relationships are observed in racial studies. The laws of heredity, metabolism, physiology, the development of racial characters, and the laws of their alteration under direct influence of the environment can on the whole be discovered by the methods of the biological sciences and by those of physics and chemistry. Only history, including written sources, archaeology, ethnography, plus linguistics and folklore studies, can throw light on the principles and course of the migrations of racial groups, their isolation, mixing, changes of number, and extinction. In other words, social laws and patterns also assert themselves in ethnic anthropology not where the dynamic laws of nature prevail but in the sphere of natural history, and in the field of the life of collectives, where the relations of the members of groups to one another and to territory have not been reinforced from the beginning of their evolution by any kind of undisturbed relationship.

The general propositions enunciated above are also applicable to elucidation of the problem of the origin and evolution of man. The laws of heredity, physiology, metabolism, and biological phenomena are almost the same for man as for the anthropomorphic apes, but the significance of natural selection underwent fundamental change in course of anthropogenesis. In a certain sense natural selection is a statistical process which finds its reflection in the mathematical theory of natural selection. The production relations that develop simultaneously with human society became the basic connections between people, while the role of selection changed sharply at just that stage of human evolution when society in the full sense of the term took shape. The effect of selection as a factor in the progressive evolution of man ceased, as is plainly visible from the fact of the relative morphological stability of the species characteristics of *Neoanthropus* from the time of the late palaeolithic.

Doubts may arise as to how far it is correct to counterpose selection as a statistical process to the course of ontogenesis as a chain of events dynamically linked. Is the whole system of relations between ontogenesis and the history of the species not thus disrupted? I would remind you of what was said earlier about ontogenetic variations. If, for example, cartilage always precedes bone in the formation of long bones, and the opposite is impossible, the rate of relative growth of the separate bones can vary within wide limits under the action of various conditions. That is why the relationship of dimensions can alter so strongly in the course of transformation of one species into another. The reconstruction of ontogenesis is most easily effected when the links are least firm. Here, as in all the cases considered above, the new can arise only in that sphere of the old where dynamic laws do not hold undivided sway.

In ending my communication, I would again recall that Anuchin never concerned himself with the problem of correlations, but I think that he would have derived satisfaction from the fact that an essential contribution to the study of this important problem has been made by Russian and Soviet scientists.

Basic Trends in the Adaptive Radiation of the Apes at the End of the Tertiary and the Beginning of the Quaternary Periods

V. JAKIMOV

Darwin's theory of the origin of man from ancient great apes is now shared by the overwhelming majority of investigators. Only individual scientists still consider it possible to regard certain non-anthropoid primates as the ancestral group for Hominids.

The strengthening of the pongid theory of the origin of man is due in no small degree to the progress of palaeontology in the field of new discoveries of fossil *Anthropoidea*. Comparative anatomical studies of the skeletal remains discovered and study of the accompanying fauna, as well as analysis of the palaeoclimatic and palaeogeographical material, have made it possible to characterize the morphological and ecological features of the various representatives of the fossil apes to a certain extent, and even to reach some understanding of their biological behavior. It has become possible to outline the most general sequences in the evolution of the various groups of *Pongidae* and to picture the line of development of man's anthropoid ancestors that led to the evolution of the earliest *Hominidae*.

Hominidae did not originate before the beginning of the Quaternary Period as is indicated by the finds of skeletal remains and very early stone tools, the first indisputable artifacts of man. It is quite evident that this event was preceded in an earlier geological epoch by the intensive evolution of various groups of fossil apes, from only one of which man's ancestors sprang. In fact, the finds of fossil anthropoids so far described indicate that the greatest burgeoning of this group of higher primates occurred in the second half of the Tertiary era, beginning in the

First published in *Trudy Moskovskogo obsjestva ispytatelej prirody*, t. 14 (1964).

Miocene Period. The pre-hominid branch of the phylogenetic tree of the primates would seem to branch off in the Miocene Period, with which the majority of researchers agree who share the theory that man arose from fossil *Pongidae* (Bunak, 1954, 1959; Nesturkh, 1954, 1960; Heberer, 1956). Bunak (1954) in particular, in characterizing "anthropoids as the direct ancestors of the earliest hominids", wrote: "It must be supposed that a variant appeared among the apes in the Miocene and Pliocene Periods with a brain capacity of 400–500 cubic centimeters and teeth of the type *Dryopithecus*, that had gone over to moving on two legs."

At the stage of anthropogenesis immediately preceding the origin of the earliest man, it is possible that there was a multiple evolutionary event in the hominoid sequence among the various members of the fossil great apes, in particular in the trend toward walking on two legs (Jakimov, 1951). The large number and wealth of forms among Tertiary anthropoids would have encouraged a broad morpho-ecological evolution characterized by extremely varied forms of adaptation to the environmental conditions.

The abundant fauna of the apes in the Tertiary era can be seen from the number of finds of skeletal remains. According to A. Remane (1956) they number around 20 genera and 30 species of Tertiary anthropoids. True, he also argues that on the criteria used to describe the fossil remains we should have to divide each of the modern species into ten genera and 20 to 30 species (Remane, 1956), but all the same, there is no doubt that the anthropoid fauna at that time was exceptionally rich as regards species.

The territorial extent of their habitat was wide and diverse as regards landscape; bone remains of these apes have been found in Africa, East and South Asia, and Central and Southern Europe. The various conditions of existence left an impression on the morphological features of the fossil *Anthropoidea*, determined their differentiation by body size even within the limits of narrow systematic groups, and were reflected in the character of their behavior which had particularly vital significance for the progressive evolution of such highly developed primates as the apes.

The palaeontological material indicates that there were two trends or sequences of evolution among the apes, namely, adaptation to life in trees and adaptation to a terrestrial existence. Both directions are characterized by the development of definite types of locomotion, and a corresponding morphological reconstruction of the skeleton, teeth, and other organs.

Adaptation to an arboreal existence conditioned the development of a special type of movement from branch to branch, or brachiation. This mode of locomotion is linked with a lengthening of the front limbs, clearly expressed in the modern brachiators, the gibbons and orangutans. As the forearm became longer than the upper arm, the hand became long and narrow, the first finger (or thumb) weakly developed and almost uninvolved in the grasping of branches, while the other fingers became longer. In the large anthropoids, like the orangutans and chimpanzees that brachiate rather more slowly than apes of smaller size (gibbons, brachitanites and siamangs), the back-to-palm plane of the phalanges of the fingers is quite curved, and that, taken with the shortening of the tendons of the surface and deeper flexors of the fingers which prevents their full extension (Straus, 1940), transforms the hand of the large anthropoids into a hook-like prehensile organ with automatically flexing fingers.

The specialized structure of the hand and of all the limbs as a whole did not promote the progressive development of the multifunction character of the hand which played an immense role in man's evolution and is so characteristic of him (Jakimov, 1947; Astanin, 1962).

The forms of adaptation of the *Pongidae* to an arboreal mode of life were quite limited because of the relatively uniform conditions of their habitat. The purely arboreal anthropoids are therefore differentiated in two main lines only — those most useful in the evolution of this group of apes.

The essential differences are in the size of the body and the type of brachiation. On the one hand, there developed fast brachiators possessing small body dimensions and many features of a clearly expressed arboreal specialization, a sequence that includes the members of the subfamilies of gibbons, i.e., the gibbons proper, the brachitanites and the siamangs.

The other line of development was that of the slow brachiators, the large apes, who also possess signs of an extreme adaptation to life in trees. These are the various species of fossil and existing orangutan. Characteristic of them is a clearly marked sexual dimorphism expressed in the greater size of the males, and powerful development of their skulls, jaws, and teeth.

At one time species belonging to both these groups were widespread in East and South Asia: bone remains of their less specialized predecessors have also been found in Miocene deposits in Europe and Africa.

Closely related to these two lines of development is a third representing apes with many signs of adaptation to life in trees and a quite marked brachiator type of locomotion, but who spend a considerable time on the ground. The various species of chimpanzee among existing large anthropoids belong to this group, and among the fossils certain members of the group of *Dryopithecus* and closely related forms like *Sugrivapithecus* and *Austriacopithecus*.

In recent years the important fact of the relatively late formation of the arboreal specialized forms constituted by the brachiators in the phylogenesis of the great apes has been established (Le Gros Clark and Thomas, 1951; Le Gros Clark and Leakey, 1951; Le Gros Clark, 1953; Bunak, 1954, 1959; Heberer, 1956; Remane, 1956). The earliest representatives of the *Pongidae*, it may be supposed, were apes that preserved features in the structure of their limbs of adaptation to running on the ground and on branches, similar to those of *Cercopithecidae*. Their hands were not specialized as a hook for clutching branches, as with the brachiators, but was used as an organ of support. The early *Pongidae*, ancestors of existing brachiators, were not narrowly specialized and were adapted in equal degree to life in trees and on the ground.

The specialized brachiators took shape late geologically speaking. Gibbons of modern structure are discovered only in Quaternary deposits (Heberer, 1956). At the same time *Propliopithecus*, *Limnopithecus*, and *Paidopithecus*, which some authors regard as more or less close ancestors of the gibbons, did not have the characteristic skeletal structure of the limbs of brachiators. *Limnopithecus*, for example, according to Leakey (1948), was very similar to *Cercopithecidae* in the structure of the front limbs. Their index of upper arm robustness was 19.3; that of existing gibbons is 13.8 to 14.3, and of *Cercopithecidae* 21.9 to 25.8. The angle of torsion of the humerus (108 degrees in *Limnopithecus*) does not exceed the limits characteristic of *Cercopithecidae* (102 to 115 degrees); in the gibbons it is significantly higher (124 to 137 degrees). It is similar with the humeral index, which is 103.6 in *Limnopithecus*, 100.8 in guenon-like forms (*Cercopithecidae*), average for 12 groups, 113.3 in gibbons, 111.3 in the siamang, and with the humeral femur index (95.0 in *Limnopithecus* and 108–112 in existing gibbons) (Heberer, 1956).

The early representatives of the apes were also not brachiator (Le Gros Clark and Leakey, 1951; Heberer, 1956). *Proconsul*, bones of which have been found in Lower Miocene deposits in Kenya, had the structure of the foot characteristic of the quadruped *Cercopithecidae*. The tarsal section was not shortened, as is usual with arboreal specialization and in existing apes, and the foot occupied a more plantigrade position. These apes which many investigators consider the probable source group for the early *Pongidae*, and possibly of the *Hominidae* as well, led a semi-terrestrial, semi-arboreal mode of life. Typical *Pongidae* like *Dryopithecus* also did not have the brachiators' differentiation of the extremities (Heberer, 1956).

The evolutionary development of the initial group of early *Pongidae* with their semi-terrestrial, semi-arboreal mode of life followed the line of the formation, on the one hand, of well-expressed adaptation to life in trees, and on the other hand, of adaptation to a terrestrial existence (see figure). Life on the ground was dangerous for animals so relatively weakly equipped with natural means of defense as the *Anthropoidea*, and required their more varied adaptation to the conditions of the environment.

In the evolution of the terrestrial *Anthropoidea* two most characteristic modes are distinguished in their adaptive development (Jakimov, 1951). One was linked with the augmentation of the dimensions of the animals and was a more or less passive form of preservation of a species with comparatively small possibilities of mastering the environment and limited ecological-morphological plasticity. The second trend was characterized by active adaptation to varied natural conditions which encouraged a wider dispersal of the species and its biological progress.

Modern gorillas belong to the first sequence, and also such fossil apes as *Gigantopithecus*, *Meganthropus*, certain *Dryopithecinae* such as *Dryopithecus giganteus* (*Indopithecus*), and the large forms of Proconsuls (*Proconsul major*).

It should also be noted that the gorillas, especially the mountain gorilla, are almost wholly terrestrial great apes, but took to life on the ground relatively recently and have therefore still not got rid of certain features of an arboreal specialization.

This was graphically shown by A. Schultz (1927) from the change in the relative dimensions of the hand and thumb in the ontogenesis of the lowland and mountain gorillas. Being secondarily terrestrial, the gorillas as inhabitants of the forest belong with other existing apes to the general vertical series of adaptive distribution of arboreal forms of *Pongidae*. Ignoring the discrepancy of the geographical range of the modern apes, three forms can be distinguished among them: inhabitants primarily of the upper level of the forest (represented by the gibbons), of the middle level (the orangutans and chimpanzees, although the latter also live partly on the ground), and of the lower level (the terrestrial gorillas). This zonal radiation of forms along the vertical, brought about in the first place by competition for food, encouraged the intensive evolution of *Pongidae* and the rapid development of features of specialization in them. Le Gros Clark (1953), in particular, demonstrated this on the example of three species of Miocene Proconsuls. Recent researches

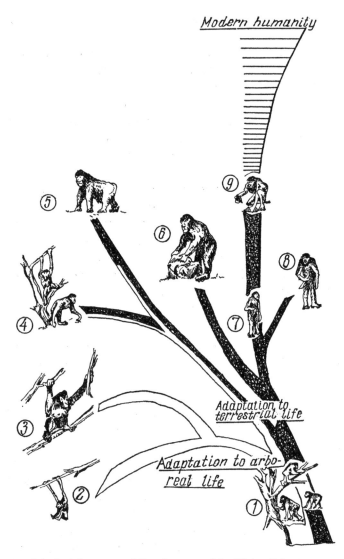

Figure 1. Principal Sequences of Development of the Higher Primates
(1) original form for higher apes;
(2) fast brachiators, small forms (gibbons, siamangs);
(3) slow brachiators, enlargement of body size (orangutans);
(4) semi-terrestrial/semi-arboreal forms, average body size (chimpanzees);
(5) secondary terrestrial forms, enlargement of body size (gorillas);
(6) gigantic terrestrial forms (*Gigantopithecus, Meganthropus*);
(7) bipedal apes, systematic utilization of objects as tools, complex forms of behavior (australopithecids);
(8) bipedal apes, utilization of objects as tools, enlargement of body size (paranthropids);
(9) fashioning of tools, beginning of labor (hominids).

and the quite numerous bone remains of *Proconsul major* have indicated that these apes were quadrupeds (Allbrook and Bishop, 1963).

The clearest picture of the development of terrestrial *Pongidae* along the path of increase of body size is given by *Gigantopithecus* — three huge mandibles and many teeth — which are known from South China (Koenigswald, 1935, 1952; Weidenreich, 1945; Pei Wen-chung, 1957; Woo Ju-kang, 1962; Dung Ti-chen, 1962). Although the majority of investigators now deny the gigantism of these South China anthropoids, in particular on grounds of the absence in the apes of an intergroup correlation between the size of the jaw and the size of the animal (Woo Ju-kang, 1962; Dung Ti-chen, 1962), *Gigantopithecus* was nevertheless much larger and stronger than modern gorillas.

According to the data of Woo Ju-kang and Dung Ti-chen not only were large teeth characteristic of the dentition of *Gigantopithecus* (especially the molars), but also there was a significant development of the front ('prelacteon') part of the alveolar arch (Bolk, 1926). The index of the relative length of its anterior part up to the pre-molars varies from 45.5 in jaw No. II to 49.6 in the largest jaw, No. III, i.e., corresponds to that of the great apes of today: viz. gorilla 45.1 to 50.0, chimpanzee 52.7, orangutan 53.5. Such a value of the index indicates that this part of the alveolar arch was quite strongly developed in *Gigantopithecus*, including the incisors and canine teeth, i.e., the jaw apparatus attained considerable size. The dentition of *Gigantopithecus* was strong, the size of the molars (M_1 and M_2), expressed in area of the crown, was 345.3 square millimeters for M_1 and 392.5 mm² for M_2, whereas these indices in the gorilla are respectively 216.2 and 284.2 mm₂, in the orangutan 167.3 and 187.5 mm² and in the chimpanzee 100.8 and 111.3 mm². There was no reduction of the last molar (M_3) in *Gigantopithecus*, which is usually defined by its size relative to the second molar (M_2); on the contrary M_3 was larger than M_2 (Dung Ti-chen, 1962).

Gigantopithecus, too, like the gorillas, had the considerable sexual dimorphism characteristic of many species of terrestrial apes. This dimorphism shows in the size of the canine teeth and in the general massiveness of the jaws (Woo Ju-kang, 1962; Dung Ti-chen, 1962). There were possibly also differences in body size and other characteristics.

The principal form of locomotion of these large terrestrial apes was in all probability a quadruped gait as in the gorillas. Against the assumption that *Gigantopithecus* and *Meganthropus* were bipedal apes is the evidence that their feet were still probably prehensile to a significant degree, i.e., not adapted for supporting such a large animal in an upright posture. "Upright walking by giants is impossible on our planet for physical reasons", writes Heberer (1956). It is possible that *Giganto-pithecus* had not reached the stage of adaptation to an arboreal existence in its evolution that the gorillas reached, but preserved the unspecialized structure of the front limbs, especially of the hand, that is characteristic of early *Pongidae* and close to the guenon-like monkeys.

The character of the fossil fauna from the caves where the bones of *Gigantopithecus* were found supports Pei Wen-chung's contention (1957) that these large terrestrial anthropoids, living in a hilly, almost woodless, terrain, ate the flesh of animals, unlike the secondarily terrestrial gorillas, dwelling in forests and completely vegetarian. According to Pei Wen-chung *Gigantopithecus* attacked young or very old individuals which were overcome without the aid of sticks, stones, or pieces of bone, (no traces of the utilization of these natural weapons have been found in the cave). Woo Ju-kang (1962), however, thinks that the structure of the dentition of *Gigantopithecus* gives evidence of a predominant vege-tarianism.

The increased body size of many terrestrial *Pongidae* and their strength-ened jaw apparatus were a useful adaptation in the struggle for existence since the circle of their potential enemies was reduced by it. This is so with the modern gorillas, the males of which can successfully defend their family groups even against such formidable predators as the leopard. At the same time, the large size of the animals made their movement slower, required a great amount of food, and reduced fecundity (Dung Ti-chen, 1962). It is possible that the formation of communities of small numbers and greater separation between them was linked with that (Semenov, 1962).

All these factors weakened these terrestrial forms of *Pongidae* in their competition with species more adapted to the conditions of the environ-ment, reduced the geographical range of their habitat, and led to the dying out of the gigantic anthropoids when environmental conditions changed greatly.

The other adaptive trend in the evolution of terrestrial *Pongidae* was characterized by complication of their forms of behavior, in particular by a high degree of "tool-using activity", and was linked with the develop-ment of the brain and the system of analyzers. Concrete examples of this evolutionary path are the australopithecines of Africa. Something similar probably occurred in the development of the fossil apes that were close ancestors of the early hominids and morphologically and genet-ically close of the African australopithecines (Jakimov, 1951).

The vital morphological feature of members of this adaptive trend was the transition of several early *Pongidae* to walking on two legs. It was predetermined by an earlier differentiation of function of the front and hindlimbs and the utilization of the former predominantly to hold objects and manipulate them, as Engels emphasized (1940b: 279). In that connection features of adaptation to a bipedal gait occurred in the structure of the limbs of such early *Pongidae* as the Miocene *Proconsul* (Le Gros Clark, 1953; Heberer, 1956). Certain hominoid features are also noted in the limb bones or *Oreopithecus* which lived at the transition from the Miocene to the Pliocene. The thigh bone of *Oreopithecus*, for example, has a strongly developed pit or fovea on its head where the round ligament (*lig. teres femoris*) is attached; this is characteristic of man but absent in existing apes, i.e., in the orangutan and gorilla (Heberer, 1956).

The idea of the bipedalism of the South African Australopithecines has been confirmed by finds of the pelvic bones of three anthropogenic *Pongidae*, *Australopithecus prometheus, A. (Plesianthropus) transvaalensis*, and *Paranthropus crassidens*, and also by Leakey's data on the foot of '*Prezinjanthropus*', discovered by him at Olduvai Gorge in 1960 (Leakey, 1961a, b; Reshetov, 1962). The massiveness of the first and fifth metatarsal bones was possibly caused by '*Prezinjanthropus*' walking predominantly on the hind legs, although its foot as a whole still preserves the structure of a grasping organ. This confirms the view of the structure of the foot of the australopithecines (Le Gros Clark, 1946), and is evidence of the early forming of such a hominoid feature as bipedalism.

Most important features of this type of adaptation were the weakening of the jaw apparatus, the systematic utilization of natural objects as tools, and the progressive development of the brain.

Comparison of the dentition of australopithecines and existing great apes indicates that the incisor-canine tooth section of the maxillary arch is considerably reduced in the former, which brings them close in this respect to *Hominidae*. Thus the index of the ratio of the 'prelacteon' part of the alveolar arch and the length of the whole arch in australopithecines does not exceed 44.1 (*Plesianthropus*), while in existing apes it is not below 45 to 50; in the earliest *Hominidae* the maximum value of the index, measured on jaw H 1 of *Sinanthropus*, is 43.5 (Jakimov, 1956). The weakening of the tooth system of australopithecine *Pongidae* in comparison with living ones shows also in the dimensions of the canine teeth and the size of the whole row of molars.

There is no great doubt that the australopithecines systematically made use of objects around as weapons of defence and attack, thus naturally compensating for their unsatisfactory natural armament. The brain of the australopithecine ape was larger than that of living apes but is hardly distinguishable from them as regards development of the regions of the cortex (Kochetkova, 1960). Thus the australopithecines, in spite of their bigger brain, did not exceed the limits peculiar to the great apes as regards the degree of complexity of its organization. Only fuller realization of the psychic possibilities inherent in such a morpho-physiological organization of the brain enabled the australopithecines to achieve a high level of systematic "tool-using" activity in the course of their adaptation to diverse environmental conditions, a level generally inaccessible to existing great apes.

The level of development of "tool-using" activity and of the brain in the various australopithecines was not uniform and did not promote the evolution of some of them in the hominid direction. In certain australopithecines there was a tendency to a general increase of body size and strengthening of the jaw apparatus which prevented their development toward man. These features of specialization are marked in the geologically later members of the australopithecines, among the various species of *Paranthropus*, and also in *Zinjanthropus*, which is distinguished by the considerable size of the jaws and molars (Jakimov, 1960). According to J. Robinson (1961) the specialization of the tooth structure of *Paranthropus* was connected with the character of the diet of these fossil anthropoids. The combination of large molars with small incisors and canine teeth was conditioned by the marked herbivorous character of *Paranthropus* and *Zinjanthropus* compared with *Australopithecus* proper, which was omnivorous and closer to *Hominidae* in diet. The character of the diet of *Paranthropus* also conditioned the formation of other features of its morphology, namely, the increase in body size, the thickening of the bones, and the development of a crest on the skull. *Paranthropus*, like other more herbivorous forms of *Pongidae*, probably utilized natural objects less systematically as tools or weapons, which retarded the development in this genus of what has been called "orientating-exploratory" activity, and diverted their evolutionary development away from the hominid direction.

The most progressive bipedal fossil anthropoids were those that systematically employed various objects as tools and weapons which became the basis of their ecology. The possible relief and landscape of the habitat of these apes was an open terrain like wooded steppes or the African savannahs.

In the course of the struggle for existence, the species in the most favorable position from the standpoint of biological adaptation and survival were those early man-like apes in which conditioned reflex connections between the animal and the objects of its activity, i.e., objects of nature, had become specially reinforced, and the activity itself has become more varied and purposeful. The influence of selection was directed toward progressive development of the brain, especially to the heightening of levels of biological behavior which was expressed in various ways but mainly in the systematic nature of the use of objects. The earlier accidental or haphazard utilization of objects as tools became necessary and took on the character of the principal pattern of further progress. This path of evolutionary development of the terrestrial great apes, which encouraged a general rise of all the vital activity and viability of the animals, and a raising of the activity of their biological behavior is an example of the aromorphous trend in biological progress (Severtsov, 1939).

In the subsequent evolution of *Hominidae*, however, a process of increasing body size is observed. The *Hominidae* must have been related to the large forms of higher primates since their ancestors were apes of average size. An interesting phenomenon is to be observed in this connection: with the attainment of a certain, and moreover significant, level of development of the brain and general complication of the psyche, increase in body size already does not exert a retarding influence on the further course of progressive evolution. The possibility develops of a growth of body size without strengthening of the natural armament, or even with its actual weakening.

A most important cause of the adaptive evolution of the anthropoid ancestors of man may have been just this weakness of their natural means of defence. It could have been made compensated by strengthening of the biological unity of these apes and the development of "a weapon armory", which encouraged more and more active mastery of the environment. Therefore the pongid ancestors of man also did not evolve along the path of increasing body size and strengthening of the teeth and jaws, or of some other form of natural armament; otherwise they would have been held back in the development of the brain and the level of higher nervous activity would have been lowered, as occurred in certain lines of evolution of terrestrial *Pongidae*. The biological progress of man's ancestors took the path of an ever-growing capacity to "equip themselves" with natural objects which they utilized as weapons and tools, and these ancestors, while not converted into powerful giants, became dangerous rivals of other great apes.

This competitive relationship should not, of course, be reduced to a sharp interspecies clash over food, hunting area, etc., leading to the direct extinction of some species groups by others, although that cannot be excluded. Much more significant was the adaptation of man's anthropoid ancestors to various environmental conditions and their more successful capacity to endure an amplitude of changes in the latter that were too much for other anthropoids.

The great adaptive possibilities of man's ancestors and the broad limits of their "adaptive stability" made it possible for them to spread widely and gradually to oust more narrowly adapted specialized forms. Extension of the environment of their habitat by modern man's ancestors, fossil great apes, and later early hominids, served as the prerequisites for the development of that special path of evolution characteristic of man, which has been called epimorphosis (Shmalgauzen, 1940).

In the course of the struggle for existence many forms of terrestrial *Pongidae* did not survive the rivalry initially with more adapted anthropoids in which hominoid features had developed and later with real *Hominidae*; they were much circumscribed in geographical area which inevitably led to the extinction of many species. In that light it becomes clear why only small remnants of a once rich fauna of Tertiary *Pongidae* are now preserved in Asia and Africa, and why the surviving forms are relics of the forest trend of adaptive radiation, which was less affected by the progressively developing ancestors of man because of their considerable morpho-ecological differences from ground-living forms.

The vitally necessary, systematic "tool-using" activity with natural objects of the highly developed fossil anthropoids was the forerunner of true human labor, and it took man's ancestors out of the framework of purely biological evolution. The mode of adaptation of terrestrial pongids to the conditions around them, in which the most vital role was played by complication of "tool or weapon activity", was transformed into a qualitatively new factor in the further progressive development of early hominids.

Problems of Race Studies

About Racial Differentiation of the Human Species. Primary Centres of Race Formation

V. ALEKSEJEV

The division of mankind into three great racial stocks — Europoid, Mongoloid, and Negroid — is widely accepted in Soviet anthropological writings. It was reflected in the first Soviet textbook on anthropology in the section written by Y. Roginskij, which summed up the results of research by Soviet specialists in the study of anthropological composition of the world population during the prewar period (Bunak, Nesturkh, Roginskij, 1941). The same concept was set out in N. Cheboksarov's well-known article dealing with racial classifications (Cheboksarov, 1951). We find the same differentiation in the textbook by Roginskij and M. Levin (1955, 1963). From the generalizing statements in the study aids, this idea has penetrated into popular writings (Nesturkh, 1955; Gladkova, 1962), and from there into the ethnographical and demographical literature. Thus, a consolidated work on the size and distribution of the peoples of the world says: "All mankind is divided into three great, or principal, races: the Mongoloid, the Europoid, and the Equatorial (or Negro-Australoid)", (*World*, 1962). This idea is accompanied by the following footnote: "Whereas there are no essential differences among anthropologists over the division of the first order, there are many different standpoints on the division into the smaller taxonomical units (branches, races of the second order, types)." We find the same idea in a reference manual on the population of the world: "Three great races are generally distinguished: the Mongoloid (yellow), the Europoid (white), and the Equatorial Negro-Australoid (black)" (*Population*, 1905). The fact is that this assertion does not quite cover all the existing standpoints.

First published in *Sovetskaja etnografija*, N1 (1969).

In the extensive writing on the study of races, various opinions have been expressed on the number not only of the secondary and minor racial divisions but also on the primary, principal races. Some writers do not recognize the original affinity of the Western African and the Eastern Australian branches of the Equatorial race, and regard them as independent racial stocks, taxonomically equivalent to the Europoids and the Mongoloids. Other authors go much further and bring out two branches within the African Negroids (Coon, 1963). There is no complete unanimity of view on this question among Soviet researchers. V. Bunak, in his earliest writings, classified the peoples of the world in a great number of genetically independent racial groups, assuming that their amalgamation on the basis of some similar features runs counter to the genealogical principle of racial classification (Bunak, 1934). In a later work, the number of the principal races he distinguished was reduced to four (Bunak, 1956b).

At the same time, there is the opposite tendency, namely, to bring together the distinct principal races into larger categories. This tendency reflects the attempt to give deeper thought to the scheme of mankind's racial division and the genetic bonds between the races, and to take account of all the existing morphological data for a reconstruction of the most ancient stages in the history of human races. It is quite natural, however, that this problem is so complex that there can be no short answer to it. Now and again, skin color is regarded as the most essential criterion of racial affinity, and in accordance with this the light-skinned races of the Northern Hemisphere — the Europoids and the Mongoloids — are contrasted to the dark-skinned races of the Southern Hemisphere — the Negroids and the Australoids (Keith, 1949; Biasutti, 1953). If skin color is not given such an essential value, and this is well justified in view of the considerable adaptability of this feature and of the probability that there are parallel series of mutability for it, the basis for such a unification and contradistinction of the Southern and the Northern groups disappears. On the contrary, other morphological facts make it possible to contrast the Western and the Eastern areas of the world, that is, to bring the Europoids together with the Negroids and to contrast the whole with the Mongoloids (Bunak, Nesturkh, Roginskij, 1941). The latter view is also supported by G. Debets, who does not, however, set out any special arguments (Debets, 1958b). The point is not how we are to group the distinct variants — contrasting the Mongoloids and the Europoids with the Negroids, or on the other hand, bringing the latter together with the Europoids and contrasting them with the Mongoloids; the important thing is that this grouping reflects the genesis of the main racial divisions, which when brought together appear as secondary branches so that the number of the principal, or we now normally say, great races comes down to two.

Consequently, in the writings of the leading modern authorities on racial science, the number of basic racial stocks fluctuates from two to five. It is true that the three-part scheme has more supporters than the others but it cannot be in any sense considered generally acceptable. Thus, the present state of mankind's racial classification on the level of the principal categories does not warrant the above-mentioned assertions by ethnographers. At the same time, the different views concerning the number of races show it may well be useful to consider this question on the strength of new data and with a comparison of the various hypotheses and their theoretical bases.

CRITICAL REMARKS CONCERNING THE THREE-PART DIVISION

When anthropology was in its infancy, the races were essentially distinguished according to a small number of features: color of hair, eyes, and skin, form of hair, structure of the soft tissues of the face, and other external traits. A vast amount of material was subsequently also brought together on such systems as blood groups, dermatoglyphics, odontology, taste and motor reflexes, and many other physiological indicators. All these features reveal a geographical differentiation, and are therefore no less suitable for bringing out racial variants and morphological features. Their importance lies in the fact that they reflect deeper processes in the vital activity of the organism than most external morphological traits. Study of these features has made the characteristics of the great races acquire exceptional completeness and may be carried out in accordance with a number of functionally unconnected systems. The absence of any close morphophysiological correlation between blood groups and palm and fingerprints, between variations of dental structure and proteins in the blood, between motor and taste reflexes, on the one hand, and morphological traits, on the other, etc., is especially important. It makes it possible to verify the reality of the existence of the great races as distinguished on the basis of morphology. This is an important stage in studying the question of whether races are merely morphological or morphophysiological concepts, and the extent to which the indicators for the various systems of organs, as they coincide, correspond to the scheme of the present-day division of mankind into three basic racial stems.

All the studies carried out up to now have shown that there is a considerable discrepancy between the variations of the different complexes of features (anthropometric, isoserological, physiological, dermatological, and odontological) on the intergroup scale within the limits of all the three great races. The existence of parallel series variations of different characteristics is rare. Summing up the data for the isoserological reactions, W. Boyd subdivided mankind into six races according to blood groups (Boyd, 1950). Subsequently he improved his scheme giving it a more ramified form and brought out thirteen races (Boyd, 1958). One's attention is drawn to the fact that Boyd's classification does not coincide with the morphological classification. In the European group he brought out four subgroups (Laponoid, North-Western, United Central and Eastern, and Mediterranean), in the Asian, two (the Asian proper and the Indo-Dravidian), and in the Pacific (as he called the Australian group), four (the Australian proper, Indonesian, Melanesian, and Polynesian).

What is important is the difference in the number of races when classified according to morphological and isoserological features (after all, any grouping may reflect the researcher's subjective approach), and the instances when there is a sharp discrepancy in the variations of the one and the other. Thus, there are known to be sharp distinctions between the peoples of India and East Asia by morphological features. These peoples are not only referred to different great races (Mongoloids and Europoids with a Negroid admixture) but according to many features are classified within them as extremes, constituting the whole range of intergroup variations for the world. The anthropological type of many peoples of India is marked by a sharp graciality and is close to the world minimum for the bizyomatic diameter. Meanwhile, the Eastern Mongoloids, especially their Siberian branch, are characterized by a large size of face which is only greater among some Indian tribes in Argentina. Against the background of these distinctions, it is surprising to find the similarity of blood groups: in India as in East Asia there is a high percentage of B and the frequency of distribution of genes within the ABO and MN systems is in general quite similar.

Odontological features provide another similar example. The Negroes and the Europeans differ sharply in pigmentation, form of hair, and structure of the soft part of the face, and are at the opposite poles of modern mankind according to these features, but are akin in the structure of dentition and in this respect are contrasted with the Mongoloids.

The Negroes and the Europeans are united by a low percentage of individuals with shovel-shaped incisors, absence of the transversal crest of the trigonide on the first lower molar, a high percentage of individuals with the Carabelli tubercle, etc. By contrast, Mongoloids have the opposite combination of features to which is also added a large percentage of enamel flows on molars (Zubov, 1964). Thus, according to odontological variations there is a clear discrepancy with the traditional scheme of mankind's division into three great races. This lack of comparability between morphological data proper and odontological data is also to be found at a lower taxonomical level.

The Polynesians, for instance, are highly peculiar as an anthropological type, and there has been no short answer in all the attempts to find the exact place for them in racial classification to accord with their morphological appearance. Among the questions which still remain open are those of whether they have or do not have a Europoid admixture, the reasons for the curious combination in their morphological type of Mongoloid and Negroid traits, and the question of their similarity with the American Indians according to anthropological data. It is this that explains the use by researchers of the same anthropological material to back up diametrically opposite concepts: the settlement of Polynesia from the West or from the East (an example is provided by the sharp discussion over Heyerdahl's hypothesis which is being carried on with extensive use of anthropological data). According to odontological variations the position of the Polynesians is quite definite: they show a considerable similarity with the peoples of South-East Asia (Riesenfeld, 1956). A craniological series from Eastern Latvia, dating from the 18th century, is on the whole marked by the Europoid complex of traits, with only a small gravitation in the Mongoloid direction. By dental structure this gravitation is much more pronounced, and the series as a whole is close to the intermediate variants (Zubov, 1965).

We find a similar picture when comparing physiological (the ability to taste phenylthiocarbamide, motor reflexes, cerumen, and color blindness) and dermatoglyphic data with morphological ones. Both physiological and dermatoglyphic traits vary over an exceptionally wide range within all the great races and their geographical distribution does not reveal any definite correspondence when maps for the distribution of each trait throughout the world are compared. In other words, territorial complexes established for each trait do not coincide either under the different systems (dermatoglyphics, and the ability to taste phenylthiocarbamide, color blindness, and motor reflexes, etc.) or with the morphological types. Thus, in summing up it is safe to say that mankind's division into three great races based on morphology is not backed up either by physiological traits or morphological ones, if morphology is taken to include additional systems like dermatoglyphics and odontology. The three big races appear to be a predominantly morphological construction and consequently do not cover the great diversity of types among modern men for all the territorially varying traits. That is a substantial shortcoming of the traditional scheme of mankind's division into three parts.

Apart from the lack of parallelism in the variations of the different systems, another possible objection to this scheme is based on the different characteristics of the great races in morphological terms and the heterogeneous structure of their geographical areas. The former implies a discrepancy between the amplitude of fluctuation of many features within the same stem and the different character of their intergroup combinations. By amplitude of fluctuation the races differ distinctly even when we deal with the features of a high differentiating value, for which the greatest distinctions between the members of the different races in fact occur. The angle between the prominence of the nasal bones and the line of facial profile on the skull among the extreme variants of the Europoid race comes to roughly $5°-6°$ ($29°-35°$), for the Mongoloids the figure is $10°-11°$ ($12°-23°$), and for the Americanoids, $15°-16°$ ($12°-28°$). The variations of these features are even more considerable among members of the Negroid stem — the Bushman series has a nasal bone angle of $5°-6°$, and similar values have been recorded in other series of African Negroes, while many groups of Papuans have a strongly protuberant nose.

Another example is the intensity of pigmentation. Negroid types are characterized by intensively dark pigmentation (although some variations do occur) and only the Australians have a somewhat lighter skin than the Negroes. Members of the Mongoloid race are also fairly homogeneous by this feature and the Eskimos, for instance, are hardly more light-skinned than the Southern Mongoloids. The Europoids show a whole spectrum of skin, hair, and eye color, ranging from sharp depigmentation (Scandinavians) to highly intensive pigmentation (population of Southern Italy, Southern France, and Spain). A third example is the horizontal flatness of the facial skeleton of which the nasomalar angle is an illustration and the determinant. Let us recall that for the Europoid series it varies from $135°-141°$. Within the Asian branch of the Mongoloid race, it varies from between $144°-150°$. The American Indians, according to available but scant data, do not differ from the Europeans in the value of this angle. It is true that the Europoid series here taken are characterized by maximum values, but even then the range of variability among the Mongoloids goes up by 4°. Thus, the Mongoloids as a whole are twice as variable according to this feature than the Europoids. The Negroids are characterized by stable values.

There are any number of such examples, but the general conclusion they suggest is already quite clear: within the great races there are different limits of fluctuations of their differentiating features, and consequently the volume of the races themselves is dissimilar in the variability proper to them. This is also expressed in taxonomical terms: each great race is a cluster of smaller variants whose number varies considerably and which are distinguished from each other by different morphological specifics. At this point we are already dealing with the problem of the different lines of intergroup variability within the limits of each of the great racial stems. For instance, the Austroloids are distinguished from the African types by a whole complex of features which includes the structure of the soft tissue of the face, pigmentation, dental structure, and form of hair. At the same time, the Northern Europeans are distinguished from the Southern only by the intensity of pigmentation. There has been only partial success in the steady effort to discover other differentiating features: differences have been discovered in the structure of dentition. The subdivision by types within the Europoid race is sufficiently objective when it comes to the Southern branch, it is more relative within the limits of the Northern branch (the Eastern groups differ from the Western not by any specific combination of features, but by the existence of a Mongoloid strain), and it is extremely difficult in Central Europe where the territorial variants are characterized by the most contradictory morphological complexes. This largely explains the highly nihilistic attitude on the part of some researchers to the genetic unity of the Europoid race (Bunak, 1956b). It is true that their standpoint has been criticized (Debets, 1958a, b), but its importance has been reduced by the fact that the features uniting all the Europoids include pigmentation, a feature with highly adaptive properties, and to some extent nose prominence. In general, adaptive features constitute a considerable percentage of the complex of differentiating racial features, and this has always created the prerequisites for parallelism in variability — let us recall the similarity of the Koisan peoples and the Mongoloids. Consequently, it is not only the dissimilar range of variability but also the different character of typological differentiation that testifies to the latter's somewhat artificial character when any attempt is made to reduce all the existing diversity of races to the three-part scheme.

The heterogeneous character of the racial areas is pronounced in a comparison of the area of the Negroid race with those of the Mongoloid and the Europoid. The latter occupy compact areas which correspond to the role of the geographical distribution of features in distinguishing racial types; however, the members of the Negroid race are split up into two areas, Australia and Africa, which are not linked with each othei. Those who argue the genetic unity of the Negroid race assume that these two areas had once been merged in one compact area linked by a bridge across Hither Asia and India. This hypothesis is backed by various indirect arguments based on an examination of scattered and highly fragmentary palaeoanthropological finds (Debets, 1951a). To this could be added as another argument the traces of Negroid and Australoid types which are widespread in Hither Asia and India. These could be regarded as vestigial, but this does not make the hypothesis that the Negroid race had a single area in antiquity any more convincing because this argument in its favor is also an indirect one. Consequently, from the standpoint of the geographical distribution of races and the geography of race formation, the division of the original ecumene into three centers of race formation does not appear to be sufficiently justified theoretically or, which is most important, backed up factually.

Finally, apart from the different characters of the racial categories of the first order and the heterogeneous structure of their racial areas, the existence of a large number of intermediate and specific racial variants also argues against mankind's division into three basic races. These variants are not shown in the existing classification. The examples are many: the Koisan peoples within the Negroid race, the Lapps who are alternately classified with the Mongoloids and with the Europoids, the Ainu who combine the features of all the big races, the Polynesians who are distinguished from the Ainu but also combine in their anthropological type the distinctive features of all three races, and finally, the African and Asian Pygmies who are now brought together in one stem and regarded as parallel variants within the West African and East Australian branch of the Tropical type. The fact that it is impossible to allocate them under the heads of the three-part division shows that the division and the existing criteria for any precise taxonomical definition are inadequate. The latter may be due to the fact that these criteria have been worked out on the basis of this same three-part scheme. On the other hand, there are many exceptions similar to those listed above which do not fit into this scheme (Europoid and Negroid features in the morphological type of the American Indians, Europoid features in the morphological type of some territorial groups of Australians, etc.).

ABOUT TWO PRIMARY CENTERS OF RACE FORMATION

Primary centres of race formation should mean the territories in which the race formation process first acquired a definite direction ultimately expressed in the formation of a definite complex of features, for instance, the Mongoloid or the Negroid. The most acute discussion has been over the question of the period to which the emergence of the primary centres of race formation should be dated. Depending on this the monocentric and the polycentric hypotheses of the origin of modern races have been formulated. The view of primary centers of race formation here set out tones down to some extent the sharpness of the discussion between the proponents of the two hypotheses. This approach does not consider the formation of racial complexes as a whole but only the emergence of these complexes in embryo — individual features and their groups which subsequently take shape as whole complexes. I think it is possible to reconcile the two propositions: the racial complexes of the first order took shape fairly late, on the whole not earlier than the upper paleolithic period or even the mesolithic, and the first distinctive features of the big races appeared fairly early and in some instances may be traced beginning from the lower paleolithic period (notably among the Mongoloids). This approach implies the stage by stage formation of races but is not a superfluous characteristic of the intensity of race formation in time; it is a reflection of the objective shift in intensity and is a result of the different raies of change of the racial complexes.

Paleoanthropological finds, illustrating the early stages in the history of the family of hominids, are known to the extremely scanty and fragmentary. Therefore, in bringing out the local groupings of primitive mankind much importance attaches to the more numerous archeological material, especially when relating to the lower paleolithic epoch where paleoanthropological finds are extremely rare. On the whole, this material makes it possible to distinguish two areas. The first of these is characterized by the overwhelming prevalence of hand axes among the stone implements. These are virtually the only form of implement known among the sites of this area and are only accompanied by splinters. The tradition of making hand axes ranged over the Southern areas of Western, Central, and Eastern Europe, the whole of Africa, the Caucasus, and Hither, Southern, and South-East Asia. In the Mousterian period there is evidence of some peculiarity of African artifacts, but this has yet to be completely understood and explained (Movius, 1949; Sorokin, 1953).

The second area is much more narrowly localized in Central and Eastern Asia. The peculiar stone implements found in some sites in this area are explained by the unusual material: at Choukowtien, for instance, implements were made of quartzite which differs from flint and requires special methods of treatment, as described by B. Bogdajevskij in his well-known book on the history of primitive implements (Bogajevskij, 1936). Apart from the peculiar material this cultural area had its own characteristic tradition in the working of it. Rough cutting implements, which have come to be designated as choppers, are the main form of implement in this area. At the same time, hand cutters have also been found, but in much smaller quantities than choppers (Larichev, 1964). Consequently, on a small territory, as compared with the former, and shut off in the North by deserts and semideserts, in the West by the vast mountain ranges of Kuan Lung and Tibet, and in the South by hundreds of kilometers of impassable jungles, there settled in the lower paleolithic epoch a local group isolated from the rest of the world and possessing specific technological techniques for the working of flint for the purpose of fabricating implements of labor. This group, although small in comparison with the rest of the population but certainly consisting of dozens and perhaps hundreds of separate small populations, was contrasted because of its isolation to the rest of the population of the ecumene, and could have served, one would assume, as the basis for the formation of the present-day Mongoloids.

To characterize the anthropological type of the most ancient population of the Eastern center, we have at our disposal extensive and well described bone material for *Sinanthropus*. F. Weidenreich, who has written most circumstantially about *Sinanthropus*, observed the similarity of features in the morphology of *Sinanthropus* and the present-day Mongoloids: broad and high face, shovel-shaped front incisors, and flatness of facial skeleton in the horizontal plane. These observations, with the exception of the shovel-shaped incisors, were made on a reconstructed skull, and it is hard to attach serious importance to them. The role of shovel-shaped incisors as a racial indicator is demonstrated by the variations in the frequency of this feature among members of different races, as the latest research proves most definitely (Carbonell, 1963; Suzuki, Sakai, 1964). Whereas for Mongoloid populations the percentage of individuals with shovel-shaped incisors usually reaches 80–90, among the Scandinavians the percentage varies below 10. Other minor details of dental structure by which *Sinanthropus* resembles the present-day Mongoloids have also been noted. Because all these are autonomous from the impact of the environment and are determined by heredity, this similarity gives grounds for saying that *Sinanthropus* is connected with the present-day Mongoloids in direct genetic succession. Incidentally, a statistical analysis carried by Roginskij shows that *Sinanthropus,* when compared with modern races by a total of many features, differs least of all from the Mongoloid races.

How was the complex of morphological features characteristic of the Mongoloids subsequently shaped? Single finds of Neanderthal skulls on the territory of China are so extremely fragmentary that they do nothing to shed light on this question. The Mongoloid complex of features is not yet fully expressed on the skulls from upper paleolithic tumuli. A small series of skulls from the Upper Cave of Choukowtien is distinguished by a fairly moderate prominence of the nasal bones but the flatness of the facial skeleton of this series is relatively small, while a skull from Liukiang although having a flat facial skeleton and nasal bones has a very small height of face and rather low orbs. This incomplete expression of Mongoloid features on upper paleolithic skulls accords with the hypothesis, well grounded in fact and theory, that the protomorphic Mongoloid type, which has been best preserved among the various groups of American Indians, is to some extent neutral (Roginskij, 1937). Neolithic series from China and the Trans-Baikal area reveal a clearly expressed Mongoloid complex. Thus, three stages may be seen in the formation of the distinctive features of the Mongoloid race: emergence of Mongoloid features in the dental structure, notably, the shovel-shaped incisors in the lower paleolithic epoch, the appearance of the tendency towards the flatness of the facial skeleton and nasal bones in the upper paleolithic epoch, and, finally, the increase in the height and perhaps in the breadth of the face and the shaping of the Mongoloid complex in its modern form in the neolithic or even earlier in mesolithic times.

The history of the Western center may be described by paleoanthropological data much less definitely, although on the whole these data are greater in number. To the extent that this definiteness may be achieved, relates only to the Western areas of the Western center — Africa, Europe, and Hither Asia — because only there have there been finds providing authentic information. No bones of the facial skeleton have come down of the Javanese *Pithecanthropus* (*Pithecanthropus IV* is much too primitive and cannot be considered as representative for the whole group) and many of the details we know about their morphology are clearly characteristic only of this insular group. We have no criteria for distinguishing typological features from this complex. Weidenreich believed the Javanese *Pithecanthropus* to be the ancestors of the Australoids, seeing them close together morphologically on the basis of the development of the sagittal fold, much too flimsy a consideration in view of the fact that on *Pithecantryopus* skulls it may well be a stadial formation.

African finds of Neanderthal men and the finds in Ngandong in Java are close to each other by a whole complex of morphological features. M. Gremjatskij was perhaps the first to bring them out in a special group of Neanderthal men (Gremjatskij, 1948), but the specific features of structure of the facial skeleton in this group are also known only on the strength of one skull from Rhodesia. Besides, all the finds in the group are very late ones, and their morphological type combines several progressive features with a clear archaism. The whole group leaves the impression of being vestigial, and could well have been an offshoot on the strength of which it is hard to judge about the straight line of evolution within the Western area. This is the more so since geographically the African finds and the finds in Ngandong are separated by a vast distance; their connection in space is as disputable as that between the African Negroes and the Australoids.

Excluding these finds, we have at our disposal paleoanthropological material virtually only for the Neanderthal group. From this group are usually distinguished the later European *paleoanthropus* who are distinguished by some specialized features by which they are farther away from the original forms than modern man. In the opinion of many students this is quite enough to exclude them from the human genealogy either fully or in part. I believe this is altogether wrong, but I do not claim my own view to be more objective than the opposite one. However that may be, by virtue of their age, late *paleoanthropus* cannot be regarded as original forms; they are here ignored regardless of the answer to the question of their place within the system and their participation in forming the modern type of man. The early West European and Palestinian *paleoanthropus* (the finds in Shanidar, before a complete description appeared, remained insufficiently clear morphologically) may claim to be such original forms which, it is true, have already gone through a long way of evolution. Among the West European finds, the facial skeletons have been preserved only on the skulls in Saccopastore and Steinheim, and among the Palestinians, in a sufficiently full form on the skulls from the Skhul cave (no numerical data have yet been published on the Kafzeh skulls).

The facial skeleton of the female skull from Saccopastore is very broad and high, which sharply distinguishes it from the Europoid series, but this is a typically Neanderthal feature. As for the Steinheim skull, it is characterized by small size of facial skeleton and in this respect does not go beyond the limits of typical modern variations. Unfortunately, it is impossible to judge about the vertical profile of the facial skeleton, but it is fairly sharply delineated in the horizontal plane. The pyriform aperture is broad, a characteristic feature of the Neanderthal type but also proper to modern types of the Tropical racial stem. It is true that by several other features, notably, the development of the superciliary fold, the Steinheim *paleoanthropus* was primitive but some archaism not only on the strength of individual features but also by their combination occurred in such a basically progressive group as the skulls from the Skhul cave. Roginskij observed in this population signs of distinctive features of all three big modern races: Negro-Australoids on the Skhul V skull, Europoid on the Skhul IV, and Mongoloid on the Skhul IX skull (the other skulls are known to be in a much worse state) (Roginskij, 1949). For the latter, I feel, there are not enough morphological grounds — the Skhul IX skull is distinguished by a considerable flatness of the facial skeleton on the level of the nasomalar points, but a single feature even of a high taxonomical value on one skull is much too small a factual basis for drawing any responsible conclusions about the Mongoloid nature of this skull, although Roginskij did so with strong reservations. As for the two other combinations, they are indeed fairly clearly expressed. The Skhul V skull is prognathous and broad-nosed and has retained all its features even after a second reconstruction (Snow, 1953). One of these features — prominence of the facial skeleton in the vertical plane — is not characteristic of European Neanderthal men and so has a special significance. By contrast, the Skhul IV skull is orthognathous and has a sharp horizontal profile and strongly prominent nasal bones.

And so, on the territory of the Western area, roughly in its central region, we find in the Mousterian epoch two morphological types one of which could be close to the modern Europoids and the other to the Australoids. Unfortunately, that is all the information to be had from the paleoanthropological data. The relative antiquity of these types is established on the basis of morphology and general theoretical considerations which are of course in themselves not indisputable. We are faced with a choice of several alternatives: (a) a Negro-Australoid combination of features — the most ancient, and Europoid originates from it; (b) the reverse relationship; (c) in the Skhul cave are representatives of an undifferentiated population within which both types occur; and (d) in the Skhul cave a mixed population has been discovered, and we find the first generation following the beginning of the crossbreeding between the Europoids and Negro-Australoids, consequently, their extremely early pre-Mousterian formation as independent racial stems must be recognized. The two latter hypotheses have been repeatedly debated. I reject the latter at once because, first, there are no data indicative of such an early, pre-Mousterian emergence of Europoids and Negro-Australoids, and second, there are no grounds for assuming that by a happy coincidence it was the first generation after the start of crossbreeding that interred its dead in the Skhul cave. Such an event is so highly improbable that it does not have to be seriously demonstrated. The first and second hypotheses also appear to be hardly acceptable because the direct transformation of a morphological type to an extent where the features of one big race are first obliterated and then the features of the other are acquired has never been observed either in paleoanthropological or in somatological studies. There remains, consequently, the third hypothesis, that of an undifferentiated population in the Skhul cave, which corresponds to the most complete empirical observations (both skulls with Europoid and Negro-Australoid features were found in the same cave, which means the appearance of morphologically heterogeneous combinations of features in the same population), and which is best justified theoretically (the existence of undifferentiated populations is a highly probable phenomenon for the Mousterian epoch).

The sharply expressed Europoid and Negro-Australoid combinations of features naturally represented deviating variants in such an undifferentiated population. On the whole (not on the strength of intragroup distribution of variants, but by mean values) it appeared to have been, according to most features, intermediate between the modern Europoids and the Negro-Australoids. The Skhul V skull, where the Negroid racial features are not sharply expressed and which by breadth of nose and prognathism looks more like the skull of an Australian than that of a Negro, appears to be closer to the average type of the whole population than the Skhul IV skull on which Europoid features are so distinctly fixed. The same applies to the Steinheim skull whose Europoid character was hardly representative of a typical group feature and was sooner a deviating variant. I am inclined to assume that the undifferentiated populations whose physical appearance combined both Europoid and Negroid features and which by average type among the modern races stood closest in the Australoids constituted the main nucleus of the population of Europe and Africa in the Mousterian period. The morphological argument in favor of this assumption is the well-known neutrality of Australoids with respect to the Europeans and the African Negroes, their intermediate place between the classical representatives of the Europoid and the Negroid races by the main features. If we were quite sure that genetic bonds had existed between the Europoids and the African Negroids, and had to imagine an original prototype, we should have given it wavy hair, dark skin but lighter than that of Negroes, broad nose, and prognathism less pronounced than that among the native population of Africa, and moderate massiveness. All these are characteristic features of the Australoid race. Add to this the fact that both the Negroes and the Europeans are similar in the age dynamics of racial features: their racial features are more pronounced with age. The children of Negroes and of Europeans have a greater similarity of racial features than do adults. In contrast, the racial features of the children of Mongoloids are most strongly expressed in childhood. This fact testifies to the relatively late separation of the Negroids and the Europoids from each other or at any rate to a later one than the separation of both from the Mongoloids. It is also another indirect indication that the Austroloid combination of features was original for both types.

It is fairly probable that on the basis of this "Australoidness" combined with characteristic Neanderthal features, both the Europoid and the Australoid complexes in their pure form were shaped in the transition to the modern type of man. Nothing need be specially said about the Europoid complex, for its protomorphic variant is fairly well known by many European finds. The Austroloid complex was also sufficiently extensively distributed not only in Africa (skull from Florisbad and Cape Flats) but also in Southern Europe (skulls from the grottoes of Menton, Markina Gora, and partially Combe Capelle). As for the typically Negroid features they must have taken form later than the Austroloid complex. At any rate, even on the skull from Fish Hoek, which has been repeatedly held close to the Negroid series, these features are less pronounced in complex than they are on Negro skulls. Thus, as for the Eastern so for the Western center of race formation, the process of race formation may be said to have been a stage by stage one. The first stage is the formation of undifferentiated populations of *paleonanthropus* distinguished by prognathism and broad nose and resembling in type Skhul V. These populations showed combinations deviating from the average type, with an accumulation now of Europoid now of purely Negroid features. Archaeologically this type may be dated to the Acheulian and the Mousterian period. The second stage is the formation of these populations, in the transition to modern man, first of the Australoid and then of the Europoid complexes in their protomorphic variants. This is the upper paleolithic epoch. Finally, the third stage is connected with the emergence of the typically Negroid combination of features in its African variant. I believe that it was finally formed not earlier than the mesolithic period, or perhaps later. At any rate, neither paleoanthropological data (the absence of earlier finds with clearly expressed Negroid features) nor morphological considerations (morphological specialization and the peculiarity of the Negroid complex) testify in favor of an earlier date.

Essay on the Graphical Presentation of the Genealogical Classification of Human Races

G. DEBETS

The scheme of genealogical classification of the races of mankind proposed in this article has been drawn up by the author with the direct participation of M. G. Levin and N. N. Cheboksarov, and is designed for exposition at the Anthropological Department of the Museum of Anthropology and Ethnography of the USSR Academy of Sciences in Leningrad. Below are set out the facts and considerations underlying the compilation of the scheme, the purpose of whose preliminary publication is to allow its broadest possible discussion.

GENERAL PRINCIPLES OF THE SYSTEM

Must the classification of the human races be a reflection of their genealogy? This is part of the general question of the relationship between phylogeny and the systematics of organisms. In general biology, the Darwinian phylogenetic principle of systematics, having withstood the numerous critical attacks, has now been almost generally recognized (Zenkevich, 1939; Paramonov, 1939). The opponents of the phylogenetic principle who insist on the morphological principle usually refer to the difficulties which arise in establishing the affinity of organisms. Such difficulties undoubtedly do exist. The instances of parallelism and convergence, whose role should not be underestimated, are of course a serious obstacle in the way of systematics on the phylogenetic principle. This obstacle is the more substantial considering that the morphological

First published in *Sovetskaja etnografija*, N1 (1958).

criterion (which should not be confused with the morphological principle) continues in practice to be the main criterion of systematics. The convergence of the morphological criterion and the morphological principle may be prevented through the broadest possible use of other criteria, namely, the palaeontological, biogeographical, physiological, and genetic.

The difficulties which arise in classifying the races of mankind on the geological principle are no greater than those in the structuring of any phylogenetic system. In some respects, they are even greater because the number of traits by which human races, especially the minor subdivisions of the anthropological classification, differ from each other are smaller in number than the number of traits differentiating the species, genera, families, and larger subdivisions of the system in general. Besides, human races, subdivisions of one hand the same species, have constantly intermingled throughout the whole of human history, and this tends greatly to complicate the determination of the degree of their affinity.

The most serious obstacle for structuring a genealogical system is the marked lag of anthropological science behind the other biological sciences on the question of the factors of race formation. Some steps to overcome this lag are now being taken by anthropologists in various countries (Coon, Garn, Birdsell, 1950; Cheboksarov, 1951), who have concentrated on the role of the geographical environment. The study of these problems has yet to reach the level which would make possible the systematic use of the data bearing on the influence exercised by the external environment on the formation of racial distinctions. In principle, however, the results of this type of research should serve as the main criterion in evaluating the genealogical importance of morphological observations.

Efforts should, nevertheless, be made to have the classification of races reflect their affinity to the greatest possible extent. Considering that this classification is required not only as a mnemonic method, and if one is to seek to make it a useful instrument in gaining a knowledge of the main conclusions which anthropological science offers to ethnographers and philologists who study the history of the formation of peoples, this classification should give the fullest possible reflection not only of the similarity but also of the affinity of the peoples in accordance with their physical traits. Equally, for the anthropologists the genealogical classification of languages is of immeasurably greater importance than the morphological one, while the classification of peoples by historico-ethnographical regions is of greater importance than the classification by economic-cultural types (Levin, Cheboksarov, 1955), although the latter could also be of much importance in clarifying various aspects of race formation.

Adoption of the genealogical principle of classification inevitably entails adoption of the principle of taxonomical non-equivalence of systematic units. In accordance with this principle, all mankind is divided into several (mostly three) great groups, each of which consists of smaller subdivisions. This principle has been accepted by most present-day anthropologists, and even the non-specialists will see that it is the correct one. That is why the genealogical tree is the most convenient for illustrating the genealogical relationships between the races and their anthropological types. In contrast to similar schemes illustrating the affinity of major subdivisions of the organic world (families, orders, classes, and types), the genealogical tree of the human races has a great number of inosculating branches, reflecting the great importance of miscegenation in the formation of anthropological types.

It was J. Deniker (1926) who laid the foundations of modern anthropological classification, and who first released it from the ethnic and linguistic subdivisions which were partially retained in its terminology but do not present any great inconvenience. The races of Deniker's classification, of which his second variant contained twenty-nine, are the generally accepted units of anthropological classification. Although the number differs with the various authors, the substance of the matter is not affected because the differences in a number of races usually depend on the up- or downgrading of the systematic rank of this or that race or subrace. A great inconvenience is the extremely inadequate stability of the nomenclature, but this is a substantial and not a fundamental aspect of the matter. The principal differences do not consist in the listing of types but in their grouping, which as V. V. Bunak (1956b) has correctly noted, is of primary importance.

Of Deniker's twenty-nine races, ten (Assyroid, Indo-Afghan, Arabian, Berber, Coastal European, Ibero-Insular, West European Adriatic, North European, and East European) have such a great number of common traits and such a compact area that almost no present-day writer has any doubt about bringing them together in one Europoid group or stem. The special view of this matter expressed by Bunak (1956b), in a highly meaningful but also highly controversial article is, in my opinion, unacceptable, and I set out the grounds for this recently in a special work (Debets, 1956a). For the same reasons, Deniker's two other races, the Eskimo and the Mongol, may be brought together in the Mongol big race.

Finally, Deniker's Negro race occupies in its morphological features as specific a place as all the ten Europoid races taken together, and this is the basis for bringing out a third big race, Negroid.

There are hardly any grounds for discussing the matter as to whether the three big races (racial stems) of mankind are stages of formation. The negative answer to this question quite obviously flows from even a superficial study of the basic characteristics of the big races.

If at the present time there had been a race with moderately dark skin, wavy hair, a developed tertiary pelage, massive facial bone structure, prognathus jaws, broad nose, thin lips, protruding upper lip, a low and dolichocephalous head with a sloping forehead and well-developed supercilliary arches, and brachymorphous proportions of the body, this race could well be considered as having retained the greatest purity of the traits of the original "common human" form. However, all these traits are scattered among the various races and are not to be found all together in any of the present-day or even of the ancient races of *Homo sapiens* (Gremjatskij, 1938; Roginskij, Levin, 1955).

It is quite natural to inquire into the degree of affinity between the big races. According to R. Biasutti (1953), the Negro-Australoid races constitute a "circle of Equatorial races", as contrasted with the "circle of Borealic races", to which the Europoids and Mongoloids belong. According to Keith (1949), the light-skinned races of the Northern Hemisphere constitute a special branch in contrast to the dark-skinned races of the Southern Hemisphere. A different conception was set forth by Ya. Ya. Roginskij (Bunak, Nesturkh, Roginskij, 1941) who believed that the earliest subdivision was into two branches, the South-Western and the South-Eastern. The former had given rise to the Negro-Australoids and Europoids, and the latter, to the Mongoloids. Because this standpoint is backed up by a number of morphological arguments, it has been accepted in the scheme presented here.

The most debatable today are the places to be assigned in the classification of the following races: the Australian, Veddoid (broad-nosed Dravidian subrace, according to Deniker), Ainu, Melanesian, Negrito, Bushman, South Indian (according to Deniker a thin-nosed Dravidian subrace), Ethiopian, Lapp, Uralic (Ugric), South Siberian (Turko-Tatar or Turanian), Polynesian, Indonesian, and all the races of the American Indians.

AUSTRALIAN RACE

In accordance with the scheme here proposed, the Australians are brought together with the Negroids into one Equatorial or Negro-Australoid big race. This is also the approach taken by many other students (Eickstedt, 1934; Cheboksarov, 1951) on the grounds of dark skin, great breadth of the nose, prognathism, and thick lips. However, the Australians quite obviously have substantial distinctions, notably their wavy hair and the well-developed tertiary pelage. In accordance with these traits, the Australians are akin to the Europoids, and some students have taken this as grounds for assuming that the Australians, or at any rate, their main element, should be included in the Europoid big race (Hooton, 1946). Those who take a third view believe that the peculiar combination of the principal traits which is characteristic of the Australians provides ground for bringing them out into a special Australoid big race equivalent in systematic terms to the Negroid and the Europoid races (Bunak, 1956b; Biasutti, 1953).

The latter view is the most circumspect. Indeed, if there is no solid ground for referring his phenomenon to any of the higher ranking classification categories, it would be better to single it out as a special category. This way out of the difficulty can only be temporary because ideally the phylogenetic systematics must be dichotomic, for it cannot be assumed that the degree of affinity between three or more races is absolutely similar. The question, consequently, may be posed only in this plane: is there any ground for selection between the Negroid and the Europoids? If there are no sufficient grounds the Australians should be kept in the systematics of mankind's races as a special stem. If there are grounds for bringing them closer together with either of the two big races (Negroid or Europoid) this should be reflected in the classification which must be as close as possible to the actual bonds between the groups.

There seems to be more ground for assuming affinity with the Negroids. The wavy, morphologically "neutral", hair of the Australians and the Europoids are intermediate between the "specialized" curly hair of the Negroids and the straight hair of the Mongoloids. It may therefore be assumed that the intermediate type of hair structure is a more ancient one, and that the ancestors of the Negroes had wavy hair. The well-developed tertiary pelage of the Australians and the Europeans is most probably a more ancient trait, and it would therefore be more correct to assume that the ancestors of present-day Negroes had more developed beards and body hair. The ancestors of the Negroes were apparently similar to the Australians in the traits which now divide the two races. In shape of skull, the Australians differ from the Negroes above all in having a retreating forehead and heavy supercilliary arches. It may be assumed that these are the marks of a more ancient form, and indeed ancient skulls with "Austroloid" features have indeed been discovered in South Africa (Drennan, 1929; Dreyer, 1935).

The Europeans' light skin, narrow nose, and orthognathism may also indeed be much later characteristics than the Australians' dark skin, broad nose, and prognathism, but it should be taken into account that even in the late palaeolithic period, that is, at the time from which the "Australoid" skulls of South Africa date, Europe was inhabited by the Cro-Magnon people who on the whole had a narrow nose and orthognathism, and consequently differed essentially from the Australians. In length of face and body proportions and several other characteristics the Australians are more remote from the hypothetical "original form" than present-day Europeans.

These facts and considerations suggest the conclusion that the Australians have a greater affinity with the Negroes than with the Europeans, and this serves as a basis for bringing the Australians and the Negroes together into one Negro-Australoid, or Equatorial, big race. There is no doubt, however, that the Australians are a part of an Oceanic branch of this big race which had developed at a very early period.

The repeated attempts to bring out several types within the Australian race (Giuffrida-Ruggeri, 1913; Birdsell, 1941) for the time being are no more than the personal views held by some researchers, and are not reflected in the scheme. Still, it appears to be appropriate to remark on the existence of a strain of curly-headed types of the Melanesian race.

VEDDOID RACE

Many students (Giffrida-Ruggeri, 1913; Montandon, 1928; Vallois, 1948; Bunak, 1956b) believe that the Veddoids are closest to the Australians, and in Deniker's classification they are designated as a "broad-nosed Dravidian subrace", an unsatisfactory name that has now been abandoned by everyone. The Veddoids are normally seen to be close to the Australians in color of skin and form of hair, the most widely but not generally accepted standpoint. Von Eickstedt, for instance, refers the Veddoids to the Europoid stem as one of the protomorphic types (Eickstedt, 1934). I do not feel that this view is acceptable. Cro-Magnon man, who should be regarded as the ancient representative of the Europoid race (Debets 1956a), does not have any specific Veddoid characteristics.

Von Eickstedt's view is also being undermined by his reference of the

"Dravidian" race proper to the Negroids. All the materials allowing a direct comparison (Sarasin, 1892–1893; Guha, 1935) show that the Veddoids have a broader nose, thicker lips, darker skin, and more wavy hair than the Dravidians. Having failed to find any real arguments in favor of Von Eickstedt's view, I have retained in the proposed scheme the most widely accepted view and included the Veddoids in the same stem as the Australians.

Mainly on the strength of the data concerning the geographical distribution of members of the Veddoid race, I have divided it into two types: the Deccan, in which the Ceylonese Veddas should also be included, and the Sunda type. For centuries, the Deccan type has been influenced by the Southern Europoids, and the Sunda type, by the Southern Mongoloids. I have thought it proper to show these influences in the scheme.

AINU RACE

The status of the Ainu is highly complicated. Their great similarity with the Europeans is obvious. That is why almost all modern authors refer the Ainu to the Europoid races (Montandon, 1928; Eickstedt, 1934; Biasutti, 1953; Vallois, 1948). A. Keith (1949), in accordance with his view of the affinity of the Europoids and the Mongoloids, assumes that the Ainu constitute an undifferentiated form of a European-Asian branch of mankind.

Soviet anthropologists (Cheboksarev, 1951; Roginskij, Levin, 1955; Bunak, 1956b), unanimously siding with L. Ja. Shternberg (1928) in this respect, hold the Ainu to be close to the Australians. Among the Western anthropologists this view, first expressed by O. Peshel, was adopted towards the end of his life by V. Giuffrida-Ruggeri (1921a). E. Hooton (1946) adopted a somewhat similar stand. It is true that he too unconditionally included the Ainu among the Europoid races, but, as I have already said, he also refers to them the main element which is a part of the Australian body.

It will hardly be correct in this instance formally to adopt the morphological criterion. Shternberg clearly showed the existence of Southern parallels in the culture of the Ainu. This fact must be reckoned with despite the obvious discrepancy in some instances between the anthropological classification and the historico-ethnographical one. By accepting the Ainu's affinity with the Europoids, we face an intractable problem.

How is it to be explained that the Ainu, being ancestors of Europoids advanced to the East, have failed to retain in their culture any Western specific features, while having a number of common features with the peoples of Oceania, without being in any way related to them in origin? If the affinity between the Ainu and the Europoids and the absence of direct affinity with the Australians were an incontestable fact, an explanation would have to be found to this involved interlacing of historico-ethnographic and anthropological relations.

Is it truly impossible to consider the Ainu race to be closer in origin to the Australian than the Europoid? To answer this question it is necessary to bear in mind that the Ainu, despite their specific features, still have some Mongoloid admixtures: The Mongoloid eyefold (epicanthus) frequently occurs among them, though not as often as among the neighboring peoples (Levin, 1949). The Ainu are less prognathous, less broad-nosed, and less thick-lipped than the Australians, but the admixture of the Mongoloid element was bound to result in a reduced prognathism, breadth of nose, and thickness of lips. Still, the Ainu are more prognathous, more broad-nosed, and more thick-lipped than their Mongoloid neighbors. (Levin, 1949; Debets, 1951b), which is especially hard to reconcile with the assumption that the Ainu have a Europoid basis. On the other hand, these facts are easily reconciled with the hypothesis that the main element of the present-day Ainu body is of Austroloid origin.

There yet remains the color of their skin. Although the Ainu are somewhat more dark-skinned than the surrounding Mongoloid peoples, the differences are not great. The sharp distinctions in skin color between the Ainu and the Australians cannot be explained only by interbreeding. One must make the assumption that the Ainu race was formed not only as the basic Austroloid element mixed with the less numerous Mongoloids, but also as the process of skin depigmentation proceeded, which fully accords with the conditions of their habitation in northern latitudes over a long period. On the strength of these facts and considerations, I have placed the Ainu race in my scheme together with the Australians within the Oceanic branch of the Equatorial stem, also remarking on the admixture of the Mongoloid element.

MELANESIAN RACE

There is no unanimous view on the origins and status of the Melanesians in the anthropological classification. On the strength primarily of the curly form of hair, some students believe them to be closer to the Negroes than to the Australians not only morphologically but also phylogenetically (Bunak, 1956b).

The geographical location of the Melanesians gives food for thought. It has been observed that the curly form of hair is formed among Melanesian children much later than among the children of African Negroes. Some local groups of Melanesians, the New Caledonians (Sarasin, 1916–1922), for example, differ from the Australians only in form of hair and are similar to the Australians on all the other counts: they have a strongly developed tertiary pelage, retreating forehead, and developed supercilliary arches. Similar variants have been discovered in the internal areas of New Guinea (Le Roux, 1948). On the strength of the data, and also of the above-mentioned considerations concerning the probability that the spiral hair forms originated from the wavy hair forms, the hypothesis was suggested that curly hair among the African and Oceanian Negroids was formed parallel to each other, and that from the genealogical standpoint the Melanesians and the Papuans are closer to the Australians than to the African Negroes. That is the hypothesis which the proposed scheme reflects.

To the two types normally brought out within the Melanesian race — the Melanesians proper and the Papuans — I found it proper to add the above-mentioned New Caledonians.

The Tasmanians are also closer to the Melanesians in form of hair, but craniologically the Tasmanian type (Morant, 1927) is characterized by exceptionally small height of face and size of cranium, which produces a special combination of features on the strength of which the Tasmanian type must be regarded as being closer to the Melanesian than to the Australian. In view of the obscurity of this question of origin of the Tasmanian type, it is shown here as a special race of the Oceanic branch.

SHORT-STATURED NEGROID TYPES (PYGMIES)

There are especial differences of view over the status of the Negrito and the Negrillos — the short-statured, dark-skinned, curly-haired groups of indigenous population of Africa and South-East Asia, which have been given the widespread though inapt designation of "Pygmies". It was J. Kollmann (1900) who hypothesized that the Pygmies, with their childlike structural features of body in general and of skull in particular, constitute a vestige of an ancient stage of mankind's development which has been preserved to our day. This hypothesis clashes sharply with man's palaeontology. All the finds of the bone remains of ancient men have proved to be absolutely not of the "Pygmy" type, but of the directly opposite, sharply hypermorphic type. A minority of anthropologists to-day insist on putting the Pygmies in a special big race, taxonomically equivalent to the Negroid, Europoid and Mongoloid (Montandon, 1928).

Some students continue to see the Pygmies as a special branch of the Equatorial (Negro-Australoid) big race (Eickstedt, 1934), but this is hard-ly acceptable either. The Negritos of the Andaman and Philippine Islands, the short-statured groups of New Guinea, and the Semangs of Malacca on the one hand, and the various groups of African Negrillos on the other, are similar only in the features which determine their membership of the Equatorial stem and by the short length of their body, but even the body proportions appear to be different. Thus Pygmies do not seem to constitute a single branch genealogically speaking even within the Equatorial stem. Some short-statured variants like the Pygmies of the Congo basin (Schebesta, Lebzelter, 1933; Gusinde, 1948) have indeed preserved some ancient features (a relatively hairy body, and a pro-truding upper lip), while others, like the Tapiro of New Guinea (Schla-ginhaufen, 1916; Bijlmer, 1923) differ from their neighbors only by the small length of their body and its functionally related proportions. On the strength of this, and also of the geographical criterion, it is possible to suggest a hypothesis that the African Negrillos are genealogically closer to the African Negroes than to the Negritos of South-East Asia, while the latter do not perhaps also constitute a genealogically uniform Negrito race within the Oceanic branch, although this traditional grouping of the Andamans, the Philippine Aëtas, and the Semangs has been preserved in the proposed scheme pending new research.

BUSHMAN RACE

The Bushman, or Koisan, race (the latter term being based on local ethnic designations, and should be preferred to the terms based on colonialist nicknames, but these have been much too widely accepted) is similar to the Negroids in form of hair, but reveals unexpected paral-lels with the Mongoloids in skin color, horizontal face profile (Woo, Morant, 1934), and even the presence of an epicanthus. The morpho-logical criterion does not in itself provide direct grounds for including the Koisans in the Negroid or the Mongoloid big races. Most authors, adopting the geographical criterion, are inclined to rank them closer with the Negroids, however, Von Eickstedt groups the Koisans with the Mongoloids (Eickstedt, 1934).

Theoretically it may well be assumed, of course, that the curly hair of the Koisans and the Negroes were formed parallel to each other, just as they have been formed among the Melanesians and the African Negroes, but this assumption requires additional evidence. There is an equally possible assumption about parallelism in the formation of features which make the Koisans akin to the Mongoloids. An argument in favor of this standpoint comes from observations of the genetic nature of the Koisan and the Mongol eyefold. These observations have suggested the conclusion that among the Mongoloids epicanthus is inherited as a dominant and among the Koisans as a recessive feature (Fischer, 1930). Combined with the typically African distribution of blood groups (Mourant, 1954) and the geographical criterion, this fact makes us incline to a majority view and to regard the Koisan race as a subdivision of the African branch of the Equatorial stem.

AFRICAN NEGROIDS

The African Negroids, who are classified by Deniker as a single Negro race, are divided in the proposed scheme into three races: the South African, the Nilotic, and the Sudanese, with the latter subdivided into two types: the Sudanese proper and the tropical type. Many authors have argued the advisability of a greater subdivision of the Negro race, but the grounds for doing so are still inadequate and the anthropological classification of the African Negroes is largely conventional. Still, I prefer these conventional subdivisions so as to maintain a more or less similar degree of detail in various parts of the scheme. I have preserved in the scheme all the groups brought out by G. Montandon (1928) whose view has been accepted by the authors of most later classifications. The paleotropical (forest) race first described by H. Johnston (1908) is presented as a mixed form with a Negrillo strain because virtually all the characteristic features of this race make it akin to the Negrillo.

DARK-SKINNED TYPES OF INDIA

The South Indian race (narrow-nosed, Dravidian, or Melano-Indian, according to Deniker) is morphologically intermediate between the Europoids and the Negro-Australoids. There is vacillation in determining its ranking in systematics, either with the Europoid (Sergi, 1911) or Negroid (Eickstedt, 1934), or even in a special Indo-African big race (Giuffrida-Ruggeri, 1913). These differences are not essential because all authors variously admit the mixed nature of this group, but what should be rejected is the idea that the South Indian race is characterized by a combination of dark skin, like that of the Negroids, and a narrow nose, like that of the Europeans. This combination of features does occur among some individuals, but cannot be regarded as a group characteristic. As I have already said, the Tamil intermediate position between the Veddoids and the Singhalese, described by P. and F. Sarasin (1892–1893), is characteristic of India in general, where a reduction in the breadth of the nose is on the whole regularly accompanied by a reduction in the intensive pigmentation of the skin, less wavy hair, and a thicker tertiary pelage. Accordingly, in the proposed scheme the South Indian race is shown as a mixed group formed as the result of a merger of Oceanic (proto-Australoid) and Europoid elements.

ETHIOPIAN RACE

The status of the Ethiopian race is similarly decided (Cheboksarov, 1936a). Its unification with the South Indian race into a single "Indo-African" branch cannot be considered advisable, because in spite of the parallel course of the process of race formation in India and in East Africa, the two races do not stem from a common non-differentiated type, and there is no need to bring them together in the classification. Morphologically, the intermediate position of the Ethiopian race is less definite than that of the South Indian. According to some features (extremely small breadth of face and high facial indicator) the Ethiopian race occupies a somewhat specific position. These features already occur on Mesolithic skulls from Kenya (Leakey, 1935), and this is perhaps evidence that the Ethiopian race is older than the South Indian.

EUROPOID RACES

The most widespread division in the classification of races of the Europoid stem is that into the light-haired Europoids of the Northern zone, the moderately dark-haired brachycephalics of the central zone (Pamiro-Alpine race), and the dark-haired meso-dolichocephalics of the Mediterranean (Montandon, 1928; Eickstedt, 1934). Soviet anthropological writers have repeatedly expressed critical remarks over the exaggeration of the taxonomical role of the cephalic index. Despite the convenience of using this greatly varying feature for diagnostic purposes (now and again one has to confine oneself to referring not only one skull but a whole series as belonging to "dolichocranial" or "brachycranial" Europoids), its genealogical importance is nevertheless not great. There has long been knowledge of instances of rapid change in the form of head in time, and also the effect of deformation caused by the form of cradle which was widely used in Hither Asia (Zhirov, 1941). It is an impossible assumption, for instance, that the brachycephalic Azerbaidzanians of the Alazan valley are more akin to the Tyrolians than they are to the dolichocephalic Azerbaidzanians of Nakhichevan or Shemakha. It is impossible to assume that the dolichocephalic Ossetians of the 16th century (Bunak, 1953) are more akin to the Arabs than to the present-day brachycephalic Ossetians. That is why one must regrettably admit that the cephalic index is suitable only for bringing out the smallest subdivisions of the anthropological classification. The division within the "light-haired branch" into a Northern and East European race in accordance with the cephalic index is not always justified, and it has already been observed (Eickstedt, 1935) that some typically "Northern" local groups have an average cephalic index as high as 85 or even 87.

We, therefore, rely mainly on the pigmentation of the hair and the eyes, restoring T. H. Huxley's xanthocroid and melanocroid races (Huxley, 1870) and adding to them a third, intermediate group. The latter may have originated not only as a result of interbreeding, but also constitute a part of the Europoid stem which did not research the stage of depigmentation characteristic of the Northern areas of Europe.

Is the color of hair and eyes the only feature serving to differentiate two of the most distinct branches of the Europoid race? With respect to the East of Europe, the answer is definitely a negative one. The Russians, for instance, clearly differ from the Georgians and the Armenians not only in pigmentation, but also in form of nose, in the development of the tertiary pelage, and the structure of the upper eyelid (Natishvili et al., 1953). Some researchers believe that the profile of the dorsum of the nose makes it possible to draw an equally sharp distinction between the Northern and the Southern Europoids as the color of hair and eyes (Keiter, 1956); however, on the Atlantic coast the problem appears to be a more complex one. Among the Irish (Hooton, Dupertuis, 1935) and the Riffs of Morocco (Coon, 1931) studied by scientists of one Harvard school, no distinctions have been discovered in the most comparable feature, the profile of the dorsum of the nose. Among the

Riffs the eyefold has been found to occur even more frequently than among the Irish, while distinctions in the development of the tertiary pelage are indefinite. It is true that there is more straight hair among the Irish than among the Riffs, but in the East of Europe the distinctions by this feature happen to be slight and indefinite. This question clearly requires further study. In the extreme West of Europe there is need to collect new and more comparable data. It may well be that alongside the "real" representatives of the Northern race, marked by insignificant occurrence of protuberant forms of nasal dorsum and a relatively weak development of the tertiary pelage, we shall also have to bring out the "depigmented Mediterraneans" who are genealogically more akin to the "real Mediterraneans" and to the "real Nordics". This idea has already been expressed by Cheboksarov (1951). We do not have enough data for a concrete solution of the problem, and the proposed scheme retains the branch of light-haired Europoids as an independent unit. In the subsequent subdivision of the three main branches of the Europoid stem I have tried to depart as little as possible from the accepted views.

The southern (Melanocroid) branch comprises the Indo-Afghan race and a cluster of Eurasian dark-haired races: the Mediterranean, Hither Asian, and Dinaric.

On the strength of the relatively rapid changes in the cephalic index, a fact noted above, I have included within the Indo-Afghan race not only the Hindu Kush, the most characteristic type for this race, and the North Indian types which includes an admixture of Veddoid and South Indian elements, but also the brachycephalic Pamiro-Ferghanese. To this race — the Central Asian interfluve race — according to L. V. Oshanin (Oshanin, Zezenkova, 1953), German anthropologists now apply the term "Turanides" (Schwidetzky, 1950). This cannot be accepted as a happy terminological find, considering that Deniker proposed that the term should be used to designate the South Siberian race which both morphologically and genealogically bears no direct relation to the Pamiro-Ferghan race. The origin of the Pamiro-Ferghan race requires further elaboration. According to V. V. Ginzburg (1951) it was formed in the process of gracilization of the Andronov type, that is, one of the proto-European variants. This may well be possible with respect to the brachycranial and relatively hypomorphic variants distinguished by palaeoanthropological data in Kazakhstan and in Kirghizia in tumuli ascribed to the Usun. If our information about the Pamiro-Ferghan race were confined to craniological data, such an assumption would have been possible also with respect to the Europoid brachycephalics of the Central Asian interfluve and the Pamirs.

Somatological studies of the Kazakhs give an idea not only of the craniological features, but also of the pigmentation of the Andronov type, which combine with the Central Asian Mongoloids to form the South Siberian race characteristic of the Kazakhs. The Andronov type must have been characterized by light eyes since the Kazakhs differ from the Mongols not only by a more protuberant nose, more intensive growth of beard, less frequent occurrence of epicanthus, and lighter pigmentation. The subsequent spread of the mixed South Siberian type into Central Asian interfluve area resulted in a paradoxical phenomenon: the Mongoloid complex of features now and again occurs here in combination with a relatively lighter pigmentation (Jarkho, 1933b).

Thus, the dark-eyed Europoid brachycephalics of the Central Asian interfluve and the Pamirs are perhaps more akin to the dark-eyed Indo-Afghans (the Eastern Mediterraneans) from which they differ only by such relatively rapidly changing features as length of body and the cephalic index. The latter has risen to the limits of brachycephaly apparently only in the last two or three thousand years, to judge by the finds which come from the area of distribution of the Pamiro-Ferghan race (Ginzburg, 1950a, b). Furthermore, there is wide use among the Tadziks and the Uzbeks of the Hither Asian type of cradle which undoubtedly leads to an increase of the cephalic index (Zhirov, 1941; Ginzburg, 1937a, b, c).

Consequently, the ancient Europoid brachycephalics of Central Asia and Kazakhstan are of different origin, and so the distinction between the two types on the strength of palaeoanthropological material entails serious difficulties.

The admixture of the South Siberian element to the Pamiro-Ferghan race is so commonplace that I have found it necessary to show this in my scheme. In the gorges of the Western Pamirs, the admixture of Mongoloid elements does not for all practical purposes occur (Oshanin, 1937).

The profound distinction between Mediterranean forms, on the one hand, and those of Hither Asia and Dinaric forms, on the other, is based on an overestimation of the importance of the cephalic index, and has not been reflected in my scheme. The Hither Asian race may well be in the same relative position to the Mediterranean as the Pamiro-Ferghan to the Indo-Afghan, but pending the completion of special studies I prefer not to depart from the established view of the independent position of this race, which occurs under various names in all the classifications.

The types and races intermediate between the races of the Southern and the Northern branches present the most difficult aspect in the Europoid classification. The Central European, Pontic, and Atlantic races, brought out in the scheme with a number of types, represent a possible variant of classification.

I have retained the traditional division of the light Europoids into the North European and the Baltic races, but in order to emphasize that the cephalic index does not lie at the basis of this subdivision I have specially noted the mesocephalic White Sea-Baltic type within the Baltic race. Consequently, the latter differs from the Northern not so much in form of head as in the presence of a small element of the Mongoloid admixture (Cheboksarov, 1936c).

URALIC-LAPONOID RACE

For a long time, the question of the niche occupied in the classification of races by the Laponoid type was decided in favor of attaching it to the Mongoloid stem (Montandon, 1928). In the recent period the opinion has gained ground that the Lapps (Saami) are an ancient form of Europoid, or specifically Alpine, race (Montandon, 1933; Eickstedt, 1934; Biasutti, 1953; Vallois, 1948).

This opinion cannot be accepted. First, palaeoanthropological data do not at all testify in favor of this assumption. Second, the existence of a Mongoloid admixture among the Lapps is quite evident: as compared with the Norwegians, the Karelians, the Russians, or the Komi, they have a less developed tertiary pelage, the face is flatter, the eyefold occurs more often, etc. (D. Zolotarev, 1928; Geyer, 1932; Schreiner, 1929). Palaeoanthropological data quite obviously testify to the existence of an ancient Mongoloid element in the area of the Kola Peninsula (Jakimov, 1953).

Nonetheless, the modern Lapps cannot be directly included in the Mongoloid big race. This is a typically intermediate form which is on the whole closer to the Europeans. Together with palaeoanthropological data, the Lapps' morphological characteristics suggest that they are a group of mixed origin. They also do have specific traits — a very long face and an incurved nose — which cannot be explained as a direct consequence of crossbreeding. At the same time, palaeoanthropology provides definite evidence against regarding these characteristics as being features of a protomorphic type. These features, together with the Lapps' short stature, are most probably relatively recent, and were formed after crossbreeding as the Lapp type took shape.

The question of the origin of the Uralic type (the Ugric race, in Deniker's terminology) is in a similar state. It is usually included in the

Mongoloid stem and only Biasutti regards this group as an ancient form of the Europoid race, alongside the Ainu (Biasutti, 1953).

In the proposed scheme the Lapp and the Uralic races are brought together in one Uralic-Laponoid race, a conception first expressed by Giuffrida-Ruggeri (1921b), but later unfortunately abandoned even by some of the authors who had shared the idea (Bunak, 1932c; 1956b). There is, of course, no doubt that the traits of the Mongoloid race are more pronounced among the Khants and the Mansi than among Lapps, but in accordance with all the main features they are intermediate between the Europoids and the Mongoloids. The incurved nose, which is characteristic of the Lapps, is equally characteristic of the Mansi (Rudenko, 1914; Debets, 1947) and also, even if to a lesser extent, of the Mari, whose physical type has long been defined by Bunak as sub-Uralic (Bunak, 1924a). The distinctions between the Lapps and the Mari are not great and boil down to a distinction in length of body, the facial, and to a lesser extent, the cephalic index.

SOUTH SIBERIAN RACE

It was Deniker who brought together the Ugric and the Turco-Tatar (Turanian) races in a Eurasian group, which in his scheme is intermediate between the Europoid and Mongoloid races. Soviet writers, following Jarkho, most frequently regard the Turanian race as a South Siberian one. At present, almost everyone inclines to the conclusion that it is of mixed origin, although it appears to have resulted from a mixture of other races of the Europoid and Mongoloid stems than the Uralo-Laponoid race (Ginzburg, Debets, Levin, Cheboksarov, 1952).

MONGOLOID RACES

Deniker's Mongoloid race is taxonomically a much higher category than the North European or the Adriatic; the authors of all later classifications sought to subdivide it. Giuffrida-Ruggeri tried to fulfil this task (Giuffrida-Ruggeri, 1921b) but was clearly unsuccessful because he was guided by some anthropometric characteristics only.

Cheboksarov's classification is the most convenient and best combined craniological and somatological criteria with the genealogical principle (Cheboksarov, 1947b). He groups the Asian races of the Mongoloid stem in two branches: the continental (Siberian) and the Southern (Pacific). These branches do not quite correspond to Deniker's North Mongolian and South Mongolian subraces, because, according to Deniker, the Northern Chinese are a part of the Northern subrace, while according to Cheboksarov, they belong to the Southern branch. The main criteria of Cheboksarov's classification are height of cranium and breadth of face. The Siberian Mongoloids are distinguished by a broad face and a low cranium, while the Pacific Mongoloids have a relatively narrow face and a high cranium.

The Siberian branch is usually regarded as a single race but this does not correspond to the degree of detail which I have adopted in my scheme as a whole. That is why it is divided into a Central Asian and a Baikal race (Debets, 1951b). On the strength of Levin's works (1958), I have singled out an Amuro-Sakhalin type which is characteristic of the Nivkhs.

The status of the Tibetans and the Eskimos remains unclear. Some writers indicated the proximity of these types (Klimek, 1930), but the geographical criterion contradicts their unification in a single race. Pending the receipt of new data it is more appropriate to single the Tibetans out as a special race intermediate between the Siberian and the Pacific branches.

With good reason, everyone regards the Eskimos as a type apart; however, the Aleuts are usually separated from the Eskimos on the strength of truly essential distinctions in the value of all the diameters and indexes of the cranium. A work dealing specially with the anthropology of North-East Asia sets out arguments in favor of bringing the Aleuts and the Eskimos together (Debets, 1951b). The fact is that the size and form of cranium characteristic of the Aleuts were apparently formed over the last few centuries. The blood groups also indicate the close kinship of the Eskimos and the Aleuts (Laughlin, 1951). By blood groups, the Eskimos and the Aleuts are not only close to each other, but are closer to the American Indians than to the Asian Mongoloids (Boyd, 1952). It is therefore hardly correct to make a sharp contraposition between the Eskimos and the American Indians. Both have a common component, although, in addition, the Eskimos appear to have a much later admixture of Asian Mongoloids proper.

POLYNESIAN RACE

There is a widely accepted and perhaps correct view that the origin of the Polynesian race (and consequently its place in the classification of races) is the most complex problem in ethnical anthropology. Indeed, the Polynesian race is classified with the Mongoloids (Vallois, 1948; Giuf-frida-Ruggeri, 1921b), the Australoids (Bunak, 1956b), or the Europoids (Eickstedt, 1934). In our day, the differences over this problem have not decreased. The usual way out of this situation — separation into a special big race — is hardly applicable in this case because it is well known that Polynesia was settled by man relatively recently when all the big races were already in existence (Bunak, Tokarev, 1951).

Morphologically, the Polynesians, as a whole, are closest to the Southern Europoids. Their slightly wavy or straight hair, relatively light skin, not very weak tertiary pelage, moderately broad and relatively prominent nose, meso- or orthognathism, not very thick lips, and the absence of or the slight expression of the Mongol eyefold make the Polynesians more akin to the Europoids than to any other race. The Europoid theory of the origin of the Polynesians, however, needs to produce a historical hypothesis which is highly intricate and not backed by any other date of the resettlement of the main nucleus of the Polynesians at least from Northern India, because it is hardly possible, without much exaggeration, to speak of an ancient spread of the Europoid race in the more proximate area of Polynesia.

The question arises as to whether it is possible to explain the origin of the Polynesian race bypassing such a complex and highly improbable historical hypothesis. Such an explanation is perhaps possible. It should be borne in mind that the nose of the Polynesians is, after all, broader and the lips thicker than those of the European group (Shapiro, 1943). These traits may be evidence that Equatorial races participated in the formation of the Polynesians. The relatively light skin and the slight waviness of the hair may also be an indication of a Mongoloid admixture. The rather broad face may also be due to Mongoloid blood. It is true that ancient forms of the Europoid race were also characterized by considerable breadth of face, but in the Southern and South-Eastern parts of the Europoid area this feature of the proto-European type must have disappeared some thousands of years before the new era, long before any possible migration to Indonesia (Swindler, 1936). Finally, the Mongol eyefold, however infrequently, does occur among the Polynesians. Only the relatively prominent nose is hard to explain by a crossbreeding with Equatorial (Australoid) and Mongoloid forms, but judging by precise craniometric data (Woo, Morant, 1934), the nose of the Australians is not very flat. In addition, ancient forms of the Mongoloid race may have also been characterized by a moderately prominent nose, evidence of which, some authors believe, is the high bridge of the nose among the American Indians.

In general, the American Indians do not differ greatly from the Polynesians. The similarity between these races is possibly not less than that between the Polynesians and the Europeans. The blood groups and other features with a clearly pronounced heredity also bring the Polynesians close to the American Indians. In the recent period these facts have come into prominence in connection with Thor Heyerdahl's bold sporting enterprise which he undertook to prove the American origin of the Polynesians (Heyerdahl, 1952; Khejerdal, 1955). Heyerdahl has some supporters among the anthropologists (Avias, 1949), but more hard-headed students indicate the possibility that the resemblance between the American Indians and the Polynesians may be due to the fact that the ancestors of both had come from Eastern Asia (Mourant, 1954).

As a result, the most probable assumption is that the Polynesians were formed in the process of interbreeding of Mongoloid and Equatorial races, and it is in accordance with this hypothesis that the Polynesians are presented in the proposed scheme.

The hypothesis of the Europoid basis of the Polynesians would have been more plausible if other Europoid types were to be found West of Polynesia. That may be the factor which has drawn attention to Deniker's "Indonesian race", preserved in some classification schemes as a subdivision of the Europoid stem (Montandon, 1928; Lester, Millot, 1939). The artificial nature of this construction is much too obvious: no people, no single ethnographic group of Indonesia, is characterized by an express combination of traits typical of the Europoids. Any description of the "Indonesian race" is usually accompanied by annotations to the effect that the race is so heavily mixed that it is no longer to be found in a pure state. Others prefer to mention an indefinite admixture of Europoid blood without further specification.

The peoples of the internal regions and the small islands of Indonesia, sometimes called the "proto-Malayans", do in fact differ somewhat from the "deutero-Malayans" who inhabit the coastal areas of the large islands. The former are mesocephalic and the latter brachycephalic. The distinctions on the strength of this trait are the most definite. It is accepted that the "proto-Malayans" have less clearly pronounced Mongoloid features; however, it remains to be proved that this recession of Mongoloid traits was caused by an admixture of the Europoid race. With respect to Southern China it has been proved that the recession of Mongoloid traits is caused by an admixture not of the Europoid but of some Equatorial type (Cheboksarov, 1947a). Pending the receipt of new data, it appears to be right to apply this conclusion to the whole of South-East Asia, including Indonesia. The "Indonesian race" is consequently the product of a mixture of an ancient population belonging to the Equatorial stem with later Mongoloid arrivals. It must of course be admitted that individuals with facial features reminiscent of the European type do occur among the peoples of Indonesia and Indochina, but Europoid facial features may in some instances be formed as the result of a combination of a Veddoid or Australoid type, on the one hand, and the ancient Mongoloids, on the other — the same way as these features were formed among the Polynesians. Besides, both in Indonesia and in Indochina there must to some extent be evidence of an admixture of Indians and Arabs, mainly in the coastal areas, among the culturally more developed peoples. That is why no special Indonesian race has been singled out in my scheme.

AMERICAN INDIANS

The problem of the origin of the American Indians continues to be the subject of a lively and sustained discussion. There is no doubt that the principal component of the American Indians is closely akin to the Mongoloids. What is controversial is the question of the origin of the admixtures in this Mongoloid basis. No one any longer has doubts about the existence of such admixtures, and the theory of the purely Mongoloid nature of the American Indians, which Hrdlička so strongly defended (Hrdlička, 1912, 1935), is now rejected by an overwhelming majority of students (Birdsell, 1951).

The basis for assuming admixtures of other than Mongoloid races is the data on the essential morphological distinctions between the American Indians and the Asian Mongoloids. In effect, these distinctions are now and again quite considerable. Back in 1910, Biasutti drew attention of the fact that the American Indians lacked the flatness of the facial skeleton characteristic of Asian Mongoloids. This observation has now been repeatedly verified statistically (Debets, 1957; Newmann, 1952). It has turned out that in flatness of face and nose the skulls of the American Indians exceed those of the Europeans to a small extent and at any rate they are much closer to them than to the skulls of the Asian Mongoloids. Some local groups (like the ancient Carancawas of Texas) have yielded values which are in no way inferior to those typical of the Europeans (nasomalaric angle 136.1; simous height 5.2; dactyal height 13.0). Only in the North-West of America is a somewhat flatter face to be found (Woo,

Morant, 1934), but still to a lesser extent than among the Eskimos, to say nothing of the Asian Mongoloids.

Some ethnic groups of American Indians studied in the recent period differ sharply from the "average type". Fragmentary data of bearded men occurring in the forest areas of South America (Wegner, 1931) have been supplemented by statistical data on the peoples of Arizona and New Mexico. Among the latter are distinguished, for instance, the Yaks (Gabel, 1949). Dark skin (No. 21 and darker, according to Lushan's scale) occurs among almost one-half of the Yaks (40 per cent), and much less frequently (not more than 3 per cent) among other peoples in the area. At the same time, compared with other neighboring peoples they have a more developed beard, less frequent prognathism, thicker lips, and broader nose. Birdsell (1951) has drawn attention to the strong development of beards among the Cahuillas and the Paiutes, based, incidentally, almost exclusively on several photographs.

These and similar other facts have induced many researchers to draw the conclusion that apart from the Mongoloids, Europoid, and Negroid elements also took part in populating America. This gave rise to the theory that America was populated along the Southern way, directly across the Pacific (apart from the main route across the Bering Straits, whose primary importance it is impossible to deny). It is quite obvious that the idea of the oceanic route playing any considerable part is much too fantastic. It is now more widely accepted that the non-Mongoloid elements penetrated into America along the same route across the Bering Straits as the ancestors of the rest of the population. This view has been elaborated in detail, for instance, by Birdsell, a student who assumes that the American Indians were formed from the Mongoloid and the Ainu types, which he calls the Amur type, and unconditionally includes in the white race.

In accordance with the view set out above on the origin of the Ainu, and considering the great number of other arguments in favor of the idea that the non-Mongoloid element took part in forming the American Indians, I show them in the proposed scheme as a branch of the Mongoloid stem, with an admixture of Equatorial elements.

As for the Europoid admixture proper, its existence for the time being remains to be proved. It is true that the bridge of the nose among some groups of Indians is as high as it is among the Europeans. This trait cannot be explained by any direct interbreeding between Mongoloids and any form of the Equatorial stem. The most acceptable now is Roginskij's (1937) hypothesis, according to which the ancestors of the American Indians were a not quite differentiated form of the Mongoloid stem. This hypothesis becomes the more probable as more data is acquired on the population of America in hoary antiquity. The latest definitions made on the basis of the radiocarbon method appear to confirm this. The age of the finds in the Sandia cave has been determined at 30,000 years (*American Antiquity*, 1956). However great the differences in defining the absolute age of the paleolithic cultures, there is no doubt that this date indicates that America was populated not in the mesolithic but in the late paleolithic period. It is quite probable that the modern types of the Mongoloid stem were not yet truly formed in that period.

Great difficulties arise in the effort to subdivide the American Indians. The inadequacy of data in accordance with descriptive traits, the destruction of many tribes by the colonists, the interbreeding of the remaining tribes with the "whites" and the Negroes, and the extensive practice of cranium deformation, all these are serious obstacles in the way of solving this problem.

Let us recall that Deniker drew a distinction between four races of the American Indians: the North American, the Central American, the South American, and the Patagonian. This may appear to be no more than a conventional geographical subdivision, but Deniker's amazing instinct served him in good stead here as well. On the whole his classification is based on fully realistic principles. Following Cheboksarov, I have brought together the South American race and the Central American, taking as the basis for this subdivision the complex of general morphological characteristics of body structure: hypomorphic in the center, and hypermorphic in the North and the South.

These three races are obviously not homogeneous, but in subdividing them we most frequently come up against extreme inadequacy of data. M. T. Newman (1951) was quite right in characterizing as impressionistic the system of Imbelloni (1938) and the similar system of von Eickstedt (1934) which have been widely accepted in the last few years. Newman does not propose another system but urges the need for a more thorough study of local groups which should precede the drawing up of worldwide schemes.

There is, nevertheless, a need for worldwide schemes, for although highly relative, they do give an idea at least of the state of our information. I have retained the Pacific type within the North American race, but was forced to subdivide the Atlantic, considering the sharp distinctions in the height of the cranium between the Dakotas, on the one hand, and the Muskogee-Algonquin tribes, on the other. The Californians who are distinguished by some "Negroid" traits stand out fairly clearly within the Central American race. The Andean and Amazonian types have been conventionally retained. As for the "Laguidans" of Imbelloni and Eick-stedt, I feel that Newman's critical remarks are well founded, and I have not included this type in the scheme. The Tierra del Fuego type appears to be more realistic, but it should be included in the Patagonian race together with the properly Patagonian Tehuelche and Araucanian types. The basis for this amalgamation is the hypermorphic type of cranial structure in virtue of which the "Australoid" traits of these types have been repeatedly observed.

Human Races Scheme

Branches	Races	Types
	Ainu	Sunda
	Veddoid	Deccan
	Australian	New Caledonian
	Tasmanian	Papuan
	Melanesian	Melanesian
		Andaman
Oceanic branch	Negrito	Malacca
		Philippine
	Bushman	Bushman
	Negrillo	Hottentot
African branch	South African	Sudanese
	Sudanese	Tropical
	Nilotic	
	South Indian	North Indian
	Ethiopian	Hindu Kush
Southern branch	Indo-Afghan	Pamiro-Ferghan
Negro-Australoid big race	Mediterranean	
	Hither Asian	Caucasian
		Dinaric
Europoid big race	Central European	Nordic
Northern branch		Valdai
		Carpathian
		Alpine
	Pontic	Pontic
Negro-Australoid big race		North Pontic
	Atlantic	
	North European	White Sea-Baltic
	Baltic	Eastern Baltic
		Vyatka-Kama
		Laponoid
	Uralo-Laponoid	Sub-Uralic
		Uralic
Siberian branch	South Siberian	Yenisei
Mongoloid big race	Baikal	Khatanga
Asian branch	Central Asian	Amuro-Sakhalin
Pacific branch	Tibetan	

	Far Eastern	Korean
		North Chinese
	South Mongoloid	Japanese
American branch	Polynesian	New Zealand
		Hawaiian
		Kamchatka
	Arctic	Aleut
		Eskimo
		Pacific
	North American	Atlantic
		Californian
		Andean
	Central American	Amazonian
	Patagonian	Patagonian
		Tierra del Fuego

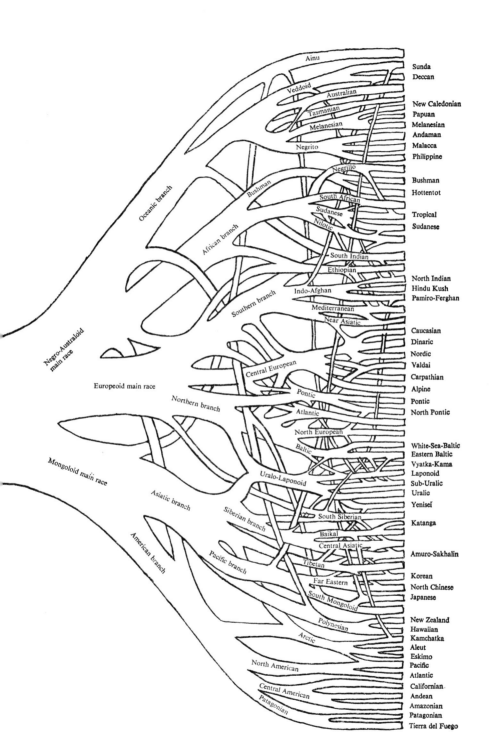

Ainu

Sunda
Deccan

Veddoid
Australian

New Caledonian
Tasmanian
Papuan
Melanesian
Melanesian
Andaman
Negrito
Malacca
Philippine

Negrillo

Bushman
Bushman
South African
Hottentot
Sudanese
Nilotic
Tropical
Sudanese

South Indian
Ethiopian
North Indian
Indo-Afghan
Hindu Kush
Mediterranean
Pamiro-Ferghan
Near Asiatic

Caucasian
Dinaric
Nordic
Central European
Valdai
Carpathian
Pontic
Alpine
Atlantic
Pontic
North Pontic

North European
Baltic
White-Sea-Baltic
Eastern Baltic
Vyatka-Kama
Uralo-Laponoid
Laponoid
Sub-Uralic
Uralic
Yeniseï

South Siberian
Katanga
Baikal
Central Asiatic
Amuro-Sakhalin
Tibetan
Far Eastern
Korean
South Mongoloid
North Chinese
Japanese

Polynesian
New Zealand
Hawaiian
Arctic
Kamchatka
Aleut
Eskimo
North American
Pacific
Atlantic
Central American
Californian
Andean
Patagonian
Amazonian
Patagonian
Tierra del Fuego

Oceanic branch

African branch

Southern branch

Central European

Northern branch

Mongoloid main race

Asiatic branch

Siberian branch

American branch

Pacific branch

North American

Central American
Patagonian

Negro-Australoid
main race

Europeoid main race

Dental Anthropology and the Historical Sciences

A. ZUBOV

Anthropological material is now known to play a big part in providing answers to many historical questions. The study of the physical types of the various populations makes it possible to establish the degree of affinity between the various groups, to trace the roots of their ancient migrations, and to judge their contacts with each other at various periods of history. In tackling historical problems, anthropology makes use of racial differences and the frequency and degree with which the various morphological features occur among the different populations. It is in this context that racial features present the main interest for the science of man. These traits, having for all practical purposes lost their adaptational importance and no longer having anything in common with the levels of biological and historical development, prove to be good indicators of the affinity of peoples and are something in the nature of "markers" which make it possible to trace the historical destinies of various groups of mankind. This kind of analysis is naturally the fuller and more precise the greater the number of authentic basic features the researcher has at his disposal. Anthropologists have always taken an interest in bringing out new differentiating features and clarifying their significance. At present, studies of populations from the standpoint of ethnical anthropology are being carried on under an extensive program including the study of blood, description and measurement of facial features, dermatoglyphics, and occasionally some physiological features.

Until recently, researchers dealt with such an important system of the human organism as the mandibular and dental apparatus on rare occasions only. Specialists have long since observed that the study of teeth

First published in *Sovetskaja etnografija*, N1 (1965).

in anthropology is highly promising because it could yield a considerable number of new differentiating features which are stable and relatively easily accessible for study. Today the scientists of many countries of the world devote increasingly more attention to the dental system. One hears more frequently such terms as "dental anthropology" or "anthropological odontology", which are used to designate independent lines in anthropology dealing with the study of teeth in anthropological terms. This relatively new branch of anthropology has three main lines: (1) ethnical or racial odontology; (2) evolutionary odontology which deals with the study of paleontological finds and questions of anthropogenesis; and (3) the general morphological line dealing with the general regularities governing the structure and development of the dental system.

The role of odontology in the study of anthropogenesis is generally known. From time to time researchers have to base their conclusions in this area on paleontological material alone; they have worked out a whole system of diagnostic indicators of the stage of evolution based on dental morphology, and especially on comparative morphology of human teeth and monkey teeth. Thus, depending on the stage of evolution, teeth help to reestablish the physical type of the men whose bones and implements are discovered in diggings. By furthering knowledge of the various stages of mankind's life, odontology links itself with the historical sciences. In this article I should like to deal not with this well-known aspect of dental anthropology, but with ethnical odontology which was shaped in its present form relatively recently and has yet to be extensively accepted. This branch of odontology commands our attention not only because it is "young" but also because it is most closely connected with the historical sciences. Like ethnical anthropology in general, it provides diagnostic, differentiating evidence which helps to establish the degree of genetic affinity between populations, bring out the traces of ancient crossbreeding, and to make judgements about the contacts between the peoples in the past and the routes of their migrations.

For a long time, scientists believed that odontology was unable to yield any racial diagnostic evidence, but in the course of research specialists gradually came to take a more optimistic view of it. Odontology, yielding new differentiating features, has recently come to have a place of honor in ethnic anthropology and has been used in solving historical problems.

Below I shall deal briefly with the development of the branch of dental anthropology which deals with the racial feature of man's dental system, describe some of the main differentiating features and the history of their discovery, and illustrate with examples the possible uses of this young branch of science of man in the sphere of the historical sciences.

Dental morphology first drew the attention of anthropologists engaged in research at the turn of the century. The study of man's evolution on the strength of paleontological finds, frequently consisting only of teeth, required a deepening and improvement of the methods used in odontological analysis. At the same time, there appeared works dealing with the racial specifics of dentition. One of the first students of teeth in the light of ethnical anthropology was the English anthropologist, Flower, who in 1885 carried out an interesting analysis of the racial distinctions on the strength of the absolute size of teeth (Flower, 1885). For his basis he took an index, subsequently known as the Flower index, which is a percentage expression of the relation between the length of the section of the alveolar arch from the first premolar to the third molar and the length of the base of the skull. Flower introduced a rubrication in accordance with the value of this index, designating the racial groups with an index of over 44 as "megalodontic"; groups with a medium magnitude of the index (42 — 43.9) as "mesodontic" and finally the group with the small dental index (under 42) as "microdontic".

The initial studies appeared to show some clearcut racial distinctions in accordance with the Flower index. The Europeans, the ancient Egyptians and the Indians turned out to be microdontic; the Chinese, the American Indians and the Malayans, mesodontic; the African Negroes bordered on the meso- and megalodontic; and the Australians, the Andamans, and the Tasmanians formed the purely megalodontic group. The groups distinguished by the value of the Flower index on the whole coincided with our modern view of mankind's division into three big races.

Soon, however, a great number of exceptions to this regularity was discovered and doubt was cast on the racial diagnostic value of the absolute size of teeth. At the same time, there was also some temporary disappointment over the value of the descriptive odontological features. The negative attitude to the prospects for the development of ethnical odontology was especially fortified by the appearance in 1905 of a monumental work by the Swiss anthropologist, M. de Terra, entitled *Essays on the Odontography of the Human Races* (Terra, 1905). He studied the teeth of a series of skulls relating to sixty different ethnic groups under a fairly extensive program and arrived at a categorical denial that odontography could be used for racial analysis. He said that the absolute size of teeth, the number of tubercles, roots, etc., do not make it possible to discover any definite regularity in distribution by ethnic groups; they merely reveal some individual variations. It later turned out that his conclusions did not accord with reality. His mistake was due, first, to the small number of many of the series he studied, and second, to the fact that in processing his measurement data and comparing them he did not take the arithmetical means but empirical values of maximums and minimums, which naturally tended to distort the actual state of affairs and suggested false conclusions. His work left a mark on odontology; even today one will hear pessimistic comments about the prospects of development of ethnic odontology with references to de Terra's conclusions.

After de Terra, work on racial odontology assumed the form of detailed descriptions of dental systems among separate groups with some authors no longer setting themselves the special aim of deciding on racial distinctions. Among such works are those of Hillebrandt (1909), Kajava (1912), Schwerz (1915), and de Jonge (1918).

From the 1920's on, however, researchers once again turned their attention to the racial odontological features and their diagnostic significance. The work of Sullivan (1920: 255–57) showed that it was possible to distinguish fairly clearly some racial groups by the number of tubercles on the second lower molar tooth which normally has either four or five tubercles. The 4-tubercle second lower molars occur much more frequently among Europoids than among other racial groups.

Hrdlička (1923: 423–38) published a study of the forms of the upper incisors and brought out some definite racial distinctions. The so-called "shovel-shaped incisors", that is, teeth which are so shaped because their lingual surface is "bordered", are highly characteristic of the Mongoloid race.

From year to year, more and more racial odontological features were coming to light. Within a few years after Hrdlička, Campbell (1925) showed that the teeth of Australian aborigines were markedly larger than those of the members of the Europoid and Mongoloid races, a fact researchers could earlier merely assume on the strength of occasional observations.

The further study of dental morphology brought out fresh valuable features. In the 1920's and 1930's, a considerable contribution to odontology was made by Hellman (1928: 157–74), Shaw (1931), Goldstein (1932: 215–35), and Nelson (1938); however, it is only in the last fifteen years that there has been a marked development of dental anthropology and its departments connected with ethnical anthropology.

In 1949 several studies simultaneously appeared which had a considerable part to play in developing odontology. The Norwegian, Selmer-Olsen (1949), published a metrical study of the teeth of the Lapps showing this group to have exceptionally small teeth, and, what was most important, presenting an excellent elaboration of odontometrical methods. The well-known American scientist, Dahlberg (1949: 138–76), carried out a detailed analysis of the descriptive features of the dentition of the American Indians, simultaneously presenting some general propositions of odontographical racial analysis. Pedersen (1949) and a year later Tratman (1950) studied an interesting feature of dentition: the interradical "flow" of enamel. This morphological detail which appears in the form of a sharpened edge of the enamel-cement border on the molars, occurs most frequently, according to these authors, among the Mongoloid groups. Tratman, comparing the dental morphology of the Malayans and the Dutch, discovered some more morphological distinctions between these two groups representing the Mongoloid and the Europoid races, respectively. The Mongoloids were found to have a more characteristic rugosity of the surface of the molars, relatively shorter roots, and an innate lack of wisdom teeth.

The Japanese odontologists, Suzuki and Sakai (1956a: 136–39; 1956b), later drew attention to such details as the internal middle accessory tubercle on the lower molars, and the so-called "deflecting wrinkle", a crest of the enamel running from the top of the mesiolingual tubercle (metaconide) to the central crevice of the grinding surface of the lower molars. These features also to some extent characterized the Mongoloid race.

There are some distinctions between the racial groups in the occurrence of various forms of the bite, the time of dentition of wisdom teeth (which appear somewhat earlier among Negroids), and the form and position of the incisors.

Not long ago I undertook a study of human molars under an extensive program on a number of skull series from different racial groups. Having made a detailed examination of their individual morphological variations, we tried to establish the intergroup distinctions on the strength of a number of fine details in the structure of the crown and the root, distinctions which in some instances were discovered with sufficient authenticity. For instance, it was shown that the so-called anterior transversal crest of the lower molars occurs more frequently among Mongoloids. The same may be said about the "cut-off" mesial root of the upper molars (the top of the root does not come to a point but appears to be cut off along a slanting line). The different racial groups have different relations between the size of tubercles on the grinding surface of the molars. In contrast to the Negroids and the Europoids, the Mongoloid groups have a metacone — the distobuccal tubercle — which is usually larger than the neighboring hypocone — the distolingual tubercle.

Verification on the strength of extensive material of the value of the features earlier noted by other authors almost in every case provided evidence for the conclusions they had made. Our material confirmed, for instance, that the above-mentioned "enamel-flow" does indeed occur considerably more often among Mongoloids. What is known as Carabelli's tubercle, the mesiolingual supplemental tubercle on the first upper molar, occurs frequently among Europoid groups.

We also reexamined the question of the diagnostic value of absolute tooth size which Flower had earlier considered. Some works, like Nelson's, while they do show the existence of real intergroup distinctions by absolute tooth size, have simultaneously revealed that these distinctions are indefinite and somewhat unsystematic. Considering this problem, we decided that it was more appropriate to use for our comparisons all the material accumulated in various writings and our own odontometric material (Nelson's work considers only a few racial groups). In addition, we decided not to use the Flower index, characterizing absolute tooth size, because it ties in the tooth size indexes with the rather greatly varying craniological feature, the length of the base of the skull. In working on the problem of the diagnostic value of absolute tooth size we introduced a new indicator, an "average module of the series" of molars, representing the sum total of the modules of the crowns of molar teeth divided by three.[1] For the sake of conveniently evaluating the values being compared we introduced three categories of values for average module of the series (for the upper molars):

a — small size (microdontism) under 10.20,
b — medium size (mesodontism) 10.20–10.49,
c — large size (macrodontism) 10.50 and over.

Introduction of the average module of the crown helped us to discern fairly definite tendencies in the distribution of absolute tooth size by racial groups. It turned out that the Papuans, East African Negroes, Bantu Negroes, Australians, Ancient Javanese (Australoids by racial type), and Eskimos could be referred to the macrodontic group; the Ossetians, Pamirians, Latgalians, Armenians, Lapps, and Bushmen to the microdontic group, and the other thirteen groups, nine of which are Mongoloid, fell in the mesodontic group. Consequently, the macrodontic group included the overwhelming majority of the Negroid series (four out of five), the microdontic, the overwhelming majority of the Europoid or series with a slight Mongoloid admixture (five out of six), while the Mongoloid groups were fairly clearly inclined to mesodontism.

[1]   In odontology, the crown module is known to be the sum of the mesiodistal and the buccolingual diameters divided by two.

These regularities do not, we find, provide any absolute criterion for diagnosing race, but it is fairly safe to say that there are definite tendencies in the distribution of absolute tooth size by racial groups.

There are also distinctions between racial groups by the crown molar index, which shows the relation between the buccolingual diameter, and the mesiodistal diameter, that is, the extent of the "elongation" of the crown. The Europoids, for instance, usually have a very high index for the second and third upper molars.

Interesting data may also be obtained by studying the relation between the size of teeth in the series. To characterize these relations, the Norwegian odontologist, Selmer-Olsen, introduced so-called "step indexes" which are percentage expressions of the relation of the size of the premolars and the molars, and the corresponding size of the first molar in the same series, which is the tooth least subject to reduction. Of especial importance are step indexes indicating the relation between the second premolar and the second molar of the upper series to the first molar of the same series. These indexes reflect the general level of tooth reduction in the jaw, giving an idea of the relative size of the variable teeth which are most subject to variation and which are reduced in the first place.

Let us note at this point that progressive reduction has always been the main trend in the evolution of the teeth of hominids; the teeth of all racial groups have been largely subjected to this process. Considering that the composition and structure of the food influence the size and form of teeth, the changes in the structure of the dental system over the last few millenia have had a different effect on the various ethnical groups, depending on when they developed food cooking techniques which relieved the chewing apparatus of a considerable part of its work. The general level of reduction may in many instances serve as a differentiating characteristic in comparing the physical types of various ethnic groups.

In the last few millenia there has been a great increase in the incidence of caries which has affected the various peoples and racial groups differently. This circumstance is also used by dental anthropologists for comparing the groups.

Diverse ritual deformations of the teeth — filing, knocking out, etc. — are also of great interest to the anthropologist and the ethnographer, and are studied by specialists.

The existence of differential racial and intergroup features provides a definite basis for the use of dental anthropology in tackling historical problems, especially those relating to ethnogenesis.

There is no need here to devote special attention to the nature of these differentiating features; I shall deal with them only briefly. Some inter-group distinctions, as I have said, result from different conditions of nutrition and differences in the structure and composition of the food. Other features may arise as a consequence of gene drift in limited populations. Some features, characteristic of big races as a whole, may be of more ancient origin. They may be the result of blood heredity among various groups of ancient hominids which played differing parts in the formation of modern racial stems.

The diagnostic value of racial odontological features would undoubtedly be enhanced if they had been thoroughly studied from the standpoint of genetics. The first few steps in this direction have already been taken. For instance, the Czechoslovakian researcher, Andrik (1960), has carried out observations over the features of dentition in mono-ovular twins, and discovered great similarities between them in a number of odontological features. A familial study of some odontological features brought out the nature of their heredity. In the 1950's, Goose and Krause (the data taken from Goose, 1963: 125–48) carried out considerable research and arrived at the conclusion that many odontological features were endogenically determined, and that "genetic factors must play the main role" in racial distinctions within the dental system.

Even if it is assumed that odontological features have not yet been adequately studied in terms of genetics, their importance should not be underestimated. If we say that today the researcher in anthropology cannot be satisfied with a statement of the phenotypical frequency of the features he is studying, that is not to say that anthropologists must abandon such studies which have already yielded a great deal for the historical and the biological sciences and may well yield more in the future. Odontological diagnostic features have increasingly commanded attention from specialists and been used by anthropologists for racial analysis. Some prominent researchers say that analysis of the racial features of each new craniological series will soon be considered absolutely inadequate without an odontological analysis. Extensive studies are being made of living individuals through the making of casts. Monographs have been published giving descriptions of dentition among some racial or territorial groups, including the work of Pedersen on the Eskimos, Moorrees (1957) on the Aleuts, and Dahlberg on the American Indians.

An odontographical map of the peoples of the world is becoming a reality, for some features.

As I have said, specialists in various countries have been making bolder and more extensive use of odontological material in connection with the questions of ethnogenesis. Here are a few examples.

The American anthropologist, Riesenfeld (1956: 505–21), tried to apply odontological data in deciding on the origin of the Polynesians. His analysis was based on a study of the frequency with which the shovel-shaped incisors and the various types of profile of the crown of the upper incisors occur among the population of Polynesia as compared with the occurrence of these features on the assumed "original" territories, Indonesia and South America. All groups of American Indians are known to have a high rate of occurrence of the shovel-shaped incisors, but this is known to be much lower in Indonesia. It would be logical to assume that if the Polynesians had arrived from America, the occurrence of shovel-shaped incisors among them would be frequent, or at any rate that the frequency would increase from West to East, from America. It has actually turned out that the frequency of occurrence of shovel-shaped incisors in Polynesia was relatively low, and that it tended to decrease from West to East. Such data cannot be ignored in deciding on the settlement of Polynesia; they provide sufficient evidence in favor of the Asian origin of the bulk of the Polynesian population.

A few years ago, V. Alekseyev expressed the view that the Latgal group has a Mongoloid "touch", which is indicated by a number of craniological features. In 1963, we made a study of a Latgalian skull series under an extensive odontological program without setting ourselves the special aim of analyzing this Mongoloid element. In processing our data, we discovered that by a number of odontological features the Latgalians showed unusual departures from the picture which is most observed in the study of Europoid series. It was discovered, for instance, that the "enamel flow" occurs on the molars of Latgalians in an average of 44 per cent of the cases (in terms of one tooth), whereas the frequency of this feature among the Europoid groups, even in the North, to say nothing of the South, normally never exceeds 25-30 per cent. The percentage of roots with a "cut-off" on the first upper molars was unusually high, and the metacone on these teeth was on average almost equal to the hypocone: according to this latter feature and the enamel flow, this group is intermediate between the Europoid and Mongoloid groups. Combined with craniological features, these data, we feel, deserve to be taken into account.

Here is an example relating to another area of the USSR.

Among the most ancient inhabitants of the territory of Siberia are the Yukagirs, who may have been the direct successors to Siberia's neolithic population. This is indicated by ethnographic, linguistic, and anthropological data. What is the verdict of odontology? An odontological study of a series of Yukagir skulls brought back by I. Zolotareva showed that according to many traits — absolute tooth size, the main tooth indexes, the number of tubercles on the molars, the specific structure of the grinding surface of the molars — the Yukagirs are similar to the neolithic series of the Trans-Baikal area. This similarity is greater than that of any of the Siberian Mongoloid series we have studied and confirms the conclusions obtained on the strength of other data.

The next example may be an illustration of how odontological data help to obtain a clearer picture of the racial composition of the group studied. A. Sharkova (1964), a student of the Anthropology Department of Moscow State University, carried out a detailed study of the morphology of the upper molars on a craniological series of Russians. Up to then there had been almost no odontographical data on the Russian population. The comparative analysis of the data obtained helped to characterize the group studied as follows: the series belongs to the Europoid big race and shows the combination of traits characteristic both of the Northern and the Southern Europoid groups (in odontological terms, the Europoid race may be quite clearly divided into the Northern and Southern groups of types). This warrants the conclusion that if we were dealing with a series of unknown origin, odontological data would have helped us to identify its racial origin.

In comparing groups to discover their affinity, origins, routes of migration, etc., there is naturally a need to have a detailed knowledge of the "odontological type" of many populations. Unfortunately, this type of material is clearly still inadequate, and further extensive odontological research into various ethnical groups is required. Odontological characteristics of a whole number of groups of the globe are now sufficiently well known. Dahlberg, for instance, has brought out a clear-cut odontological type of the peoples of the Mediterranean and the Middle East. This type is distinguished by the following features:[2] (1) explicit microdontism; (2) a considerable degree of reduction of the metacone on the upper molars; (3) strong reduction of the tubercles of molars (on the lower up to 4 and even up to 3, and on the upper, to 3-2); (4) a particularly low frequency of formations like enamel flow, transversal crest, protostilid, shovel-shaped incisors, that is, highly clearly expressed and emphatic "Europoidness"; (5) a high frequency of forms of reduction on the lateral incisor — a reduction in size (low "incisor index") through a conical form to complete innate absence of this tooth; and (6) high crown indexes for the second and third upper molars.

---

[2]   Alongside Dahlberg's data (Dahlberg, 1949) we have supplemented the characteristic of the type with our own results.

The whole mass of Northern Europoid groups is distinguished from the above-mentioned type by somewhat larger tooth size (a tendency to mesodontism), a toning down of the Europoid features as expressed in some increase in the frequency of occurrence of enamel flow, lesser general reduction, lesser reduction of the metacone, appearance of some specific features like higher frequency of the two-root lower cuspid (Razdobarina, 1963), a very high frequency of the Carabelli tubercle, etc.

A characteristic Melanesian odontological type is Negroid according to the principal characteristics (microdontism, extremely slight reduction, high indexes for the relation of the size of premolars and the second molar to the size of the first molar), but distinguished by a high frequency of Carabelli's tubercles (very strongly developed) and various other details which virtually never occur among the African Negroes (shovel-shaped incisors, enamel flow) which create the impression of some shift towards Mongoloidness but occur here with lesser frequency than among Mongoloid groups.

Further research is bound to give depth and to add to our knowledge of the odontological types of the world, but work in this area, we feel, can already be of considerable benefit to anthropology specifically in that sphere of it which is of direct practical importance for the historical sciences.

Genetic-Geographical Zones of Eastern Europe by ABO Blood Groups

V. BUNAK

MAPPING THE FREQUENCY OF *ABO* GENES

The frequency of blood groups has been determined for a vast number of small and large population groups in the European part of the USSR. The data assembled has been used for some time now to compile geographical gene maps of the *ABO* factors. Such maps had already been compiled for Europe as a whole, and for Eastern Europe in the 1930's by various authors in other countries (Steffan, 1932; Steffan and Wellisch, 1936; Streng, 1935; Boyd, 1939; Mourant, 1958). Since the last maps and tables published by Mourant and his co-authors (1958), there has been comparatively little new material on Eastern Europe. Therefore, it has not been possible to employ computers to the extent needed for thorough analysis and statistical processing of all the data available. The compilation of new maps of the geographical distribution of the *ABO* blood factors in Eastern Europe has become urgently necessary since authors in other countries have been employing the data available without breaking them down into ethnic groups, and have been arbitrarily generalizing characteristics established for small populations. The boundaries of the gene and geographical zones of Eastern Europe delineated on Mourant's maps are clearly incorrect. For these reasons we have undertaken the compilation of new maps.

Army intakes provided abundant data for the investigation of gene distribution. Data on conscripts is processed at present in Austria. In the past, information on the frequency of blood factors was collected

First published in *Voprosy antropologii*, vyp. 32 (1969).

and processed in Switzerland, Poland, Finland, Sweden, and in other countries to some extent.

The data of blood banks and donor points has also been drawn on for geographical studies of gene distribution. Donor data can be employed provided that (1) the blood groups of all donors originally offering blood are determined without selection of definite serological variants; (2) there is a predominance of aborigines in the donors offering blood at the given station; (3) there is information in the questionnaire about the origin of the examinee; and (4) at small donor stations it is possible to make exact extracts from their journals.

Unfortunately these conditions are seldom satisfied. The approach made by us with the support of the Learned Council of the USSR Ministry of Health to blood banks only yielded satisfactory information about small populations in the European part of the USSR. The blood banks and donor stations in large cities dispose of a wealth of material on the frequency of ABO blood groups, but it is not uniform in origin. Tens of thousands of the people investigated at big donor institutions are suitable for establishing the characteristics of the population of the whole country or of major parts of it but are of little use for separate areas. In the donor data collected in Moscow and Leningrad (Solovjeva, 1964; Umnova, 1967), for example, the two groups, although almost uniform according to the data obtained on the spot by different investigations, show quite probable differences between the two areas.

Basic material on the frequency of blood groups is given by the work of various authors who have made studies to obtain control data for hospital practice and for comparisons of the populations of different areas. The development of work along these lines was encouraged by the Standing Commission on the Study of Blood Groups working in Kharkov under the leadership of Prof. V. Ja. Rubashkin (1929). From 1928 to 1932 the Commission published four volumes of its *Bulletin* which contained dozens of papers on various areas and ethnic groups. Similar bureaux organized in Leningrad by Prof. Vishnevskij under the Institute of Ethnography of the USSR Academy of Sciences were operating at the same time. From the mostly unpublished data of the Leningrad Bureau we extracted and included in our tables several groups for which there were no doubts about the origin of the subjects examined and the technique used to determine blood groups. In the 1930's blood groups were studied on a wide scale by the Institute of Anthropology of Moscow University. Summaries of the data of various authors were published in Besedin (1927) and Kratkije (1940).

In recent years Ukrainian anthropologists have had the opportunity of employing data of the blood banks in all regions of the Ukrainian SSR, totalling more than 250,000 observations. The new Ukrainian material which we grouped for five areas proved to agree closely with data collected earlier, but the concentration of the q gene in the new series for the South-Western districts was reduced by 0.02–0.03. It is difficult to determine which material is the more significant, but the numerical size of the new series definitely gives it priority. By kind permission of the Ukrainian anthropologists V. D. Djachenko and E. N. Danilova, we have been able to include material presented by them in our tables of the frequency of blood groups in the Ukraine.

In compiling our original summaries, all available published and unpublished data were considered, but in the final tables only those groups were included for which the locality of the observations and the predominant ethnic composition of the groups studied could be established, and for which the data were comparable and had no marked, inexplicable deviations. If the frequency of the q gene varied between 22 and 28 per cent in five groups out of six, but was 10 per cent in one, the latter was not included in the general characteristic. No age or sex distinction was made in the material available so that we were only able to employ summarized characteristics that included all adults of both sexes.

The material assembled was divided according to regions for Russian, Ukrainian, and Belorussian populations, and for a number of Union and Autonomous Republics for Finnish and Turkic groups. The number of ethnic groups taken into account in any one area varied between two and twelve; the total number considered exceeded 200. The summary tables employed to compile our maps and the bibliography pertaining to them are lodged in the Institute of Ethnography of the Academy of Sciences, and it is proposed to publish them in a special edition. In this article only the generalized characteristics of separate territorial and ethnic groups based on the processing of the material assembled are given.

METHODOLOGICAL NOTES

One of the best methods of population analysis of *ABO* blood groups is that developed by S. Rosin (1956). He employed the system of rectangular coordinates established by F. Bernstein (1925) for the frequency of each gene whose sides record the variations. Submitting this system to an arc cosine transformation, Rosin constructed a diagram that enabled the probable deviation of any combination of genes from the general average to be calculated, and thus proceeded to the grouping and unification of local groups. In studies of large areas that are not ethnically uniform, Rosin's method, which is valuable for comparing related populations, is not effective since the geographical distribution of the various deviations from the average serological type then acquires major significance.

The first basic problem arising in population studies of blood groups is to determine the gene equilibrium, and with it the reliability of the quantitative characteristic of gene frequency. The most precise means of doing this is to calculate the frequency of the three genes according to frequency of blood groups, and then to make reverse calculations of the frequency of blood groups by several different formulae, employing the calculated gene frequency (Boyd, 1939; Race and Sanger, 1958; Wiener, 1943).

This method, which is justified for calculations to an accuracy of five decimal places, is of little use when restricted to three decimal places. The square root of the frequency of group O, i.e., the gene frequency, and the square of the concentration of gene r, i.e., the frequency of group O, differ within limits of 0.001 to 0.002, depending on the arithmetic technique employed and more than half of the general total differences between the calculated and empirically found frequencies fall to the share of discrepancies of the frequency of AB group. It is easy, however, by employing small auxiliary tables to find how far the actually ascertained AB frequency differs from the theoretical one and whether a supplementary check of the equilibrium of the group is required without resorting to Fisher's formula which requires much calculation. The imbalance of a group and the need to exclude it from the general characteristic can sometimes be established without special calculations; in other cases the difference d (the difference between the total frequency and unity) is a sufficient indication of equilibrium expressed in fractions of Bernstein's standard deviation (Bernstein, 1925). To determine the standard deviation we employed Boyd's nomograms. In our experience a relative deviation exceeding two units (acceptable as the limit for equiponderant groups) does not in fact always mean a significant deviation from equilibrium. When for example, the sum of deviations is small (0.002), the ratio exceeds two even for a numerically small deviation from unity (e.g., 0f 0.005), which cannot by any means always serve as an index of imbalance in the frequency of genes in a given population.

The second problem is to determine the homogeneity of several populations within an area, and the absence or presence in a given locality of

groups differing significantly from each other. The problem of homogeneity often has to be resolved in several stages: first, uniting the initial
populations of the locality; then, finding the district characteristics;
and finally, generalizing the findings for several districts in order to obtain
the characteristic of a zone. The various methods of computation available give rather differing results.

In view of the differences, we give a short description of the methods
we adapted. We found the cumulative characteristic for a population
consisting of several parts by multiplying the frequency of each factor
in the component populations by the relative weight in the whole group,
i.e., by n_a/N_s (where n_a is the number of observations in a single population, and N_s the number in the summary), and then adding together
the weighted frequencies. With a noticeable divergence in the frequency
of the united groups, the difference between the frequency of the genes
in a given population group and the total population was calculated, the square of the difference was taken, its ratio to the frequency
of the gene in the total group calculated, and the sum of the relative
quantities found. All calculations were made in percentages. To find
the value of χ, the sum obtained was multiplied by $N: 100$, N being
taken as the sum of the frequency of genes expressed in absolute quantities. If any individual population gave χ exceeding the table value of
the 5 per cent probability factor, it was excluded from the generalized
series, and the cumulative characteristic was recalculated. For the most
part the result stood up well in the initial stages of calculation when two
groups were compared, and it was seldom necessary to repeat the whole
cycle of calculations.

We thus obtained a generalized figure for eight regional groups of the
Russian population, five for the Ukrainian population, one for the Belorussians, and twenty-three different ones for Finnish, Turkic, and other
ethnic groups of Eastern Europe (Tables 1 and 2).

THE DISTRIBUTION OF BLOOD GROUPS IN EASTERN
EUROPE AS A WHOLE

The following frequencies of the *ABO* blood groups and the corresponding genes were established for the territory of Eastern Europe; for
comparison with the population of the continent as a whole we took
gene frequencies compiled from the basic summaries of blood group
frequencies given in the well-known works of A. Mourant (1958),

Table 1. *Frequency of ABO Blood Groups (in percentages) and the Corresponding Genes (in thousandths) for Main Ethnic Groups*

Locality	N	O	A	B
Russians				
Archangel and Vologda Regions	583	34.1	31.4	27
Perm and Kirov Regions	3 500	28.4	34.6	29
Pskov, Novgorod, and Smolensk Regions	791	29.8	38.6	23
Upper Volga (Kalinin, Yaroslavl, Kostroma, Ivanovo and Vladimir Regions)	3 292	34.2	37.4	21
Middle Volga (Gorky, Ulyanovsk, Penza, Kuibyshev, Saratov, Volgograd, Orenburg and Astrakhan Regions)	12 849	32.7	37.5	21
Don Regions (Riazan, Tambov, Lipetsk, Voronezh, Rostov)	2 596	32.2	39.9	21
Regions between the Don and Desna (Tula, Kaluga, Orel, Briansk, Kursk)	2 180	34.2	37.2	20
Krasnodar and Stavropol Territories	1 410	29.5	40.4	19
Moscow (city)	31 896	38.5	37.8	20
Leningrad (city)	16 423	35.1	37.0	20
Belorussians				
Belorussian SSR	2 879	36.2	37.2	20
Ukrainians				
North-Eastern Zone of the Ukraine (Poltava, Sumy, Chernigov and Kharkov Regions)	28 195	37.3	36.6	19
Northern zone (Volhynian, Zhitomir, and Rovno Regions)	34 286	30.2	39.5	22
Central zone (Vinnitsa, Kiev, Khmelnitsky, and Cherkassy Regions)	54 414	34.6	38.8	19
Southern zone (Dniepropetrovsk, Zaporozhye, Nikolaevsk, Odessa, Kirovograd, Kherson Regions)	98 964	36.7	36.5	20
Western zone (Transcarpathian, Lvov, Ivano-Frankovsk, Ternopol, Chernovitsy Regions)	42 777	33.5	37.8	21

p	q	r	D	D/S	I
0.224	0.202	0.574	−0.012	1.50	1.030
0.258	0.225	0.517	−0.021	6.00	1.027
0.279	0.186	0.585	−0.014	2.00	1.129
0.260	0.160	0.580	−0.007	2.00	1.135
0.264	0.162	0.570	0.002	1.43	1.138
0.280	0.161	0.559	0.011	2.97	1.165
0.258	0.155	0.587	0.002	0.51	1.139
0.298	0.164	0.538	0.006	1.00	1.190
0.265	0.156	0.579	0.001	0.91	1.147
0.257	0.150	0.593	0.001	0.67	1.144
0.255	0.147	0.598	−0.005	1.56	1.149
0.246	0.140	0.614	0.004	3.33	1.141
0.277	0.166	0.557	0.009	1.76	1.154
0.267	0.143	0.590	0.002	2.22	1.169
0.248	0.145	0.612	0.008	20.00	1.129
0.261	0.156	0.583	0.005	4.17	1.142

Table 2.   *Frequency of ABO Blood Groups (in percentages) and the Corresponding Genes (in thousandths) for Ethnic Groups on the Territory of their Basic Population*

Ethnic Group	N	O	A	B
Moldavians	6 130	32.3	40.8	19.8
Lithuanians (in Kaunas)	4 477	39.0	36.6	19.5
Letts	1 160	32.2	36.6	24.2
Estonians	2 778	33.8	35.5	22.4
Finns (Leningrad Region)	179	31.9	41.3	21.8
Karelians	1 931	38.8	29.8	26.8
Western Finns	12 955	34.5	41.6	17.3
Eastern Finns	6 547	30.1	44.1	18.3
Lapps	1 225	31.8	55.3	7.8
Komi-Zyrians	2 549	34.6	30.0	26.8
Komi-Permyaks	2 111	33.7	29.4	29.4
Udmurts	2 550	34.2	30.1	28.0
Maris*	594	33.0	24.0	34.8
Chuvash	3 529	30.3	29.2	33.5
Kazan Tatars	3 199	30.0	31.6	30.3
Moksha-Mordovians	403	28.0	37.0	23.0
Erzya-Mordovians	522	34.7	29.3	26.0
Karagash	418	37.8	29.2	28.7
Nogais	131	30.5	36.7	31.7
Bashkirs	4 051	29.6	34.9	26.6
Astrakhan Kalmucks	414	25.7	22.9	40.0
Astrakhan Kazakhs	290	35.8	26.2	32.2
Nenets** (Archangel Region)	606	28.1	28.7	26.0

1 Maris — formerly called Cheremis — Ed.
11 Nenets — formerly called Yurak-Samoyeds — Ed.

R. Khérumian (1951), P. Steffan (1932), W. Boyd (1939), and P. Steffan and P. Wellisch (1928–36).

Frequency of Blood Groups and Genes

Blood groups and genes	Range of variation	Eastern Europe predominant classes	All continents range of variation	mean class
O	25–39	30–35	25–85	46–65
A	18–53	26–70	5–85	26–45
B	8–35	8–24	0–40	13–24
r	48–63	56–60	35–95	56–75
p	18–37	(1) 20–25 (2) 26–30	7–48	21–30
q	6–35	(1) 16–20 (2) 20–25	0–35	16–25

Thus, for the population of Eastern Europe as a whole a relatively small proportion of blood group *O* (and the corresponding *r* gene) is charac-

p	q	r	D	D/S	I
0.278	0.145	0.567	−0.001	0.43	1.173
0.236	0.132	0.632	−0.010	4.35	1.136
0.260	0.183	0.557	−0.013	2.55	1.119
0.251	0.169	0.580	−0.001	0.29	1.109
0.270	0.146	0.584	0.024	1.60	1.170
0.203	0.186	0.611	−0.015	3.75	1.021
0.281	0.128	0.591	0.005	1.04	1.213
0.305	0.140	0.555	0.008	3.33	1.237
0.371	0.067	0.562	0.002	0.50	1.490
0.216	0.196	0.588	0.0	0	1.026
0.208	0.208	0.584	0.017	4.25	1.000
0.209	0.592	0.592	0.009	2.73	1.013
0.177	0.246	0.574	0.004	1.90	0.916
0.203	0.231	0.556	0.020	5.88	0.964
0.225	0.217	0.558	0.014	3.78	1.010
0.281	0.194	0.525	−0.005	0.50	1.121
0.220	0.199	0.581	0.0	0	1.027
0.187	0.183	0.630	0.019	2.34	1.004
0.185	0.185	0.595	0.054	3.38	1.045
0.243	0.199	0.558	0.018	5.80	1.058
0.186	0.304	0.510	0.004	0.36	0.855
0.176	0.215	0.609	0.014	4.67	0.947
0.228	0.282	0.490	0.012	1.26	0.930

teristic, with little variation outside the lower limit of the average class. The frequency of blood group A and its corresponding p gene remained within the limits of the average class, the lower variant of the average class being predominant in a significant part of the population. The frequency of blood group B and genotype q varied within the limits of the average class. For comparison the gene index first proposed by Wellisch $(p + r) : (q + r)$ is calculated. The index is higher, the higher is the frequency of p and the lower the frequency of r. In Eastern Europe an index of 1.1 is predominant, which indicates a slight preponderance of p and a small proportion of r. Apart from the $A>O>B$ variant (European according to Ottenberg), an $O>A>B$ variant (intermediate type) was also found, and others as well. When gene ratios rather than blood group ratios were considered, gene r (with unverified exceptions) was numerically first in all populations. Gene frequency rather than phenotype is now almost exclusively employed for comparative purposes.

In Eastern Europe gene q comes first within the relative wide scale of variation, and gene p third. While the frequency of p fell more markedly with a rise in frequency of q, the proportion of r changed less noticeably.

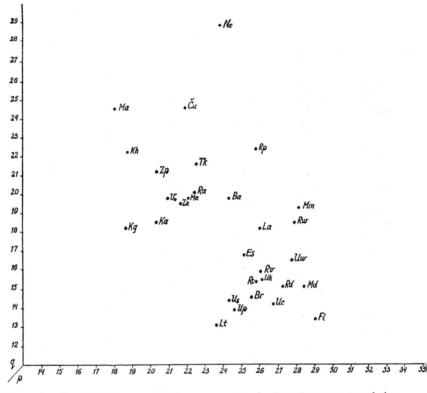

Figure 1.   Combined frequencies of genes *r* and *q* in East European population.
Designation of ethno-territorial groups:

R, Russians; Ra, Archangelsk and Vologda; Rp, Vyatka and Perm; Rw, Western;
Rv, Volga; Rd, Don; Rc, central; U, Ukrainians; Up, North-Eastern; Uw, North-
Western; Uc, central; Uk, Western (Carpathian); Us, Southern steppes; Ba, Bashkirs;
Br, Belorussians; Cu, Chuvash; Es, Estonians; Fi, Finns (Finland); Ka, Karelians;
Kg, Karagash; Kh, Kazakhs; La, Letts; Lt, Lithuanians; Ma, Mari; Md, Moldavians;
Mm, Moksha-Mordvinian; Ne, Nenets; Tk, Kazan Tatars; Vo, Udmurts; Zk, Komi-
Zyrians; Zp, Komi-Permyaks.

The distribution of populations according to the combined frequency of
q and *p* is shown in Fig. 1. A low frequency of gene *q* often goes hand
in hand with a high concentration of gene *p*; conversely the scatter
along the other coordinate, characterizing the variability of gene *r*,
frequency is less marked.

The frequency of the three genes in adjacent populations, when they
consist of separate marriage circles (demes) proves as a rule to vary.
The divergence of the frequency of the separate genes is occasionally as
much as 10 per cent, but such a discrepancy is only encountered in a
small number of studies. In groups from a single area and of a single

ethnic type, which include hundreds of investigations, the frequency divergence rarely exceeds 0.1 of the gene index. In general, variation of the gene index falls noticeably with increase in the number of observations. In comparative population studies one is occasionally forced to limit oneself to a small-scale investigation because of the smallness of the population or its inaccessibility for study. A variety of geographical ethnic, historical, and other factors must then be taken into account for comparative purposes.

In neighboring populations the frequency of the three genes often varies more when they are composed of different marriage circles than in a widely separated population, or in unified, summarized groups. Examples can be found both in our tables of blood groups and in the researches of many authors who have compared separate populations and generalized groups by serological and somatic indices (Bunak, in print; Davydova, in print). This is not the sole possible type, of course. Local differences often become ironed out and the summaries diverge much more, but the first type of variation in blood group frequencies is comparatively common. An example of this is found in France when cantonal indices are compared with area ones, and area characteristics with departmental results (Khérumian et. al., 1959). A divergence in the frequency ratio of genes in related or adjacent populations that are ethnically homogeneous is usually linked with the isolation of the population group and the effect of special factors created by isolation, but such an interpretation does not apply everywhere. The circle of marriage relations as a rule does not encompass more than 4000 or 5000 persons. In populations of such size (demes) special isolation factors cannot express themselves (Bunak, 1965a). When the difference in gene frequency between related groups does not reveal any definite geographical tendency, it must be taken as a chance variation of sampling. With large groups and more samples the effect of chance deviations is reduced and deviations of the mean become less significant (Saller, 1960).

The pattern of groups composed of natives of different parts of an area also does not lessen the effect of chance in sampling but rather increases it. When because of that it is necessary to limit a survey to a definite number of investigations in order to characterize the *ABO* combination of any area, it is better to sample two or more points correctly selected for the pattern of the district as a whole. The divergence of related local groups as regards *ABO* blood groups, even when it is statistically reliable, rarely exceeds the limits of one class, incidentally, and seldom of 1.5 classes, i.e., 5 to 8 per cent or 0.01 of the gene index. Therefore the polymorphism of separate populations does not exclude the possibility of obtaining a generalized pattern and of compiling a geographical gene map. It can be taken as established that a difference or similarity in the concentration of genes in adjacent areas corresponds to a genetic connection between the populations of the groups compared, although this connection occasionally relates to the remote past.

The scale of the variation of *ABO* blood group frequencies over the territory of Eastern Europe is 15 to 19 thousandths. With the exception of several not numerous and peripheral populations most of the groups investigated varied within the limits of two classes, classes IV and V in our classification; see the following table.

Classification of Gene Frequency and Gene Composition

Classes	Gene Concentration (per cent)	
	p and q	r
II	10–15	46–50
III	16–20	50–55
IV	21–25	56–60
V	25–30	61–65
VI	31–35	65–70

When the number of groups compared falls within the limits of 1000, the frequency difference in one class seldom reaches the criterion x^2 of statistical probability; when it is confined to a definite area and has a clear geographical trend, the group divergences become significant even when not statistically reliable.

GEOGRAPHICAL MAPS OF THE DISTRIBUTION OF GENE FREQUENCY

On Mourant's map two zones are distinguished — a North-Eastern one with a gene p frequency of 20–25 per cent (our Class IV), and a South-Western zone with a p frequency of 25–30 per cent. The boundary between them is a straight line running from Lake Onega to approximately the mouth of the Ural river. He established frequency zones for gene q as follows: an Eastern zone, lying in Western Siberia but partly embracing the land between the Ural and Volga rivers, with a gene concentration of 20–25 per cent (class IV); an adjacent zone belonging to class III, occupying the greater part of Eastern Europe with a tongue or salient extending West to the Niemen; and a third zone with a gene frequency of 10–15 per cent embracing the area of the East coast of the Baltic and the Ukraine.

Our data distinguish the same zones but with boundaries different to those on Mourant's map (see Figs. 2–4). The zone of low gene p concentration (21–25 per cent) includes the territory of the Northern Russian regions and the republics and national areas of the Northern Urals and the Middle Volga. The lowest gene p frequency is among the Mari and Chuvash (18–20 per cent); among the Northern Finnish peoples (Karelians and Komi) p frequency is slightly above 20 per cent, and among the Kazan Tatars and Bashkirs it does not exceed the limits of class IV. Over the rest of the territory of Eastern Europe a class V concentration predominates (26–30 per cent), and is found in varying degrees among the Russian, Belorussian, and Ukrainian populations, and the Letts and Estonians. In Finland gene p frequency is on the boundary of classes IV and V, reaching a maximum of 37 per cent (class VII) among the Lapps. In mapping gene frequency we have rounded off fractions of several thousandths to include a population in the class predominating in the area investigated.

For gene q two zones are distinguished coinciding territorially with those for the p gene. Gene q frequency was highest among the Mari and Chuvash (around 24 per cent). In other Finnish and Turkic nationalities its concentration fell to the lower limit of class IV, and among the Zyrians and Mordvinians to the boundary value of 19 per cent. Gene q concentration was also at this boundary figure among Archangelsk and Vologda Russians, but because of the special features of contact groups we included the Northern Russian populations in class IV for gene q. In the bulk of the Russian population gene q concentration was 16–17 per cent (class III). It was also necessary to include the Belorussians, Letts, Estonians, and Karelians in this type because they had a boundary value. In the Ukraine q frequency was around 3 per cent less than in Central Russia. A boundary value of 14 per cent predominated, but the whole of the South-West Ukraine was more correctly separated off and included in class II. The population of Finland also fell in this group. The Kola Lapps, as with gene p, occupied a special place, their gene q concentration being less than 10 per cent, but the Lapps are less differentiated from mixed Swedes and Norwegians as regards gene q than for gene p.

Gene r frequency varied comparatively little in the general pattern and had no territorial link. Class IV concentration (55–60 per cent) predominated. Class III was found only in three Russian groups with no

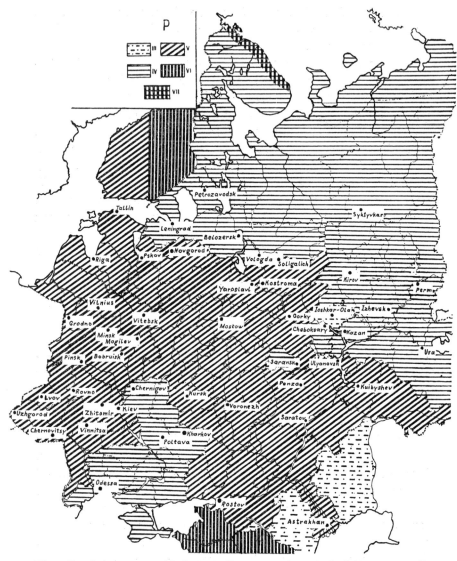

Figure 2.   Gene *p* geographical zones. Frequency of genes: I, 5–10 per cent; II, 11–15 per cent; III, 16–20 per cent; IV, 21–25 per cent; V, 26–30 per cent; VI, 31–35 per cent; VII, 36–40 per cent.

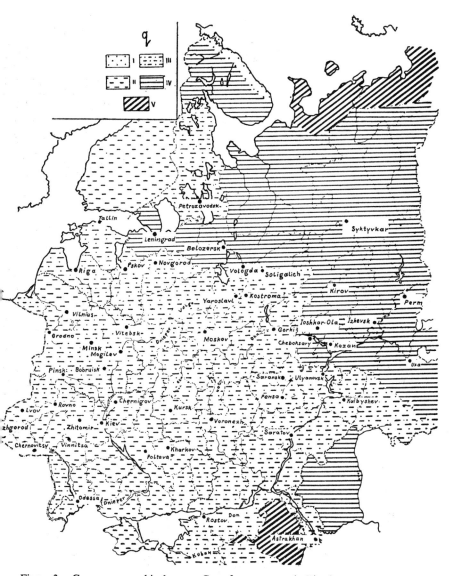

Figure 3.   Gene *q* geographical zones. Gene frequency: as in Fig. 2.

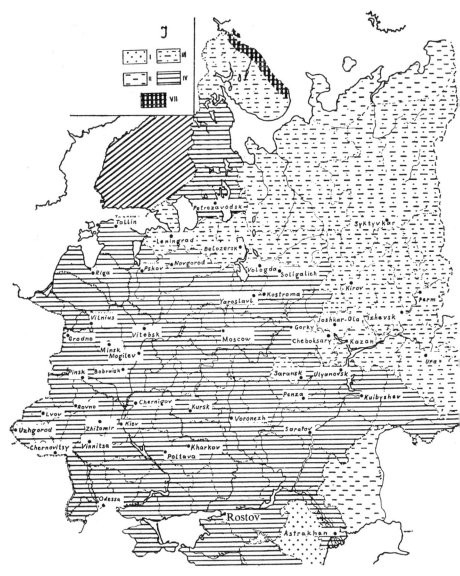

Figure 4. Zones by gene index $\mathrm{I} = (p + r):(q + r)$. Index frequencies: II, 46–50 per cent; III, 56–60 per cent; IV, 51–55 per cent; V, 61–65 per cent; VI, 66–70 per cent.

link between them, and among the Chuvash and Mordvinians. Class V (60–66 per cent) was established in two Ukrainian groups and among the Lapps. The gene index varied from 1.10 to 1.18 among Russians, Ukrainians, Belorussians, and the Baltic peoples. In two Northern Russian groups it was 1.03. Among the Finnish and Turkic peoples of the Transvolga the index was a little above 1.00, and for the Mari and Chuvash was just below unity.

In the combined concentration of the three genes two zones could be distinguished in Eastern Europe: (1) a principal zone embracing the Central, Southern, and West; (2) a second zone embracing the North and the Transvolga. The pattern of gene concentration for the two zones was as follows:

Zone	Gene Concentration		
	p	q	r
Principal	Class V (25–30%)	Class III (15–20%)	Class IV (56–60%)
Northern and Eastern	Class IV (20–25%)	Class IV (20–25%)	

Within the limits of each zone there was a variation with a tendency to shift toward the upper or lower boundary value of the class, and in a few cases to deviate slightly from the boundary value.

COMPARATIVE PATTERN OF *ABO* BLOOD GROUP ZONES IN EASTERN EUROPE

EUROPE

ABO blood groups have been determined for the overwhelming bulk of the population of Western Europe. In many countries the results of mass surveys have been published and various separate monographs. From a review of the published material the changes in gene frequency in definite directions, from East to West or from North to South, reveal a certain order in the shift of gene concentration, not excluding individual foci that do not fit into the general pattern or that vary within the limits of one class. A sample of the most typical ethnic groups in Western Europe that characterize the general trend of variation of gene concentration is given in Table 3.

Table 3. *ABO Blood Group Frequencies (in percentages) and the Corresponding Genes (in thousandths) among the Peoples of Western Europe and Middle East*

Locality of investigation	Authors	N	O
	Poles		
Warsaw	Amzel and Halber*	2 928	33.7
Lodz	Halber and Mydlazski*	1 962	32.4
Poznan	Halber and Mydlazski*	765	31.2
Cracow	Halber and Mydlazski*	345	27.3
	Romanians		
Moldavia	Necrasov**	1 960	32.1
Oltenia	Rammeantsu**	1 870	33.9
Muntenia	Popoviciu**	1 278	33.5
	Bulgarians		
Sofia	Ganev*	6 060	32.1
	Czechs and Slovaks		
Czechoslovakia	Vlčkova and Vlček (1962)	174 206	33.2
	Hungarians		
Budapest	Somogy and Angyal*	1 000	33.1
Debrecen	Verzar and Weszeczky*	1 500	31.0
	Serbs		
Yugoslavia	Verzar and Weszeczky*	6 863	32.5
	Greeks		
Athens	Diamantoupolos*	1 200	42.0
	Swedes		
Various places	Hesser*	633	37.9
	Norwegians		
Oslo, etc.	Host*	615	37.9
	Danes		
Copenhagen	Rosling*	2 354	43.9
	Germans		
Leipzig	Sucke*	1 000	34.5
Dresden	Christiansen*	1 171	35.3
Hamburg	Haselhorst*	8 680	39.2
Munich	Kruse*	1 300	42.5
Bonn	Crome*	1 300	38.3
	French		
Whole country	Khérumian (1951)	207 588	44.0
	British		
East Anglia	Penrose (1954)	1 000	43.2
Scotland (Glasgow)	Matta*	746	49.6
Ireland (Dublin)	Boyd (1939)	399	55.2
	Spaniards		
Catalonia	Rigalt*	1 890	43.1
	Italians		
Tuscany	Abruzzese*	800	43.0
Sicily	Nicoletti*	540	45.9
	Berbers		
Algeria	Penrose (1954)	206	52.9
	Copts		
Egypt	Penrose (1954)	1 476	31.2
	Syrians (Christians)		
Beirut	Parr*	2 091	37.8
	Syrians (Muslims)		
Beirut	Parr*	1 777	35.0
	Turks		
Istanbul	Babakan*	500	33.8

* Work cited by W. C. Boyd (1939).
** Work cited by A. Manuila (1951).

AB	r	p	q	I	D/S
8.5	.574	.250	.173	1.103	0.6
8.3	.570	.276	.156	1.165	0.5
8.0	.558	.272	.177	1.129	1.0
9.0	.522	.298	.192	1.148	1.0
8.7	.567	.286	.148	1.195	—
7.8	.582	.274	.144	1.180	—
6.3	.579	.275	.136	1.194	—
8.1	.567	.308	.123	1.268	0.9
8.1	.576	.283	.138	1.203	—
6.3	.576	.294	.139	1.217	1.5
12.2	.557	.274	.149	1.177	4.3
7.4	.574	.288	.138	1.211	—
3.7	.648	.254	.102	1.069	1.0
6.5	.616	.301	.073	1.331	1.9
4.4	.616	.304	.083	1.316	0.5
3.7	.663	.259	.082	1.238	1.5
7.5	.588	.284	.127	1.220	0.2
6.2	.596	.294	.110	1.261	0.2
4.4	.626	.283	.098	1.256	—
4.9	.652	.272	.070	1.280	1.8
5.1	.619	.308	.068	1.349	1.4
8.5	.663	.274	.061	1.294	—
2.7	.658	.295	.048	1.350	—
4.3	.704	.224	.065	1.213	1.9
1.7	.744	.186	.076	1.134	1.3
1.2	.657	.290	.053	1.334	0.5
5.4	.657	.254	.084	1.229	1.1
3.4	.678	.213	.118	1.119	1.5
3.4	.727	.203	.064	1.176	—
10.3	.559	.248	.190	1.077	—
7.7	.615	.281	.092	1.267	4.2
9.3	.592	.255	.144	1.151	2.4
8.8	.581	.293	.116	1.254	1.6

A concentration of gene p of 25 to 30 per cent and of gene r of 55 to 60 per cent, as in the principal zone of Eastern Europe, is to be noted in countries adjoining the Western boundary of that zone, viz. Poland, the German Democratic Republic, Czechoslovakia, Hungary, Romania, and Yugoslavia; in Bulgaria the frequency of gene p exceeds the limits of class V by 0.008. In Romania as a whole the frequency of genes p and q is the same, but in the center of the country, Transylvania, especially among the Szeklers who speak Hungarian, and deeper in the arc of the Carpathians and in the Dobrudja, the frequency of gene p rises to 32–35 per cent (Manuila, 1958). The frequency of gene q among the populations of these countries varies between 11 and 14 per cent, i.e., is 3 or 4 per cent lower than in Eastern Europe. The gene index exceeds 1.2 but does not go as high as 1.3.

To the West of the Federal Republic of Germany, in the Netherlands, Belgium, Great Britain, France, Spain, and North Italy, the concentration of gene p, with minor exceptions, remains within the limits of class V, but is often above its upper limit. The frequency of gene r is above 60 per cent, often as high as 70 per cent. The frequency of gene q in class I is between 6 and 10 per cent, i.e., 4 to 6 per cent lower than in the adjacent zone, and 8 per cent lower than in Eastern Europe; the fall in q concentration is less than the rise in r concentration. The gene index is between 1.2 and 1.3. Foci of higher p concentrations are to be found not in the extreme West, as might be expected, but predominantly in the valley of the Upper Danube and in the Alps, especially in the Western Alps, merging with a belt of higher p concentration in the Balkans. The Scandinavian countries differ from the West in a certain drop in r concentration; in Scotland and Ireland, on the contrary, r concentration is above 70 per cent, while p concentration remains within the limits of class IV. In Southern Italy, Sardinia, and among the Berbers of Algeria, the general features are less definitely expressed; certain groups have a similar gene concentration to the Scottish and Irish regions, while the r frequency in others is low (60 per cent) and the p concentration is rather higher. In Egypt, Syria, and Turkey the frequency of gene r is low (62 per cent), that of gene p remains within the limits of class II, while that of gene q varies.

These two principal zones are distinguished in Western Europe with several less marked areas. The zone bordering on the East European region, lying between Vistula and the Elbe, and covering most of the Balkan Peninsula, can be provisionally called 'Central European' and the Western region 'Atlantic'.

Characteristics of the West European Zones

Zone	Gene concentration (per cent)		
	p	*q*	*r*
Central European	25–30	10–15	55–60
Atlantic	25–30	6–10	66–70

Within the limits of these zones there is a vaguely defined region of foci of higher *p* concentration, up to 35 per cent, stretching along the mountain ranges of the Carpathians and Western Alps. Foci of higher *p* concentration are also noted in places on the Southern peninsulas, on the Rhine, and in Great Britain. The territorial extent of these foci, however, remains unclear because they have been found mainly in the urban population. A secondary variety, deviating from the Atlantic picture mainly by variation of *r* frequency can be distinguished in Scandinavia, Scotland, and Ireland, and in the Western and Eastern Mediterranean.

Let us now pass to a survey of blood group distribution over the territory of Western Siberia adjacent to Eastern Europe. The aboriginal population of the taiga and tundra belts of Western Siberia at present consists of small isolated groups of 1000–2000 persons leading a hunting or reindeer-herding existence, with agriculture in places. As to blood groups the populations that have been investigated prove to be non-uniform. This can be explained in part by the smallness of the populations and random errors of sampling, and partly by the heterogeneous composition of the West Siberian population which has proved to be less homogeneous than earlier investigators, who had included West Siberia in the region of high frequency of group B, had suggested. An increase in gene *q* frequency is found among the Buryats of Transbaikalia but in Western Siberia a *q* frequency exceeding 20 is only found in isolated populations of comparatively recent origin.

We shall confine ourselves here to giving only summaries of the principal ethnic groups from our tables (Bunak, ms.) without going into details of all the available material.

Among the Mansi[1] several populations have been investigated which proved not to be uniform in gene concentration of the *ABO* system. In the Pelym group the gene index was 1.57 and in the Ivdel group a little lower; but in the Berezovo subgroup recently investigated the index is less than unity (0.982). Two populations of another Ugrian

[1] Mansi — formerly called Voguls — Ed.

group differed markedly, the mean gene index of the Khanti[2] being 1.106.

The Ugrians are related to the ancient population of Western Siberia. No other, older group has survived in Western Siberia, but in the opinion of ethnographers survivals exist outside this area, e.g., the Yukagirs of the Lower Kolyma. The 113 Yukagirs investigated by I. M. Zolotareva (1964) differed essentially as regards blood groups from both the Ugrians and the Buryats. The following gene figures (p 0.272; q 0.064; r 0.63) and a gene index of 1.28 were found among them. Thus the Yukagirs have a much lower r gene frequency than either the Atlantic groups or the Lapps with a similar q frequency.

In historical times two other ethnic groups migrated from the foothill steppes of the Sayan Mts. and the Altai to the forest belt of Siberia, viz. the Kets[3] and the Nenets. The Kets at present are settled in six small, isolated groups. Their gene index is 1.040. The Selkups,[4] a people speaking a language of the Nenets group, have a similar index. The Nenets of the Taimyr Peninsula and estuary of the Yenisei have a gene index of 1.10–1.05, but the Western Nenets in the Bolshaya Zemlya tundra have a lower index (0.97–0.99).

The highest q gene frequency outside Western Siberia is found among the Buryats whose gene index is 0.840. Whereas the gene index among the Evenks[5] in the forest zone to the North of Transbaikalia between the Yenisei and the Lena is as high as 1.30, to the West in the mountains and steppe zone of the Sayan Mountains and the Altai and in the steppe country as far as the Caspian, the index remains low among the Turkic peoples, but not as low as among the Buryats. Its variation between 1.1 and 0.9 indicates that the pre-Turkic population of the steppes up to the middle of the first millenium A.D. did not have such low serological indices as the Buryats. From the sixth to the twelfth centuries the Turks of the Aral steppes moved to the Lower and Middle Volga and to the wooded steppe country along the Tom and Tobol rivers. The formation of groups of mixed descent led to a higher concentration of gene q. It must be supposed that this shift was affected by the settling of the Nenets, whose original region is placed in the Sayan Mountains; nevertheless, the regions in Eastern Europe where the Turkic foreign element was significant only differ as regards gene q by 3 or 4 per cent from regions where Turks did not penetrate. It therefore follows that a comparatively

---

[2]   Khanti — formerly called Ostyaks — Ed.
[3]   Kets — formerly called Yenissei Ostyaks — Ed.
[4]   Selkups — formerly called Ostyak-Samoyeds — Ed.
[5]   Evenks — formerly called Tungus — Ed.

high concentration of gene q was inherent to the population of Eastern Europe before the appearance of Turkic peoples there.

The geographical distribution of *ABO* gene frequencies in Europe can be regarded as a kind of clinal variation with a high concentration of gene q somewhere in Asia and a gradual fall in concentration from the Urals to the Atlantic Ocean. In fact, a reduction of gene q concentration in the Western regions is traceable in Europe. The ancient population of the forest zone of Western Siberia before the spread of the Nenets and Turks had a low gene q concentration. There is not a single population group among the Mansi, Khanti, or Selkups in which gene q frequency is higher than among the Maris on the Middle Volga. Even if it is supposed that there was a considerable migration of West Siberia tribes into Eastern Europe in antiquity, this debatable fact would not establish an Eastern (Siberian) origin for the serological type of the population in the central part of Eastern Europe. It is much more probable that it is a type formed locally in the distant past rather than a link in a single Asiatic-European series of variants. The migration of tribes from the region of the Dnieper and Nieman to the central part of Eastern Europe led to a small reduction in the concentration of gene q in the principal East European zone. The original serological type is better preserved in the North and in the Transvolga. The lowering of the gene index among the Transvolga Finns was probably reinforced when Turkic peoples in whom q concentration was in all probability comparatively high (Bulgars, Tatars) penetrated to the Middle Volga.

FACTORS PRODUCING CHANGES IN *ABO* GENE FREQUEN-CIES

The territorial disparity of *ABO* serological types, and equally of other serological and racial anthropological subdivisions, is a long-established fact. The variants of certain serological types like somatic complexes are confined to definite and large areas, which points to their great antiquity. The question of the interconnections of the two categories of anthropological features remains significant and is closely linked with the problem of the factors governing the differentiation of serological types. Analyzing of the distribution of *ABO* gene concentration in Europe provides vital data for evaluating the theory of serological differentiation.

1. The automatic genetic processes in small populations that preserve a stable level over many generations are considered a factor in the

differentiation of the ratios of blood groups. In these conditions the proportion of heterozygous forms is reduced and there is a corresponding reinforcement of homozygosity. Formulae by which the rate of isogame-tation can be calculated (Ignatjev, 1940) have been derived for di-allelic genes. With three alleles at a locus, as with blood groups, the rate of isogametation is altered somewhat but in all cases a substantial shift in the frequency of homozygous forms is only possible after scores of generations. It takes 139 generations to halve the frequency of di-allelic genes, i.e., 2500 years. Such conditions are hardly likely to be realized in human populations (Bunak, 1965).

A less significant shift in the frequency of heterozygotes, which does not weaken the fitness of the group, a condition for the preservation of a certain level of heterozygosity, can develop, specialists think in a much shorter space of time (Nemeskeri and Thoma, 1961; Rychkov, 1964a, 1965a). No convincing evidence for this theory has been produced up to the present, i.e., definite exception to Hardy's rule, shifts in the tempo of formation of the organism or in morbidity rates, etc. (Morton and Chung, 1959; Gadzhiev, 1968; Bunak, in print; Davydova, in print). It is still uncertain as to what shift in the relationship of blood group frequencies the development of isogametation should be related. In addition it has not been established at what size of the marriage circle (deme) the process of isogametation acquires marked expression of any kind (Bunak, 1965 a,b).

2.   Changes in gene concentration may be the results of loss of an allele with elimination of a small part of it from the group. This hypothesis was developed in the Soviet literature by Roginskij (1947) regarding the origin of the aborigines of America, in whom gene p and especially gene q are either completely absent or rare. The effect of accidents of sampling is stronger when a group is an isolated, small initial group with few samples taken from the initial population. When several groups are separated from the parent stem an identical deviation resulting from chance is improbable. At the same time one can hardly consider charac-teristic the settling of a broad territory through the spread of a single population after it had separated off from the original group. The peopling of Siberia proceeded quite otherwise, apparently.

3.   The frequency of *ABO* factors in groups differentiated according to pathological conditions or diseases of some sort differs as a rule from their distribution in the mass of the population. That fact, incidentally, is not always clearly or reliably expressed, as was noted in the 1920's (Rubashkin, 1929), but the search for the correlation between blood groups and various morphological and physiological characteristics was

not widely developed because the nature of the supposed connection was still quite unclear. At present a marked shift in this field has been noted. Immunological investigations have shown, for example, that the smallpox virus contains an antibody similar to the isoantibody anti-A (Pettenkofer et al., 1960; Harris et al., 1963). Therefore, since group *B* is more stable vis-à-vis smallpox, it will have an advantage over group *A* and a wider distribution. This view is directly confirmed by comparison of the smallpox death rate, the severity of the disease, and the statistics on its distribution in the various states of India (Vogel, 1964; 1965; Komarovich and Rychkov, 1966).

Analogous findings, whether immunological or statistical or both, have been obtained for many other microbial infections, viz., plague, syphilis, and infantile diarrhoea (Vogel, 1964). Pathological states developing only at later ages do not have as vital an effect on the fertility of the infected persons and on the frequency of the *ABO* factors in populations. The diseases mentioned, however, also affect children and young individuals, and therefore take on the significance of a selection factor. A difference from the gene *A* frequency in the mass population has also been noted in certain diseases of the vital organs, such as cancer of the stomach, gastric and duodenal ulcers, diabetes melitus, pernicious anaemia, etc. (Khérumian et al., 1959), although the difference in many cases is not great. The correlation between sickness and blood factors occasionally proves to be high, for example +0.623 for smallpox and group *O*. Exactly the same or similar value has been established for the correlation between blood groups and diverse morphological and serological characteristics, although most of them have been proved unreliable, dissimilar, or slight in various populations (Kirk, 1961). In Manuila's view (Manuila et al., 1945; Manuilla, 1958) a deviation from the serological type of the mass population has not been proved for various illnesses. All the same, the coincidence of the results obtained by Vogel employing various techniques on different populations are scarcely to be explained by chance. The heightened concentration of group *B* in India, Egypt, and other countries suggested by Vogel, where severe epidemics of plague and smallpox often occur, reveals one of the possible factors of serological differentiation in that region of the inhabited world. It is not the sole one, and of course is not universal. Its effect in Western Siberia, where the frequency of group *B* is low (and also in Europe) cannot be of any significance.

The heightened selective effect of serological incompatibility of the foetus and mother has occasioned a vast literature. Since the first circumstantial theoretical study of the question (Brues, 1954) work has appeared that partially confirms the effect of this factor and extends its significance to include incompatibility of the gametes themselves (Matsunaga and Itho, 1958; Hiraizumi, 1964). More recent investigations of Japanese material (Matsunaga, 1962) have shown that the effect of serological incompatibility of the foetus and mother has not always been noticeably manifest in Japan. Its effect is dissimilar in different zones (Volkova, 1965), and most likely leads to maintenance of heterozygosity at the level characteristic of the group.

Much attention is being given to the problem of the role of mutations in the transformation of serological types. The special calculations of leading mathematical geneticists (Holden, Fleischhacker, and Fischer) and others have shown that a 10 per cent shift in gene A frequency can be brought about with an average rate of mutation only after the lapse of scores of millenia, and consequently is outside the limits of the possible epoch of the formation of contemporary geographical gene zones. The rate of mutation can vary greatly in accordance with circumstances; reconstruction of the protein structure of the organism through the effect of micro-organisms of the environment during the period of initial adaptation could provide the stimulus for a real acceleration of the mutation process. Various views are possible on that subject, but the general trend of the reconstruction of ABO factors does not provoke much disagreement. As to the numerical relationship of the three genes and their interconnections, the view is firmly established that the initial antigen of the ABO system was antigen H, which is present in all three blood groups, including group O (Hirszfeld and Amzel, 1940; Morton and Chung, 1959). The total quantity of substances H and A, and H and B, remains constant; the more A and B there is, the less H. The formation of antigens A and B occurs through several intermediate stages; antigens A_1 and A_2, etc., established by way of absorption, are differentiated by successive reductions of agglutinating activity, and so also are B_1 and B_2. The alleles A_4 and A_5 have a low proportion of the agglutinating effect characteristic of A_1. Then A_c, B_c and O_c (full antigens) complete the stage of antigen formation. Hirszfeld called them the "isoserological pleiades" and noted transitional forms that were also distinguishable in modern populations (Hirszfeld, 1947, 1948). Antigens A_1 and A_2 differ only quantitatively, but are represented by special alleles of a single locus A_1, A_2. As regards the other A varieties, their genetic basis is quite unclear. The differentiation of A and B signifies two different trends of evolution which Hirszfeld calls the 'Northern' (A) and the 'Eastern' (B) mutation. The existence of similar receptors in primates and other mammals deserves greater attention (Potapov, 1962; Komarovich and Rychkov, 1964), but does not lessen the force of Hirszfeld's conclusions.

In spite of the great attention given to the dynamics of the frequencies of blood groups, no indisputable indications have yet been found of a change of gene composition in a population in the absence of migration, mixing, or specific conditions of isolation (Penrose, 1945; Morton and Chung, 1959; Mourant, 1959).

In Eastern Europe the relationship of the *ABO* genes is of great antiquity, preceding the differentiation of the modern ethnic groups (Finnish and Slavonic). In favor of a remote neolithic or mesolithic age for the formation of the serological type of Eastern Europe are the geographical gene zones of Western Europe and the frequencies of *ABO* factors.

When we differentiate serological types that differ by 5 per cent in gene concentration, ten or fifteen types can be distinguished over the whole inhabited world. The figure is less if we take a wider gradation of classes. In all cases the serological and the racial, somatological complexes do not coincide territorially for either the major or the minor racial subdivisions (Oschinsky, 1959). The essence of the difference is that racial features are more closely linked with a definite area. Convergent or parallel formation of complexes of racial features is rarely encountered. On the contrary serological complexes are less closely linked with definite geographical regions (similar *ABO* gene concentrations are found at the most varied latitudes), and arise much more often by way of parallel development. Serological types are polyareal by nature.

SUMMARY

1.   Soviet investigators had already in the 1920's collected much material on the blood group frequencies of the population of the European part of the USSR. The data accumulated was employed by specialists in other countries to compile summaries and geographical gene maps. On the maps of Streng and Steffan, and in recent years on Mourant's gene maps which have acquired wide renown, the characteristics of the territory were drawn without distinction of the ethnic composition of the population, and the relative size of the populations were used to determine blood groups. The boundaries of the *A* and *B* factors on Mourant's maps do not correspond to the data available.

2.   To compile a new map we reviewed all the published investigations, and, as far as possible, also the unpublished ones, made a critical selection of the data, calculated indices of the equilibrium of groups, and obtained characteristics for generalized groups satisfying the criterion of x^2.

The summaries compiled are lodged with the Institute of Ethnography of the USSR Academy of Sciences, and are proposed for special publication. In the present communication only the characteristics of the general groups from which the maps were compiled are given (Tables 1 and 2).

3. Two geographical gene zones are distinguished in Eastern Europe: the first and principal one embraces the Central, Southern, and Western areas, and the second the Northern area and the Transvolga regions. The gene r frequencies in both zones are almost identical (55-60 per cent); gene p frequency in the principal zone is 25-30 per cent, and 5 per cent lower in the Eastern zone; gene q frequency is 15 to 20 per cent in the principal zone and 5 per cent higher in the Eastern zone.

4. Two main zones are distinguished in Western Europe, the central and Atlantic; gene q concentration in the first is 5 per cent lower than in Eastern Europe and 8-10 per cent lower in the second; the frequency of factor r is as high as 70 per cent.

5. Contrary to previous views there are no ancient ethnic groups in Western Siberia with a gene q frequency exceeding 10-15 per cent; the region of high concentration of this gene lies beyond Lake Baikal among the Buryats. In the mountain and foothill steppe belt of the Sayan and Altai Mountains, the gene frequency is higher than in Siberia. The penetration of Turkic tribes into the forest zone of Siberia from this region formed mixed types. In the preceding epoch Ket and Samoyed tribes had moved from this same region into the forest zone of Siberia. Among the present members of these ethnic groups the gene index is also rather low, and the gene q frequency raised.

6. The clinal hypothesis of the gene distribution in Eurasia is partially substantiated as regards the European territory, but is not well grounded as regards Western Siberia.

7. It is most probably that the serological type in Eastern Europe was formed locally in the distant past, in neolithic or mesolithic times.

8. A review of the hypotheses suggested to explain the differentiation of blood groups and changes in their frequency does not make it possible to consider the effect of any particular factor to be established as significant for Europe as a whole, except the migration and mixing of ethnic groups.

9. Serological complexes and anthropological racial types evolve independently, at different times, and do not coincide with either major or minor subdivisions. Serological types have little connection with geographical regions and are polyareal.

Bibliography

LIST OF ABBREVIATIONS

AZ	*Antropologicheskij zhurnal* [Anthropological Journal] (Moscow).
DGO	*Doklady Geograficheskogo obsjestva SSSR* [Papers of Geographical Society of USSR] (Moscow-Leningrad).
ICAES	*International Congress of Anthropological and Ethnographical Sciences* (Moscow).
IGAIMK	*Izvestija gosudarstvennoj akademii istorii materialnoj kultury* [Proceedings of the State Academy of Material Culture History] (Leningrad).
KSIE	*Kratkije soobsjenija Instituta etnografi ANSSSR* [Brief Reviews of the Institute of Ethnography, AS USSR] (Moscow).
KSIIMK	*Kratkije soobsjenija Instituta istorii materialnoj kultury* [Brief Reviews of the Institute of Material Culture History] (Moscow).
MGU	Cf. *Vestnik MGU.*
NAA	*Narody Azii i Afriki* [Peoples of Asia and Africa] (Moscow).
NTE	*Narodna tvorchist ta etnografija* [Folk Art and Ethnography] (Kiev), (In Ukrainian).
NZ	*Nauka i zhizn'* [Science and Life] (Moscow).
RAZ	*Russkij antropologicheskij zhurnal*, from 1932 — *Antropologicheskij zhurnal* [Russian Anthropological Journal, from 1932 — Anthropological Journal] (Moscow).
SA	*Sovetskaja arkheologija* [Soviet Archaeology] (Moscow).
SE	*Sovetskaja etnografija* [Soviet Ethnography] (Moscow).
SGAIMK	*Soobsjenija gosudarstvennoj akademii istorii materialnoj kultury* [Bulletin of the State Academy of the History of Material Culture] (Leningrad).
SMAE	*Sbornik Muzeja Arkheologii i Etnografii* [Collection of Museum of Archaeology and Ethnography] (Leningrad).
TIE	*Trudy Instituta etnografii AN SSSR* [Proceedings of the Institute of Ethnography AS USSR] (Moscow).
UZMGU	*Uchenyje zapiski Moskovskogo gosudarstvennogo universiteta* [Transactions of Moscow State University] (Moscow).
VA	*Voprosy antropologii* [Problems of Anthropology] (Moscow).
VAN	*Vestnik Akademii nauk SSSR* [State Academy of Sciences Herald] (Moscow).
Vestnik MGU	*Vestnik Moskovskogo gosudarstvennogo universiteta.*
VDI	*Vestnik drevnej istorii* [Ancient History Herald] (Moscow).
VF	*Voprosy filosofii* [Problems of Philosophy] (Moscow).
VI	*Voprosy istorii* [Problems of History] (Moscow).

NON-RUSSIAN LANGUAGE PUBLICATIONS

Abdushelishvili, M. G.
1964 *The Anthropology of Georgia's Ancient and Modern Population* (Tbilisi).
Allbrook, D. and W. W. Bishop
1963 "New Fossil Hominoid Material from Uganda", *Nature* 147:4873.
American Antiquity
1956 *Seminars in Archaeology*, 1955 (= *American Antiquity* 22: no. 2 Supplement).
Andrik, P.
1960 "Lebka, obličay a chrup jednovajcových dvojčiat", *Acti Facultatis Rerum Natural Univ. Comenianae* IV:9–10.
Aul, Yu. M.
1964a "On the Anthropology of Russians Living along the Eastern Borders of the Estonian SSR. Works in Anthropology", *Proceedings of Tartu University* 155 (Tartu).
1964b "Data on Lett Anthropology. Works in Anthropology", *Proceedings of Tartu University* 155 (Tartu).
1964c "Anthropological Investigations in Vodj and Izhory Living in the West of Leningrad District. Works in Anthropology, I", *Proceedings of Tartu University* 155 (Tartu).
1964d "Estonian Anthropology", *Proceedings of Tartu University* 158 (Tartu).
  See also Russian language bibliography.
Avias, Y.
1949 "Les groupes sanguins des Néo-Caledoniens", *L'Anthropologie* 53.
Bernstein, F.
1925 "Zusammenfassende Betrachtungen über die erblichen Blutstrukturen des Menschen", *Zs. indukt. Abstammungs u Vererbungslehre* Bd. 37.
Best, E.
1924 *The Maori* vols. 1–2 (Wellington).
Biasutti, R.
1953 *Le razze ei popoli della terra* 1 (Turin).
Bijlmer, H. Y.
1923 *Anthropological Results — New Guinea* 7 (Leiden).
Birdsell, Y. B.
1941 "A Preliminary Report on the Trihybrid Origin of the Australian Aborigines", *American Journal of Physical Anthropology* 28: no. 3.
1951 "The Problem of the Early Peopling of the Americas as Viewed from Asia", *Papers on the Physical Anthropology of the American Indians* (New York).
Blegen, C. W.
1940 "Athens and the Early Age of Greece", *Athenian Studies Presented to W. S. Ferguson* (Cambridge).
1963 *Troy and the Trojans* (New York).
Bolk, L.
1926 "Das Problem der Menschwerdung", *Vortrag auf der 25. Versammlung der Anatomischen Gesellschaft zu Freiburg* (Jena).
Boyd, W. C.
1939 "Blood Groups", *Tabulae Biologicae* 17 (The Hague).
1950 *Genetics and the Races of Man* (Boston).
1952 *Genetics and the Races of Man* (Boston).
1953 "Contribution of Genetics to Anthropology", *Anthropology Today*, ed. by Kroeber (Chicago).
1958 "Genetics and the Races of Man", Boston University Lecture.

Bromley, Ju. V.
1968c   *The Archaic Form of the Communal Family* (Moscow).
   See also Russian language bibliography.
Brues, A. M.
1954   "Selection and Polymorphism in the *ABO* Blood Groups", *Amer. J. Phys. Anthrop.* 12.
Bunak, V. V.
1928a   "Des Caractères Morphologiques Indissolublement Liés aux Variations Physiologiques Normales", *Bull. de la Soc. des Formes Humaines* 4 (Paris).
1928b   "Un Pays de l'Asie Peu Connu: Le Tanna-Touva", *Archive International de l'ethnographie* 29 (Leiden).
1932b   "The Craniological Types of the East Slavic Kurgans", *Anthropologie* 10 (Prague).
1932c   "Neues Material zur Aussonderung Anthropologischer Typen unter der Bevölkerung Osteuropas", *Zeitschr. für Morphologie und Anthropologie* 30.
1965b   "Der Verwandschaftsgrad der Bevolkerung kleiner Ländlichen Gemeinden", *Acta Genet. Med. et Gematol.* 14 (Rome).
1968   *The Evolution of the Elementary Unit of Population (Dem) and its Anthropological Significance* (Moscow).
   See also Russian language bibliography.
Campbell, T. D.
1925   "Dentition and Palate of the Australian Aboriginal", *The Keith Sheridan Foundation Publications* no. 1 (Univ. of Adelaide).
Carbonell, V.
1963   "Variations in the Frequency of Shovel-Shaped Incisors in Different Populations", *Dental Anthropology* (Oxford-London-New York-Paris).
Chepurkovskij, E. M.
1902   *Archiv für Anthropologie*, Bd. X.
1911   "Anthropologische Studien" *Archiv für Anthropologie*, Bd. X (N.F.), Heft 2–3 (Braunschweig).
   See also Russian language bibliography.
Coon, C. S.
1931   *Tribes of the Rif* (Cambridge).
1963   *The Origin of Races* (London).
Coon, C. S., Garn, and J. B. Birdsell
1950   "Races", *A Study of Race Formation in Man* (Springfield).
Dahlberg, A. A.
1949   "The Dentition of the American Indian", *The Physical Anthropology of the American Indian*, W. S. Laughlen (ed.) (Viking Fund, New York).
Darwin, Ch.
1900   *The Variation of Animals and Plants under Domestication* (New York).
Deniker, J.
1926   *Les races et les peuples de la terre* (Paris).
Drennan, M. R.
1929   "An Australoid Skull from the Cape Flats", *Journal of the Royal Anthropological Inst.* 59.
Dreyer, T. F.
1935   "A Human Skull from Florisbad, Orange Free State", *Koninklijke Akademie van Wetenschappen te Amsterdam Proceedings* 38.
Echanove Trujillo, C. A.
1948   *Sociologia mexicana* (Mexico).
Eickstedt, E. V.
1934   *Rassenkunde und Rassengeschichte der Menschheit* (Stuttgart).
1935   "Anlage und Durchführung von Rassenkundlichen Ganuntersuchungen", *Zeitschrift für Rassenkunde* 2.

Engels, F.
1940a *The Origin of the Family, Private Property and the State* (London).
1940b "The Part Played by Labour in the Transition from Ape to Man", *Dialectics of Nature* (London).

Erdland, P.
1914 *Die Marshall-Insulaner Münster in Wien*.

Fischer, E.
1930 "Versuch einer Genanalyse des Menschen mit Besonderer Berücksichtigung der Anthropologischen Rassensystem", *Zeitschr. für Induktive Abstammungs- und Vererbungslehre* 54.

Flower, H. W.
1885 "On the Size of the Teeth as a Character of Race", *Journal of the Anthropological Institute of Great Britain and Ireland* 16.

Fortes, M. and E. E. Evans-Pritchard (eds.)
1940 *African Political Systems* (London).

Francis, E.
1965 *Ethnos und Demos (Soziologische Beiträge zur Volkstheorie)* (Berlin).

Gabel, N. E.
1949 "A Comparative Racial Study of the Papago", *University of New Mexico Publications in Anthropology* (Albuquerque, New Mexico).

Geyer, E.
1932 "Die Anthropologische Ergebnisse der Lapland-Expedition", *Mitteilungen der Anthropologischen Gesellschaft in Wien* 62.

Giuffrida-Ruggeri, V.
1913 *L'uomo attuale: una specie collectiva* (Rome).
1921a Su l'origine dell'uomo, *Nuove teorie e documenti* (Bologna).
1921b "Prime linee di un'antropologia sistematica dell'Asia", *Archiv per l'antropologia e la etnologia* 47.

Gjerstad, E.
1963 *Legends and Facts of Early Roman History* (London).

Goldstein, M. S.
1932 "The Cusps in the Mandibular Molar Teeth of the Eskimo", *American Journal of Physical Anthropology*.

Goose, D. H.
1963 "Dental Measurement: An Assessment of its Value in Anthropological Studies", *Dental Anthropology* (Oxford-London-New York-Paris).

Grosse, E.
1894 *Die Anfänge der Kunst* (Leipzig).

Guha, B. S.
1935 "Racial Affinities of the Peoples of India", *Census of India* 1931 (Simla).

Harris, R., G. Harrison, and C. Rondle
1963 "Vaccinia Vizus and Human Blood Group A Substance", *Acta Genet.* 13.

Heberer, G.
1956 "Die Fossilgeschichte der Hominoedea", *Primatologia, Handbuch der Primatenkunde* vol. 1, Herausgegeben von H. Hoper, An. Schultz, D. Stark (Basel-New York).

Hellman, M.
1928 "Racial Characters in Human Dentition", *Proceedings of the American Philosophical Society* 68: no. 2.

Heyerdahl, T.
1952 *American Indians in the Pacific* (London).

Hillebrandt, E.
1909 "Beitrage zur Morphologie der Zähne", *Pester Medchirugische Presse* nos. 17–18 (Budapest).

Hiraizumi Yuichiro
    1964   "Prezygotic Selection as a Factor in the Maintenance of Variability", *Cold Spring Harbor Symposia in Quantitative Biology* 29.
Hirschberg, W.
    1965   *Wörterbuch der Völkerkunde* (Stuttgart).
Hirszfeld, L.
    1947   "The Transition Forms of Blood Groups", *J. Immunol.* 55.
    1948   "Nouveaux Aspects des Mutations Sérologiques", *Rev. Immunol.* 12.
Hirszfeld, L. and R. Amzel
    1940   "Etude sur les pléiades isosériques du sang", *Annal. Institut Pasteur* 65.
Hogbin, H. J.
    1934   *Law and Order in Polynesia* (London).
Hooton, E. A.
    1946   *Up from the Ape* (New York).
Hooton, E. A. and C. W. Dupertuis
    1935   "The Physical Anthropology of Ireland", *Papers of the Peabody Museum* 30: nos. 1–2.
Hrdlička, A.
    1912   "The Bearing of Physical Anthropology on the Problem under Consideration", *The Problem of the Unity or Plurality and the Probable Place of Origin of the American Aborigines* (= *American Anthropologist, n.s.* 14).
    1923   "Variation in Dimensions of Lower Molar in Man and Anthropoid Apes", *American Journal of Physical Anthropology* no. 4.
    1935   "Melanesians and Australians and the Peoples of America", *Smithsonian Miscellaneous Collections* 94: no. 11.
Huxley, J. S.
    1932   *Problems of Relative Growth* (London).
Huxley, T. H.
    1870   "On the Geographical Distribution of the Chief Modifications of Mankind", *Journal of the Ethnological Society of London* n.s. 11.
Imbelloni, J.
    1938   "Tabla clasificatoria de los 'Indios'", *Revista de la Sociedad Argentina de Ciencias Naturales* 12.
Jackson, J. E.
    1959   "Some Aspects of the Negro Question in the United States", *World Marxist Review* 2: no. 7 (July).
Johnston, H.
    1908   *George Grenfell and the Congo* (London).
Jonge, Th. E. de
    1918   *Odontologische Studien Osterreichische Zeitschrift fur Stomatologie*, XVI, Ht. no. 1.
Kajava, I.
    1912   "Die Zähne der Lappen. Anthropologische Zahnstudien", *Verhandlungen der Gesellschaft Finnischer Zahnärzte* 9.
Katz, F.
    1958   The Evolution of Aztec Society. *Past and Present* no. 13.
Keiter, F.
    1956   Geschichtzüge in Italien und Libyen", *Homo* 7: nos. 2–3.
Keith, A.
    1949   *A New Theory of Human Evolution* (New York).
Khérumian, R.
    1951   *Génétique et anthropologie des groupes sanguins* (Paris).
Khérumian, R. and J. Moulec
    1959   "Les groupes sanguins *ABO* dans les gancers et les ulcères de l'estomac et du doudénum", *Revue d'hématol.* 14: no. 2.

Khérumian, R., E. Ropatz and J. Moulec
1959 "Repartition des groupes sanguins dans le departement de la Seine-Maritime", *Revue d'hématol.* 14: no. 5.

Kirk, R.
1961 "Blood Group Interaction and the World Distribution of the *ABO* Gene *p* and the *Ph* Gene *r/cde*", *Amer. J. Human Genet.* 13: no. 7.

Klimek, S.,
1930 "Kraniologische Beiträge zur Systematik der gelben Rasse", *Verhandlungen der Deutschen Gesellschaft für physischen Anthropologie.*

Koenigswald, G. H. R. von
1935 "Eine Fossil Sängetierefauna mit Simia aus Südchina", *Proc. Koninkl. Akad. Wet. Amsterdam* 38: pt. 3.

1952 "Gigantopithecus blacki, von Koenigswald a Giant Fossil Hominid From the Pleistocene of Southern China", *Anthropol. Papers Amer. Mus. Nat. Hist.* 43:4.

Kollmann, J.
1900 "Neue Gedanken über das alte Problem von der Abstammung des Menschen", *Correspondenz Blatt der Deutschen Gesellschaft für Anthropologie, Ethnologie und der Urgeschichte* 31.

Kubbel, L.
1967 *On the Origin of Statehood in the Western Sudan* (Moscow).

Labouret, M.
1934 *Les Manding et leur langue* (Paris).

Laughlin, W. S.
1951 "The Alaska Gateway. Viewed From the Aleutian Islands", *Papers on the Physical Anthropology of the American Indian* (New York).

Leakey, L. S. B.
1935 *The Stone Age Races of Kenya* (London).
1948 "Fossil and Subfossil Hominoidea in East Africa", *R. Broom Commemorative.*
1961a "Exploring 1,750,000 Years into Man's Past", *National Geographic Magazine* 120:4.
1961b "New Finds at Olduvai Gorge", *Nature* 189:4765.

Le Gros Clark, W. E.
1946 "Significance of the Australopithecinae", *Nature* 147:4873.
1953 "Growth and Body Proportions in Relation to the Systematics of the Higher Primates", *Proc. Linn. Soc.* 164:3 (London).

Le Gros Clark, W. E. and L. S. B. Leakey
1951 "The Miocene Hominoidea of East Africa", *Fossil Mammals of Africa* (= *Brit. Mus. Nat. Hist. No.* 1) (London).

Le Gros Clark, W. E. and D. P. Thomas
1951 "Associated Jaws and Limb Bones of Limnopithecus Macinnesi", *Fossil Mammals of Africa* (= *Brit. Mus. Nat. Hist.* no. 1) (London).

Lenin, V. I.
1963 *Collected Works* (Moscow).
See also Russian language bibliography.

Leroi-Gourhan, A.
1964 *Le geste et la parole. I. Technique et langage* (Paris).
1965 *Le geste et la parole. II. La memoire et les rythmes* (Paris).

Le Roux, C.
1948 *De Bergpapoea's van Nieuw Guinea* (Leiden).

Lester, O. and J. Millot
1939 *Les races humaines* (Paris).

Lounsbury, F.
1964   "The Structural Analysis of Kinship Semantics", *Proceedings of the 9th International Congress of Linguistics* (The Hague).

Maget, M.
1953   *Guide d'étude directe des comportements culturels* (Paris).

Makarius, R. et L.
1961   *L'origine de l'exogamie et du totemisme* (Paris).

Manuila, A.
1951   "Recherches serologiques et anthropologiques chez les populations de la Roumanie et des regions voisins", *These, L'Université de Genève* (Zürich).
1958   "Blood Groups and Disease – Hard Facts and Delusions", *J. Amer. Medic. Association* 167: no. 17.

Manuila, A., M. Sauter and M. Vestemeanu
1945   "Etude de $\sqrt{16.685}$. Correlations entre le groupe sanguin et d'autre caractères morphologiques examinés en Europe Centrale", *Arch. Suic. Anthrop. Génét. Annexe*.

Marx, K.
1966   *Capital* (Moscow).

Marx, K. and F. Engels
1970   *Selected Works* 3 (Moscow).

Matsunaga, E.
1962   "Selective Mechanism Operating on *ABO* and *MN* Blood Groups with Special Reference to Prezygotic Selection", *Eugenic Quarterly* 9.

Matsunaga, E. and S. Itoh
1958   "Blood Groups and Fertility in Japanese Population with Special Reference to Intra-Uterine Selection Due to Maternal-Foetal Incompatibility", *Annal Huite au Genet*, v. 22.

Montandon, G.
1928   *L'ologénése humaine* (Paris).
1933   *La race, les races* (Paris).

Moorrees, C. F. A.
1957   *The Aleut Dentition* (Harvard Univ. Press, Cambridge).

Morant, Q. M.
1927   "A Study of the Australian and Tasmanian Skulls Based on Previously Published Measurements", *Biometrica* 19: nos. 3–4.

Morgan, L. H.
1871   *Systems of Consanguinity and Affinity of the Human Family* (Washington).
1877   *Ancient Society or Researches in the Lines of Human Progress from Savagery through Barbarism to Civilization* (Chicago).
1881   *Houses and House-Life of American Aborigines* (Washington).

Morgan, W. and W. Watkins
1948   "The Detection of a Product of the Blood Group *O* Gene and the Relation of So-called *O*-Substance to the Agglutinogenes *A* and *B*", *British J. Experim. Patholog.* 29.

Morton, N. and C. Chung
1959   "Are the *MN* Blood Groups Maintained by Selection?", *Amer. J. Human Genet.* 11.

Mourant, A. E.
1954   *The Distribution of Human Blood Groups* (Oxford).
1959   "Human Blood Groups and Natural Selection", *Cold Spring Harbor Symposia on Quantitative Biology* 24.

Mourant, A., A. Kopec, and K. Domanievska-Sobczak
1958   "The *ABO* Blood Groups", *Comprehensive Tables and Maps of World Distribution* (Oxford).

Movius, H.
1949 "Early Man and Pleistocene Stratigraphy in Southern and Eastern Asia". *Papers of the Peabody Museum of American Archeology and Ethnology* 19: no. 3 (Cambridge, Mass.).

Nelson, C. T.
1938 "The Teeth of the Indians of Pecos Pueblo", *American Journal of Physical Anthropology* 23.

Nemeskeri, J. and A. Thoma
1961 "Ivad and Isolate in Hungary", *Acta Genet.* 11 (Rome).

Newman, M. T.
1951 "The Sequence of Indian Physical Types in South America", *Papers on the Physical Anthropology of the American Indian* (New York).

Newmann, G. K.
1952 "Measurements and Indices of American Indian Varieties", *Yearbook of Physical Anthropology.*

Nilsson, M. P.
1932 *The Mycenaean Origin of Greek Mythology* (Berkeley).

1933 *Homer and Mycenae* (London).

Oschinsky, L.
1959 "A Reappraisal of Recent Serological, Genetic and Morphological Researches on the Taxonomy of the Races of Africa and Asia", *Anthropologica* 1.

Pedersen, P. O.
1949 "The East Greenland Eskimo Dentition", *Meddelelsez on Grønland* 142 (Copenhagen).

Pei Wen-chung
1957 "Giant Ape's Jaw Bone Discovered in China", *American Anthropologist* 59:5.

Penrose, L.
1954 "Quelques principes sur la frequence des genes et sa stabilité dans les populations humaines", *J. Genet. Humaine* 7:3.

Pettenkofer, H., Q. Maasen, and R. Bickerich
1960 "Antigen-Gemeinschaft zwischen menschlichen Blutgruppen und Enterobacteriaceen", *Zs. Immun. Forschung* Bd. 119.

Race, R. and R. Sanger
1958 *Blood Groups in Man* (Oxford).

Remane, A.
1956 "Palaeontologie und Evolution der Primaten, besonders der Nicht-Haminoiden", *Primatologia. Handbuch der Primatenkunde*, Bd. 1, Herausgegeben von H. Hofer, A. H. Schultz, D. Stark (Basel-New York).

Riesenfeld, A.
1956 "Shovel-Shaped Incisors and a Few Other Dental Features Among the Native Peoples of the Pacific", *American Journal of Physical Anthropology* 14: no. 3.

Robertson Smith, W.
1907 *Lectures on the Religion of the Semites* (London).

Robinson, J.
1961 "The Australopithecines and their Bearing on the Origin of Man and Stone Tool-making", *South African J. Sci.* 57:1.

Rohan Csermark, G. de
1967 "Le première apparition du terme 'ethnologie'", *Ethnologia Europaea* 1: no. 3.

Rosin, S.
1956 "Die Verteilung der *ABO* Blutgruppen in der Schweiz", *Archiv. der J. Klaus Stiftung.* Bd. 31; H. 1-z (Zürich).

Ryberg, I. S.
1940   *An Archaeological Record of Rome, from the Seventh to Second Century B.C.*
(London).

Sahlins, M. D.
1958   *Social Stratification in Polynesia* (Seattle).

Saller, K.
1960   *Lehrbuch der Anthropologie*, begründet von R. Martin. 10 Lieferung: "Blut-
weisse und Blutgruppen" (Stuttgart).

Sarasin, F.
1916–1922   *Nova Caledonia* (Berlin).

Sarasin, F. and P.
1892–1893   *Die Weddas von Ceylon* (Wiesbaden).

Schebesta, P. and V. Lebzelter
1933   *Anthropology of the Central African Pygmies in the Belgian Congo* (Prague).

Schlaginhaufen, O.
1916   "Pygmäenrassen und Pygmäenfrage", *Vierteljahrschrift der Naturforschenden
Gesellschaft* 61: no. 1.

Schmidt, W. and W. Koppers
1924   *Völker und Kulturen* (Regensburg).

Schreiner, A.
1929   *Die Nord-Norweger* (Oslo).

Schreiner, K.
1939   *Crania Norvegica* (Oslo).

Schultz, A. H.
1927   "Studies on the Growth of Gorilla and of Other Higher Primates with
Special Reference to a Fetus of Gorilla Preserved in the Carnegie Museum",
Mem. Carneg. Mus. 11.

Schwerz, F.
1915   "Die Volgerschaften der Schweiz von Urzeit bis zu Gegenwart", *Studien und
Forschungen zur Menschen und Völkerkunde* 13 (Stuttgart).

Schwidetsky, I.
1950   "Turaniden-Studien. Akademie der Wissenschaft und der Literatur in
Mainz", *Abhandlungen der Mathematisch Naturwissenschaftlichen Klasse*
Jahrgang no. 9.
1959   *Das Menschenbild der Biologie* (Stuttgart).

Selmer-Olsen, R.
1949   "An Odontometrical Study on the Norwegian Lapps" (= Skrifter Utgitt av
Norske Videnskaps-Akademie i. Oslo 1) *Mat-Naturv. Klasse* no. 3.

Seminars in Archaeology,
1955   (= *American Antiquity* 22: no. 2. Supplement).

Semper, K.
1873   *Die Palau-Insel im Stillen Ozean* (Leipzig).

Sergi, G.
1911   *L'Uomo* (Turin).

Shapiro, H. L.
1943   "Physical Differentiation in Polynesia. Studies in the Anthropology of
Oceania and Asia", *Papers of the Peabody Museum* 20.

Shaw, J. C. M.
1931   *The Teeth, the Bony Palate and the Mandible in Bantu Races* (London).

Snow, Ch.
1953   "The Ancient Palestinian Skull V Reconstruction", *Amer. School of Prehistoric Research* Bulletin 17.

Southall, A. W.
1953   "Alur Society", *A Study in Processes and Types of Domination* (Cambridge).

Starikov, V. S.
1966 "Catalogue of the Kitan Script (first variant)", *XI Pacific Science Congress* (*Tokyo, 1966*) (Moscow).
See also Russian language bibliography.

Steffan, P.
1932 *Handbuch der Blutgruppenkunde* (Munich).

Steffan, P. and P. Wellisch
1928–1936 "Die Geographische Verteilung der Blutgruppen", *Zs. für Rassenphysiologie* Bd. 2–7.

Straus, W.
1940 "The Posture of the Great Ape Hand in Locomotion and Its Phylogenetic Implications", *Amer. J. Phys. Anthropol.* 27:2.

Streng, O.
1935 *Die Blutgruppenforschung in der Anthropologie* (Helsinki).

Sullivan, L.
1920 "Differences in the Pattern of the Second Lower Molar Tooth", *Amer. J. Phys. Anthropol.* no. 3.

Suret-Canale, J.
1958 *Afrique noire occidentale et centrale* (Paris).

Suzuki, M. and T. Sakai
1956a "The Tuberculum Accessorium Mediale Internum in Recent Japanese", *Journal of Anthropological Society of Nippon* 64: no. 4.
1956b "On the 'Deflecting Wrinkle' in Recent Japanese", *Journal of Anthropological Society of Nippon* 65:49.
1964 "Shovel-Shaped Incisors Among the Living Polynesians", *Amer. J. Phys. Anthropol.* n.s. 22: no. 1.

Swindler, D. R.
1936 *A Study of the Cranial and Skeletal Material Excavated at Nippur* (Philadelphia).

Terra, M. de
1905 *Beiträge zu einer Odontographie der Menschenrassen* (Universität Zürich, Parchim. i. M. Druck von H. Freise).

Thompson, L.
1945 *The Native Culture of the Mariana Islands* (Honolulu).

Tokarev, S. A.
1967b "Die Grenzen der ethnologischen Erforschung der Völker industrieller Länder", *Ethnologia Europaea* 1: no. 1.
See also Russian language bibliography.

Tratman, E. K.
1950 "A Comparison of the Teeth of People of Indo-European Racial Stock with the Mongoloid Racial Stock", *Yearbook of Physical Anthropology* no. 3.

Vallois, H. V.
1948 *Les races humaines* (Paris).
1961 "The Social Life of Early Man: the Evidence of Skeletons", *Social Life of Man* (New York).

Vlčkova, M. and E. Vlček
1962 "Blood Groups of the *ABO* and *Rh* Systems in Czechoslovakia", *IA1* 92.

Vogel, F.
1964 "Neuere Untersuchungen zur Populationsgenetik der *ABO*-Blutgruppen. Bericht über die 8 Tagung Deutschen Gesel.", *Anthrop. Homo.* Bd. 13.
1965 "Blood Groups and Natural Selection", *Proc. 10 Congress Soc. Blood Transfus.* (Stockholm-Basel).

Vogel, F. and M. Chakravartti
1966 "*ABO* Blood Groups and Smallpox in a Rural Population of West Bengal and Bihar", *Humangenetik* 3.

Vogel, F., J. Dehnhert, and W. Helmbold
1964 "Über Beziehungen zwischen den *ABO* Blutgruppen und der Säuglings-dyspepsie", *Humangenetik* 1.
Wegner, R. N.
1931 *Zum Sonnentor durch Altes Indianerland* (Darmstadt).
Weidenreich, F.
1945 "Giant Early Man From Java and South China", *Anthropol. Papers Amer. Mus. Nat. Hist.* 40:1.
Westermarck, E.
1901 *History of Human Marriage* (London).
Wiener, A.
1943 *Blood Groups and Transfusion* (Springfield).
Williamson, R. W.
1924 *The Social and Political Systems of Central Polynesia* 1-3 (Cambridge).
Wirz, O.
1922, 1925 *Die Marind-anim von Holländisch-Süd-Neu-Guinea* Bd. I, II (Hamburg).
Woo, T. L. and Q. M. Morant
1934 "A Biometric Study of the 'Flatness' of the Facial Skeleton in Man", *Biometrika* 26.
Woo Ju-Kang
1962 "The Mandibles and Dentition of Gigantopithecus Palaeontol", *Sinica*, n.s.d. no. 11 (whole ser. no. 146).

RUSSIAN LANGUAGE PUBLICATIONS

Abramzon, S. M.
1951 "Formy rodo-plemennoj organizatsii u kochevnikov Srednej Asii" [The Forms of Clan-Tribal Organization among the Nomads of Central Asia], *TIE* 14.
Agajev, A. G.
1968 "Funktsija jazyka kak etnicheskogo priznaka" [The Function of Language as an Ethnic Indication], *Jazyk i obsjestvo* (Moscow).
Akaba, L. Kh.
1961 "Etnograficheskoje izuchenija abkhazov za gody Sovetskoj vlasti" [Ethnographical Studies of Abkhazians for the Years of Soviet Power], *Trudy Abkhazskovo instituta jazyka, literatury i istorii* 32 (Sukhumi).
Akimova, M. S.
1952 "Antropologicheskij tip lezgin" [The Anthropological Type of the Lezghin], *KSIE* 16.
Akimova, M. S. and M. A. Bulatova
1947 "K antropologii avartsev" [On the Avar Anthropology], *KSIE* 2.
Aleksandrov, V. A.
1964 "Russkoje naselenije Sibiri XVII — nachala XVIII vv. (Jenisejskij kraj)" [The Russian Population of Siberia, the 17th to the Beginning of the 18th cent. (The Yenisei Region)], *TIE* 87.
Aleksejev, V. P.
1960 "Nekotoryje voprosy razvitija kisti v protsesse antropogeneza (o meste kiik-kobintsa sredi neandertalskikh form)" [Certain Problems of the Development of the Hand in the Course of Anthropogenesis (On the Place of the Kiik-Koba Man among Neanderthal Forms)], *TIE* 50 (n.s.).
1961 "O smeshannom proiskhozhdenii uralskoj rasy" [On the Mixed Origin of the Uralic Race], *Voprocy arkheologii Urala* 1 (Sverdlovsk).

1962 *Rod, plemija, narodnost, natsija (istoricheskije formy obsjnosti ljudey)* [Clan, Tribe, Nationality, Nation (Historical Forms of the Community of People)] (Moscow).

1963 "Antropologicheskij dannyje k probleme proiskhozhdenija tsentralnych predgorij Kavkasskogo khrebta" [Some Anthropological Data on the Origin of the Range of Caucasus], *TIE* 82 (n.s.).

1964 "Antropologicheskije issledovanija v SSSR" [Anthropological Studies in the USSR], *SE* 4.

1967 *Kraniologija narodov Vostochnoi Evropy i Kavkaza v svjazi s problemami ikh proiskhozhdenija* [The Craniology of the Peoples of Eastern Europe and Caucasus as Related to their Origin] (Moscow, Doctorate thesis).

i.p. *Drevnejshije evropeoidnoje naselenije Srednej Azii i jego potomki* [The Ancient Europoid Population of Central Asia and its Descendants].

Aleksejev, V. P. and Ju. V. Bromley

1968 "K izucheniju roli pereselenij narodov v formirovanii novykh etnicheskikh obsjnostej" [On the Studies of the Role of the Peoples Migrations in the Formation of New Ethnic Communities], *SE* no. 2.

Aleksejev, V. P., A. L. Mongajt and A. I. Pershits

1968 *Istorija pervobytnogo obsjestva* [The History of Primitive Society] (Moscow).

Aleksejeva, T. J.

1955 "Antropologicheskij tip naselenija Chuvachii" [The Anthropological Type of the Population of the Chuvach Republic], *KSIE* 23.

1956 "Antropologicheskij sostav naselenija Volgo-Okskogo bassejna (k probleme slavjano-finskikh vzaimootnoshenij v Povolzhje)" [The Anthropological Composition of the Population of the Volga-Oka Basin (On the Problem of Slav-Finnish Relations in the Volga Region)], *TIE* 33 (n.s.).

1958 "Etnicheskaja prinadlezzhnost' sitskarej v svete dannykh antropologii" [The Ethnic Affiliation of the Sitskary in the Light of Anthropological Information], *SA* no. 1.

1965 "Antropologicheskije materialy k etnogenezu vostochnykh slavjan" [Anthropological Materials on the Ethnogenesis of Eastern Slavs], *SA* no. 3 (1964) (translated in *Homo* Bd. 16, Hf. 3).

Aleksejeva, T. J. and B. A. Vasiljev

1959 "K voprosu o geneticheskom rodstve russkoj mesjery i tatar — misharej" [On Genetic Relationships between the Russian Meshchera and Mishari Tatars], *KSIE* 31.

Amlinskij, I. E.

1955 *Zhoffrua Sent-Iler, ego borba protiv Kjuvje* [Geoffroy Saint-Hilaire and His Struggle with Cuvier] (Moscow).

Andrianov, B. V.

1961 *Narody Afriki* [The Peoples of Africa] (Moscow).

1964 *Naselenije Afriki* [The Population of Africa] (Moscow).

1967 "Problema formirovanija narodnostej i natsij v strankakh Afriki" [The Problem of Formation of Nationalities and Nations in African Countries], *VI* no. 9.

1968 "Khozjajstvenno-kulturnyje tipy i istoricheskij protsess" [Economical-Cultural Types and the Historical Process], *SE* no. 2.

Andrianov, B. V., M. Ja. Berzina, S. I. Bruk, Ja. R. Vinnikov, F. W. Kamenetskaja, and V. I. Kozlov

1961 *Karta narodov mira* [The Map of the Peoples of the World] (Moscow).

Anisimov, A. F.

1936 *Rodovoje obsjestvo evenkov (tungusov)* [Evenks (Tungus) Clan Society] (Leningrad).

Anisimov, S. F.

1955 "Sootnoshenije kategorij zakona, prichinnosti, neobkhodimosti i sluchajnosti"

[The Relationship between the Categories of Law, Causality, Necessity, and Chance], *VF* no. 6.

Annaklychev, Sh.
1961   *Byt rabochikh-neftjanikov Nebit-Daga i Kum-Daga* [The Life of the Oil Industry Workers of Nebit-Dag and Kum-Dag] (Ashkhabad).

Anokhin, G. I.
1964   "O materialnoj kulture farertsev" [On the Material Culture of the Faroese], *SE* no. 6.

Anokhina, L. A. and M. N. Shmeleva
1964a *Kultura i byt kolkhoznikov Kalininskoj oblasti* [Culture and Everyday Life of the Collective Farmers of the Kalynin Region] (Moscow).
1964b "Nekotoryje problemy etnograficheskogo izuchenija sovremennogo russkogo goroda" [Some Problems of Ethnographical Study of the Modern Russian Town], *SE* no. 5.
1968   "Ispoizovanije anketno-statistichoskikh dannykh pri etnograficheskom izuchenii goroda" [On the Use of Questionnaires and Statistical Data in Ethnographic Studies of the Town], *SE* no. 3.

Antipina, K. I.
1962   *Osobennosti materialnoj kultury i prikladnogo iskusstva juzhnykh kirgizov* [Peculiarities of the Material Culture and Applied Arts of the Southern Kirghiz] (Frunze).

Anuchin, D. N.
1889   "O geografichescom raspredelenii rosta muzhskogo naselenija Rossii (po dannym o vseobsjej voinskoj povinnosti v imperii za 1874–1883 gody)" [On the Spatial Distribution of Male Population in Russia According to Height (Based on Data Obtained from Reports on the Implementation of the Law of Universal Military Service, 1874–1883)], *Zapiski Russkogo geograficheskogo obshestva po otdeleniju statistiki* 7:1 (St. Petersburg).
1900   "Beglyj vzgljad na proshloje antropologii i na jee zadachi" [A Passing Glance at the Past of Anthropology and its Tasks], *RAZ* no. 1.

Arkhangel'skij, A. M.
1961   *Plemja, narodnost, natsija kak istoricheskij formy obsjnosti ludej* [Tribe, Nationality, and Nation as Historical Forms of the Community of People] (Moscow).

Artanovskij, S. N.
1967   *Istoricheskoje jedinstvo chelovechestva i vzaimnoje vlijanije kultur* [The Historical Unity of Mankind and Mutual Cultural Influence] (Leningrad).

Arutjunjan, Yn. V.
1966a "Sotsialnaja struktura selskogo naselenija" [Social Structure of the Rural Population], *VF* no. 5.
1966b "Podvizhnost' sotsialnoj struktury sela" [Mobility of Village Social Structure], *Vestnik MGU, serija filosofii* no. 3.
1968   "Opyt sotsialno-etnicheskogo issledovanija (Po materialam Tatarskoj ASSR)" [Some Experience of Socio-ethnic Research (On the Data of the Tatar ASSR)], *SE* no. 4.

Arutjunov, S. A.
1961   "Etnicheskaja istorija Japonii na rubezhe nashej ery" [The Ethnic History of Japan on the Eve of A.D.], *TIE* 23.
1964   "Problemy istoriko-kulturnykh svjazej Tikho-okeanskogo bassejna" [The Problems of the Historico-Cultural Connections of the Pacific], *SE* no.4.
1965   "Novyje cherty v japanskom zhenskom natsionalnom kostjume" [New Features in the Japan Female National Dress], *SE* no. 4.
1968   *Sovremennyj byt japontsev* [The Everyday Life of Modern Japanese] (Moscow).

Arutjunov, S. A. and D. A. Sergejev
1969 *Drevnije kultury aziatskikh eskimosov (Uelenskij mogilnik)* [The Ancient Cultures of the Asiatic Eskimo (Uelensky Burial Ground)] (Moscow).

Astanin, L. P.
1962 "Proportsii kisti primatov" [Proportions of the Hands of Primates], *VA* no. 10.

Atlas narodov mira [*Atlas of the Peoples of the World*]
1962 ed. by S. J. Bruk and V. S. Apenchenko (Moscow).

Aul, Yu. M.
1958 "O vzaimootnoshenijakh estontsev i latyshei po antropologicheskim dannym" [Anthropological Evidence of Relations between Estonians and Letts], *KSIE* 29.
See also non-Russian bibliography.

Averkijeva, Ju. P.
1941 *Rabstvo u indejtsev Severnoj Ameriki* [Slavery among the North American Indians] (Moscow-Leningrad).
1961 "Razlozhenije rodovoj obsjiny i formirovanije ranneklassovykh otnoshenij v obsjestve indejtsev severozapadnogo poberezhja Severnoj Ameriki" (Disintegration of Clan Community and Formation of Early Class Relations in Indian Society of the North-West Coast of North America], *TIE* 20.
1967 "Jestestvennoje i obsjestvennoje razdelenije truda i problema periodisatsii pervobytnogo obsjestva" [Natural and Social Labor Differentiation and the Problem of the Primitive Society Periodization], *Ot Aljaski do Ognennoj Zemli. Istorija i etnografija stran Ameriki* (Moscow).

Averkijeva, Ju. P., S. A. Arutjunov and Yu. V. Bromley
1969 "VIII Mezhdunarodnyj kongress antropologicheskikh i etnograficheskikh nauk" [The 8th International Congress of Anthropological and Ethnological Sciences], *SE* no. 1.

Aziatskaja chast' SSSR [Asian Part of the USSR] 1960 (Moscow).

Baller, E. A.
1969 *Prejemstvennost' v razvitii Kultury* [Continuity in Development of Culture] (Moscow).

Baltijskij etnograficheskij sbornik [The Baltic Ethnographic Collection of Articles]
1956 *TIE* 32.

Bardavelidze, V. V.
1957 *Drevnejshije religioznyje verovanija i obrjadovoje graficheskoje iskusstvo gruzinskikh plemen* [The Ancient Religious Beliefs and the Ritual Drawings of the Georgian Tribes] (Tbilisi).

Bashkirov, P. N.
1937 "Proportsii tela v razlichnykh konstitutsionalnykh tipakh" [Bodily Proportions of Various Constitutional Types], *UZMGU* 10 (anthropology).

Belitser, V. N.
1951 "Narodnaja odezhda udmurtov. Materialy k etnogenezu" [Folk Dress of the Udmurts. Data on Ethnogenesis], *TIE* 10.

Bernshtam, A. N.
1934 "Problema raspada rodovykh otnoshenij u kochevnikov Asii" [The Problem of Clan System Decline among the Asiatic Nomads], *SE* no. 6.

Berzin, J. O., M. A. Vitkin and I. L. Andrejev
1966 "Vystuplenija na diskussii o sotsialnykh strukturakh Vostoka" [Speeches at the Discussion on Social Formation in the East], *Obsjeje i osobennoje v istoricheskom rezvitii stran Vostoka* (Moscow).

Berzina, M. Ja.
1962 "Narody Ameriki" [The Peoples of America], *Chislennost' i rasselenije narodov mira* (Moscow).

1968   "Etnicheskij sostav naselenija Kanady" [The Ethnic Composition of Canadian Population], *SE* no. 1.

Berzina, M. Ja. and S. I. Bruk
1962   *Karta narodov Indonezii, Malji i Filippin* [The Map of the Peoples of Indonesia, Malaya, and the Philippines] (Moscow).

Besedin, G.
1927   "K voprosu o gruppovom (po krovi) raspredelenii russkikh" [On the (Blood) Group Distribution of Russians], *RAZ* nos. 1–2.

Bibliografija trudov Instituta etnografii im. N. N. Miklukho-Maklaja 1900–1962 [The Bibliography of the Institute of Ethnography named after N. N. Miklukho-Maklay 1900–1962] 1967 (Leningrad).

Blavatskaja, T. V.
1966   *Akhejskaja Gretsija* [Achean Greece] (Moscow).

Bogajevskij, B. L.
1936   *Tekhnika pervobytno-kommunisticheskogo obsjestva* [Implements in Primitive Communist Society] (Moscow-Leningrad).

Bogatyrev, P. G.
1964   "Problemy izuchenija materialnoj i dukhovnoj kultury naselenija Karpat" [The Problems of Research of the Material and Spiritual Culture of the Carpathian Population], *SE* no. 4.

Bogina, Sh. A.
1968   "Nekotoryje voprosy razvitija americanskoj natsii" [Some Problems of Development of the American Nation], *SE* no. 4.

Bogoraz-Tan, V. G.
1932   "Severnoje olenevodstvo po dannym khozjajstvennoj perepisi 1926–1927 gg." [The Northern Reindeer–Breeding in the Data of the Economic Census], *SE* no. 4.
1939   *Chukchi. II. Religija* [The Chukchee. II. Religion] (Leningrad).

Bolshov, L. N. and N. V. Smirnov
1965   *Tablitsy matematiceskoj statistiki* [Tables for Mathematical Statistics] (Moscow).

Boriskovskij, P. I.
1957   *Drevnejsheje proshloje chelovechestva* [The Earliest Past of Mankind] (Moscow-Leningrad).
1970   "Problemy stanovlenija chelovecheskogo obsjestva i arkheologicheskije otkrytija poslednikh desjati let" [Problems in the Making of Human Society and the Archeological Discoveries of the Last Ten Years], *Leninskije idei v isuchenii istorii pervobytnogo obsjestva, rabovladenija i feodalisma* [Moscow).

Brazilia. Ekonomika, politika, kultura [Brazil. Economy, Policy, Culture] 1963 (Moscow).

Bromley, Yu. V.
1968a   "Osnovnyje napravlenija etnograficheskikh issledovanij v SSSR" [Principal Directions of Ethnographical Researches in the USSR], *VI* no. 1.
1968b   "Nauka o narodakh mira" [Science on the Peoples of the World], *NZ* no. 8.
1969a   "Kongress antropologov i istorikov v Japonii" [The Congress of Anthropologists and Ethnologists in Japan], *VAN* no. 1.
1969b   "Etnos i endogamija" [Ethnos and Endogamy], *SE* no. 6.
    See also non-Russian bibliography.

Bromley, Yu. V. and M. S. Kashuba
1969   "Nekotoryje aspekty sovremennykh etnicheskikh protsessov v Jugoslavii" [Some Aspects of Modern Ethnic Processes in Yugoslavia], *SE* no. 1.

Bromley, Yu. V. and O. I. Shkaratan
1969   "O sootnoshenii istorii, etnografii, sotsiologii" [On the Correlation of History, Ethnography, and Sociology], *SE* no. 3.

Bronnikova, M. A.
1964   *Ontogenez aggljutinogenov krovi* [The Ontogenesis of Blood Agglutinogens]
       (Moscow).
Bruk, S. I.
1959a *Karta narodov Kitaja, MNR, Korei* [The Map of the Peoples of China, MPR,
       and Korea] (Moscow).
1959b *Karta narodov Indokitaja* [The Map of Peoples of Indochina] (Moscow).
1960   *Narody Perednej Azii (karta)* [The Peoples of the Near East (Map)] (Moscow).
1964   *Osnovnyje problemy etnicheskoj geografii (metodika opredelenija etnicheskogo
       sostava naselenija, printsipy etnicheskogo kartografirovanija)* [Basic Problems
       of Ethnic Geography (Methodology for Determining the Ethnic Composition
       of the Population, Principles of Ethnic Cartography)] (Moscow).
Bruk, S. I. and N. N. Cheboksarov
1961   "Sovremennyj etap natsionalnogo razvitija narodov Azii i Afriki" [Con-
       temporary Stage in the National Development of the Peoples of Asia and
       Africa], *SE* no. 4.
Bruk, S. I., N. N. Cheboksarov, and Ya. V. Chesnov
1969   "Problemy etnicheskogo razvitija stran zarubezhnoj Asii" [Problems of
       Ethnic Development in Countries of Alien Asia], *VI* no. 1.
Bunak, V. V.
1922   "Antropologicheskij tip donskikh kazakov" [The Anthropological Type of
       Cossacks of the Don], *RAZ* 12: nos. 1-2.
1924a "Antropologicheskij tip cheremis" [The Anthropological Type of the
       Cheremis], *RAZ* 13: nos. 3-4.
1924b "Neskolko dannykh k voprosu o tipichnykh konstitutsijakh cheloveka"
       [Some Data on Typical Human Constitution Types], *RAZ* vyp. 1: v. 13.
1929   "Cherepa zheleznogo veka iz Sevanskogo rajona Armenii" [Iron Age Skulls
       from the Sevan District, Armenia], *RAZ* 17: nos. 3-4.
1932a "Geograficheskoje raspredelenije rosta prizyvnogo naselenija SSSR po
       dannym 1927 goda" [The Geographical Distribution of Stature Among
       Inductees in the USSR as of 1927], *AZ* 2.
1934   "Rasy" [The Races], *Bolshaja meditsinskaja entsiklopedija* 28 (Moscow).
1940   "Normalnyje kostitutsionnyje tipy v svete dannykh o korreljatsii otdelnykh
       priznakov" [Normal Constitutional Types in the Light of Data on the Correla-
       tion of Individual Characteristics], *MGU* (Anthropology) 34.
1948   "Antropologicheskije issledovanija v Zakarpatskoj oblasti USSR" [Anthropo-
       logical Studies in the Trans-Carpathian Region of the Ukrainian SSR], *KSIE* 4.
1953   "Cherepa iz sklepov gornogo Kavkaza v sravnitelno-antropologicheskom
       osvesjenii" [Skulls from Crypts in the Mountains of the Caucasus in a
       Comparatively Anthropological View], *SMAE* 14.
1954   "Sovremennoje sostojanije problemy evoljutsii stopy u predkov cheloveka"
       [Present State of the Problem of the Evolution of the Foot in Man's Ancestors],
       *Bonch-Osmolovskij G. A., Skelet stopy i goleni iskopajemogo cheloveka iz
       grota Kiik-Koba, Paleolit Kryma* vyp. 3 (Moscow-Leningrad).
1956a "Antropologicheskije issledovanija v juzhnoj Belorussii" [Anthropological
       Studies in Southern Belorussia], *TIE* 93.
1956b "Chelovecheskije rasy i puti ikh obrazovanija" [Human Races and Ways of
       Their Formation], *SE* no. 1.
1958   "Zakonomernost' otnositelnogo rosta kak osnovnogo faktora formoobrazov-
       anija v pozdnem (postembrionalnom) ontogeneze" [Patterns of Relative
       Growth as the Main Factor in Form Derivation in Late (Postembryonal)
       Ontogenesis], *Tezisy dokladov VI Vsesojuznogo Sjezda anatomov, gistologov i
       embriologov* (Moscow).
1959   "Cherep cheloveka i stadii jego formirovanija u iskopaemykh ljudej i sovre-

mennykh ras" [The Human Skull and its Stages of Development in Fossil Men and Contemporary Races], *TIE* n.s. 49.

1963   "Russkoje naselenije v Zabajkalje" [The Russian Population of the Trans-Baikal Region], *TIE* n.s. 82 (Moscow).

1965a   "Izuchenije malykh populjatsij v antropologii [Study of Small Populations in Anthropology], *VA* vyp. 21.

See also non-Russian bibliography.

Bunak, V. V., M. F. Nesturkh, and Ya. Ya. Roginskij
1941   *Antropologija* [Anthropology], Bunak (ed.) (Moscow).

Bunak, V. V., V. I. Kozlov, and M. G. Levin
1963   "O predmete i zadachakh etnografii" [On the Subject and Objects of Ethnography], *SE* no. 1.

Bunak, V. V. and S. A. Tokarev
1951   "Problemy zaselenija Avstralii i Okeanii" [Problems of the Settlement of Australia and Oceania], *TIE* n.s. 16.

Bunak, V. V.
i.p.   *Izmenenija tipa russkogo naselenija Sibiri pod vlijanijem smeshenijai obosoblenija* [Changes in the Type of the Russian Population of Siberia through Mixing and Isolation].

MS.   *Svodnyje tablitsy raspredelenija krovjanykh grupp ABO naselenija SSSR* [Summaries of the Distribution of *ABO* Blood Groups in the Population of the USSR].

Busygin, J. P.
1966   *Russkoje Selskoje naselenije Srednego Povolzhja* [The Russian Rural Population of the Middle Volga Basin] (Kazan).

Butinov, N. A.
1951   "Problemy ekzogamii (po avstralijskim materialam)" [The Problems of Exogamy (on Australian Data)], *TIE* 14.

1960   "Razdelenije truda v pervobytnom obsjestve" [Labor Differentiation in Primitive Society], *TIE* 54.

1962   "Proiskhozhdenije i etnicheskij sostav korennogo naselenija Novoj Gvinei" [The Origin and Ethnic Composition of the Native Population of New Guinea], *TIE* 80.

1968   *Papuasy Novoj Guinei* [The Papuans of New Guinea] (Moscow).

Butinov, N. A. and Ju. V. Knorozov
1956   "Predvaritelnoje soobsjenije ob izuchenii pismennosti ostrova Paskhi" [Preliminary Report on Research into the Easter Island Script], *SE* no. 4.

1964   *Predvaritelnoje soobsjenije o deshifrovke kitanskogo pisma* [Preliminary Report on Deciphering the Kitan Script] (Moscow).

1965   *Predvaritelnoje soobsjenije ob issledovanii protoindijskikh tekstov* [Preliminary Report on Research into the Proto-Indian Texts] (Moscow).

"Byt kolkhoznikov kirgizskikh selenij Darkhan i Chichkan" [The Everyday Life of the Collective Farmers of Kirghiz Villages of Durkhan and Chichkan] 1958 *TIE* 34.

Cheboksarov, N. N.
1936a   "Negroidy i evropeoidy v Vostochnoj Afrike" [The Negroids and the Europoids of East Africa], *AZ* 1.

1936b   "Gruppy krovi i daltonism u komi" [Blood Types and Daltonism Among the Komi], *AZ* 2.

1936c   "Iz istorii svetlykh rasovykh tipov Evrasii" (From the History of Light-Skinned Racial Types of Eurasia), *AZ* 2.

1947a   "K voprosu o proiskhozhdenii kitajtsev" [On the Question of the Origin of the Chinese], *SE* no. 1.

1947b   "Osnovnyje napravlenija rasovoj differentsiatsii v Vostochnoi Asii" [The Main Lines of Racial Differentiation in Eastern Asia], *TIE* n.s. 11.

1951 "Osnovnyje printsipy antropologicheskikh klassifikatsij" [Fundamental Principles of Anthropological Classifications], *TIE* n.s. 16.

1964 *Problemy proiskhozhdenija drevnikh i sovremennykh narodov* (vstupitelnoje slovo na simpoziume VII MKAEN) [Problems of the Origin of the Ancient and Modern Peoples. (Opening Address at the Symposium of VII KAES)] (Moscow).

1966 "Etnicheskije protsessy v stranakh Juzhnoj i Jugo-Vostichnoj Azii" [Ethnic Processes in the Countries of South and South-East Asia], *SE* no. 2.

1967 "Problemy tipologii etnicheskikh obsjnostej v trudakh sovetskikh uchenykh" [Problems of Typology of Ethnic Units in the Works of Soviet Scientists], *SE* no. 4.

Chepurkovskij, E. M.
1913 "Geograficheskoje raspredelenije formy golovy i tsvetnosti krestijaskogo naselenija" [Geographical Distribution of Head Shapes and Hair Color in the Peasant Population]. *Trudy Antropologicheskogo otdela* 28, 2nd issue (Izvestija Obsjestva Ljubitelej jestestvoznanija, antropologii i etnografii) (Moscow).
See also non-Russian bibliography.

Chernetsov, V. N.
1964 "Izcheznuvsheje iskusstvo (uzory, vydavlennyje zubami na bereste u mansi)" [The Vanished Art: Mansi Designs, Pressed by Teeth on Birch Bark], *SE* no. 3.

Chili. Politika, economika kultura [Chile. Policy, Economy, Culture] 1965 (Moscow).

Chislennost' i rasselenije narodov mira [Numerical Strength and Distribution of the Peoples of the World] 1962 (Moscow).

Chistov, K. V.
1968 "Folklor i etnografija" [Folklore and Ethnography], *SE* no. 5.

Chitaja, G. S.
1948 "Etnograficheskije issledovanija v Gruzinskoj SSR" [Ethnographical Researches in Georgian SSR], *SE* no. 4.

1952 "Zemledelcheskije sistemy i pakhotnyje oreudija Gruzii" [Agricultural Systems and Arable Implements of Georgia], *Voprosy etnografii Kavkaza* (Tbilisi).

Chlenov, M. A.
1969 *Ocherki po etnicheskoj istorii narodov Tsentralnykh Molukk (Indonezija)*, Author's abstract of a dissertation (Moscow).

Chyrakzade, V. A.
1965 "O proizvodstvennom byte rabochikh shelkovoj promyshlennosti g. Nukhi" [On the Working Lifeways of the Workers of the Silk Industry in Nukha], *Azerbajdzhaskij etnograficheskij sbornik* 2 (Baku).

Davydova, G. M.
1963 "Antropologicheskije issledovanija sredi semejskikh russkikh Zabajkalja" [Anthropological Investigations of the Semei Russians of the Trans-Baikal Region], *TIE* n.s. 82.

i.p. *Antropologicheskije tipy russkikh starozhilov Sibiri* [Anthropological Types of Old Russian Settlers in Siberia].

Debets, G. F.
1933 "Tak nazyvajemyj 'vostochnyj velikoruss' (k voprosu o pranarodakh protorasakh)" [The So-called "Eastern Great Russian" (On the Problem of Proto-peoples and Proto-races)], *AZ* 1-2.

1934 "Book Review", *Antropologicheskij zhurnal*, 1-2.

1938 "Rasy jazyki Kultura", *Nauka o rasakh i rasizm* (Moscow-Leningrad).

1941 "K probleme rasovogo tipa 'protofinnov'" [On the Problem of the "Proto-Finnish" Race Type], *UZMGU* 63.

1947   "Selkupy" [Selkups], *TIE* n.s. 11.
1951a   "Zaselenije Juzhnoj i Perednej Asii po dannym antropologii" [Peopling of Southern Asia and Near East According to Anthropological Data], *TIE* n.s. 16.
1951b   "Antropologicheskije issledovanija v Kamchatskoj oblasti" [Anthropological Research in the Kamchatka Region], *TIE* n.s. 17.
1956a   "O printsipakh klassifikatsii chelovecheskikh ras" [On the Principles of Classification of Human Races], *SE* no. 4.
1956b   "Antropologicheskije issledovanija v Dagestane" [Anthropological Studies in Daghestan], *TIE* n.s. 33.
1957   "Sorok let sovetskoj antropologii" [Forty Years of Soviet Anthropology], *SA* 1.
1958a   "O printsipakh klassifikatsii chelovecheskikh ras" [On Principles of Classification of the Human Races], *SE* no. 1.
1958b   "Opyt graficheskogo izobrazhenija genealogicheskikh klassifikatsij chelovecheskikh ras" [Essay on the Graphical Presentation of the Genealogical Classification of Human Races], *SE* no. 4.
1960   "Antropologicheskije tipy" [Anthropological Types], *Narody Kavkaza* 1 (Moscow).
1961   "O putjakh zaselenija severnoj polosy Russkoj ravniny i Vostochnoj Pribaltiki" [On the Ways by Which the Russian Plain and Eastern Baltic Region Were Settled] *SE* no. 6.
Debets, G. F., M. G. Levin, and T. A. Trofimova
1952   "Antropologicheskij material kak istochnik izuchenija voprosov etnogeneza" [Anthropological Data as a Source in the Research of Ethnogenesis], *SE* no. 1.
Denisova, R. Ja.
1956   "Antropologicheskij tip livov" [The Livonian Anthropological Type], *TIE* n.s. 32.
1963   "Antropologiceskij tip vostochnykh litovtsev" [The Anthropological Type of Eastern Lithuanians], *Izvestija Academii Nauk Latvijskoj SSR* 9.
Djachenko, V. D.
1953   "Antropologicheskoje issledovanija gagauzov Moldavskoj SSR" [An Anthropological Study of the Gagauz in the Moldavian SSR], *KSIE* 15.
1965   *Antropologichnij sklad ukrainskogo naroda* [The Anthropological Type of the Ukrainian People] (Kiev).
Djakonov, I. M.
1959   *Obsjestvennyj i gosudarstvennyj stroj Drevnej Mesopotamii* [The Social and State System of Ancient Mesopotamia] (Moscow).
Dolgikh, B. O.
1960   "Rodovoj i plemennoj sostav narodov Sibiri XVII v" [Clan and Tribal Structure of the Siberian Peoples in the 17th Century], *TIE* n.s. 55.
1963   "Proiskhozhdenije dolgan" [The Origin of the Dolgans], *TIE* 34.
Drobizheva, L. M.
1967   "O sotsialnoj odnorodnosti respublik i razvitii natsionalnykh otnoshenij v SSSR" [On the Social Uniformity of Republics and the Development of National Relations in the USSR], *Istorija SSSR* no. 1.
Dung Ti-chen'
1962   "Morfologicheskij osobennosti skeletnykh ostatkov i zubov gigantopiteka v svjazi s jego polozhenijem v sisteme primatov" [Morphological Features of the Skeletal Remains and Teeth of Giganthopithecus in Connection with its Position in the System of Primates], *VA* 13.
Dzhekson, D. E.
1957   "K teoreticheskoj otsenke negritjanskogo voprosa v SShA" [On the Theoretical Estimation of Negro Question in the United States], *Problemy mira i sotsializma* no. 7.

Dzhunusov, M. S.
1966 "Natsia kak sotsialno-etnicheskaja obsjnost'" [Nation as a Social and Ethnic Community], *VI* no. 4.
Efendiev, M. M. and A. I. Pershits
1955 "O susjnosti patriarkhalno-feodalnykh otnoshenij u kochevnikov-skotovodov" [On the Essence of Patriarchal-Feudal Relations Among Nomadic Cattle Breeders], *VI* 1.
Efimov, A. V.
1966 "Sotsialnyi aspekt biologicheskoj kategorii rasy" [The Social Aspect of a Biological Category of Race], *Protiv rasizma* (Moscow).
Ekvador. Istoriko-etnograficheskije ocherki [Ecuador. Essays in History and Ethnography] 1963 (Moscow).
"Etnicheskije protsessy i sostav naselenija v strankakh Perednej Azii" [Ethnic Processes and Composition of the Population in the Near East Countries] 1963 *TIE* 83.
Etnograficheskoje izuchenije byta rabochikh [Ethnographical Study of the Workers' Life] 1968 (Moscow).
Etnografija russkogo naselenija Sibiri i Srednej Azii [Ethnography of the Russian Population of Siberia and Middle Asia] 1969 (Moscow).
Fainberg, L. A.
1964 *Obsjestvennyj stroj eskimosov i aleutov. Ot materinskogo roda k sosedskoj obsjine* [Eskimo and Aleut Social Systems, From the Matriclan to the Neighbor Community] (Moscow).
Frantsev, G.
1964 "Kultura" [Culture], *Filosofskaja entsiklopedija 3* (Moscow).
Gadzhiev, A. G.
1964 "Dannye po gruppam krovi narodov Dagestana" [Information on Blood Types Among the Peoples of Daghestan], *VA* 17.
1965 *Proiskhozhdenije narodov Dagestana (po dannym antropologii)* [The Origin of the Peoples of Daghestan according to Anthropological Data] (Makhachkala).
1968 *Antropologija malykh populjatsij Dagestana* [Anthropology of Small Populations in Daghestan], Dissertation (author's abstract) (Moscow).
Gadzhieva, S.
1960 *Materialnaja kultura kumykov XIX–XX vv* [The Material Culture of the Kumyks in the 19th and 20th Centuries] (Makhachkala).
Gantskaja, O. A. and L. N. Terentjeva
1965 "Etnograficheskije issledovanija natsionalnykh protsessov v Pribaltike" [Ethnographic Researches in the National Processes in the Baltic Countries], *SE* no. 5.
Gardanov, V. K.
1967 *Obsjestvennyj stroj adygskikh narodov (XVIII-pervaja polovina XIX v.)* [Social System of the Adyghe Peoples (18th to the first half of the 19th cent.)] (Moscow).
Gardanov, V. K., B. O. Dolgikh, and T. A. Zhdanko
1961 "Osnovnye napravlenija etnicheskikh protsessov u narodov SSSR" [The Principal Directions of Ethnic Processes Among the Peoples of the USSR], *SE* no. 4.
Gerasimov, M.
1937 "Paleoliticheskaja stojanka Malta" [Maltan Palaeolithic Camp Site], *Paleolit SSSR* (Moscow).
Ginzburg, V. V.
1934 "Izogemaggljutinatsija u gornykh tadzhikov" [Isogemagalutination Among Tadzik Highlanders], *AZ* 1–2.
1936 "Antropologicheskij sostav naselenija Zapadnogo Pamira — po materialam N. V. Bogojavlenskogo" [The Anthropological Composition of the Popula-

tion of Western Pamirs — Based on N. V. Bogoyavlensky's Results], *AZ* 1·

1937a *Gornyje tadjiki.* *Materialy po antropologii tadzhikov Karategina i Darvasa* [Tadziks of the Mountains, Materials on the Anthropology of Tadziks in the Kara-Teghin and Darvaz Areas] (Moscow-Leningrad).

1937b "Izuchenije krovjanogo davlenija u gornykh tadzhikov" [A Study of Blood Pressure Among Tadziks of the Highlands], *AZ* 2.

1937c "Izogemoagglutinatsija u turkmen" [Isogemoagglutination among Turkmenians], *AZ* 2.

1949 "Tadzhiki predgorij" [Piedmont Tadziks], *SMAE* 12.

1950a "Pervyje antropologicheskije materialy k probleme etnogeneza Baktrii" [The First Anthropological Material on the Problem of the Ethnogenesis of Bactria], *Trudy Sogdijsko-Tadzhiksoj Arkheologicheskoj Ekspeditsii* 1, *Materialy i issledovanija po arkheologii SSSR* 15.

1950b "Materialy k paleoantropologii vostochnykh rajonov Srednej Azii" [Material for a Palaeoanthropology of the Eastern Regions of Central Asia], *KSIE* 11.

1951 "The Marxical Anthropology of Ireland", *Paper of the Peabody Museum* XXX:1–2.

1957 "Drevnije i sovremennyje antropologicheskije tipy Srednej Azii" [Ancient and Modern Anthropological Types of Central Asia], *TIE* n.s. 16.

1964 *Rasa sredneaziatskogo mezhdurechija i jeje proiskhozhdenije* [The Race of the Central Asian Interfluve and its Origin] (Moscow).

1967 "Teorii proiskhozhdenija rasovogo tipa sredneaziatskogo mezhdurechja" [Theories Concerning the Origin of the Racial Type of the Central Asian Interfluve], *Tezisy dokladov nauchnoj sessij, posvjasjennoj itogam raboty Instituta etnografii AN SSSR (Leningradskoje otdelenije) za* 1966 *god* (Leningrad).

Ginzburg, V. V., G. F. Debets, M. G. Levin, and N. N. Cheboksarov

1952 *Ocherki po antropologii Kasakhstana* [Essays in the Anthropology of Kazakhstan] 14.

Gladkova, T. D.

1962 *Chelovecheskije rasy* [The Human Races] (Moscow).

1963 "Antropologicheskij otdel objsestva ljubitelej jestestvoznanija, antropologii i etnografii" [The Anthropology Department of the Society of Lovers of Nature Study, Anthropology and Ethnography], *TIE* n.s. 85.

1966 *Kozhnyje uzory kisti i stopy obezjan i cheloveka* [Skin Patterns of Ape and Human Palm and Footprints] (Moscow).

Godelier, M.

1965 "Ponjatije aziatskogo sposoba proizvodstva i marksistskaja skhema razvitija obsjestva" [The Concept of the Asian Mode of Production and the Marxist Scheme of Social Development], *NAA* no. 1.

Gokhman, I. I.

1963 "Materialy k antropologii jelogujskikh ketov" [Some Materials on the Anthropology of the Kets of Eloquy], *KSIE* 38.

Grekov, B. D.

1948 *Vinodolskij statut ob objsestvennom i politicheskom stroje Vinodola* [The Vinodol Statute on the Social and Political System of Vinodol] (Moscow-Leningrad).

1953 *Kijevskaja Rus'* [Kievan Rus'] (Moscow).

Gremjatskij, M. A.

1938 "Priznaki 'vysshikh' i 'nizshikh' ras i antropogenez" [Features of "Higher" and "Lower" Races and Anthropogenesis], *Nauka o rasakh i rasizm* (Moscow).

1941 "Antropologicheskij tip komi (permjakov)" [The Komi-Permyak Anthropological Type], *UZMGU* 63.

1948 "Problema promezhutochnykh form ot neandertalskogo tipa cheloveka k sovremennomu" [The Problem of Intermediate and Transitional Forms from the Neanderthal Type to the Modern Type of Man], *UZMGU* 115.

Grenier, A.
1912 *Bologne villanovienne et etrusque* (Paris).

Gromov, G. G.
1966 *Metodica etnograficheskikh ekspeditsij* [The Methods of the Ethnographic Expeditions] (Moscow).

Gulijev, G. A.
1961 "Etnografia Azerbajdzhana za 40 let" [The Ethnography of Azerbaijan for Forty Years], *SE* no. 4.

Gulyga, A. V.
1965 "Ponjatije i obraz v istoricheskoj nauke" [Conception and Image in Historical Science], *VI* no. 9.

Gumilev, L. N.
1967 "O termine 'etnos'" [On the Term "Ethnos"], *DGO* issue 3.

Günter, R.
1959 "Sotsialnaja differentsiatsija v drevnejshem Rime" [Social Differentiation in Earliest Rome], *VDI* no. 1.

Gurevich, A. I.
1967 *Svobodnoje krestjanstvo feodalnoj Norwegii* [The Free Peasantry of Feudal Norway] (Moscow).

Gurvich, I. S.
1963 "Etnicheskaja istorija severo-vostoka Sibiri" [The Ethnic History of the North-Eastern Siberia], *TIE* 89.
1965 "O rabote sektsij VII mezhdunarodnogo kongressa antropologicheskikh i etnograficheskikh nauk" [On the Work of the Section of the Seventh International Congress of Anthropological and Ethnological Sciences], *SE* no. 6.
1966 *Etnicheskaja istorija severo-vostoka Sibiri* [Ethnic History of the North-Eastern Siberia] (Moscow).
1967 "Nekotoryje problemy etnicheskogo razvitija narodov SSSR" [Some Problems of Ethnic Development of the USSR Peoples], *SE* no. 57.

Gusinde, M.
1948 *Urwaldmenschen am Ituri* (Vienna).

Guslistyj, K. G.
1958 "Stan I zavdannia rozvitku etnografichnoj nauki v Ukrainskij RSR" [The State and Development of Ethnographical Science in the Ukrainian SSR], *NTE* no. 4. (In Ukrainian).
1963 *Voprosy istorii Ukrainy i etnicheskogo razvitija ukrainskogo naroda* [Problems of Ukrainian History and the Ethnic Development of the Ukrainian People] (Kiev).

Guslistyj, K. G., V. F. Gorlenko, and Ja. P. Priljapko
1967 "Rabota nad istoriko-etnograficheskim atlasom na Ukraine" [Working on Historical-Ethnographical Atlas of Ukraine], *SE* no. 1.

Gviana: Gajana, Frantsuzskaja Gviana, Surinam [Guiana: Guyana, French Guiana, Surinam] 1969 (Moscow).

Ignatjev, M. V.
1940 "Issledovanija po geneticheskomu analizu populatsii. Soobsjenije 1–2" [Studies in the Genetic Analysis of Populations, Issue 1–2], *UZMGU, Antropologija* 34.
1957 "Biometricheskije problemy v antropologii" [Biometrical Problems in Anthropology], *SE* no. 1.

Ismagilova, R. N.
1963 *Narody Nigerii* [The Peoples of Nigeria] (Moscow).

"Issledovanija po materialnoj kulture mordovskogo naroda" [The Study of Material Culture of the Mordvinian People] 1963 *TIE* 36.

Itogi Vsesojuznoj perepisi naselenija 1959 *goda. SSSR (Svodnyj tom)* [Returns of the All-Union Census of Population, 1959. USSR (Summaries)] 1963 (Moscow).
Itogi Vsesojuznoj perepisi naselenija 1959 *goda. RSFSR.* [Returns of the All-Union Census of Population, 1959. RSFSR] 1963 (Moscow).

Its, R. F.
1964   *K probleme sootnoshenija klassov i gosudarstva (Po materialam janshanskikh itszu)* [On the Problem of the Relationship Between Classes and the State (on the Material of the Jan Shan I-tsu)] (Moscow).

Its, R. F. and A. G. Jakovlev
1967   "K voprosu o sotsialno-ekonomicheskom stroje janshanskoj gruppy naroda I" [On the Question of the Socioeconomic System of the Jan Shan Group of the I People], *Obsjina i sotsialnaja organizatsija u narodov Vostochnoj i Jugo-Vostochnoj Azii* (Leningrad).

Ivanov, M. S.
1967   "Sovremennyje protsessy v Irane" [Modern Processes in Iran], *SE* no. 5.

Ivanov, S. V.
1954   "Materialy po izobrazitelnomu iskusstvu narodov Sibiri XIX-nachala XX v" [Data on the Folk Arts of the Siberian Peoples, from the 19th to the Beginning of 20th Cent.), *TIE* 22.
1961   "Sovremennoje iskusstvo narodov Sibiri (skulptura)" [The Modern Folk Art of the Siberian Peoples (Sculpture)], *SE* no. 6.
1969   *Skulptura narodov Severa* [The Sculpture of the Peoples of the North] (Moscow-Leningrad).

Ivanovskij, A. A.
1904   "Ob antropologicheskom sostave naselenija Rossii" [On the Anthropological Composition of the Population of Russia], *Izvestija obsjestva ljubitelej jestestvoznanija, antropologii i etnografii* 205 (Moscow).
1911   "Naselenije zemnogo shara. Opyt antropologicheskoj klassifikatsii" [World Population. An Attempt at an Anthropological Classification], *Izvestija Obsjestva ljubitelej jestestvoznanija, antropologii i etnografii* 121 (Moscow).

Jakimov, V. P.
1947   "Razvitije skeleta perednich konechnostej cheloveka i nekotorykh mlekopita-jusjikh" [Development of the Skeleton of the Front Limbs of Man and Certain Mammals], *Zoologicheskij Zhurnal* 26: no. 4.
1951   "Rannije stadii antropogeneza" [The Early Stages of Anthropogenesis], *TIE* n.s. 16:1
1953   "Antropologicheskaja kharakteristika kostjakov iz pogrebenij na Bolshom Olenjem Ostrove (Barentsevo more)" [Anthropological Characteristics of Skeletons from Burials at Bolshoj Olenij Island (Barents Sea)], *SMAE* 15.
1956a "Atlantrop, novyj predstavitel drevnejshikh gominid" [Atlanthropus, a New Member of the Early Hominoidea], *SE* 3.
1956b "Nachalnyje etapy zaselenija Vostochnoj Pribaltiki" [Initial Phases in the Settlement of Eastern Baltic Region], *TIE* n.s. 32.
1960   "Otkrytije kostnykh ostatkov novogo predstavitelja avstralopitekovykh v Vostochnoj Afrike" [Discovery of Fossil Remains of a New Member of the Australopithecinae in East Africa], *VA* no. 4.
1962   "Replika Opponentam" [Reply to My Opponents], *VA* 9.

Jarkho, A. I.
1932a "Gandzhinskije Tjurki" [Turks of Ghandja], *AZ* no. 1.
1932b "Unifikatsija opredelenija mjagkikh chastej litsa" [Standardization in Determinations of Facial Soft Tissue], *AZ* 1.
1933a "Turkmeny Khorezma i Severnogo Kavkaza. Antropologicheskij ocherk o dlinnogolovom evropeoidnom komponente turetskikh narodnostej SSSR" [Turkmenians of Khorezm and North Caucasus. An Anthropological Essay

on the Long-headed Europoid Component of Turkish Peoples in the USSR], *AZ* 1–2.

1933b "Antropologicheskij sostav turetskikh narodnostej Srednej Azii" [The Anthropological Composition of the Turkish Nationalities of Central Asia], *AZ* 3.

1952 "Antropologicheskij tip kara-kalpakov" [The Kara-Kalpak Anthropological Type], *Trudy Khorezmskoj Archeologo-Etnograficheskoj expeditsii* 1 (Moscow).

Jefimov, A. V.
1964 "K voprosu o vozniknovenii i razvitii natsij v Latinskoj Amerike" [Concerning the Origin and Development of Nations in Latin America], *Natsii Latinskoj Ameriki* (Moscow).

1966 "Sotsialnyj aspect biologicheskoj kategorii 'rasa'" [The Social Aspect of the Biological Category of "Race"], *Protiv rasizma* (Moscow).

Jershov, N. N.
1968 "K istorii razvitija etnograficheskoj nauki v Tadzhikistane" [On the History of Development of Ethnographical Science in Tadzikistan], *SE* no. 4.

Jevropejskaja chast'SSSR [European Part of the USSR] 1968 (Moscow).

Kabo, V. R.
1968 "Pervobytnaja obsjina okhotnikov i sobiratelej (po avstralijskim materialam)" [The Primitive Community of Hunters and Gatherers (Australian Material)], *Problemy istorii dokapitalisticheskikh obsjestv* (Moscow).

1969 *Proiskhozhdenije i rannjaja istorija aborigenov Avstralii* [The Origin and Early History of the Australian Aborigines] (Moscow).

Kagarov, E. G.
1937 "Perezhitki pervobytnogo kommunizma v obsjestvennom stroje drevnikh grekov i germantsev" [Survivals of Primitive Communism in the Social Organization of the Ancient Greeks and Germans], *TIE* 15.

Kaltakhchian, S. T.
1966 "K voprosu o ponjatii 'natsija'" [On the Question of the Concept "Nation"], *VI* no. 6.

1969 *Leninizm o susjnosti natsii i puti obrazovanija internatsionaloj obsjnosti ljudej* [Leninism on the Essence of the Nation and Ways of Forming an International Community of People] (Moscow).

Kanajev, I. I.
1963 *Ocherki iz istorii sravnitelnoj anatomii do Darvina* [Essays from the History of Comparative Anatomy before Darwin] (Moscow-Leningrad).

Karakashly, K. T.
1964 *Materialnaja kultura azerbajdzhantsev Severo-Vostochnoj i Tsentralnoj zon Malogo Kavkaza* [The Material Culture of Azerbaijanians of North-Eastern and Central Areas of Small Caucasus] (Baku).

Karapetjan, E. G.
1958 *Armjanskaja semejnaja obsjina* [Armenian Family Community] (Erevan).

Kasimova, R. M.
1960 "Antropologischeskoje issledovanije sovremennogo naselenija Kurinskoj oblasti" [An Anthropological Study of the Modern Population of the Kura District], *VA* 5.

Kelle, V. and M. Kovalzon
1969 *Kurs istoricheskogo materializma* [Course in Historical Materialism] (Moscow).

Kharadze, R.
1960–1961 *Gruzinskaja semejnaja obsjina* [Georgian Familian Community], 1–2 (Tbilisi).

Khejerdal, T.
1955 *Puteshestvije na "Kon-Tiki"* [The "Kon-Tiki" Expedition] (Moscow).

Khit', G. L.
1961 "Raspredelenije grup krovi v naselenii Pamira" [Blood Type Distribution Among the Pamiri], *VA* 8.
Khlopin, I. N.
1968 "Segmentatsija v istorii pervobytnogo obsjestva" [Segmentation in the History of the Primitive Society], *VI* no. 8.
Khomich, L. V.
1966 *Nentsy* [The Nenets] (Leningrad).
1969 "O soderzhanii ponjatija 'etnicheskije protsessy'" [On the Meaning of the Term "Ethnic Processes"], *SE* no. 5.
Kilchevskaja, E. V. and A. S. Ivanov
1959 *Khudozhestbennyje promysly Dagestana* [Crafts of Daghestan] (Moscow).
Kisljakov, N. A.
1936 *Sledy pervobytnogo kommunizma u gornykh tadzhikov Vakhio-bolo* [The Traces of Primitive Communism Among the Mountain Tadziks of Vakhio-Bolo] (Moscow-Leningrad).
"K itogam raboty VII Mezhdunarodnogo Kongressa antropologicheskikh i etnograficheskikh nauk (MKAEN) (3–10 avgusta 1964 g. v Moskve)" [The Results of the VII International Congress of Anthropological and Ethnological Sciences (ICAES) (August 3–10, 1964, Moscow)] 1965 *SE* no. 3.
Knorozov, Yu. V.
1963 *Pismennost' indejtsev maja* [Maya Script] (Moscow-Leningrad).
Knyshenko, Yu. V.
1965 *Istorija pervobytnogo obsjestva i osnovy etnografii* [The History of Primitive Society and the Basis of Ethnography] (Rostov-on-Don).
Kobychev, V. P. and A. J. Kobakidze
1967 "Osnovy tipologii i kartografirovanija zhilisja narodov Kavkaza (materialy k Kavkazskomu istoriko-etnograficheskomu atlasu)" [The Principles of Typology and Mapping of the Caucasian Peoples' Dwellings (Data from the Caucasus Historical-Ethnographical Atlas], *SE* no. 2.
Kochetkova, V.I.
1960 "Metod rekonstruktsii osnovnykh dolej mozga iskopajemykh gominid po ikh endocranam" [Method of Reconstruction of Principal Lobes of the Brain from the Endocrania of Fossil Hominoidae], *VA* 3.
Kogan, D. M.
1967 "Svjazi gorodskogo i selskogo naselenija kak odna iz problem etnografie goroda" [The Urban-Rural Population Connections as One of the Problems of Urban Ethnography], *SE* no. 4.
Koleva, T. A.
1969 "O nekotorykh voprosakh razvitija obychajev (na bolgarskom materiale)" [On Certain Problems Bearing on the Development of Customs (on Bulgarian Material)], *SE* no. 1.
Komarovich, N. I. and Yu. G. Rychkov
1964 "O gruppakh krovi cheloveka i ikh filogeneze" [On Human Blood Groups and Their Phylogenesis], *VA* 18.
1966 "Sistema ABO (H) grupp krovi, immunitet k ospe" [The ABO (H) Blood Groups and Smallpox Immunity], *VA* 23.
Korsunskij, A. R.
1963 *Obrasovanije rannefeodalnogo gosudarstva v Zapadnoj Jevrope* [The Formation of the Early Feudal State in Western Europe] (Moscow).
Kosven, M. O.
1932 "Vnov' otkrytaja forma gruppovogo braka" [The Recently Discovered Form of Group Marriage], *SGAIMK* nos. 3, 4.
1940 "Matriarkhat. Etnograficheskije materialy" [The Matriarchate. Ethnographic Material], *UZMGU* 61; *Istorija* 11.

1946 "K probleme gruppovogo-braka" [On the Problem of Group Marriage], *KSIE* no. 1.

1948 *Matriarkhat. Istorija problemy* [The Matriarchate. The History of the Problem] (Moscow-Leningrad).

1952 "O periodizatsii pervobytnoj istorii" [On the Periodization of Primitive History], *SE* no. 3.

1957 *Ocherki istorii pervobytnoj kultury* [Essays in the History of Primitive Culture] (Moscow).

1960 "K voprosu o vojennoj demokratii" [On the Question of the Military Democracy], *TIE* n.s. 54.

1963 *Semejnaja obsjina i patronimija* [The Family Community and Patronymy] (Moscow).

Kozlov, V. I.

1967a "Nekotoryje problemy teorii natsii" [Some Problems of the Theory of the Nation], VI no. 1.

1967b "O ponjatii etnicheskoj obsjnosti" [On the Concept of Ethnic Community], *SE* no. 2.

1969 *Dinamika chislennosti naroda* [Dynamics of the Numerical Strength of Peoples] (Moscow).

Kozlova, K. I.

1967 *Istorija pervobytnogo obsjestva i osnovy etnografii* [The History of Primitive Society and the Basis of Ethnography] (Moscow).

1968 "Spetsifika etnicheskoj obsjnosti marijtsev v period prisojedinenija k Rossii" [Specific Features of the Mari at the Time of Unification with Russia], *SE* no. 6.

"Kratkije sobsjenia Instituta: Muzeya antropologii" 1940 *MGU* (Moscow).

Krichevskij, Je. Ju.

1936 "Sistemy rodstva- kak istochniki rekonstruktsii razvitija sotsialnoj organizatsii avstralijskikh plemen" [Kinship Systems as Records for Reconstruction of the Social Organization of the Australian Tribes], *TIE* 4.

Krjukov, M. V.

1967a *Formy sotsialnoj organizatsii u drevnikh kitajtsev* [The Forms of Social Organization of the Ancient Chinese] (Moscow).

1967b "O sootnoshenii rodovoj i patronimicheskoj (klanovoj) organizatsii" [On the Correlation Between Clan and Patronymic (Clan) Organization], *SE* no. 6.

Krjukova, T. A.

1956 *Materialnaja kultura marijtsev* [The Material Culture of the Mari], (Yoschkar-Ola).

Krupjanskaja, V. Yu.

1960 "K voprosu o problematike i metodike etnograficheskogo izuchenija sovetskogo rabochego klassa" [On the Problem and Methodology of Ethnographical Study of the Soviet Working Class], *VI* no. 11.

Krupjanskaja, V. Yu. and M. G. Rabinovich

1964 "Etnografija goroda i promyshlennogo poselka" [The Ethnography of Town and Industrial Settlement], *SE* no. 4.

Krupjanskaja, V. Yu., L. P. Potapov, and L. N. Terentjeva

1961 "Osnovnyje problemy etnograficheskogo izuchenija narodov SSSR" [The Main Problems of the Ethnographical Research of the USSR Peoples], *SE* no. 3.

Kryvelev, I. A.

1961 "Preodolenije religiozno-bytovykh perezhitkov u narodov SSSR" [The Overcoming of the Day-to-Day Religious Survivals of the Peoples of the USSR), *SE* no. 4.

Kuba. Istoriko-etnograficheskije ocherki [Cuba. Historical-ethnographical Essays] 1961 (Moscow).

Kubanskije stanitsy. Etnicheskije i kulturno-bytovyje protsessy na Kubani [Cuban Townships. Ethnic, Culture and Day-to-Day Life Processes in Cuba] 1967 (Moscow).

Kudrjavtsev, B. G.
1949   "Pismennosti ostrova Paskhi" [Script of Easter Island], *SMAE* 11.

"Kultura i byt tadzhikskogo kolkhoznogo krestianstva" [Culture and Mode of Life of the Tadzik Collective Farm Peasantry] 1954 *TIE* n.s. 24.

Kultura indejtsev. Vklad korennogo ndaselenija Ameriki b mirovuju kulturu [The Culture of the American Indians. Contribution of the Aboriginal Population of America to the World Culture] 1963 (Moscow).

Kultura i byt kolkhoznogo krestjanstca adygeiskoj avtonomnoj oblasti [Culture and Mode of Life of the Kolkhoz Peasantry of the Adighe Autonomous Region] 1964 (Moscow-Leningrad).

Kultura i byt narodov stran Tikhogo i Indijskogo okeanov [Culture and Mode of Life of the Peoples of the Pacific and Indian Ocean Countries] 1966 (Moscow-Leningrad).

Kultura i byt narodov Zarubezhboj Jevropy [Culture and Mode of Life of the Peoples of Alien Europe] 1967a (Moscow).

Kultura i byt kazakhskogo kolkhoznogo aula [Culture and Mode of Life of the Kazakh Kolhoz Aul] 1967b (Alma-Ata).

Kultura i byt narodov Severnogo Kavkaza [Culture and Mode of Life of the Peoples of the North Caucasus] 1968 (Moscow).

Kusher (Knyshev), P. I.
1950   "Metody kartografirovanija natsionalnogo sostava naselenija" [Methods of Mapping the National Composition of the Population], *SE* no. 4.

1951   *Etnicheskije territorii i etnicheskije granitsy* [Ethnic Territories and Ethnic Boundaries] (Moscow).

Kuvenjova, O. F.
1966   *Gromadskij pobut ukrainskogo seljanstva* [The Social Lifeways of the Ukrainian Peasantry] (Kiev). (In Ukrainian).

Larichev, V. Ye.
1964   "K voprosy o lokal'nykh kul'turakh nizhnego paleolita Vostochnoj i Tsentral'noj Azii" [About Local Cultures of Lower Paleolithic in Eastern and Central Asia], *Arkheologija i etnografia Dal'nego Vostoka* [Archaeology and Ethnography of Far East] (Novosibirsk).

1966   "K voprosu o lokalnykh kulturakh nizhnego paleolita v Vostochnoj i Tsentral'noj Azii" [About Local Cultures in the Lower Paleolithic Period in Eastern and Central Asia], *Arkheologija i etnografia Dal'nego Vostoka* [Archaeology and Ethnography of the Far East] (Novosibirsk).

Larkin, B. G.
1964   *Orochi* [The Orochis] (Moscow).

Lashuk, L. P.
1967a   "Istoricheskaja struktura sotsialnykh organizmov srednevekovykh kochevnikov" [The Historical Structure of Social Organisms of Medieval Nomads], *SE* no. 4.

1967b   "O formakh donatsionalnykh etnicheskikh svjazej" [On the Forms of Pre-National Ethnic Ties], *VI* no. 4.

1967c   "O kharaktere klassoobrazovanija obsjestv rannikh kochevnikov" [On the Nature of Class Formation in Early Nomad Society], *VI* no. 3.

1968   "Opyt tipologii etnicheskikh obsjnostej srednevekovykh tjurok i mongolov" [Experiment in Typology of Ethnic Communities Among the Medieval Turks and Mongols], *SE* no. 1a.

Lekomtsev, Yu. K.
1964 "Distributsija fonem i generatsija slogov (na materiale graficheskikh slogov klassicheskogo tibetskogo jazyka)" [The Distribution of Phonemes and Generation of Syllables Employing the Graphic Syllables of Classical Tibetan], *Voprosy struktury jazyka* (Moscow).
Lenin, V. I.
1960 *Sobranije sochinenij* 14.
See also non-Russian bibliography.
Levin, M. G.
1941 "Kraniologicheskij tip khantov i mansi" [The Craniological Type of the Khanti and Mansi], *Kratkije soobsjenija NII Antropologii MGU za 1938–1939 gody* (Moscow).
1947 "Sovetskaja antropologija za 30 let" [Soviet Anthropology During Thirty Years], *SE* no. 4.
1949 "Antropologicheskije issledovanija na Amure i Sakhaline" [Anthropological Research in the Amur and Sakhalin Areas], *KSIE* 5.
1954 "K voprosu o juzhno-sibirskom antropologicheskom tipe" [On the Question of the South Siberian Anthropological Type], *KSIE* 21.
1958a "Etnicheskaja antropologija i problemy etnogeneja narodov Dalnego Vostoka" [Ethnic Anthropology and Problems of the Ethnogenesis of the Peoples of the Far East], *TIE* n.s. 36.
1958b "Gruppy krovi u chukchej i eskimosov" [Blood Types Among the Chukchi and Eskimos], *SE* no. 9.
1959 "Novyje materialy po gruppam krovi u eskomosov i lamutov" [New Data on Blood Types Among the Eskimos and Lamuts], *SE* 3.
1962 "O nekotorykh voprosakh antropologii severnoj Sibiri" [On Some Problems of North Siberian Anthropology], *VA* 12:
Levin, M. G. and N. N. Cheboksarov
1951 "Drevneje rasselenije chelovechestva v Vostochnoj i Jugo-Vostochnoj Azii" [The Ancient Settling of Mankind in Eastern and South-Eastern Asia], *TIE* n.s.16.
1955 "Khozjajstvenno-kulturnyje tipy i istoriko-etnograficheskije oblasti" [Economic-Cultural Types and Historical-Ethnographic Regions], *SE* no. 4.
1957 "Obsjije svedenije" [General Notions], *Ocherki obsjej etnografii* [Essays in General Ethnography] (Moscow), p. 10.
1962 "Obsjije svedenija (jazyki, rasy, narody)" [General Information (Languages, Races, Peoples)], *Ocherki obsjej etnografii Avstralija i Okeanija, Amerika, Afrika* vyp. 1 (Moscow).
Levin, M. G. and L. P. Potapov (eds.)
1961 *Istoriko-etnograficheskij atlas Sibiri* [Historical-Ethnographical Atlas of Siberia] (Moscow-Leningrad).
Levman, R. S.
1948 K voprosu ob antropologicheskom tipe bessarabskikh moldavan [On the Anthropological Type of Moldavians Living in Bessarabia], *KSIE* 4.
1950 *Antropologicheskije tipy korennogo naselenija Moldavskoj SSR (k probleme etnogeneza moldavan)* [The Anthropological Type of the Indigenous Population of the Moldavian SSR. On the Ethnogenesis of the Moldavians], Candidate Diss. Thesis (Moscow).
Likhtenberg, Ju. M.
1960 "Avstralijskije i melanezijskije sistemy rodstva" [Australian and Melanesian Kinship Systems], *TIE* n.s. 54.
Lobacheva, N. P.
1967 "O formirovanii novoj svadebnoj obrjadnosti u narodov Uzbekistana" [On the Formation of the New Wedding Ceremony of the Peoples of Uzbekistan], *SE* no. 2.

Malinovskij, A. A.

1945   "Fiziologicheskije istochniki korreljatsii v strojenii chelovecheskogo organizma" [Physiological Sources of Correlation in the Structure of the Human
Organism], *Zhurnal obsjej biologii* 6: no. 4.

1948   "Elementarnyje korreljatsii i izmenchivost chelovecheskogo organizma"
[Elementary Correlations and the Variability of the Human Organism],
Trudy Instituta tsitologii, gistologii i embriologii 2: issue 1 (Moscow).

1960   "Tipy upravljajusjikh biologicheskikh sistem i ikh prisposobitelnoje znachenije" [Types of Biological Control Systems and Their Adaptive Sig-
nificance], *Problemy kibernetiki* no. 4 (Moscow).

Maretin, Ju. V.

1961   "Obsjina minangkabau i jeje razlozhenije (pervaja tret XX v.)" [Minangkabau
Community and its Break-up in the First Third of the 20th Cent.], *TIE* n.s. 73.

Maretina, S. A.

1967   "Obsjina u gornykh narodov Assama" [The Community Among the Moun-
taineers of Assam], *Obsjina i sotsialnaja organizatsija u narodov Vostochnoj i
Jugo-vostochnoj Azii* (Leningrad).

Mark, K. Ju.

1960   "Etnicheskaja antropologija mordvy" [The Ethnic Anthropology of the
Mordvinians], *TIE* n.s. 63.

Markarjan, E. S.

1963   *Khajastany koltntesakanneri yntanyky jev yntanykan kentsaghy* (Yerevan).
(In Armenian).

1969   *Ocherki teorii kultury* [Essays on the Theory of Culture] (Yerevan).

Masanov, E. A.

1966   *Ocherk istorii etnograficheskogo izuchenija kazakhskogo naroda v SSSR*
[An Essay on the History of Ethnographical Studies of the Kazakh People in
the USSR], (Alma-Ata).

Miklashevskaja, N. N.

1953   "Nekotoryje materialy po antropologii narodov Dagestana" [Some Materials
on the Anthropology of the Peoples of Daghestan], *KSIE* 19.

1959   "Novyje paleoantropologicheskije materialy s territorii Dagestana" [New
Paleoanthropological Materials from Daghestan], *Materialy po arkheologii
Daghestana* 1 (Makhach-Kala).

1960   "Antropologicheskij sostav naselenija Dagestana v alanokhazarskoje
vremja" [The Anthropological Composition of the Population of Daghestan
in the Period of Settlement of the Alans and Khazars], *VA* 5.

Minakov, E. I.

1961   *Plemja, narodnosti, natsija kak istoricheskije formy obsjnosti ljugej* [Tribe,
Nationality, and Nation as Historical Forms of the Community of People]
(Tiraspol).

Monogarova, L. F.

1967   "Sovremennyje etnicheskije protsessy na Zapadnom Pamire" [Modern
Ethnic Processes in the Western Pamir]. *SE* no, 4.

Nadzhimov, K.

1958   *Antropologichekij sostav naselenija Surkhan-Darjinskoj oblasti* [The Anthropological Composition of the Population of Surkhan-Darja District] (Tashkent).

Narodnoje Khozjajstvo Tatarskoj ASSR [Economy of the Tatar ASSR] 1966 (Kazan).

Narody Afriki [The Peoples of Africa] 1954 (Moscow).

Narody Avstralii i Okeanii [The Peoples of Australia and Oceania] 1956a (Moscow).

Narody Sibiri [The Peoples of Siberia] 1956b (Moscow-Leningrad).

Narody Perednej Azii [The Peoples of the Near East] 1957 (Moscow).

Narody Ameriki [The Peoples of America] 1959 vols 1–2 (Moscow).

Narody Kavkaza [The Peoples of Caucasus] 1960 vol. 1 (Moscow).

Narody Kavkaza [The Peoples of Caucasus] 1962 vol. 2 (Moscow).

Narody Juznoj Azii [The Peoples of South Asia] 1963a (Moscow).
Narody Srednej Azii i Kazakhstana [The Peoples of Central Asia and Kazakhstan] 1963b vols. 1–2 (Moscow).
Narody Jevropejskoj chasti SSSR [The Peoples of the European Part of the USSR] 1964 vols. 1–2 (Moscow).
Narody Zarubezhnoj Jevropy [The Peoples of Alien Europe] 1965a vols. 1–2 (Moscow).
Narody Vostochnoj Azii [The Peoples of East Asia] 1965b (Moscow-Leningrad).
Narody Jugo-Vostochnoj Azii [The Peoples of South-East Asia] 1966 (Moscow).
Naselenije zemnogo shara [Population of the World] 1965 (Moscow).
Natishvili, A. N., et al.
  1935 "Materialy ekspeditsii 1950 goda po antropologii sovremennogo naselenija Gruzinskoj SSR" [Materials of the Expedition of 1950 on the Anthropology of the Contemporary Population of the Georgian SSR], *Trudy Instituta eksperimentalnoj morfologii an Gruzinskoj SSR.* 4.
Natsii Latinskoj Ameriki [The Nations of Latin America] 1964 (Moscow).
Nemirovskij, A. J.
  1959 "K voprosu o vremeni i znachenii tsenturiatnoj reformy Servija Tullija" [On the Question of the Time and Importance of the Centuriate Reform of Servius Tullius], *VDI* no. 2.
  1962 *Istorija rannego Rima i Italii (Vozniknovenije klassov i gosudarstva)* [A History of Early Rome and Italy (Emergence of Classes and State)] (Voronezh).
Nesturkh, M. F.
  1954 "Iskopajemyje gigantskije antropoidy Azii i ortogenetichescaja gipoteza antropogeneza Vejdenrejkha" [Fossil Giant Anthropoidea of Asia and Weidenreich's Orthogenetic Hypothesis of Anthropogenesis], *UZMGU* 166.
  1960 *Primatologija i Antropogenez* [Primatology and Anthropogenesis] (Moscow).
  1965 *Chelovecheskije rasy* [The Human Races] (Moscow).
Neusykhin, A. I.
  1929 "Vojennuje sojuzy germanskikh plemen okolo nachala nashej ery" [Military Alliances of the German Tribes Close to the Beginning of Our Era], *Trudy Instituta istorii Rossijskoj assotsiatsii nauchno-issledovatelskikh institutov objestvennykh nauk* 3 (Moscow).
  1956 *Vozniknovenije zavisimogo krestjanstva kak klassa rannefeodalnogo obsjestva v Zapadnoj Jevrope 6–8 vv.* [The Emergence of the Dependent Peasantry as a Class of Early Feudal Society in Western Europe in the 6th–8th Centuries] (Moscow).
  1967 "Dofeodalnyj period kak perekhodnaja stadija razvitija ot rodoplemennogo stroja k rannefeodalnomu (na materiale istorii Zapadnoj Jevropy rannego srednevekovja)" [The Pre-Feudal Period as a Transition Stage in the Development from the Clan-Tribal Systems to the Early Feudal System (on Material from the History of Western Europe in the Early Middle Ages)], *VI* no. 1.
Nikolskij, V. K.
  1950 "Antinauchnost' burzhuaznogo mifa ob iskonnosti semji i chastnoj sobstvennosti" [The Unscientific Nature of the Bourgeois Myth of the Primordial Nature of the Family and Private Property], *Uchenyje zapiski Moskovskogo oblastnogo pedagogicheskogo instituta* 14.
Obsjina i sotsialnaja organizatsija u narodov Vostochnoj i Jugo-Vostochnoj Azii [Community and Social Organization of the Peoples of East and South-East Asia] 1967 (Leningrad).
Ocherki istorii russkoj etnografii folkloristiki i antropologii [Essays in the History of Russian Ethnography and Anthropology] 1956–1968 iss. 1, 2, 3, 4 (Moscow).
Ocherki obsjej etnografii. Obsjije svedenija. Avstralija, Okeanija, Amerika, Afrika [Essays in Ethnography. General Information. Australia, Oceania, America, Africa] 1960 (Moscow).

Ocherki teorii kulture [Essays on the Theory of Culture] 1969 (Yerevan).

Olderogge, D. A.

1946a "Koltsevaja svjaz' rodov, ili trekhrodovoj sojuz (gens triplex)" [Clan King or the Gens Triplex], *KSIE* no. 1.

1946b "Trekhrodovoj sojuz v Jugo-Vostochnoj Azii" [The Gens Triplex in South-East Asia], *SE* no. 4.

1947 "Iz istorii semji i braka. Sistema lobola i Razlichnyje formy kuzennogo braka v Juzhnoj Afrike" [From the History of the Family and Marriage. The Lobola System and Various Forms of Cousin Marriage in South Africa], *SE* no. 1.

1949 "Parallelnyje teksty tablits s ostrova Paskhi" [The Parallel Texts of the Tables From Easter Island], *SMAE* 11.

1951 "Malajskaja sistema rodstva" [The Malayan Kinship System], *TIE* 14.

1952 "Proiskhozhdenije narodov Tsentralnogo Sudana" [The Origin of the Central Sudanese Peoples], *SE* no. 2.

1958 "Nekotoryje voprosy izuchenija sistem rodstva" [Some Problems of Studying Kinship Systems], *SE* no. 1.

1959 "Sistema rodstva bakongo v XVII veke" [Bacongo Kinship System in XVII Century], *TIE* 52.

1960a "Osnovnyje cherty razvitija sistem rodstva" [Major Features in the Development of Kinship Systems], *SE* no. 6.

1960b "Zapadnyj Sudan v XV–XIX vv. Ocherki po istorii i ictorii kultury" [Western Sudan from 15th to 19th Cent. Essays in History and History of Culture], *TIE* n.s. 53.

Orlova, A. S.

1958 *Afrikanskije narody. Ocherki kultury, khozjajstva i byta* [The African Peoples. Essays in Culture, Economy, and Life] (Moscow).

Oshanin, L. V.

1926 "Tysjacheletnjaja davnost' dolikhotsefalii u turkmen i vozmozhnyje puti jeje proiskhoshdenija. Opyt obosnovanija skifo-sarmatskogo proiskhozhdenija turkmensgogo naroda" [Millenium-old Dolichocephaly Among the Turkmenians and its Probable Origin. An Attempt at Proving the Descent of the Turkoman People from Scythian and Sarmat Tribes], *Izvestija Sredazkomstarisa* 1 (Tashkent).

1927 "Materialy po antropologii Sredmej Azii. Kirgizy juzhnogo poberezhja Issyk-Kulja" [Materials in the Anthropology of Central Asia. The Kirghiz of the Southern Shore of Lake Issyk-Khul], *V. V. Bartoldu-druzja, ucheniki i pochitateli* (Tashkent).

1927–1928 "Materialy po Antropologii Srednej Azii. Uzbeki Khorezma, 1–2" [Materials in the Anthropology of Central Asia. Khorezm Uzbeks], *Bjulleten' sredneaziatskogo universiteta* nos. 16–17 (Tashkent).

1928 "Nekotoryje dopolnitelnyje dannyie k gipoteze skifo-sarmatskogo proiskhoshdenija turkmen" [Some Additional Information in Support of the Hypothesis of the Origin of the Turkomans From Scythians and Sarmats], *Izvestija Sre dazkomstarisa* 2 (Tashkent).

1937 *Iranskije plemena zapadnogo Pamira* [The Iranian Tribes of the Western Pamir] (Tashkent).

1957 "Antropologicheskij sostav i voprosy etnogeneza tadzhikov i uzbekskikh plemjon juzhnogo Tadzhikistana" [Anthropological Composition and Problems of Ethnogenesis of the Tadziks and Uzbek Tribes Living in Southern Tadzikistan], *Trudy Instituta Istorii, Arkheologii i Etnografii AN Tad. SSR* 62 (Dushanbe).

1957–1959 *Antropologischeskij sostav naselenija Srednei Azii i etnogenez jeje narodov* [The Anthropological Composition of the Population of Central Asia and the Ethnogenesis of Its Peoples] Parts 1–3 (Yrevan).

Oshanin, L. V. and V. K. Jasevich
1929 "K sravnitelnoj antropologii etnicheskikh grupp prishlykh iz Peredney Azii arabov i jevrejev i etnicheskikh grupp Uzbekistana — uzbekov i tadjikov" [On the Comparative Anthropology of Ethnic Groups Migrant From the Near East: Arabs and Jews and Indigenous Ethnic Groups of Uzbekistan. Usbeks and Tadziks], *Materialy po antropologii naselenija Uzbekistana* 1 (Tashkent).

Oshanin, L. V. and V. I. Zerenkova
1953 *Voprosy etnogeneza narodov Srednej Azii v svete dannych antropologii* [Problems of Soviet Central Asian Ethnogenesis in the Light of Anthropological Data] (Tashkent).

Osipov, G. V.
1964 *Sovremennaja burzhuaznaja sotsiologija* [Contemporary Bourgeois Sociology] (Moscow).

Paramonov, S. Ja.
1939 "Dolzhna li biosistematika byt' filogeneticheskoj?" [Must Biosystematics be Phylogenetic?], *Uspekhi sovremennoj biologii* 10: part 3.

Pavlenko, A. P.
1967 "Predvaritelnyje dannyje intonograficheskogo issledovanija zvukov indo-nezijskogo jazyka" [Preliminary Data for an Intonographic Investigation of the Sounds of Indonesian], *Jasyki Jugo-Vostochnoj Azii* (Moscow).

Pershits, A. I.
1953 "O vojennoj demokratii (k voprosu o periodizatsii istorii pervobytnogo obsjestva)" [On "Military Democracy". On the Question of Periodization of the History of Primitive Society], *SE* no. 2.

1956 *Problemy istorii pervobytnogo obsjestva v sovetskoj etnografii* [Problems in the History of Primitive Society in Soviet Ethnography] (Moscow).

1960 "Razvitije form sobstvennosti v pervobytnom obsjestve kak osnova perio-dizatsii jego istorii" [The Development of Forms of Property in Primitive Society as the Base of Periodization of Its History] *TIE* n.s. 4.

1961a "Khozjajstvo i obsjestvennyj stroj Severnoj Aravii v XIX — pervoj treti XX m." [Economy and Social Structure in North Arabia in the 19th to the First Third of the 20th Centuries], *TIE* n.s. 69.

1961b "Plemja, narodnosti, natsija v Saudovskoj Aravii" [Tribe, Nationality, Nation in Saudi Arabia], *SE* no. 5.

1964 "Aktualnyje problemy sovetskoj etnografii" [The Urgent Problems of the Soviet Ethnography], *SE* no. 4.

1967 *Rannije formy semji i braka v osvesjenii sovetskoj etnograficheskoj nauki* [Early Forms of Family and Marriage in the Light of Soviet Ethnography] 7: no. 2.

Pershits, A. I. and N. N. Cheboksarov
1967 "Polveka sovetskoj etnografii" [Half Century of Soviet Ethnography], *SE* no. 5.

Pimenov, V. V.
1965 *Vepsy* [The Vepses] (Moscow-Leningrad).
1967 "O nekotorykh zakonomernostjakh v razvitii narodnoj kultury" [On Certain Laws in the Development of Folk Culture], *SE* no. 2.

Pisarchik, A. K.
1954 "Etnograficheskaja rabota v Tadzhikistane" [Ethnographical Studies in Tadzikistan], *Izvestija AN Tadzhikskoj SSR. Otdelenije obsjestvennykh nauk vyp.* 6 (Dushanbe).

Popov, A. A.
1931 "Pojezdka k dolganam" [Trip to Dolgans], *SE* no. 3-4.
1936 *Tavgijtsy Materialy po etnografii avamskikh i vedejevskikh tavgijtsev* [The

Tavgi. Materials for Avam and Vedejevo Tavgis Ethnography] (Moscow-Leningrad).
1948   "Nganasany" [The Nganasans], *TIE* n.s. 3.
Population 1965 *Naselenie zemnago shara* [Population of the World] (Moscow).
Porshnev, B. F.
1966   *Sotsialnaja psikhologija i istorija* [Social Psychology and History] (Moscow).
1969   "Myslima li istorija odnoj strany?" [Is the History of a Single Country Conceivable?], *Istoricheskaja nauka i nekotoryje problemy sovremennosti* (Moscow).
Potapov, L. P.
1947   "K voprosu o patriarkhalno-feodalnykh otnoshenijakh u kochevnikov" [On Patriarchal-Feudal Relations Among the Nomads], *KSIE* no. 3.
1954   "O susjnosti patriarkhalno-feodalnykh otnoshenij u kochevykh narodov Srednej Azii i Kazakhstana" [On the Essence of the Patriarchal-Feudal Relations Among the Nomadic Peoples of Soviet Central Asia and Kazakhstan], *VI* no. 6.
1957   *Proiskhozhdenije i formirovanije khakasskoj narodnosti* [The Origin and Formation of the Khakass Nationality] (Abakan).
1962   "Etnograficheskoje izuchenije sotsialisticheskoj kultury i byta narodov SSSR" [The Ethnographical Study of the Socialist Culture and Day-to-Day Life of the USSR Peoples], *SE* no. 2.
Potapov, M. I.
1962   "O filogeneze gruppovykh antigenov cheloveka" [On the Phylogenesis of Human Group Antigens], *Zhurnal obsjej biologii* no. 6.
Potekhin, I. I.
1951   "Vojennaja demokratija matabele" [The Matabele Military Democracy], *TIE* n.s. 14.
1955   "Formirovanije natsionalnoj obsjnosti juzhno-afrikanskikh bantu" [The Formation of National Unity of the South African Bantu], *TIE* n.s. 29.
1957   "Zadachi izuchenija etnicheskogo sostava Afriki v svjazi s raspadom kolonialnoj sistemy" [The Problems of Research of the African Ethnic Composition in View of Disintegration of the Colonial System], *SE* no. 4.
"Problemy istorii pervobytnogo obsjestva" [The Problems of the History of Primitive Society] 1960 *TIE* n.s. 54.
Problemy izmenenija sotsialnoj struktury sovetskogo obsjestva (Metodologicheskije problemy) [Problems of Change in the Social Structure of Soviet Society (Methodological Problems)] 1968 (Moscow).
"Proiskhozhdenije i etnicheskaja istorija russkogo naroda po antropologicheskim dannym" [The Origin and Ethnic History of the Russian People According to Anthropological Data]. 1965 *TIE* n.s. 88 (Moscow).
Proiskhozhdenije osetinskogo naroda [The Origin of the Ossetian People] 1967 Ordzhonikidze.
Puchkov, P. I.
1968   "K analizu etnicheskoj situatsii v Okeanii" [Towards an Analysis of the Ethnic Situation in Oceania], *VI* no. 10.
Puljanos, A. N.
1963   "K antropologii karaimov Litvy i Kryma" [On the Anthropology of Crimean and Lithuanian Karaims], *VA* 13.
Razdobarina, L.
1963   "Chastota dvukhkornevogo nizhnego klyka v raznykh etnicheskikh gruppakh" [Frequency of the Two-Root Lower Cuspid in Various Ethnic Groups], *Archive of the Anthropology Department* (Moscow University).
Razlozhenije rodovogo stroja i formirovanije klassovogo obsjestva [Disintegration of Clan Society and Formation of Class Society] 1968 (Moscow).

Reshetov, Ju. G.
1962 "Novyje nakhodki iskopajemykh primatov v usjelje Oldovaj, Tanganjika" [New Finds of Fossil Primates at Olduvai Gorge, Tanganyika], *VA* 11.
Robakidze, A. I.
1968 "Osobennosti patronomicheskoj organizatsii u narodov gornogo Kavkaza (V svjazi s voprosom o sootnoshenii patronomii, roda i semji)" [Peculiarities of the Patronomic Organization Among the Peoples of the Caucasus Mountains (In Connection With the Question of Correlation of Patronymy, Clan and Family)], *SE* no. 5.
"Rodovoje obsjestvo" [Clan Society] 1951 *TIE* 14.
Roginskij, Ja. Ja.
1934 "Materialy po antropologii tungusov Severnogo Pribajkalja" [Materials on the Anthropology of the Tungus of the North Baikal Region], *AZ* 3.
1937 "Problema proiskhozhdenija mongolskogo rasovogo tipa" [The Problem of the Origin of the Mongolian Racial Type], *AZ* no. 2.
1941 Chelovecheskije rasy" [Human Races], V. V. Bunak, M. F. Nesturkh, and Ja. Ja. Roginskij, *Antropologija* (Moscow).
1947 "Zakonomernosti prostranstvennogo raspredelenija grupp krovi u cheloveka" [Patterns of the Spatial Distribution of Human Blood Groups], *TIE* 1.
1949 *Teorii monotsentrizma i politzentrizma v probleme proiskhozhdenija sovremennogo cheloveka i jego ras* [Theories of Monocentrism and Polycentrism in the Problem of the Origin of Modern Man and His Races] (Moscow).
1959 "O nekotorykh rezultatakh primenenija kolichestvennogo metoda k izucheniju morfologicheskoj izmenchivosti" [On Certain Results of Application of the Quantitative Method to Study of Morphological Variability], *Arkhiv anatomii, gistologii i embriologii* 36: no. 1.
1960 "K voprosu o vozrastnykh izmenenijakh rasovykh priznakov u cheloveka (v utrobnom periode i v detstve)" [On the Question of the Age Changes of Racial Features Among Men (in the Uterine Period and in Childhood)], *TIE* n.a. 50 (Moscow).
Roginskij, Ja. Ja. and M. G. Levin
1955 *Osnovy antropologii* [Principles of Anthropology] (Moscow).
1963 *Antropologija* [Physical Anthropology] (Moscow).
Rozhdestvenskaja, S. B.
1964 "Opyt obrabotki etnograficheskikh materialov pri pomosji sjetnykh mashin" [Some Experience in Treating Ethnographical Data By Means of Computers], *SE* no. 3.
Rozov, N. S.
1961 "Antropologicheskije issledovanija korennogo naselenija zapadnoj Sibiri" [Anthropological Studies of the Indigenous Population of Western Siberia], *VA* 6.
Rubashkin, V. Ja.
1929 *Krovjanyje gruppy* [Blood Groups] (Moscow-Leningrad).
Rudenko, S. I.
1914 "Antropologicheskoje issledovanije inorodtsev Severo-Zapadnoj Sibiri" [Anthropological Research of Native Peoples in North-Western Siberia], *Zapiski Akademii Nauk po fiziko-matematicheskomu otdeleniju* 33: no. 3 (St. Petersburg).
1916 "Bashkiry. Opyt etnologicheskoj monografii, I, fizicheskij tip bashkir" [The Bashkirs. An Attempt at an Ethnological Monograph, part I, Physique], *Zapiski Russkogo geograficheskogo obsjestva po otdeleniju etnografii* 43:1 (St. Petersburg).
1955 *Bashkiry. Istoriko-etnograficheskije ocherki* [The Bashkirs. Essays in History and Ethnography] (Moscow-Leningrad).

Russkije Istoriko-etnograficheskij atlas [The Russians. Historical-Ethnographical Atlas] 1967 (Moscow).

Rychkov, Yu. G.

1964a "Antropologicheskoje issledovanije protsessa izoljatsii na Pamire i Kavkaze" (Anthropological Investigation of the Process of Isolation in the Pamirs and Caucasus], VII *ICAES* (Moscow).

1964b "Projskhozhdenije rasy sredneaziatskogo mezhdurechja" [The Origin of the Race of the Central Asian Interfluve], *Problemy etnicheskoj antropologii Srednej Azii. Nauchnije trudy Tashkentskogo universiteta* 285 (Tashkent).

1965a "Nekotoryje aspekty serologicheskikh issledovanij v antropologii" [Aspects of Serological Researches in Anthropology], *VA* 19.

1965b "Osobennosti serologicheskoj differentsiatsii narodov Sibiri" [Features of the Serological Differentiation of the Peoples of Siberia], *VA* 21.

Saburova, L. M.

1967a *Kultura i byt russkogo naselenija Priangarja* [Culture and Day-to-Day Life of the Russians in the Angara Valley] (Leningrad).

1967b "Literatura o novykh obrjadakh i prazdnikakh za 1963–1966 gg." [The Literature on New Customs and Holidays for 1963–1966 Years], *SE* no. 5.

Samarin, G. A.

1948 "Etnograficheskije i folklornyje raboty v Kirgizskoj SSR" [Ethnographical and Folklore Studies in Kirghiz SSR], *SE* no. 1.

"Selo Vyrjatino v proshlom i nastojasjem" [The Village of Vyrjatino in Past and Present] 1958 *TIE* 41.

Semenov, Ju. I.

1962 *Vozniknovenije chelovecheskogo obsjestva* [The Origin of Human Society] (Krasnojarsk).

1963 Rev.: H. V. Vallois, "The Social Life of Early Man, the Evidence of Skeletons. Social Life of Man" (New York, 1961), *VA* no. 14.

1964 *Gruppovoj brak, jego priroda i mesto v evolutsii semejno-brachnykh otnoshenij* [Group Marriage, Its Nature and Place in the Evolution of Familial-Marital Relations] (Moscow).

1965a "O periodizatsii pervobytnoj istorii" [On the Periodization of Primitive History], *SE* no. 5.

1965b "O nekotorykh voprosakh stanovlenija chelovecheskogo obsjestva" [Some Problems of the Formation of the Human Society], *VE* no. 6.

1966a *Kak vozniklo chelovechestvo* [How Mankind Originated] (Moscow).

1966b "Kategorija 'sotsialnyi organizm' i jeje snachenije dlja istoricheskoj nauki" [The Category of "Social Organism" and Its Implications for Historical Science], *VI* no. 8.

1968 *Razvitije tekhniki v kamennom veke* [Development of Technology in the Stone Age] (Leningrad).

"Semja i semejnyj byt kolkhoznikov Pribaltiki" [Family and Familial Life of the Collective-Forms of the Baltic Lands], 1962 *TIE* n.s. 27.

Sergejeva, G. A.

1967 *Archintsy* [The Archins] (Moscow).

Severtsov, A. N.

1939 *Morfologicheskije zakonomernosti evolutsii* [Morphological Patterns of Evolution] (Moscow-Leningrad).

Sharevskaja, B. I.

1964 *Staryje i novyje religii Tropicheskoj i juzhnoj Afriki* [Ancient and Modern Religions of Tropical and Southern Africa] (Moscow).

Sharkova, A.

1964 "Verkhnije moljary russkikh" [The Upper Molars of Russians], student paper, *Archive of the Anthropological Department* (Moscow University).

Shelepov, G. V.
1968 "Obsjnost' proiskhozhdenija- priznak etnicheskoj obsjnosti" [Common Origin Being an Indicator of Ethnic Community], *SE* no. 4.

Shirokogorov, S. M.
1923 *Etnos* [Ethnos] (Shanghai).

Shluger, S. A.
1936 "Materialy po antropologii moldavan" [Materials in Moldavian Anthropology], *AZ* 4.
1941 "Antropologicheskoje issledovanije nentsev" [An Anthropological Study of the Nenets], *Kratkije soobsjenija NII Antropologii pri MGU za* 1938-1939 *gody* (Moscow).

Shmalgauzen, I. I.
1939 "Znachenije korreljatsij v evoljutsii zhivotnykh" [The Significance of Correlation in the Evolution of Animals], *Pamjati akademika A. N. Severtsova* 1 (Moscow-Leningrad).
1940 *Puty i zakonomernosti evoljutsionnogo protsessa* [Paths and Patterns of the Evolutionary Process] (Moscow-Leningrad).

Shtaerman, E. M.
1967 "Problemy kultury v zapadnoj sotsiologii" [Problems of Culture in Western Sociology], *VF* no. 1.

Shternberg, L. Ya.
1928 "Ajnskaja problema" [The Ainu Problem], *SMAE* 8.
1933 *Semja i rod u narodov severo-vostochnoj Azii* [Family and Clan of the Peoples of North-Eastern Asia] (Leningrad).

Sibirskij etnograficheskij Sbornik [The Siberian Ethnographical Collected Articles] 1952-1963 vols. 1-5.

Sjepanskij, Ja.
1969 *Elementarnyje ponjatija sotsiologii* [Elementary Concepts of Sociology] (Moscow).

Sjure-Kanal', Zh.
1965 "Traditsionnyje obsjestva v Tropicheskoj Afriki i marksistskaja kontseptsija 'aziatskogo sposoba proizvodstva'" [Traditional Societies in Tropical Africa and the Marxist Concept of the "Asian Mode of Production"], *NAA* no. 1.

Smirnov, S. R.
1956 "Obrazovanije i puti razvitija severo-sudanskoj narodnosti" [The Formation and the Ways of Development of North Sudan Nationality], *TIE* n.s. 34.

Smirnova, Ya. S.
1967 "Natsionalno-smeshannyje braki u narodov Karachajevo-Cherkesii" [Mixed Marriages of the Peoples of Karachai-Circassia], *SE* no. 4.

Smoljak, A. V.
1963 "O nekotorykh etnicheskikh protsessakh u narodov Nizhnego i Srednego Amura" [Some Ethnic Processes of the Peoples of the Lower and Middle Amur Basin], *SE* no. 3.
1966 *Ulchi* [The Olcha] (Moscow).

Snesarev, G. P.
1969 *Relikty domusulmanskikh verovanij i obrjadov u uzbekov Khoresma* [Relics of the Pre-Moslem Beliefs and the Rites of the Khwarazmian Uzbeks] (Moscow).

Sokolova, V. K.
1965 "Rabota simpoziumov na VII Mezhdunarodnom Kongresse antropologicheskikh i etnograficheskikh nauk" [The Work of the Symposia of the 7th International Congress of Anthropological and Ethnological Sciences], *SE* no. 1.

Solovjeva, T. G.
1964 "Gruppy krovi sistemy *ABO* i *Rh*-faktor v ikh vzaimosvjazi u donorov i

nedonorov Leningrada" [*ABO* Blood Groups and *Rh*-factor in their Interconnections with Donors and Non-Donors of Leningrad], VII *ICAES*
(Moscow).

Sorokin, V. S.
1953   "O lokalnykh raslichijakh v kulture nizhnego paleolita" [On the Local
Differences in the Culture of the Lower Paleolithic Period], *SE* no. 3.

Sozina, S. A.
1967   *Sotsialnyj stroj i kultura drevneindejskoj tsivilizatsii Chibcha-muiskov (Kolum-
bija) v seredine 16 veka.* Avtoreverat dissertatsii [The Social System and
Culture of the Ancient Indian Civilization of the Chibcha-Muisca (Colombia)
in the Mid 16th Century. Summary of Cand. Diss.] (Moscow).

Starikov, V. S.
1967   *Materialnaja kultura kitajtsev severo-vostochnykh provintsij KNR* [The
Material Culture of the Chinese, of the North-Eastern Provinces of the CPR]
(Moscow).
        See also non-Russian bibliography.

Stelmakh, G. Je.
1964   *Istorichnij rozvitok silskikh poselen na Ukraini* [The Historical Development
of Country Settlements in Ukraine] (Kiev). (In Ukrainian).

Stepermanis, M. K.
1960   "Razvitije etnograficheskoj nauki v Sovetskoj Latvii" [The Development of
Ethnographical Science in Soviet Latvia], *SE* no. 3.

Studenetskaja, Je. N.
1967   "Odezhda narodov Kavkaza (o sobiranii materialov dlja Kavkazskogo
istoriko-etnograficheskogo Atlasa)" [The Dress of the Caucasian Peoples
(on Collecting Data for the Caucasian Historical-Ethnographical Atlas)] *SE*
no. 3.

Sukhareva, O. A. and M. A. Bikzhanova
1955   *Proshloje i nastojasjeje selenija Ajkyran* [Past and Present of the Village of
Ajkyrhan] (Tashkent).

Suret-Canale, G.
1965   "Traditionnyje obsjestva v tropicheskoj Afrike i marxistskaja konseptsija
'aziatskogo sposoba proizvodstva'" [Traditional Societies of Tropical
Africa and the Marxist Concept of the "Asian Mode of Production"],
Narody Azii i Afriki 1.

Taksami, Ch.
1967   *Nivkhi* [The Nivkhs] (Leningrad).

Tarojeva, R. F.
1965   *Materialnaja kultura karel* [The Material Culture of the Karelians] (Moscow-
Leningrad).

Terentjeva, L. N.
1960   Kolkhoznoje krestjanstvo Latvii [The Kolkhoz Peasantry of Latvia], *TIE* 59.
1969   "Opredelenije svojej natsionalnoj prinadlezhnosti podrostkami v natsionalno-
smeshannykh semjakh" [The Determination of Their National Affiliation by
Teenagers in Nationally-Mixed Families], *SE* no. 3.

Terletskij, P. Je.
1953   "O novom metode etnicheskogo kartografirovanija" [A New Method of
Ethnic Mapping], *SE* no. 1.

Tipy selskogo zhilisja v stranakh zarubezhnoj Jevropy [Types of Rural Dwelling in the
Countries of Alien Europe] 1968 (Moscow).

Tokarev, S. A.
1929   "O sistemakh rodstva u avstralijtsev" [On the Systems of Kinship Terminologies Among the Australians], *Etnografija* no. 1.
1946   "Engels i sovremennaja etnografia" [Engels and Modern Ethnography],
Isvestija AN SSSR, serija istorii filologii 3: no. 1.

1949 "K postanovke problem etnogeneza" [On the Statement of Problems of Ethnogenesis], *SE* no. 3.

1957 *Religioznyje verovanija vostochnoslavjanskikh narodov XIX- nachala XX vv* [The Religious Beliefs of the Eastern Slav Peoples from the 19th to the Beginning of the 20th Cent.] (Moscow).

1958a *Etnografia narodov SSSR* [Ethnography of the Peoples of the USSR] (Moscow).

1958b "K voprosu o metodike izuchenija terminologii rodstva" [On the Methods of Studying Kinship Terminology], *Vestnik MGU.*

1958c "Proiskhozhdenije obsjestvennykh klassov na ostrovakh Tonga" [The Origin of Social Classes in the Tongan Islands], *SE* no. 1.

1958d "Sovetskaja etnografija za 40 let" [Soviet Ethnography for Forty Years], *Vestnik istorii mirovoj Kultury* no. 2.

1964a "Problema tipov etnicheskikh obsjnostej" [Problem of the Types of Ethnic Communities], *VF* no. 11.

1964b *Rannije formy religii i ikh razvitije* [Early Religious Forms and Their Development] (Moscow).

1964c *Religija v istorii narodov mira* [Religion in the History of the Peoples of the World] (Moscow).

1966 *Istorija russkoj etnografii* [The History of Russian Ethnography] (Moscow).

1967a "O zadachakh etnograficheskogo izuchenija narodov industrialnykh stran" [On the Problems of Ethnographic Studies of the Peoples of Industrial Countries], *SE* no. 5.

1968a "Novoje o proiskhozhdenii ekzogamii i o totemizme" [New Facts about the Origin of Exogamy and Totemism], *Problemy antropologii i istoriceskoj ethnografii Azii* (Moscow).

1968b *Osnovy etnografii* [The Basis of Ethnography] (Moscow).
See also non-Russian bibliography.

Tolstov, S. P.
1931 "Problemy dorodovogo obsjestva" [The Problems of the Preclan Society], *SE* nos. 3–4.

1934 "Genezis feodalizma v kochevykh skotovodcheskikl obsjestvakh" [Genesis of the Feudalism in Nomadic Cattle-Breeding Societies], *IGAIMK* 103.

1935a "Vojennaja demokratija i problema 'genetichoskoj revolutsii'" [Military Democracy and the Problem of the "Genetic Revolution"], *Problemy istorii dokapitalisticheskikh obsjestv* (Moscow).

1935b "Perezhitki totemizma i dualnoj organizatsii u turkmen" [The Survivals of Totemism and Dual Organization Among the Turkmens], *Problemy istorii dokapitalisticheskikh obsjestv* nos. 9–10.

1946 "K voprosu o periodizatsii pervobytnogo obsjestva" [On the Question of the Periodization of Primitive Society], *SE* no. 1.

1947a "Vystuplenije v diskussii po probleme ekzogamii" [Speech in a Discussion on the Problem of Exogamy], *SE* no. 3.

1947b "Sovetskaja shkola etnografii" [The Soviet Ethnographical School], *SE* no. 4.

1948 *Drevnij Khorezm* [Ancient Khoarazm] (Moscow).

1957 "Sorok let sovetskoj etnografii" [Forty Years of Soviet Ethnography], *SE* no. 5.

1960 "Osnovnyje teoreticheskije problemy sovremennoj sovetskoj etnografii" [The Principal Theoretical Problems of Modern Soviet Ethnography], *SE* no. 6.

Tolstov, S. P. (ed.)
1954–1966 *Narody mira. Etnograficheskije ocherki* [The Peoples of the World] (Moscow).

Trofimova, T. A.
1962 *Drevneje naselenije Khorezma i sopredelnykh oblastej po dannym paleoantro-*

pologii [The Ancient Population of Khwarazm and Adjacent Regions in the Light of Paleoanthropological Information] (Moscow).

Trofimova, T. A. and N. N. Cheboksarov

1941   "Severouralskaja ekspeditsija Muzeja Antropologii" [The North Urals Expedition of the Anthropology Museum], *Kratkije soobsjenija o nauchnykh trudakh NII Antropologii pri MGU za* 1938–1939 *gody* (Moscow).

Trudy Khorezmskoj arkheologo-etnograficheskoj ekspeditsii [Proceedings of the Khwarazmian Archaeological-Ethnographical Expedition] 1952–1959 vols. 1–4 (Moscow).

Trudy Kirgizskoj arkheologo-etnograficheskoj ekspeditsii [Proceedings of the Kirghiz Archaeological-Ethnographical Expedition] 1956–1960 vols. 1–4 (Moscow).

Trudy Tuvinskoj kompleksnoj arkheologo-etnograficheskoj ekspeditsii [Proceedings of the Tuva Archaeological-Ethnographical Expedition] 1960–1966 vols. 1–2 (Moscow).

Tumarkin, D. D.

1954   "K voprosu o formakh semji u gavajtsev v kontse XVIII-nachale XIX v" [On the Question of Family Forms Among the Hawaiians at the End of the 18th and the Early 19th Centuries], *SE* no. 4.

Umnova, M. A.

1967   *Izoimunnyje svojstva krovi cheloveka i ikh znachenije v klinicheskoj praktike* [The Iso-Immune Properties of Human Blood and Their Value in Clinical Practice] Dissertation (Author's Abstract) (Moscow).

Vajnshtejn, S. I.

1967   "Ornament v narodnom iskusstve tuvintsev" [Ornament in the Folk Art of the Tuvinians], *SE* no. 2.

Vardumjan, D. S.

1962   "Armjanskaja etnografija za gody Sovetskoj vlasti" [The Armenian Ethnography for the Years of Soviet Power], *SE* no. 5.

Vardumjan, D. S. and E. T. Karapetjan

1963   *Semja i semejnyj byt kolkhoznikov Armenii* [The Family and Family Life of the Armenian Collective Farmers] (Yerevan). (In Armenian).

Vasilevich, G. M.

1930   "Nekotoryje dannyje po okhotnichjim obrjadam i predstavlenijam u tungusov" [Some Data on Tungus Hunting Customs and Beliefs], *Etnografija* no. 3.

1969   *Evenki* [The Evenks] (Leningrad).

Vasiljeva, G. P.

1968   "Sovremennyje etnicheskije protsessy v Severnom Turkmenistane" [Contemporary Ethnic Processes in Northern Turkmenistan], *SE* no. 1.

1969   *Preobrazovanije byta i etnicheskije protsessy v Severnom Turkmenistane* [Transformation of Everyday Life and Ethnic Processes in Northern Turkmenistan] (Moscow).

Vdovin, I. S.

1965   *Ocherki istorii i etnografii chukchej* [Essays in History and Ethnography of the Chukchi] (Leningrad).

Venesuela. Ekonomika, politika, kultura [Venezuela. Economy, Policy, Culture] 1967 (Moscow).

Vichnjanskajte, A.

1960   "Etnograficheskije issledovanija v Litve v 1940–1960 godakh" [Ethnographical Studies in Lithuania, 1940–1960], *SE* no. 3.

Vijres, A. O.

1960   "Estonskaja sovetskaja etnografija (1940–1960)" [Estonian Soviet Ethnography (1940–1960)], *SE* no. 3.

Vinnikov, I. N.

1936   "Chetvertoje izdanije knigi F. Engelsa 'Proiskhozhdenije semji, chastnoj sobstvennosti i gosudarstva'" [The Fourth Edition of Engels' "The Origin of the Family, Private Property, and the State"], *Voprosy istorii doklassovogo obsjestva* (Moscow-Leningrad).

Vinnikov, Ja. R.
1969 *Khozjajstvo, kultura i byt selskogo naselenija Turkmenskoj SSSR* [Economy, Culture and Day-to-Day Life of the Rural Population of the Turkmen SSR] (Moscow).

Vitov, M. V.
1964 "Antropologicheskije dannyje kak istochnik po istorii kolonizatsii russkogo Severa" [Anthropological Data as a Source for the Study of the History of Colonization in Northern Russia], *Istorija SSSR* no. 6.

Vitov, M. V., K. Ju. Mark, and N. N. Cheboksarov
1959 *Etnicheskaja antropologija vostochnoj Pribaltiki* [Ethnic Anthropology of the Eastern Baltic Basin] (Moscow).

Vlastovskij, V. G.
1958 "Sravnitelnyj analiz korreljatsij na primere trubchatykh kostej cheloveka i zhivotnykh" [Comparative Analysis of Correlation, Taking the Long Bones of Man and Animals as an Example], *SA* no. 2.

Volkova, L. S.
1965 *Nesovmestimost' materi i ploda po krovjanym gruppam ABO* [*ABO* Blood Groups Incompatibility of Mother and Embryo], Dissertation (Author's Abstract) (Moscow).

Volotskij, M. V.
1937 "Novyi daktiloskopicheskij indeks" [A New Dactyloscopic Index] *Uchonye zapiski MGU* 10.
1941 "Novyj daktiloskopicheskij index i jego raspredelenije po zemnomu sharu" [A New Dactyloscopic Index and Its Distribution Across the World], *Kratkije soobsjenija NII Antropologii pri MGU za 1938–1939 gody* (Moscow).

Voprosy etnicheskoj istorii estonskogo naroda [Problems of the Ethnic History of the Estonian People] 1956 (Tallin).

"Voprosy etnicheskoj istorii narodov Pribaltiki" [Problems of the Ethnic History of Baltic Peoples] 1959 *Trudy Pribaltijskoj objedinennoj kompleksnoj ekspeditsii* 1 (Moscow).

"Voprosy etnicheskoj istorii mordovskogo naroda" [Problems of the Ethnic History of the Mordvinian People] 1960 *TIE* n.s. 63.

"Voprosy istorii doklassovogo obsjestva" [Problems in the History of Preclass Society] 1936 *TIE* 4.

"Vostochnoslavjanskij etnograficheskij sbornik. Ocherki narodnoj materialnoj kultury russkikh, ukraintsev i belorussov v XIX-nachale XX vv" [The Eastern Slav Ethnographical Collected Articles. Essays in Folk Material Culture of Russians, Ukrainians, and Belorussians from the 19th to the Beginning of the 20th Centuries) 1956 *TIE* 31.

Vsemirnaja istorija [World History] 1957 vol. 3 (Moscow).

World 1962 *Chislennost' i rasselenije narodev mira* [World Population Numbers and Distribution] (Moscow).

Yelnitskij, L. A.
1958 "U istokov drevnerimskoj Kultury i gosudars tvennosti" [On the Origins of Ancient Roman Culture and Statehood], *VDI* no. 3.

Yeremejev, D. J.
1967 "Jazyk kak etnogeneticheskij istochnik (iz opyta leksicheskogo analiza turetskogo jazyka)" [Language as an Ethnogenetical Source (Some Experience of Linguistic Analysis of the Turkish Language)], *SE* no. 4.

Zarubezhnaja Azija [Alien Asia] 1959 (Moscow).

Zarubezhnaja Evropa [Alien Europe] 1966 (Moscow).

Zenkevich, L. A.
1939 "Sistema i filogenija" [System and Phylogeny], *Zoologicheskij zhurnal* 18.

Zenkevich, P. I.
1937 "K voprosu o faktorakh formoobrazovanija dlinnykh kostej cheloveche-skogo skeleta, I" [On the Factors of Formation of the Long Bones of the Human Skeleton], *Antropologicheskij zhurnal* no. 1.
1940 "K voprosu o faktorakh formoobrazovanija dlinnykh kostej chelovecheskogo skeleta, II" [On the Factors of Formation of the Long Bones of the Human Skeletons], *UZMGU* 34.

Zhakov, M. P.
1933 "K postanovke geneticheskikh problem istorii doklassovogo obsjestva" [On the Consideration of the Genetic Problems in the History of Preclass Society], *IGAIMK* 100.

Zhdanko, T. A.
1964 "Etnograficheskoje izuchenije protsessov razvitija i sblizhenija sotsialistiche-skikh natsij v SSSR" [Ethnographic Studies of Processes Characterizing the Development and Cohesion of Socialist Nations in the USSR], *SE* no. 6.

Zhirov, E. V.
1941 "Raznovidnosti brakhikefalii" [Varieties of Brachycephaly], *KSIIMK* 10.

Zhukovskaja, N. L.
1965 "Iz istorii religioznogo sinkretizma v Zabajkalje" [On the History of Religious Syncretism in Transbaikalia], *SE* no. 6.

Zinich, V. T.
1963 *Sotsialistichni peretvorenn'a parostki novogo kommunistichnogo v kulturi ta nobuti robitnikov Radian'skoj Ukraini* [Socialistic Transformation and New Communist Shoots in the Culture and Everyday Life of the Laborers of Soviet Ukraine] (Kiev). (In Ukrainian).

Zolotarev, A. M.
1931 "Proiskozhdenije ekzogamii" [The Origin of Exogamy], *IGAIMK* 10: nos. 2–4.
1933 "Novyje dannyje o gruppovom brake" [New Data on Group Marriage], *SE* nos. 3–4.
1939 *Rodovoj stroj i religija ulchej* [The Clan Society and the Religion of the Ulcha] (Khabarovsk).
1940 "K istorii rannikh form gruppovogo braka" [On the History of the Early Forms of Group Marriage], *Uchenije Zapiski Istoricheskogo fakulteta Moskovskogo Oblastnogo Pedagogicheskogo Instituta* 2 (Moscow).
1941 "Antropologicheskije issledovanija v Priamurje" [Anthropological Studies in the Amur Basin], *Kratkije soobsjenija NII Antropologii pri MGU za 1938–1939 gody* (Moscow).
1964 *Rodovoj stroj i pervobytnaja mifologia* [Clan Society and Primitive Mythology] (Moscow).
MSa "Proiskhozhdenije ekzogamii" [The Origin of Exogamy].
MSb "Ocherk istorii rodovogo stroja" [Essays on the History of the Clan System].

Zolotarev, D. A.
1928 *Kolskije lopari* [The Lapps of Kola] (Leningrad).

Zolotareva, I. M.
1962 "Antropologicheskoje issledovanije nganasan" [An Anthropological Study of the Nganasans], *SE* no. 6.
1964 "Raspredelenije grupp krovi u narodov Severnoj Sibiri" [Blood Group Distribution Among the Peoples of Siberial, VII *ICAES* (Moscow).
1965 "Antropologicheskoje issledovanije dolgan" [An Anthropological Study of the Dolghan], *SE* no. 3.

Zubov, A. A.
1964 *Nekotoruje antropologicheskije aspekty morfologii postojannykh bolshikh*

korennykh zubov sovremennogo cheloveka [Some Anthropological Aspects of the Morphology of the Molars of Modern Man] (Moscow).

1965 "Antropologicheskaja odontologija i istoricheskije nauki" [Dental Anthropology and the Historical Sciences], *SE* no. 1.

Zvorykin, A. A.

1967 "Opredelenije kultury i mesto materialnoj kultury v obsjej kulture" [Definition of Culture and Place Occupied by the Material Culture in Civilization], *ICAES* 4 (Moscow).